The Grey Filly

Virgil S. Cross

Greetings

Virgil S. Cross

E.M. Press, Inc.
Manassas, VA

This book is dedicated with deep affection and gratitude to my wife, Lois, without whose support and help in editing and mastering the computer, this work could not have been accomplished.

Virgil S. Cross

FOREWORD

It is said that everyone has a book within him or her. Virgil Cross's life beginning with his first childhood recollection through his life with Ethel, The Grey Filly, is one that few can imagine happening. Yet the events are factual and, I believe, accurately recalled. I have personally known Virgil for over 30 years and can verify many of the stories he has related. In *The Grey Filly*, Virgil shares the adventures of a very active life.

There is adventure, humor, sadness, failure, pride, tragedy, tenderness, and ruggedness all combined into a book that few can put down until it is read. The strong family bond that was present made it possible for the Crosses to make the most of adversity, capitalize on situations, and obtain success. The talents of each family member were developed. Even with Ethel's handicap, all were able to live and mature as a happy and normal family with strong bonds to each other and their community.

At the start of the book, the writing style on the author's childhood days was simple and then as he grew older the style took on maturity. Starting with the chapter titled Polio, toward the end of the book, the carefree life and writing became one of dedication, deep feeling, and understanding of relations with others. The book illustrates that regardless of what life may "deal you," with perseverance, intelligent planning, cooperation, and support of a loving family, adversities can be overcome.

Richard E. Ohms, Ph.D.

Dr. Ohms is a much sought-after, internationally-known production consultant.

INTRODUCTION

The Grey Filly is not a Western novel about a horse, although most of the action occurs in the West.

Virgil Cross is a man with a story to tell. From his photographic memory and notes he compiled over the years, he is able to recall in fascinating detail the life of his family, neighbors, associates, and the historical events of the early settlers in South Idaho. The love story of Virgil and his wife, two people dedicated to one another, will stay with you for a long time.

The story begins with the activities of a very adventurous small boy with a penchant for getting into and out of trouble and continues through the challenges of his adolescence and manhood. There is fast-moving action which touches on Indian skirmishes, cattle and sheepmen's wars, a lost gold mine in the Teton Mountains, work with the FBI during and after World War II, and contacts with several famous people.

What you are going to read about a now 87-year-old man's journey through life will enlighten and enrich your world.

THE MAGIC OF LOVE

*Love is like magic and it always
will be,
For love still remains life's
sweet mystery!
Love can transform the most
commonplace
Into beauty and splendor and
sweetness and grace!
Love is unselfish, understanding
and kind,
For it sees with its heart
and not with its mind!
Love is the answer that
everyone seeks—
Love is the language that
every heart speaks—
Love can't be bought, it is
priceless and free,
Love like pure magic
is a sweet mystery!*

—Helen Steiner Rice

THE GREY FILLY

CORPUS CHRISTI

My first memory of an event occurred in Corpus Christi, Texas, in 1909. I was about three years old, sitting on a pier with my father. He was bringing in a fish and I stepped closer to the edge of the pier. My father said, "Virg, please step back, you could fall in." I stepped back, barefooted, and screamed. I had stepped on a catfish and the spine had penetrated deeply into my heel, causing terrific pain. The spine had broken off, leaving only a little stub sticking out of my flesh. A fishing companion pulled it out with his teeth and sucked the hole repeatedly, spitting out what he said was poison. Father took me home and Mother put poultices on it for several days.

The train that ran on the railroad track near our house frequently stopped for passengers and freight whenever a customer waved a red flag. My brother, Farrell, and his friend, Orville Griggs, both about eight years old, decided it would be fun to stop the train. Our folks were in town, and Freida, the hired girl, was trying to keep us out of trouble. Farrell found a large red bandana and they tied the corners to a long stick and waited for the train. It came clicking along, huffing and puffing, with black smoke rising from the smokestack. They were standing by the track waving the flag, while I was standing down the embankment. With a squeal of the drivers, the train slid to a stop. Two men climbed down. They each grabbed a boy and asked, "Why did you flag us?"

A frightened Orville said, "We just wanted to see if you would stop." When the men flipped the boys over their knees and started spanking them with long leather gloves, I ran for the house. I could hear the children yelling in pain. They were still crying when the folks arrived shortly after. Mother put cold cream on Farrell's blistered bottom.

"Farrell, you deserved this spanking. You should know better than to interfere with grown-up business."

I remember, vaguely, that Mother made me learn my ABC's and to count to one hundred. She had a McGuffey reader, and I could read in it when I was five.

Perhaps what I remember most vividly was the Great Snake Killing with Farrell. On that day my father said, "Boys, it may storm. I have to go to the office. Do not leave the place." Mother was in Houston recovering from an abdominal operation. Frieda, a robust German girl,

1

was keeping house and looking after us. She had a heavy German accent with vats and yahs, which we mimicked. We lived in a house about 2 miles from the center of Corpus Christi, a very small but fast-growing town.

The house was on top of a small knoll, perhaps about 150 feet across and nearly 3 feet above the flat plain. It faced the railroad tracks which bordered the fence on the vast King Ranch on the other side. The railroad track with its banks and cuts was full of holes. On the King Ranch in the chapparel there was an abundance of rodent holes in the rich soil. This area was out of bounds to us because of the large number of rattlesnakes and coral snakes.

About 10 o'clock, a big black cloud moved in from the Gulf of Mexico. Rain came down in solid sheets, which people called a cloudburst. In 2 hours it rained over 10 inches, stopping as suddenly as it began. Our house was like an oasis, surrounded by a circle of water less than 50 feet away. It and the railroad track were all that could be seen above the water.

We were standing outside with Freida, looking at the track. Freida said, "Vat's dat swimmink to der house?"

Farrell said, "It's a snake!"

I yelled, "There's another!"

Freida grabbed a hoe. Farrell and I picked up long poles that we used for stick horses and we started to kill snakes that were coming from every direction, trying to find dry ground. The rattlers swam with their heads up and rattles above the water. We were laughing and yelling, "I'll get this one—Freida, get that one!"

"Yah, I vill!"

It was fast and furious for almost 2 hours. We waded out into shallow water to meet them. We found that if we stood apart, the snakes would try to swim between us and we could close in.

Father came home about 6 o'clock. When he saw what we had done, he was aghast at what could have happened. He would not let us gather up the snakes, fearing some would be alive. He put on rubber boots and used a pitch fork to pile them up.

Farrell and I argued, "I counted 36."

"I counted 38, I am right. I am older and smarter than you."

Dad said, "Regardless who is right, there are a lot of snakes."

The three years in Texas were pleasant years. We lived in a nice house. The food was good. Our parents were always smiling and laughing. Every night we were read to. Kipling was the favorite author. I dreamed of Moguli and Baghera, the panther. Robinson Crusoe, the Arabian Nights, Greek mythology, Hercules, Hector, Achilles, The Trojan Horse, Proserpina, Robin Hood, and The Northmen Myths were in the reading sessions until we were nine years old and reading stories in books and magazines.

The family moved to Portland, Oregon in 1912 because Al Cross, my father, had caught maleria and he wanted to get to a healthier climate. He had been very successful in selling real estate. I remember one of the few quarrels my parents ever had. Father said, "I don't want to take all of that money with me. I will take $300 above the train fare and leave the rest of it on deposit in the company, where it is drawing interest."

"Al, something might happen. We can hide it and keep it safe."

"Ora, there have been some train robberies lately and I don't want to lose it all." He had several thousand dollars in the company from his commissions.

It could have been the meat was spoiled in the sandwich from the vendor on the train. I was sick most of the way to Portland. Men in the front of the car shot out of the windows at passing posts and such. The conductor didn't seem to mind until the passengers complained. I guess it was a carry-over from the early days when the passengers carried guns and shot at almost anything that moved.

We stayed at a hotel for a few days while the folks looked for a place to buy. I learned later that they paid $2,000 down on the house, the balance to be due in six months. This would give them time to get their money from the Texas real estate company.

We moved into a nice house at 1415 East Halsey Street in Portland. Father found a good job as supervisor in the OWRNS railroad. He wrote a letter asking the company in Corpus Christi to send his money to him. They replied that they couldn't pay him now. The president of the company had absconded with $500,000 and his redheaded secretary. They thought he was in Brazil. They offered Father 20 acres of what is now downtown Corpus Christi. They said the company would eventually be solvent and would be able to pay him in full. He decided to wait for his money.

I entered school. My desk was in the front row near the teacher. I didn't get very much attention, as I already knew how to read, and arithmetic was easy. The teacher would take one glance at my slate and say, "That is fine, Virg," and spend her time with the other students.

An incident occurred that I would always remember. I was walking homeward with three classmates through an area that was not completely settled. There were lots that were not cleared of brush, trees, and berry and hazelnut bushes. We were nearly opposite a woman hoeing in her garden. I had heard some of the classmates saying, "Tony is a Dago," and I asked, "Tony, are you a Dago?"

The woman let out a yell. "He is a Dago, but you a sonabitch. I killa you!" She started after me with the hoe. I ran across the road into the brush and woods. She barely missed me with the hoe. I could always run like a rabbit and went through a small opening easier than she could in her long dress. I crawled under some wild blackberry

3

bushes and lay still, trying not to pant. She finally gave up and left the area. I sneaked out and went toward home. It was a wonderful feeling to be safe. Near home I met my father, who was looking for me.

"What happened, Son?"

I told him truthfully the whole story.

"You embarrassed Tony and his mother by calling Tony a Dago, which is a slurring word for Italian. Remember this: You have no right to embarrass anyone without just cause. Do you think you are better than Tony just because he is Italian?"

"I am an American."

"Tony is just as American as you are. How would you like it if they said you are an Indian, a half-breed or a breed?"

"I am not, and I would be mad if they did."

"Virg, you are one-fourth Indian, or a quarter-breed. We are proud of our Indian blood, but we don't tell anyone. Our skin is very white and no one would suspect it. When you embarrass someone, you make an enemy. Friends are more rewarding. Use the person's proper name and never say Dago, Wop, Kike, Chink, Mex, coon or nigger. Regardless of their color, they are adults. Address them as Mr. or Mrs."

After my terrible scare, this lecture was engraved forever on my mind.

The second grade was a repetition of the first. I was not aware that I couldn't hear well.

That summer, after working for two years in the car shops of the railroad, my father was eligible for a family railroad pass. The family went back to Illinois where both parents were reared. I remembered my grandfather as a small man who spoke quietly with affection to me and my brother. The fact that my grandfather would not touch a gun during target practice with my father's old .22 that he had left behind made a lasting impression. When we were alone, I asked my father, "Why wouldn't Grandfather shoot at the target or touch a gun?"

"When he came back from the war, he would not shoot anything. Someone else had to kill the hogs when we butchered." Grandfather had been a sharpshooter and had served four years in the Army during the Civil War. He had been in the Manassas or Bull Run, the Wilderness, and with Sherman. He had never been hit, but sometimes had holes in his clothes. Sharpshooters did not march head on, but remained at the edges of the fighting. When he marched in the Veterans' Parade, he wore a sharpshooter medal.

Ora Cross had kinfolk in the Missouri Ozarks, cousins she had not seen for years. She took my brother and me and boarded a train for a few hours' ride. We were met at the station in Gainesville by a tall, slim, bushy-haired, heavily black-whiskered man.

"Ora, I'm your cousin Jeb."

4

After the suitcases were loaded, the five of us climbed into an old black surrey. Soon we left the flatlands and went on a dirt road that led through a draw toward distant hills. It was hot and dusty. The team was slow and my seat was tired and hurting. I don't remember going to bed.

Refreshed the next morning after a breakfast of grits, ham, bisquits and gravy, I was feeling good. Jeb and Sara Lee had a passle of kids, some older, same age, and younger. They were anxious to show their cousins around. Right after breakfast people began to arrive on horseback, muleback, in wagons and buggies. All were cousins, second cousins, aunts and uncles. Ora Farrell Cross was something. She had graduated from college. They were proud of her.

It was to be a three-day doings. To my surprise they marked off three 6-foot circles and started to play marbles. Horseshoe games were being played by the men. The women were gossiping, talking, and preparing the evening meal. It seemed that everyone brought some kind of food. Chickens, ham, sausage, pies, wild game, yams, vegetables. Someone brought a boar hog that Jeb had asked for.

My brother Farrell was three years older. Portland was famous for its marble championships, and Farrell had won the championship of the fifth grade. He asked if he could play and was rebuffed, "Sonny, these men are good shooters. You are not old enough." The player was in the bottom ring where you worked your way up.

Farrell said, "I can beat you."

"Go ahead, Sonny."

Farrell won the lag and promptly knocked the two crockies out of the 6-foot circle. He moved up to the first ring and stayed there until he got tired. I couldn't play marbles worth a darn and I was just another young'un.

To get rid of us, the mothers sent me and four other children with buckets down to a creek to catch crayfish. It was fun, wading barefoot, getting wet and reaching under the bank to get a crayfish, trying not to get pinched. We took a different route back through the oak woods to the house. There was an opening in the dense woods. I smelled a strong, sour smell. The clearing had a big, boiler-like thing with some curling pipe. There were barrels full of yellow corn that smelled, stacks of wood, and a lot of small kegs.

"What is that?" I asked.

"That is the still."

"What's a still?"

"You dummy, a still makes liquor. We never say 'still' or talk about it."

The dinner was really a picnic with the food on a table and everybody lining up and helping themselves. I was sitting at a table. An elderly man asked, "Young'un, what did you do today?"

5

"We had fun. We played hide and seek. Then we caught a whole bunch of crawfish, and we saw the still."

The silence was instantaneous. There was a long hush. I wished I could hide.

Finally: "Young'un, we never, ever say still and don't you forget it."

After the picnic, lanterns were lit. There was banjo playing, fiddling, singing, and dancing. It was still going on when I went to bed. The last thing I heard was, "Swing your partner."

One or two days later, Cousin Jim said to me, "Let's go watch the hogs." The first pen had several hogs in it. They were motionless, snoring, only flicking an ear occasionally to get rid of a fly. Jim said, "After they eat the mash from the still they are drunk and just lay there and grow fat."

In another pen was the boar with two young sows.

"Virg, don't get in there. He's a mean'un. See those tusks? He can rip you open with them."

The boar went over to one of the sows, sniffed and nosed under her tail and leisurely mounted her. It looked like a whirling corkscrew that entered the gilt. Both the boar and sow stood still with eyes closed. The boar gave a hunch once in a while.

"Why does he do that?"

"Pa sez that a boar sez 'ever jig I make a pig and sometimes three or four.' They fuck for hours. Don't say 'fuck' around grownups or you'll get a whuppin."

Back at school in Portland, the third grade started all wrong. I was in the back seat in the far corner. It seemed that I couldn't understand the teacher. She started calling me stupid. Then she told me I was dumb. My mother couldn't understand why I couldn't get my school work done. Teacher said I didn't pay any attention to her instructions. Rowena Cook was the pretty girl of the class. All of the boys were crazy about her except me. I thought girls were messes. At recess one day the boys were talking about girls. I didn't enter into the conversation. One of the boys said he saw Rowena's pants. He was asked what color they were.

"They were not bloomers. They were short pants and I could see her bare knees." I, without thinking, said, "I suppose you want to fuck her." The boys all laughed. At noon one of the boys told the teacher, "Virg said he wanted to fuck Rowena." The teacher called in another teacher. They took me out in the hall and beat me with a strap, calling me a stupid, dumb monster. Someone told my mother about the whipping. The talk with my mother was a painful one. She explained to me that fuck was a rude, crude word that refined or nice people never used. If I used this word I could expect to be punished.

"Virg, if you remember never to say anything that you do not want

6

to be repeated, you will keep out of trouble." Then she explained to me how babies are made.

I failed the third grade. My parents discovered I could not hear. A specialist removed growths from my ears, which cured the hearing problem, but the "stupid" and "dumb" remarks remained deep-rooted in my mind.

When we returned from our trip to the East, Father was notified that the company in Texas was bankrupt and there would be no more interest payments on the money they owed him. He had been back to work only two weeks when the I.W.W. called for a strike and he was unemployed. It was a tough time for the Cross family. We moved out of a nice house to a shack with a hydrant and no inside plumbing. We ate lots of liver at 5¢ a pound. My father dug cesspools, and my mother did housework and washing. Odd jobs barely kept the family in food. That summer the family took a ride up the Williamette River to the hop fields, where my parents picked hops.

I was walking along a path by the river with some other children. We came to some bushes, and someone threw a clod into a hornets' nest. They all started to run. I heard a scream. A 2-year-old girl had been left alone and the hornets were buzzing and stinging her. I ran back, picked her up and ran crying as the hornets were stinging my face and neck. Older people rushed out and helped us. I was deathly sick. The camp doctor gave me some shots. It was three days before my eyes were open enough to see. Everyone came around and said what a hero I was. Happily, the little girl also completely recovered.

IDAHO

An ad in *The Portland Oregonian* stated that workers were needed on the new rich irrigation tract at Twin Falls, Idaho. With only a few dollars and a suitcase with his good clothes, my father rode freight trains to Idaho. He sent most of his $40 a month to us. After three months my mother had saved enough for the train fare to Twin Falls. They didn't charge for my 3-year-old sister who was born in Portland.

Father was manager of a developing apple orchard that was owned by a New York syndicate. Mother cooked for the two hired men. The grocery bill was paid by the syndicate and Mother was allowed to buy anything she wanted. To me it was paradise, being able to eat all I wanted of meat, milk, pies, and other dishes that used to be portioned out.

My brother and I thinned apples at 5¢ an hour. By the time the Fourth of July arrived, we had saved nearly $5 apiece. There was to be a celebration in the nearby town of Hansen. Our parents let us each take a whole dollar to spend. This turned out to be quite a task. We tried the merry-go-round first at 5¢ a ride. The ferris wheel the same. The penny toss games didn't deplete the capital very fast. Food and drink were expensive— 10¢ for a big hamburger and 5¢ for all the ice-cold lemonade you could drink. One hundred fire-crackers cost a dime. We took them home. Balloons were 1¢ and 5¢. We were completely worn out trying to spend the dollar. In spite of being stuffed with food and drink, I won the 50-yard dash for 8- to 10-year-olds and received half a dollar. So I actually returned home with 55¢.

After one year our family had saved enough to buy a cow, a team of horses (Slim and Madge), and a wagon. With the help of a long-time friend, Harry Davis, my father rented a farm on the Gooding tract, named after U.S. Senator Frank Gooding. The house was a tar paper shack. There was one long room with a canvas-covered sleeping porch on each side. We two boys slept on one side, our parents and Evelyn on the other side.

Water was hauled two barrels at a time for the house and Daisy, the Jersey cow. The horses were taken to the river a mile away. After irrigation water was turned on in the spring, water was hauled for the house only.

We had never had a dog. We dreamed of having one of our own and made much over the neighbors' dogs. When our father came back from town one day, he brought with him a small, stocky, yellow ball of fur. The color was the gold, brown, and white of a collie. The nose was not pointed, but short, with a rather heavy jaw. The paws were so big for such a small pup that they looked ludicrous. Father said, "He will grow into them." And he did. We named him Rover. He was our close companion for many years. He loved to chase tumbleweeds as they rolled with the wind across the bare fields.

Fortunately, 45 of the 60 acres of arable land was planted in red and white clovers for seed. Father didn't know very much about raising clover seed. He contacted the county agent and, following his advice, raised an unusually good crop of clover seed. The family got up at daylight, mowed and shocked the ripe seed while the dew was still on to keep it from shattering. A rainy weekend helped. The neighbors traded work during threshing. The women helped each other with cooking for the crews. They vied as to who could put out the best meals. I was relegated to the kitchen. My mother and I scalded and plucked eight large fryers for one meal.

Our 10-bushel yield per acre of red clover seed was almost unheard of. The price was 45¢ per pound. The stack of 120-pound sacks of seed got higher and longer each day. Father, with a shotgun by his side, and Rover slept on the pile at night. Each sack was worth $60, or twice a man's monthly wage.

This very profitable first year marked the beginning of a short-lived prosperous period. The landlord built another room onto the house for a living room. The new oak table and chairs, with a buffet to match, were Mother's pride and joy. The Edison phonograph with its diamond needle was in constant use. Neighbors called to hear Phillip Sousa's band, Caruso, and to laugh at the Uncle Josh records. Every fall after the crop was harvested, father would order a keg of iced oysters shipped in from Portland. This went into oyster stew for a neighborhood party that ended up with tables of Rook.

The cow herd had increased from Daisy to five head. A substantial cream check paid the grocery bill and more. Two Percherons, each weighing 1,800 pounds, did the heavy work. Father had a sizable savings account in the bank and when a neighboring 80 acres came up for sale, he bought it, paying $6,000 of the $20,000 down and to pay $1,000 a year, plus interest. The Luckenga place had a good house, with a windmill and tank, but no indoor plumbing. Being naturally gifted, Father put in a sink, toilet, and bathtub. The housewarming was quite a party. There was a constant flushing by pulling the chain of the high water closet. It was a new experience for many of the guests.

I dreamed through grade school. My mother saw to it that I studied enough to pass and that was all I cared about. It seemed to me that the teachers didn't like me and I thought they were on the stupid side. Anyway, I never communicated with them unless I had to. My mother despaired of my barely passing grades. When she contacted the

9

teachers at P.T.A. meetings, they left her with the impression that I was just plain slow and it was difficult for me to learn. When I was in the fifth grade, she attended school one day to see what the problem was.

The arithmetic class that day was on addition. The blackboard was two-sided. The teacher would write a column of numbers on one side and turn it over, and the students would compete to see who could be first with an accurate answer. Mary Elizabeth Thomas was the champion. It was an optional challenge deal. Near the end of the class, Mrs. Haight said, "Does anyone want to challenge our champion, Mary Elizabeth?" Herb Clark and Ruth Bevington did. As usual, Mary Elizabeth beat them, but just barely. The teacher remarked how good Mary Elizabeth was and how exceptionally good in mathematics—and no wonder because her father was a banker. Then she said, "Does anyone else want to try?" I had never challenged, but wanted to show off before my mother, and held up my hand.

"What is it, Virgil?"

"I would like to challenge Mary Elizabeth."

The teacher laughed and turned to the class and said, "Virgil thinks he can beat Mary Elizabeth!" I was stung by the ridicule.

"I can beat her."

"All right. Class, be quiet while I write the numbers on the board."

Mary and I, each with a piece of chalk in the right hand and an eraser in the left, waited for the boards to be turned over. My mother was embarrassed by my brashness and thought it would be impossible for me to win—but she did hope for a miracle. The blackboards were turned. Mother told my father that night that I moved my piece of chalk down the first column, wrote the number, up the second and down the third without even hesitating. I finished and turned around when Mary Elizabeth was getting started on the fourth column of 10-digit figures. The teacher checked my answer. It was correct. She, the class, and Mary Elizabeth were dumbfounded.

"Class, one time doesn't mean all that much. We will try again and see if Virgil is really that good." The result was the same. Mary Elizabeth was red-faced and glaring at me.

I asked, "Would you like to try for a third?" The bell rang.

At home, Mother admonished me for being a smart-aleck.

"I don't care. That teacher is partial to the town kids. She gives them the good grades and all I ever get is an old 'C' or worse."

Clem Ault and Herb Clark were classmates starting in the fourth grade. In fact, they lived on adjoining farms. Fortunately, all three families were responsible people with principles, manners, and education above average. Being country boys, we were looked down on by the town kids. I felt that and was sure Clem and Herb felt the same way. The townspeople had nicer clothes. Their shoes didn't need

to have manure cleaned off them. It seemed that the town k\
stayed together. I liked to help people and was very outgoing. B -g
gullible, I always believed everyone, and was often getting hurt or
getting into trouble. It was difficult to understand why people said
things to hurt other people. My father told me, "When you say
something derogatory about someone else, you are actually running
yourself down, because people think you have something to hide and
are calling attention to someone else.

"Son, your life is an adventure like a story. You can control it and
make it very interesting, or you can merely live, work, and die. Do not
hesitate to try new things as long as they do not harm you or other
people. Sharing and caring can be said in one word—helping. If you
help, are honest and pleasant, the whole world is yours to enjoy. Hitch
your wagon to a star and you'll be rewarded."

This message was repeated to me in various ways all through my
adolescent years and accounted for my having many unusual
experiences.

TRAPPING

We three children, Farrell, age 14, myself, 11, and Evelyn, 6, were seated at the breakfast table with our parents, eating cracked wheat that had been soaked the day before, scrambled eggs, two slices of bacon each, and a pitcher of milk.

"Finish your breakfast, you have plenty of time," Mother said. I was really impatient to get started.

My father cautioned, "Remember to get back as quickly as you can. It is your turn to herd the hogs to glean up the scattered grain heads on the wheat stubble."

I scraped my plate clean. "May I go now?" I asked. Before breakfast I had completed my morning chores, measuring out feed for the hogs, filling their water trough, and currying Slim and Madge. I went out the door, grabbed the four No. 1 Victor traps, and called to Rover. I walked briskly across the road and through the fence belonging to our neighbor, Martin Silk. The field had been in hay, with only the stubble left. I was not thinking of my surroundings, but of cleaning up a stack of muskrat hides on stretchers, of sending them off and getting a check in the mail. Then I could get that .22 rifle from Sears-Roebuck catalog at which I had looked so many times that the page was almost worn out. Rover ran around looking for a rabbit to chase.

It was Saturday morning, October 1, a typical Idaho fall day with bright warm sunshine and a very blue October sky. A slight chill in the air suggested winter's approach. In the shady spots there were sparkling patches of frost. The willows and poplars still had leaves that showed many shades of green, yellow, and light brown, depending on the exposure to the chilly winds. It was the first day of trapping season. I had been anticipating this day for a long time, and had read the book about trapping muskrats and talked with trappers. I knew there were muskrats in this bend of the Big Wood River because I had seen them swimming in the wide spot that had grassy banks and soil they could burrow in, and I had marked the bank in several places where muddy water was coming out of their underwater burrows.

The first set was to be by a large willow which I had blazed. With a one-bladed Barlow knife, I cut a branch off the willow to stake out the trap.

A voice said, "What are you doing?" I looked up to see a tall, slim man who wore a Stetson hat, Levis, and polished boots.

"You must be Mr. Silk. I am going to trap muskrats. I hope you will let me trap on your land."

"It will be fine for you to trap on this side of the river, but not on the other because the traps and dog could bother my cats. Have you ever trapped before?"

"No, but I have read about it and talked to a lot of people."

"Would you like me to tell you how to do it?"

"I sure would."

"You mean, you surely would. First, you want to stake your trap so it won't get lost. Then trim the stake so that when the rat gets into the ring of the trap it will slip over the short-cut branch and will not slip back. The rat will drown immediately and will not suffer. If he can get at his leg, he will gnaw it off." He showed me how to trim the stake and set the trap.

I thanked him and started to set the rest of the traps. Rover came nosing about, getting in my way. I slapped him and told him to go away.

Mr. Silk said, "Boy, you never hit an animal. They remember the hit more than they will remember two hundred good things. Remember, they are your friends. They can't help it that you are their owner. Call Rover to you." Then he petted Rover, who really knew no commands. He sat down and talked to Rover and made friends with him. Then he told Rover to sit and gently sat him down and praised him, holding his hand over Rover's head. When he told Rover to sit again, the dog did so and was rewarded.

"Virgil, you are going to want a horse. Make friends with him first by blowing in his nose. That is the way horses make friends with each other. An Indian cowboy taught me that. I am looking for one of my cats. Have you seen one?"

"We have been feeding a black cat with a white face for three or four days."

"That is my cat. I'll go over and pick him up."

Martin Silk walked over to his horse, patted and talked to him, mounted and rode away. I set my traps in four different underwater holes, staked them and trotted home. I was just in time to hear my mother say, "Would you like to have dinner with us Sunday, Mr. Silk?"

"I surely would. What time?"

"Two o'clock."

Martin tipped his hat and said, "Thank you, Mrs. Cross."

That is the way the Cross family met Martin Silk.

At the supper table that night my mother said, "He is really the English gentleman. His grammar is perfect and he is so polite."

My father said, "He was one of the first settlers here and it is rumored that he had shoot-outs with gunmen in the Lincoln County

13

...nd sheep wars and with Indians. He is still alive, hale and
..y, almost 90—and they are not. Ed Bowers saw him shoot a hawk
ou. of the air with a pistol."

"Finish your dinner, Virgil," my mother said. I had been rapt in a
violent fantasy. There were Indians charging toward Martin who was
calmly shooting them down with a pistol in each hand as he galloped
toward them. Also he was shooting at outlaws who were trying to steal
cattle, picking them off one by one.

I had a difficult time going to sleep after setting my four traps for
the first time. I dreamed of a large muskrat in each trap. According to
the price list of Funsten and Company, fur buyers in St. Louis, a large
prime muskrat would bring at least a dollar or even a dollar and a half.
Six muskrats would buy the Stevens single-shot .22 rifle. Catching a
lot of rats would mean money to buy a lot of things. I would start a
bank account and save money.

I was already awake when my mother called, "Time to get up,
boys." The morning was nippy. Pants, shirt, and socks were hurridly
put on over the long-handled underwear that had a drop seat.

The pigs squealed and grunted for their breakfast of grain wet with
warm skim milk fresh from the separator. Typically, they crowded to
the spot where the mixture was being poured into the trough. I liked
the pigs and talked to them and scratched their backs. Pigs have it
really easy—all they have to do is eat and sleep. Feeding milk to the
lone calf took only a little time. By the time I had washed and combed
my hair, breakfast was ready. The blessing was short. The successful
clover crop had changed the diet of our family. Sunday breakfast was
special—bisquits, sausages, eggs, and gravy.

"Take it easy, Virgil. You have to wait until breakfast is over, so
enjoy your food."

Finally, I could leave. Over my red plaid mackinaw coat I put a
burlap potato bag to carry the rats back. I tried to whistle "Buffalo
Gals" as I skipped along. Rover was running back and forth, trying to
find something to chase. The chain of the first trap was in place. I
pulled it up and it was still set. To replace it in the underwater hole
meant rolling up my sleeve and putting my arm in ice-cold water over
my elbow. Rubbing took away the cold pain. The chain of the next set
was out of sight, too far to reach. Cutting a willow limb and leaving a
stub of a small branch at the end retrieved the chain. The big rat had
drowned. I showed it to Rover and told him what a fine big muskrat it
was. The next trap yielded a toe and it was also unset. The last trap
contained another large drowned rat. In a week the total number was
11 hides that were properly skinned and stretched according to a
U.S.D.A. Bulletin on muskrat farming and care. My mother helped me
package the furs and mail them to Funsten Fur Company in St. Louis.
Their advertisement said it would take 10 days or two weeks. After a

week I started looking for the mail. Two weeks later the letter came while I was at school.

"Let me help you open it," Mother said. "You don't want to tear the check."

"All right, but please hurry!"

The check was for $15.78. This was a lot better than driving a hay derrick 10 hours a day for 50¢!

"Tomorrow is Saturday and we will go to town. If you wish, you can put your money in the bank where it will be safe and you can draw some of it out or add to it. You will get a bank book and blank checks."

"Can I put the money in the bank and write a check to Sears-Roebuck for my rifle?"

"That would be easier and cheaper than a money order."

Saturday evening I asked my father to help me order the rifle.

He said, "Virgil, before we order this rifle, there are several things you must agree to. You are never to take the gun out of the house without our permission. You are never to load the gun in the house. You are never to point the gun at anyone—loaded or unloaded. If you break any of these rules, what do you think we will have to do?"

"I suppose you will sell the gun."

"Right. I will have to go with you for a while until you learn to hunt safely for yourself and everyone else."

It seemed like forever waiting for the box from Sears to arrive. My father said they were probably waiting until the check cleared. It was a happy time when the gun was taken out of the box and put together. This was followed by a period of supervision by my father on gun safety. It was nearly two months later that I killed a jackrabbit on my first solo hunt. I skinned the rabbit for a grateful Rover.

No gun was ever better cared for. The Les smoke-improved black powder shells demanded that the gun be cleaned after every use to prevent corrosion of the barrel. I trapped Wood River and ponds during October and November for the next eight years. My savings account slowly grew larger.

Skunks were plentiful and easy to trap. A note to my parents from my teacher said, "Either Virgil stops trapping skunks or he stays home from school." I stopped trapping skunks.

I was hunting cottontail rabbits for food in the lava flow, a mile or so from home. There were pockets in the lava 5 to 8 feet below the top of the flow. These could be a few feet to many feet across. The pockets were full of rich soil and the sagebrush, safe from fire, grew 6 to 8 feet tall and 8 or more inches thick.

Clem, my long-time friend, said, "What makes those long scratches and shreds the bark on the sagebrush?" We climbed down into the hollow. There in the snow were cat tracks almost as large as

15

Rover's footprints. Bobcats.

"Clem, bobcat hides bring $7.50 each and the sheepmen pay $2.50 bounty. Let's get four Victor coyote traps and go in as partners. We will have to trap only on Saturdays and Sundays."

"Why only Saturday and Sunday?"

I was thinking about what Martin Silk had said about drowning muskrats. "It would not be right for the animals to suffer longer than necessary."

We discussed the matter with my father, who said, "You will have to check the traps morning and evening. You can take turns looking at them."

Clem didn't have any money, so I offered to buy the traps and he could pay his share out of his half of the income. We shot jackrabbits and wired their hind legs about 4 feet up on the sagebrush, after slitting their bellies. The trap was wired to the base of the sagebrush and covered with sagebrush bark. The four traps were placed in promising locations over a half-mile. We had barely enough weight to spring the large double-springed No. 3 Victor traps. Because lava looks the same all over, we marked the locations with white flags. Clem stayed overnight with me and in the morning we set out, riding Slim and carrying the Stevens .22 and a gunny sack.

The first trap had a large, freshly-caught male which we shot. The third set had another large male. We were so excited!

The next day, Sunday, we pulled our traps. A big female with a beautiful coat was the catch. We reset our traps every weekend, moving to new territory until we were several miles from home. There was never a weekend that we didn't get at least one of the big cats. Money was rolling in. Some of the hides brought as high as $12.50. We had sold over $200 worth of hides and bounty.

Then, on a Saturday morning, there was a bob kitten about the size of a housecat in the first set. It was caught by a hind leg. A piece of sagebrush had caught in the jaws and held them partly open so the leg was not broken. My first thought was that I must shoot it so it wouldn't suffer, but when I raised the .22, it looked at me so pitifully that I couldn't pull the trigger. I took off my coat and spread it over the kitten. Holding it wrapped in the coat while stepping on the springs at both ends of the trap to open the jaws wasn't easy. When the springs were pushed down by the weight of my feet, the jaws of the trap opened and I was able to lift the kitten out. Limping, he scrambled out of the lava pocket.

I unwired the trap and put it in the gunny sack. I also picked up the other three traps. When I got home I hung the traps on the side of the granary.

"Are you through trapping?" my father asked.

"I am not going to trap anything that will not drown immediately."

"I am very proud of you for following your conscience. Money isn't everything. Peace of mind and liking yourself is important. Remember, like yourself for what you are doing and have done. If you can't like and respect yourself after doing something—don't do it, regardless of how much it costs."

I trapped muskrats and mink all through grade school and until my junior year in high school. I always had a bank account, small though it was, and had a few dollars available to spend.

MARTIN SILK

No one knew of Martin Silk's background. It was evident from his manner and accent that he was an Englishman. His intelligence and knowledge of literature and world affairs indicated that he was extremely well-educated. No one ever heard him mention anything about his early life, or why he came to America. He had money. When he arrived in Salt Lake City, he took the stage coach to Shoshone, Idaho. He purchased a horse and buggy, loaded his baggage and guns, and drove to Toponis (now called Gooding, Idaho). After looking around at land, he purchased 160 acres of bottom land bordered by Big Wood River. This land was partly irrigated from the river and had a patented water right. He filed on an additional 160 acres of land that was not cultivatable because of a lava flow, one of the remnants of the seven lava flows that kept forcing Snake River south to its present course.

He apparently did not know much about cattle and free range because cattle are always confined within fences in England. The former owner, Ed Bowers, and his wife were hired to help with the cattle and cook. The first thing Martin did was to order barbed wire and cedar posts. Ed told him, "The other cattlemen and sheepmen are not going to like these fences. They will not like having to drive their herds 3 miles around through the lava rocks."

"This is my land," Martin said. "That is what they will have to do. It may take them a while to get used to it, but they will."

Martin attended some of the socials, dances, box suppers, and picnics the first few years. The town really buzzed with rumors when two carloads of red brick, lumber, and a windmill and tank were set off at the siding in Toponis. A bricklayer from Salt Lake and two local carpenters built a two-story brick house complete with windmill, tank, and running water, and a toilet that had the water closet touching the ceiling with a long chain for flushing. There was a curved cement walk leading to the driveway and a lawn with newly planted trees and a couple of lilac bushes.

Martin had an open house with the help of three women who served food and drink. It was the talk of the area. People came from miles around. The main attraction was the flush toilet. Most of them had never used one and they stood in line to try it.

One lady said, "Mr. Martin, I'll bet someone is coming to live in this house."

18

His reply was, "You could be right."

The town became Gooding, and Gooding County was formed from Lincoln County. It had a courthouse. The records in the courthouse showed that Martin Silk had applied for a marriage license for Martin Silk, age 34, and Emily Broadhurst, age 24. In such a small place this soon became public knowledge.

A short time later, a beautiful young woman, an older woman and a man stepped off the pullman at the railroad station and were greeted by Martin who was driving a shiny new buggy with red spokes and a fringed, tasseled top. Their luggage and boxes were loaded onto the spring wagon driven by a hired hand. Emily attended socials and dances and visited Martin's few friends. Everyone expected to hear the announcement of the wedding. The whole community was stunned when after about a month, Emily, the older woman, and man, baggage and all, took the train to New York.

Mrs. Bowers said Martin was never the same . He stopped all social life. He seldom smiled, but was always courteous and polite.

Shortly after this tragic set-back, the Lincoln County cattle and sheepmen's war broke out. It started with the cattlemen having a good time stampeding sheep to death. They burned sheep wagons and even killed some Basque sheepherders The sheepmen brought in gunmen and the slaughter began. Historians claim 30 to 40 people were killed. One of the last incidents that caused the governor to bring in the militia to stop the hostilities was when the sheepmen put out a herd of sheep in an advantageous location. They had riflemen hidden strategically, and a cattleman and his two sons and two cowboys were killed while stampeding the sheep.

The Silk herd was taken off the open range to prevent trouble, and part of his ranch was put into pasture. Martin wanted to improve his herd. He was informed that there was a young registered whiteface bull at Richfield.

Record of inquest at Gooding County courthouse:

Judge: "What is your name?"
"Martin Silk."
Bailiff: "Put your hand on the Bible. Do you swear to tell the truth, the whole truth, and nothing but the truth?"
"I do."
Judge: "Mr. Silk, you brought in two bodies of men, saying you shot them in self-defense. Did you shoot them in self-defense?"
"I did."
Judge: "Have you ever seen or talked to these men before?"
"I have never seen or talked to them before."
Judge: "How can you justify the killing of these men?"
"Your Honor, I was going to Richfield to the Draper ranch to buy a

young bull. I left my ranch at 9 o'clock yesterday morning. I took the trail through the lavas, not wanting to go on the main road from here to Shoshone to Richfield. There has been so much trouble. I did not want any hassle. I did not meet anyone until after I left the lavas. I stopped at the saloon and restaurant in Richfield, had a drink and ate lunch. The bartender told me how to get to Draper's ranch. There were three or four other customers and I did not recognize any of them.

"It was about 2 o'clock when I arrived at the Maroni Draper ranch. Draper and I looked over his herd. I checked over the Hereford bull and decided to buy him. I also bought a heifer that was in heat so he would follow, and a 4-year-old cow that would lead. I stayed all night at the Draper ranch and left at daylight. Had a little trouble getting the cattle to trail, but once we got into the lavas we made good time.

"While I was busy trailing the cattle, I was still nervous and looking out for trouble. I had not seen anyone. There was a tug at my coat sleeve and boom boom at the same time. I flopped over the saddle horn as if I were hit, flopping one arm and acting as if I had trouble staying in the saddle. They didn't shoot anymore. I guess they thought I wouldn't last very long. Out of gun-shot range they were following me but not very fast. Ahead of me there was a bend in the trail that hid me from their sight. There was a break in the ridge on the right. I turned and rode back a couple hundred yards and climbed over the lava ridge to where I could watch the trail. I got there just in time. They were trotting their horses and talking, looking for tracks. When they were opposite, I raised my gun and shot twice as fast as I could pull the trigger. They both fell off their horses, dead. The horses ran a short distance and stopped. I rolled the men into their slickers and tied them on their saddles. Then I went back to gather the cattle. I trailed the cattle into my ranch, leading the two horses. Then I brought the bodies into town and reported to the sheriff."

Judge (to the six-man jury): *"Do you have any questions?"*

The foreman, after consulting the jury, said, *"There are no questions, Your Honor."*

Judge: *"Will the jury convene and reach verdict."*

After 15 minutes the jury filed back in and sat down.

Judge: *"Has the jury reached a verdict?"*

Foreman: *"We have, Your Honor. It is justifiable homicide, for self-defense."*

There is no record of the following story, but it was often-told.

When Martin Silk settled on his ranch there was still Indian trouble. Every spring Chief Little Thunder led his band of 40 or more back from winter quarters in Nevada. They gathered and dried camas roots for flour, and caught and dried the large and very abundant salmon trout from Big Wood River. They ate wood or rock chucks which

20

numbered thousands in the Camas plains area. When they camped by the river near the eastern boundary of his farm, Martin was apprehensive, and after considerable thought he rode out and met Chief Little Thunder. They had a friendly talk. An understanding was reached. Martin's cattle and horses would not be touched, and his property would not be stolen or molested. In return, he would let the chief pick out one fat cow. This arrangement went on for three years.

Martin got up at his usual time one morning and rode a mile up the river to the upper pasture in the far corner of the ranch. He walked his horse on the grass, observing the cattle and feed. When he went through a willow patch, there were two Indians skinning a heifer. One of the young Indians grabbed a bow and shot an arrow that didn't enter, but scratched Martin's hip. The other Indian was just bending his bow when Martin shot and killed him. The first Indian ran away through the willows. Martin rode the mile to the Indian camp, asked the chief and two of his counselors to come with him. When the Indians searched the area, looked at the cut on his hip, they gave the peace sign and said, "Still friends."

Martin Silk died at age 91. He left $50,000 to the Catholic Church, his ranch and some cattle to a nephew who had to live on the ranch without mortgaging it for 10 years. His life remains largely a mystery, but he was a good friend.

GROWING UP

It happened during the Christmas holidays. My brother Farrell and I were skating down the river. Rover was harnessed to the flexible flyer sled. We were close to the hill, ready to slide down. Two boys about our size ran across the ice toward us. The older, Ivan Parks, was carrying a 410 shotgun. They ran alongside as we were skating on each side of the sled. Ivan pointed the gun as if he were going to shoot Rover. Farrell said, "Stop pointing that gun at Rover."

"I am going to shoot that dog. My father is feeding sheep here and he said to shoot every dog." He pulled the trigger. The blast to the shoulder left Rover lying on his side quivering from shock. Farrell kicked off his skates instantly. The Parks boy was reloading his gun when Farrell's shiney stick caught him on the back of the head. It was a good thing that he was wearing a heavy stocking cap. The blow was a hard one. He sprawled out face down on the ice. In the meantime, I had kicked off my skates. My first blow caused his brother to slip on the ice and land with me on top. His heavy clothes hampered him from getting up and I pounded his face with both fists until he couldn't raise his arms anymore. The Parks boys both lay on their backs whimpering. Farrell unloaded the 410. He took the end of the barrel in his hand and broke the stock off on the ice. He threw the two pieces off into the thick willows.

Getting Rover home was a problem. He sat up crying with his leg hanging loosely from his shoulder. We took turns pulling the sled while the other rode, holding Rover.

Rover was put in a box in back of the stove. Fortunately, he had a very heavy coat and was heavily muscled. The wound was where he could reach it, and he licked it constantly. He allowed many of the shot pellets to be picked out with tweezers. For three weeks he lay there quietly, only asking to go out to relieve himself or to sit leaning against the wall to eat. In a month he ran with only a slight limp.

The reaction to the incident by the Cross family was one of unbelievable anger and indignation. The Parks' sheep were being fed on the Fales' ranch. Bill Fales was a good friend of my father. Father called Bill and asked him to have Roscoe Parks call him. At dinner he said, "Boys, you are going to have trouble at school with the Parks boys."

"They are only visiting. They go to school at Declo."

The sheepman never called, and things simmered down for the time

22

being.

It was late in November the next year. Ice was forming on the river, making it difficult to trap as it had to be broken and my arm got achingly cold pulling traps. I decided to pull the traps for the year.

Two of the older Parks boys, then in their late teens or early 20s, had been hauling hay every day by the Cross ranch. There had been no contact or confrontation. My father had warned us to be careful, as the Parks family had a reputation for being arrogant and lawless.

The light snow cracked and squeaked under my feet, the sky was clear, the sun almost warm. There was not a rat in any of my six traps. I heard a voice say, "Ivan, there he is. Go beat him up." My father had gone to the neighbors. Evidently the Parks men thought I was home alone and Ivan could get even for the beating he had taken the year before. Ivan took off his coat, and I shucked mine. They put a piece of stick on Ivan's shoulder and told me to knock it off. I had seen this before and the fellow that knocked off the chip always got hit really hard first. I immediately hit Ivan with a right to the nose. We were evenly matched in size and strength. When Ivan fell on me, they let him continue to punch. When I was on top, they pulled me off and held me until Ivan got in a punch or two before they let me go. The second time this happened there was a shot. My father was standing on the bank with a shotgun pointed in the air.

"We are going to have a fair fight." he said. "There is to be no kicking, biting or hitting when one is on the ground. They will fight 2 minutes and rest one. You (pointing to the older Parks man) will keep time. You are also your brother's second and you may give him advice between rounds. You (pointing to the other) will be the referee and I will see to it that you do it correctly." He handed his Ingersoll watch to the timekeeper, broke the shotgun open and reloaded. The gun was never pointed in any way that could be considered menacing.

The fight began anew. Two evenly-matched boys stood toe to toe and rained punches on each other. During the rest break, my father said, "Virg, he has a hard head and you aren't really hurting him. This time, feint with your left like I've taught you and hit him in the belly with your right. He will bend over, then hit him as hard and as fast as you can in the face until he quits—and he will."

It worked, and Ivan gave up, whimpering and crying. Both were badly bruised. Father, with his left hand, handed the gun to me, saying, "Be careful, it's loaded."

The older Parks boy was to his left and slightly behind him. He started to take a step with his arm raised and fist closed. Father had anticipated an attack from the rear. Pivoting on his left foot, he swung a low right into the midsection which actually doubled the man over. Without hesitating, he charged the older Parks and luckily landed a punch to the jaw that allowed him to pound the man at will until he

23

collapsed. Grabbing the other Parks by the hair, he slapped him until he cried. With both of them sitting on the ground, he gave them a lecture about people's rights, shooting the dog and what kind of crumbs they were, and promised that if there were anymore trouble he would have a meeting with their father which wouldn't be pleasant. It was pointed out to them that he had never aimed the gun at them or referred to it as he had been hunting and was just passing by.

"Virg, hand me the gun. I am going to count to 10 and you had better run as fast as you can." He counted one, and they took off running as fast as they could. This ended the Parks confrontation. Either they were finished hauling or they used another route, because no more loads of hay were hauled on the road past the Cross ranch.

Our farm was bordered by a road that was the main route the sheepmen used to drive their flocks to the hills. The drives started in May. Sheepmen were notorious for letting their herds graze on the unattended fields beside the road. Most fences were of two or three strands of barbed wire, and the sheep could walk right under the wire and into the fields. The sheepmen were old-timers, a rough, tough arrogant breed as a whole. They regarded the new settlers as interlopers. Many farmers came home from a shopping trip to town to find 20 or more acres of a crop ruined after being grazed by a band of one or two thousand sheep. Herders got bonuses for these acts. A day's grazing for a thousand ewes and lambs was worth several hundred dollars in weight gain.

On a Saturday the Cross family rode to town in the canvas carry-all behind Slim and Madge. I was left behind to tend the irrigation water, to see that the proper amount of water was running down each corrugate. Too little meant that the water would not reach the end of the field or soak up the 2 feet of soil between corrugates. Too much would wash and waste water. I was busy, as the water had not been set very long.

The wind was blowing from the direction of the house toward me. I thought I heard a bell. Looking toward the house a quarter-mile away, I saw the white top of a sheep wagon. I knew the sheep would be ahead of the wagon and possibly already grazing in our field of white clover near the house. I grabbed my Stevens single-shot .22 rifle, which I always carried for shooting rock chucks, called Rover and ran for the house. When I climbed over the dike at the north side of the 10-acre clover seed field, I was furious, sick at heart, and mixed up at the sight of the field almost completely covered by grazing sheep, and sheep were still coming in from the road. The herder was sitting on the ditch bank holding a long staff. His dog charged for Rover and immediately ran away howling and limping from the larger dog.

I yelled, "Get those sheep out of here. Take them out, Rover."

The herder said, "Don't run the sheep. They will bloat." White

24

clover is very lethal to sheep and cattle because the high protein content of the legume makes them susceptible to bloating. If a cow or a sheep is made to run so that they are heated, it causes excess gas, creating too much pressure on the lungs and the animal suffocates.

The herder walked toward me, holding the end of his staff in both hands. I cocked my rifle and pointed it at the herder's belly with my finger on the trigger. "If you don't sit down by the time I count three, I will shoot you. One, two...." He sat down. Rover had been taking the sheep out as fast as they could run. He had them back in the road in a hurry. In the road the sheep started to drop. The herder didn't dare move them until they cooled off. Over 20 died. The herder and camp tender skinned the sheep. They also sent for a wagon to haul away the carcasses. They were almost through skinning when my family came home. My father asked the herder for whom they were working. The herd belonged to Senator Gooding. Father took a sheep pelt with the G brand in red paint on it and put it in his barn.

The herder asked, "What are you going to do with that?"

"That is going to be evidence." About that time, Will Deasy, one of our neighbors, stopped by and looked at the sheep and damage. Father said, "Take a good look. I may need you as a witness. I am going to show the sheepskin to John Thomas and Senator Gooding and ask them for damages."

Will said, "Al, the Senator was entering the First National Bank as I drove by it."

Slim and Madge were hitched up; Father loaded the sheepskin in and trotted the team 3 miles to town. Senator Gooding was in the bank talking to his partner and manager, John Thomas. Dad waited at the desk.

"What can I do for you, Al?" asked Mr. Thomas.

"I want to speak to Senator Gooding."

The Senator said, "How can I help you?"

"Senator, your herder sat on a ditch bank in my field and watched a herd of sheep eat in my white clover field. I contacted your herder; I have a hide that one of your herders skinned off a bloated sheep."

"How many bloated?"

"I would guess about 20."

The Senator swore and said, "That is a big loss!"

"That is not the only loss. I have witnesses and the loss to the clover crop is at least $250 to $300."

"Well, I am not going to pay it."

"Mr. Gooding, you give me a check for $250 now or I will file a claim in small claims court and you will have to pay it and court costs. I will also get out a newspaper story and a Senator can't afford that kind of publicity."

Dad took the check and deposited it.

25

That evening when we were doing chores, he asked me, "Would you really have shot him?"

"He was trying to get close enough to hit me with his staff. If he came any closer, I would've shot him in the knee—if my gun had been loaded."

"Virg, you showed good judgment. The last thing you want to do is shoot someone for whatever reason."

Our six milk cows furnished the main source of cash income for living expenses. Turning the crank of the DeLaval separator to separate the cream from the milk was a morning and nightly chore. Cream was kept cool and sold to cream buyers based on the percent of butterfat in it. The skim milk was fed to the hogs. Herding the cows on a vacant square mile of undeveloped sagebrush fell to me. I rode Slim, the untrusty horse. This piece of land was almost bisected by a slow-moving canal. Several small feeder ditches came out of each side of the canal to furnish water for the farms. Cheat grass grew in the sagebrush and was excellent feed until the heads became dry and unpalatable. On the banks of the ditches and canal, grass grew rapidly. After breakfast it was my job to board Slim and herd the cows to the grazing area a mile away. Actually, the herding consisted of just following the cattle while they grazed. The gently flowing, 3-foot-deep canal was safe and ideal for a 12-year-old boy to swim in. By a silent but mutual agreement, the Cross cattle used the west side of the canal and the Coppinger girls, Mirth and Wilma, herded their cows on the east side.

There was a headgate that diverted water on both sides. The slightly deeper hole below it was ideal for swimming. Noon was a rest period for the cows, and shade from trees near the headgate made a handy stop for the three herders to take a swim and cool off. The girls wore their bloomers and shirts. I wore my shorts, which said "Cupid" on the seat because my mother had made them out of a Cupid flour sack. Swimming usually lasted about half an hour, then half an hour for the underwear to dry out before we could finish dressing. I thought the girls were rather forward, especially after they stopped and watched a bull service a cow. They made remarks about it that I couldn't hear and laughed after the conversation. A wet girl in bloomers and shirt did not look at all interesting.

What happened next might not have happened if their 18-year-old sister, Helen, had not married the hired man. The couple lived in the bunk house on her parents' ranch. The bedroom windows faced the foot of the bed. When the window was open, the shade lacked almost 2 inches of reaching the bottom. They left the coal oil lamp with a bullseye reflecting on the bed away from the window. In the summer the girls slept on the sleeping porch. Their parents slept upstairs on the other side of the house. The girls could hear occasional laughter and other sounds. They decided to watch. There were poplar trees close to

26

the bunkhouse window, and they could lean against a tree and look into the window, which was eye high.

Fred, the sister's husband, was nearly 30 and appeared to be experienced. The couple was busy exploring sex acts. After watching the couple's love-making for nearly two weeks, the girls got the idea that I might be able to do it to them. The next day, after the ditch rider had checked and measured the streams at 11 o'clock, the girls decided to go swimming.

"Let's swim without our clothes," said Wilma. "It's such a mess to wait for our clothes to dry." I thought it was a good idea and we all stripped and jumped in. They were bashful at first and kept just their heads and shoulders above the water. They finally waded over with the water coming up to their navels and gradually only to their knees. It was the first time I had seen a naked female. Thirteen-year-old Wilma had a black curly bush below her navel. It turned me on.

"Look," said Mirth to her sister. "It is bigger than Fred's! It is longer but smaller around." All three were so sore the next day, nothing happened. My mother noticed my walking gingerly and asked what was the matter.

"I'm chafed from riding bareback."

She gave me a washpan full of warm water with boric acid in it and a small, nearly empty bottle of Vasoline, saying, "Keep it in your pocket. We have another full bottle." This cured the problem. The Vasoline came in handy, especially with 11-year-old Mirth.

For the next six weeks, until the feed dried up, the girls watched by night and we practiced by day. The week Wilma didn't swim was somewhat of a relief for me.

I spent the rest of the summer helping with the haying and irrigating. I visited the girls and we tried to get together under the ruse of playing hide-and-go-seek in the barn with one of the girls watching. Their mother always took a long time gathering eggs and setting hens in the barn. Wilma said, "Ma is suspicious of us." Anyway, we only got to play hide-and-seek. The Coppinger family moved to Montana that fall.

Uncle Jack and his wife, Alpha, father's half-sister, came out for a visit from Illinois. Uncle Jack Wharton could see how well his brother-in-law was doing. He went back to Illinois, quit his job as a telegrapher and moved to Idaho. The renting of a farm was easy, but he lacked the necessary capital to get started. Getting credit or a loan from a Gooding bank was a problem. Father, over the protest of Mother, cosigned Jack's note for $1,250. It didn't seem much at the time. Later it would seem like a fortune.

Magic Dam on Big Wood River was the source of the all-important irrigation water. If it filled, water was abundant and crops were profitable. The developers had counted on heavy snowfall every year.

27

What followed were two dry years. There was not enough water to make a cash wheat crop, and we had only one cutting of hay instead of the usual three. Uncle Jack had to borrow more. Father couldn't make the payments on the place. After two years of drought, the bank foreclosed. Having to move from a good house and farm of our own to a house without plumbing again was heart-rending for the family. During this period I had grown tall and slim. It could have been my Indian ancestry that accounted for my unusual wiry strength.

The sinking of the Luisitania by a German U-Boat left questions as to why. Headlines read that thousands were killed in France. World War I didn't make much impression on a 12-year-old. We had meatless Tuesdays and wheatless Thursdays. Grade school children knitted washrags for the soldiers. My washrag kept getting bigger and bigger. Finally, the teacher unraveled it and rolled the yarn into a ball and gave up on me. There were Victory Stamps at 25¢ each at the post office. I was very proud when I saved enough stamps to buy a $50 war bond.

I was riding my bicycle into town to get a library book; I could hear bells, horns blowing, and shooting before I reached town. People were dancing in the streets. I thought they had gone crazy. Then I heard the war was over and rode back home as fast as I could to tell my parents. They were elated. That evening my father said, "This means the end of high prices for farmers. I will sell the wheat tomorrow." He was right, as wheat was selling for half as much a month later. The lower prices did not affect our family much, as our five cows and 200 laying hens brought an income that took care of living expenses.

The Business Men's Club had a telegraph wire to the 1918 World Series with a board diamond and men that were placed on it as the wire came in. Walter Johnson was my idol. Uncle Jack, who could understand Morse Code, placed some profitable bets.

It was either 1919 or 1920 when the big event happened. We got our first car. A Model T Ford touring car with side curtains and all. It was reliable except it kicked back on the crank when you advanced the spark too far before cranking to start it. The backfire could break an arm. Sometimes it stopped due to trash or lint getting on the mag post under the seat. The coil box sometimes got jarred and we had to rearrange the coils. A rock was hazardous to the thin tires, which also picked up horseshoe nails left by many generations of horses. A tire pump, jack, patches, and boot patches were a must. We could go farther than we could with Slim or Madge and get back in time to milk.

Mother cooked chickens and made up other goodies for a picnic. We piled into the car and headed for Hagerman Valley. It was July 24, the day the Mormons celebrated as the day they arrived in Salt Lake, commonly called "the Mormon Fourth of July." This celebration was the big annual annual event of the area.

Just going to Hagerman Valley was a treat. It was an oasis, a valley bordered by 400-foot lava cliffs on the east, Snake River on the south and west as it meandered its way through the lava flows westward to the Columbia. The Gooding tract was so new that very few ranches had shade trees except a few who had water rights under the Carey Act. Others had only the Wood River for irrigation water.

When you reached the top of Justice Grade and looked down into Hagerman Valley, everything was green. The tall trees, poplar and maple, green pastures, fruit orchards, and clear, cold streams of spring water. It was such a contrast to the sun-baked and dusty sagebrush desert, spotted with irrigated fields and tar paper shacks of the farms, whose water had to be hauled from the river or from wells of the few people who had them in the Gooding area.

Justice Grade was steep with hairpin turns that angled back and forth within a distance of about four blocks. In order to drive it safely, one had to keep one foot on the low pedal and the other foot on the brake. It was a terrifying descent. My mother would keep her eyes closed.

Actually, the valley was the result of Lake Bonneville, the huge inland sea, and the seven large lava flows that covered a vast area in Utah, Idaho and Nevada. The Great Salt Lake is a remnant of Lake Bonneville. The high-water mark can be seen on the hills high above Ogden. When it broke through the hills to the west end of the Salt Lake Valley, Snake River was formed. It flowed westward to the Columbia to the ocean. The river would be dammed for a period of time and deposit soil. During this period there were seven huge lava flows which started in the north and continued to the south. A lava flow would block or dam up the river, and the river would change its course southward again. The channels of the old river were not completely blocked, leaving many channels 300 to 400-feet deep underground, carrying spring water that came out of the lava walls of the canyon for almost 31 miles, creating many clear, cold springs. Some of the springs, like Thousand Springs, Blue Lakes and Clear Lakes are as large or larger than many rivers.

The celebration was held in Caltharp Park. It had an artificial lake, auditorium, stage, benches, and heavenly green grass. The shade of the trees felt good, as we rarely had any shade at home. There were horse races on the gravel road in front; a band played. Foot races were held for kids of all ages. I had been practicing with my brother Farrell. My father said, "Put on an extra pair of socks." I did. I won a whole silver dollar.

The last event of the day was Grandma Vader. She had to be in her late eighties or early nineties. What a character she was! All of 5 feet tall, maybe a 100 pounds, walked as if she were 6 feet tall and as spry as a cricket. Her voice was surprisingly clear, sharp, and penetrating. You could hear almost every word she said. She came out on the stage in a long dress and a bonnet, with a hoe in her hand. Her story started with their stop at the river near the spot where Owsley's ferry later operated. It was in August of 1870. They were on their way to Oregon with a wagon train. The feed was good; it was an ideal place to rest the horses and cattle for a few days. A trapper rowed across the river, talked to her husband, saying what a desirable area of land was untouched in the valley across the river. For supplies the trapper agreed to take her husband to look at it. He found what he thought was an ideal piece of land, 160 acres, bordered by a big spring, Billingsley Creek on the west, and the canyon wall rising nearly 300 feet to the east. They had to go to Glenns Ferry to take the Three Island Crossing to get across the river, then drive 40 miles back to Hagerman Valley. They filed on the land, built a log cabin, putting in the small glass windows that they had so carefully guarded all the way across the plains from Missouri. There was water, salmon, and trout in the streams. Deer and antelope were abundant. Indians were catching salmon by the hundreds at the upper Salmon Falls and drying them for food and trade. The trapper said, "They are generally peaceful and friendly, but there are a few renegades that go around stealing and killing. The Bannocks, Nez Perce, and Blackfeet are causing trouble, but they seldom wander down this far. The soldiers at Fort Boise have pretty much cleaned up this area. At the rate people are coming west, this will be settled in a few years and the Indians will be crowded out."

This is what we saw and heard after her introductory talk. She beckoned toward the door backstage and a small girl, about 12, came out in a long dress and bonnet, hoe in hand.

"Becky and I were hoeing in the garden." So they hoed a few steps. Grandma looked sideways for an instant and said, "Becky, don't stop hoeing. Don't look up."

"Yes, Mama."

"There are three Indians with guns sneaking up on us in the rocks by the canyon wall. Keep on hoeing, don't look up. When we get to the end of the row, I'll say, 'Run.' Run for the cabin door. If I don't make it, bar the door. The double-barreled Greenier is loaded and ready. Shoot if they try to come through the window." They hoed on to the end of the row (closer to the stage door). Grandma Vader said, "Run, Becky!" They both ran through the cabin door. Grandma came out with the shotgun.

"The three Indians fired their muzzle loaders at us, one hitting the door jam, one the window sill. I cocked both hammers back. The Indians were reloading."

She continued her pantomime of the Indians reloading, pouring in powder and tamping the bullets with their ramrods.

"Two of them were standing so close together I could not see past them, so I aimed at them. Boom. The 16 No. 4 buckshot downed both

30

of them. The other Indian started to run and I shot at him, and he , got up, staggered and ran. I grabbed the barrel end of the shotgun to finish him off, but he outran me." The laughter and clapping of the crowd interrupted her at this point. She was holding the gun and panting.

"My husband and sons found him dead about a half-mile away. They buried them and covered their graves with rocks."

Grandma Vader and her great-granddaughter bowed to the audience amid cheers and applause. She could have been a famous actress.

For once the Ford went home without any delay. We had enjoyed a wonderful outing and change of scenery.

Almost every evening in the summer, Farrell, Clem, Herb, and I rode our horses a mile and a half to the river for a swim before supper. Other boys often were swimming in Wood River. A 2-by-12 plank was lodged in rocks and weighted with rocks, serving as a diving board. The water was about 10 feet deep. The only way the swimmers could reach the bottom of the pool was to jump in holding a rock of at least 15 pounds. The pool was lined with lava rocks, worn smooth and rounded by ages of water flowing over them.

Little Virgil Morrison was standing on the end of the diving board trying to get courage to dive the 10 feet down into the water. The older boys were egging him on by calling him coward, chicken, and other belittling names. He slipped as he jumped and his head hit the end of the diving board. He sank like a rock. Clem was in the water close to the end of the board. He dived, trying to reach Virgil as he sank down. Clem came up, saying, "I can't reach him!" I picked up a large rock, which took me to the bottom quickly. I started to swim in a circle on the bottom. Just as I was forced to go up because of bursting lungs, I touched a hand, grabbed onto a wrist. When we broke the surface, I was badly strangled. Clem and Herb helped us to the bank. Little Virgil was not breathing. Emerson Gill was working to be an Eagle Scout and had taken life-saving and artificial respiration. He immediately placed Virgil on his stomach, head to one side, and started to push on his chest and count. One boy got on a horse to go for help. Water gushed from Virgil's mouth during the first few pushes, but within minutes Emerson was rewarded by a cough, then more coughs and whimpering. Virgil lay there breathing with his eyes half-open, probably dazed from hitting his head on the board. A car drove up and a couple put a coat around him and took him home.

Old man Reed was a neighbor. He wasn't really old—we just called him that. He was small, slim and narrow-faced. He had a tall, slim, underfed daughter named Ruth, about my age, and a son who appeared to have Down's Syndrome. We thought Reed was mean and stingy. His stock always looked as if they were being starved. All three of us had worked for him as derrick boy or herding his sheep on weekends, and all of us had become fed up with his nagging, miserly ways, poor lunch, and his never being satisfied with our work.

I started driving derrick for Mr. Reed when I was almost 11. You helped attach the cables to the net and led the horse to pull it up the derrick. When the load was tripped atop the stack, you backed the horse to lower the net, or slings, as they were called. Then you rearranged the slings on the ground and forked any loose hay onto them, and waited for the buckrake, driven by Mr. Reed, to bring in another load. For this I received a dollar a day and lunch, which usually consisted of beans, bread, and fried potatoes. He was what was called a "belly robber" who scrimped on food to save money, and his family looked it. I felt guilty to take all I wanted to eat because there was so little on the table, and always left the table hungry. He made remarks like, "Boy, you sure eat a lot. I don't see how your folks can afford to keep you!"

I had worked five days when he stated, "A dollar a day is too much to pay you. From now on it will be 50¢ a day." It was Saturday evening and he grudgingly paid me the $5. When I told my father about the cut in wages, he called Reed and told him I was worth more than that at home. Reed called on Monday morning saying that he would pay a dollar a day, but father told him I was needed at home.

A year later, Reed was grazing feeder lambs on the crop residue left after harvesting. His fences were only three-strand barbed wire and the lambs had to be herded. On Saturday and Sunday I herded them for a dollar a day. It was easy work, but a boring 10 hours. Sheep are about the most stupid of all farm animals. It was about 10 o'clock and the sheep had been grazing for 3 hours when he drove up. He looked at the flock and said, "Some of them are missing."

"They are all there."

This didn't convince him, so we put the sheep against a steep ditch bank and counted them as they went by. You count sheep with fingers—one finger on the right hand for each sheep and one finger on the left hand for 10. My tally was correct.

"They are all there."

"Just barely."

"You owe me $2."

He took a dollar, a half-dollar, a quarter, two dimes and five pennies from his purse. When I started to walk away, he asked, "Where do you think you are going?"

"I quit."

"Cross, who is going to herd these sheep?"

"You are—if they are herded."

On the way home, I met Clarence Pauls, who said, "I thought I saw you herding Reed's sheep." I told him the whole story. He laughed, "Reed is so tight he can't eat tomatoes because he can't pass the seeds!" Old man Reed got even with me in spades. It happened like this.

Mr. Reed raised watermelons. We decided to try to steal some just for spite. We knew that the Reeds always went to town Saturday afternoon. One Saturday late in August we met at my house. We pitched horseshoes while watching the Reed house half a mile away. Sure enough, about 12:30, the Reed Ford came down the road on the way to town. All we had to do was walk down the road and through the fence to the patch. As we were thumping melons to find ripe ones, we heard a car coming from the opposite direction. As the patch was in plain sight from the road, there was only one place to hide—lie face down in the patch.

The car stopped. We heard the car door slam, and knew we had been had. A voice said, "Hello, boys." Sheepishly, we stood up. There was old man Reed with a grin on his face. With a very pleasant voice he said, "Boys, why don't you just come to me and ask for a melon. I would have been glad to give you one. There wasn't any need to act like thieves. There are lots of good melons here. Let's pick out one and we will cut it and eat it. Here is a real nice one." He picked up a big melon, carried it over to a bench in the yard and sliced it up with his knife.

"Eat it up, boys. Don't let it go to waste."

We almost cleaned it up. We thanked Mr. Reed and started walking down the road to the Cross home. Reed called to us, "You are welcome to another any time." We were thinking that we had been mistaken about old man Reed. He was a fine fellow after all.

When we had gone about three blocks down the road, Herb stopped suddenly, rushed to the side of the road, slipped off his suspenders and squatted and groaned. Within a minute or so, Clem and I were in the same predicament. We all had to make at least six similar stops in the next quarter-mile. We looked back toward Reed's and saw the old man waving at us. He had doped the melon with croton oil.

For the boys to be faithful to each other and willing to defend each other at the drop of a hat for eight grades was very unusual. Clarks owned their farm, had money. They drank skim milk and put lard on their popcorn. It was a common practice for people to be miserly and skimp on food. The Aults were well fed but had little money for clothes. The Crosses didn't have much money, but we butchered hogs and a beef because Father said, "We don't get too much out of this life, but we'll eat well."

When we reached the age of 14, we had to have hunting licenses. Clem could not afford the $2.50 license fee. Herb and I decided that he had to hunt with us. Al Laws was a notoriously mean game warden. He was big, rough, and abusive to smaller offenders. We rehearsed a plan in case he caught us and checked our licenses. We had been hunting in the sagebrush and had six birds. We were cleaning them so they would not taste of the sage they had been eating. Al Laws sneaked up on us. "Let me see your licenses."

Herb and I took off running. Clem stood still. The warden chased us, yelling for us to stop. We let him catch us after running about 50 yards. Laws grabbed me by the collar and threw me to the ground hard. I got up and said, "If you touch me again, my father will beat the hell out of you."

"Who is your father?"

"A. W. Cross."

"Boys, I'll have to take you in because you don't have a license."

We produced our licenses, and he looked around. Clem and the birds were long gone.

"Why did you run?"

"We were afraid of you."

"You are liars. I'll get you yet!"

When we reached my home, Clem came out of the barn to meet us, and we skinned the birds.

HIGH SCHOOL

When I received my large junior high school diploma, it never occurred to me to stop going to school, although many of my classmates dropped out. Herb Clark, Clem Ault, and Marshall Smith all stayed in school. As a freshman I was a little over 5 feet tall and weighed a few pounds over 100. I was growing, and like a puppy I had large feet and hands. My posture, like my father's, was ramrod straight. I was slightly pigeon-toed. My father said I would be a sprinter. I did run a lot and was faster than most of my classmates.

My father said, "Pigeon toes come from your Indian ancestry. Indians with pigeon toes could run faster and more quietly on narrow trails. This came from thousands of years of heredity. The splay-footed were eliminated because they made too much noise and could not run fast enough to escape from their enemies or secure game for food. The same thing is true of blacks because their feet do not turn out, and only the fastest survived the charge of lions and other enemies."

My freshman year started out unfortunately. Just before going to school, I threw a rope over Slim's neck and the heavy metal snap at the end swung around and broke one of my front teeth, leaving a gap that made me very self-conscious. I would put my hand in front of my face when I talked.

Shortly after school started, I really got into trouble. Several of us waited for the school wagon in the shelter of a straw stack near the road. We could hear the constant rustling of mice that had gathered in the straw to spend the winter. Sid Kelly said, "Let's catch some and take them to school."

"I'll put my lunch in my coat pockets, and we can put the mice in my lunch bucket, which has ventilation holes." Everyone had mittens on, and in a short time there were a dozen or more mice scrambling around in my lunch bucket. The first period that morning was an assembly, which began with the singing of the national anthem. That is when the lid came off the bucket. A girl noticed a mouse as she sat down and she shrieked. Then all hell broke loose as girls ran out into the hall. I laughed for a short while only. Mr. Hampshire collared Sid and me and took us to the office. We admitted our guilt and were suspended; we could only come back if accompanied by our fathers.

My father said, "Don't embarrass the family like this again. This is the last time I'm going to school with you."

The second mistake was correcting the general science teacher.

35

Because of the newness of the Gooding Tract, teachers with college degrees were scarce. Most of the high school teachers had only two years of normal school and training to teach in grade school only. Mrs. Collins, the science teacher, was a farm housewife who probably had a minimum of time to prepare for her classes. She never realized how inadequate she was as a teacher. When she explained that an object fell down because it was heavier than air or water, and that was called gravity, I held up my hand.

"What is it, Virgil?"

"Mrs. Collins, according to the dictionary, gravity is the attraction of things to the center of the earth." She got all red in the face and made no comment. Even though I proved she was wrong, she never forgave me and apparently black-balled me with the rest of the teaching staff.

Ray "Rosy" Rosenbaum was huge for a freshman. He weighed over 150 pounds and was 6 feet tall. He was a bully. When he tried to shove me on the school steps, I ducked down. He tripped over me and fell down the steps, losing skin on both elbows and knees. I laughed. This was the start of a vendetta. Rosy would shove, push or slap me every chance he got, making life miserable for me. When I told my father about it, he said, "Why don't you go to the principal?"

"I did, and he didn't do anything about it. Rosy is on the football team and all the teachers think he is great."

"Virg, if you slip up on Rosy, give him a good punch or two into the face and surprise him, then grab him. He will not be able to hit you back because you are too close. You will lose the fight that day, but there is another day."

"He will beat me up."

"He is doing that now. Can you run faster than Rosy?"

"He can't catch me if I have a clear path."

"Try hitting and running. Eventually he will get tired of being hit and leave you alone."

On a Monday morning students were talking in the hall, waiting for the bell to ring for the first class. Rosy was talking and laughing with a couple of the football players. I slipped up behind him, stepped out and hit him with a hard left and right to the face. The surprised and enraged bully tried to hit me, but ended up wrestling with me. Mr. Hampshire, the principal, saw us and stopped the scuffle. He threatened to take us to his office and paddle us if we did it again. Rosy growled, "I'll fix you but good!"

I was scared, but out of bravado I said, "You'll have to catch me first."

During the noon hour, I grabbed my lunch bucket, sneaked out through the basement to an empty school wagon and ate my lunch there. Through the celluloid windows I could get an occasional glimpse of Rosy frantically looking for me. It was a typically beautiful, warm fall day. All the students were outside during the noon hour, playing ball or pump pump pullaway. The 10-minute warning bell brought a rush to the two front doors at either end of the school building. I slipped up in the rear of the crowd. Rosy was two steps ahead of me. A quick survey of the crowd spotted the Ag teacher standing on the other stairway with his back toward me. I slipped up two steps, swung a long, looping, round-house right that landed smack on the right ear. It not only startled Rosy, but slightly stunned him. By the time he recovered, I was safe on the other stairway, talking to the Ag teacher.

This cat and mouse game went on for almost a month. Rosy became very wary and the whole school knew what was going on. They bugged Rosy by saying, "Here comes Virg!" and Rosy would whirl around and square away, much to their delight. The cat didn't always lose. In fact, the cat was winning about one in every five encounters. The mouse got really battered sometimes. The Crosses had a pair of boxing gloves, and my father boxed with me and gave me instructions. We attended some local boxing matches. One of the boxers was partially stunned by a blow to the head and staggered around the ring. His opponent rained a flurry of punches until he went down for good.

"Virg, if you see that Rosy is hurt like that, keep on hitting him until he goes down."

This gave me an idea how to end the battle once and for all. I carried my lunch to school in a half-gallon Karo syrup pail with holes punched in the lid for ventilation. I always had a pint Mason jar for milk. On that day Rosy rode a horse to school so that he would not have to catch his school wagon, and he planned to fix me.

I saw Rosy's wagon leave. Mine was a little late. Confidently, I walked toward my wagon. I looked up and there was Rosy. I ducked under a long right swing, brought my lunch bucket overhand, hitting him squarely on the forehead. Rosy almost went down and started to stagger around. The bucket had come loose from the bail. When the school wagon driver pulled me off Rosy, I was completely exhausted from punching the unprotected face, which was a mess of cuts and bruises. My hands were swollen and cut, but I had no other injuries. When I told my father about the fight, he said the lunch bucket should not have hurt Rosy that much. I told him that I had the milk jar filled with water.

"Virg, you have won the battle and it is time to stop it. Monday, go up to Rosy and say, 'Shall we stop this fighting, shake hands and be friends, or do you want to fight some more?'"

This is exactly what I did. I held out my hand and Rosy took it. I had no other fights in high school. I didn't know it, but the big boys had talked about me and decided they didn't want to mess with me. All I wanted was to be left alone.

During my sophomore year, Doc Ikard, a veterinarian who coached football, paid absolutely no attention to me. Later I found out that he had it in for me because I was a Cross. Doc was quietly romancing a senior girl. My brother Farrell was going with her openly. One day when I was getting my shoes, I happened to jar one of his dress shoes and it rattled. I found a round aluminum condom box labeled "Agnes, Mabel and Becky." It contained only Becky. A week later I checked the shoe again and Agnes and Mabel were there, but no Becky. I knew Farrell would not talk about it, so I never mentioned it to him.

I went out for football in my junior year. I had gained 3 inches in height and weighed 150 pounds. Very few of the seniors were much larger, with only Rosy at 6' 3" and 170 pounds. Farrell also went out for football. Ikard refused to give him a suit, saying he was too small. He was only 5' 5" tall and weighed 125. I played center and linebacker or roving center, as it was called in those days. The football formations called for the center to pass the ball between his legs directly to the ball carrier. Jim Coon, the first string center, was no longer larger than me. I was faster and stronger, and thought I would have no trouble being the starting center. After the first week of drills and fundamentals, which I was sure I had mastered, the first lineup was posted, and I was second-string center. In the scrimmages I completely dominated Jim. In order to run plays through the line, the coach had the guards help Coon keep me from making a tackle. During the first two games at home, Ikard let me suit up but assigned me to hold one end of the yardage chain. The next game was away from home. Ikard took 18 players and left me at home. The only reason he kept me on the squad was that he needed me to have 11 men to scrimmage against.

My father said, "Why don't you quit?"

"I want to play and there is another year. Ikard might be gone and we would have a new coach."

In the middle of the season I was really working Jim Coon over in scrimmage. In one play, I charged, knocking him into the ball carrier, and he was out with two broken ribs for the rest of the season. I thought I would get to play then and really show what I could do. Ikard moved Andy Frederickson from end to center. Herb now weighed 170 pounds and was a regular guard. Clem and Smitty made the trips, but never got to play. Coaches rarely substituted in those days. The final blow was when the coach scheduled a second team game with Richfield and left me at home.

I wanted to play basketball and asked Ikard if I could go out, but was told that I wasn't needed. Only eight men were allowed to suit up for a game. Nine players were out for basketball and Ikard practiced with them as he was on the town team. My appeal to the superintendent fell on deaf ears. Apparently, Ikard also held this against me.

After football season I got my front tooth bridged in by Dr. Miller.

It really helped my appearance, as well as my self-confidence. Girls and teachers commented on how much better I looked. Most of my classmates were dating and dancing. I had not done either.

The L.D.S. Church had dancing classes in their church on Saturday afternoon. Music by a Victrola played "Sleepy Time Gal" and "Mollie and Me." Farrell and I had sent for Arthur Murray's dance lessons by correspondence. Farrell played saxophone in a band and could dance fairly well. I had started to grow and was somewhat awkward. The Murray kit helped some. I had a perfect sense of time, and dancing became easier and fun. When I asked Mary Elizabeth Thomas, the banker's daughter, to go to the New Year's school dance, she stared at me and said, "Who do you think you are?"

This really crushed me to the extent that I didn't date in high school, though I went to the dances. Some of the town girls refused to dance with me when I first started to dance. As I improved, I never asked them to dance again. Actually, I would dance only once with about five different girls. Emily Rhodes was one of my steady partners. I liked her, but the only other people who danced with Emily were her brothers. She was lucky if she got to dance four dances. Emily was tall, blonde, and beautiful. Her face, hands, and feet were normal for her height. Otherwise, she was just plain fat—in fact, very fat. Her Scandinavian mother had insisted the children clean off their plates, or else. Emily always had a smile and we liked to talk to each other. I wanted to ask her for a date, but I was afraid the fellows would make fun of me for dating a big fat girl.

Then there was Elma Miller (Pinky), the ranger's daughter, who came down to school from Fairfield. She had the most beautiful red hair. She was tall, well built, and good-looking, an only child reared in the back woods and allowed to run free. She had a whispered reputation. The Cougar Ranger Station was in the forest above Fairfield and in the summer Pinky would ride her horse and camp out by herself. She even broke horses to ride. I liked to talk to her about fishing, hunting, and camping. We had walked outside from the dance a couple of times and done some petting. I wanted to ask her for a date, but Mary Elizabeth's rebuff still bothered me.

In May of my junior year, it was evident that it would be one of the driest years in history. There wasn't much snow in the mountains and there would be only enough water for one crop of hay instead of the usual three, and the only grain that would mature was early maturing barley. We had previously had three good years in a row and with the cows, hogs, and chickens we could weather it through. Father said he and the neighbors could put the hay up and if Farrell and I could find jobs for the summer, we should take them. My problems were solved just after school was out in May. Riley Smith, a sheepman, drove up to our ranch in his Model T pickup. He greeted my father at the barn and said, "I need a sheepherder for a week. Can you spare Virg?"

"Riley, you can have him all summer if you want."

"If I don't need him, I'll pay him two days' wages. I checked the sheep and the feed is good. I suspect the herder is late starting them out to feed in the morning."

I was delighted to accept the job. I packed my suitcase with extra clothes, toothbrush, and paste. I didn't take a razor, as I only shaved every 10 days or so.

When Riley called at midnight, I got out of bed and sleepily dressed and climbed into the car. Riley explained what he wanted done and my duties while herding. The sheep camp was about 10 miles above the ranger station on Camas Creek. We could drive the car within a mile of the camp. It was a little after 4 o'clock in the morning when we stumbled in pale moonlight to a hill a quarter of a mile above the camp. At 5 o'clock there was a streak of light in the east. At 6 o'clock it was getting light with the combination of mountains, sunlight, and clouds edged with gold breakers. At 7 o'clock smoke started to come out of the chimney of the sheep wagon. The two dogs barked as the door opened and the sheep were started out to graze.

Riley said, "That does it. Those sheep should have been grazing by 5:30. The grass is soft from dew and more palatable. It is also cool, and the sheep will eat more and get heavier. They do not like to eat when it is hot."

I carried my suitcase down to the camp wagon. The border collies, Doug and Sam, were father and son. I had worked with them before and they acted glad to see me. They looked as if they had not been fed too well. Their coats were ragged and full of burrs. Riley greeted the herder and asked how the lambs were doing. Herman, the heavy-set, paunchy herder, said, "The feed is good and they have really been putting on weight."

"Herman, will you catch that lamb for me?"

Herman pointed out the lamb to Doug and Sam and said, "Hold him, boy." They separated the lamb and turned it into the arms of Herman. Riley felt the flesh over the ribs, loin and leg. He asked me to check the lamb's flesh. Every sheepman has a number of bum or orphan lambs, when the ewe dies, has triplets, or refuses to claim the lamb. If a foster mother isn't found, they are killed or given away to be raised on a bottle. Smiths had been furnishing lambs to the Crosses to raise. The ribs of the lamb were thinly covered, the loin narrow, and the leg was not filled out. I was not very tactful as I blurted out, "I think this lamb is skinny."

Riley Smith turned to Herman, "Can you rustle up some breakfast?" It didn't take him long to whip up some sour dough bisquits, bacon, eggs, and potato cakes. While the herder was doing the dishes, the sheepman took me for a walk. He had the map of his range allotment from the forest service, which had been granted to the Smith sheep for nearly 20 years. It was roughly 2 miles wide, following a meandering creek up to a ridge on each side. The area was calculated to be long enough to feed the 700 ewes and 1,000 lambs until about the middle of September.

"The camp tender will bring in the supplies you order each week, and move the wagon to fresh feed and see how you are getting along. I am taking Herman back to Gooding."

We shook hands and I called the dogs and started herding the sheep. I had the sheep out of their bed grounds and feeding at 5 o'clock. That was no problem, as I had been getting up at that time to milk cows. I was busy cleaning up the camp wagon, cooking, and brushing and feeding the dogs, in addition to herding the sheep. The two border collies were veterans, which made rounding up the sheep an easy chore. Sam would be waved to go to the right and Doug to the left. Sheep get used to dogs and vice versa, and the dogs brought the sheep back at a leisurely walk. By this time the sheep that tended to stray had been nipped enough that they followed the flock.

Barney had been a sheepherder's saddle horse all his life. The first day I put a rope on his halter and took off the hobbles that he wore in the daytime. Lazy Herman had not removed his hobbles at night and the pasterns were raw, chaffed, and sore. I washed them with soap and warm water with a little sheep dip added to discourage the flies. Barney appreciated getting curried and brushed. Every morning I blew breath in his nostrils as Martin Silk had taught me, and gave him a cupful of oats with a teaspoon of brown sugar morning and evening. He started following me like a dog, without hobbles, while I was herding. I tied him up at night.

The Smith grazing permit started in the early spring on the sagebrush flats near Magic Dam on the Big Wood River, at an elevation of around 4,000 feet. As the season progressed, the sheep were moved deeper and deeper into the hills and mountains as the feed matured in the higher elevations. The range area followed up a small, clear, cold stream that had trout in beaver dams. The camp was now into the foothills with mountains in the background on both sides. The camp wagon was always placed upwind and above the sheep because of the strong odor of dirty wool. It was placed near trees but never under them because of the danger from lightning. The first week I had a visitor, Ranger Ed Miller. I invited him to share with me the last of a leg of lamb that I had baked. The ranger was checking to see that the sheep were staying in their alloted grazing area. I didn't mention that I knew his daughter.

Riley Smith was pleased with the condition of the lambs. The supplies included a steak, a beef roast in addition to bacon, eggs, and fresh vegetables. In addition to food, I had ordered books to read, and

Mother sent me the *Saturday Evening Post* and *Country Gentleman* which contained continued stories I had been reading. In addition to ordering a cook book, I gave Smith a letter addressed to Miss Elma Miller, Ranger Station, Fairfield, Idaho.

After sheep are moved to new bed grounds, they are uneasy the first night. I was taught that a good herder should walk around them periodically at night with the dogs, keeping a steady conversation. The day of the third move had been hot in the morning. A mass of cumulonimbus clouds moved in. That night the full moon would shine intermittently as the clouds passed across its face. Lightning flashed in the distance, followed by the rumble of thunder. The storm was rapidly moving closer, being pushed by west winds from the Pacific Ocean following the Columbia Gorge to Snake River Canyon and South Idaho plains. Picking my way in the poor light around the 1,700 ewes and lambs took some time. Doug and Sam were whining and acting as uneasy as the sheep. I had just finished the round and was taking off my slicker when there was a tremendous flash of lightning and a crash of thunder that shook the ground. The sheep bolted downhill. I stood there for a few minutes, shaken and bewildered as to what to do. I knew that cattle stampeded, but had never heard of sheep doing it unless pushed by man. Sam, the older dog, responded to my whistle and was sent after the sheep to turn them. I caught up with them half a mile down the hill. Sam had turned them back and was holding them. All the run was out of them and they stood panting with their heads down. It started to rain. I whistled for Doug several times with no results. I was cussing him for being a no-good, worthless dog, running off when he was frightened. In fact, he was no better than the sheep.

When daylight came, I became aware that many of the sheep were missing. There was one black sheep as a marker for every hundred ewes, or a total of 150 lambs and ewes. I was heartsick. I had to find those sheep, and needed the assistance of the missing dog. It was still raining when Sam and I moved the sheep back to camp at daybreak. I hurriedly fixed a breakfast of hot cakes and bacon, and fed Sam. Hanging the field glasses around my neck, I went out on the wagon tongue to look around. I thought I heard a bell. It was a bell! Looking to the left, I saw a band of sheep slowly moving toward the camp. Doug was herding them back. I sent Sam to help the tired and bedraggled Doug. The band of sheep had split when they bolted and Doug had taken the ones that went left. Fortunately, the route they traveled was quite smooth without any rock to cause pile-ups. The count showed all black sheep present. Doug and Sam shared a pile of pancakes with bacon grease and a pound of bacon. The rest of the day was spent finding the seven sheep with broken legs or backs, shooting and skinning them. I cooled a carcass in the ice-cold beaver dam just a little way down the creek, then pulled it up 20 feet high on a rope over a tree limb. Flies would not bother it at that height. Wrapped in burlap and pulled high in the shade during the day, meat would keep for several days.

Ed Miller, the forest ranger, dropped by as I was about to start the evening meal of lamb chops. He complimented me on the way I was conducting the grazing of the sheep. The week's grazing area would be roughly 4 square miles divided into seven sections. That day had been a typical day as the sheep were started to graze on a new section back toward the old section. The dogs and I followed them. I carried a book, my .22 rifle for shooting grouse or scaring away coyotes, and field glasses around my neck. There was usually very little herding to do. When the sheep had grazed for 4 or 5 hours, it was time to turn them back to camp. The sheep liked to rest in the shade of the pines, chewing their cuds and sleeping, until it cooled off in the afternoon. This usually gave sheep dogs and herder a chance to nap and read before they started the sheep grazing back toward camp before the sun went down.

My father had made us aware of the beauty and wonders of nature, which helped dispel most of my feeling of loneliness. It was very pleasant at times to just sit and watch the white fleecy clouds drift across the blue sky, or to watch the colors of sunrise or sunset. The hush of dawn was special as the creatures of the world awoke and made their presence known, and there was a new day in my life.

I had a lot of reading material. One of the books was about geology and I looked for minerals in the outcrops. The book emphasized that silver, lead, zinc, and gold were usually found in quartz in granite batholiths. I could recognize quartz and granite. There was much white, green, and even pink quartz in the endless seams of hard, multicolored granite deposits in the Sawtooth Mountains. The whole area was mineralized, with many outcrops showing a paper-thin streak of galena. A big pine tree had blown down, leaving a big hole in the rocky hillside. I climbed over the roots to take a look at the newly exposed rock. There, boggling my mind, was a foot-wide vein of quartz streaked with shiny bright yellow. As it was time to start the sheep back to camp, I picked up a piece to take with me. I dreamed of finding gold, becoming rich, buying a sheep ranch, a Buick or even a Willys Knight. It had to be gold! My father had told me how to tell real gold from "fool's gold" (iron pyrite). When you hit it with a hammer, real gold will flatten out, but pyrite will shatter. After the sheep were bedded down for the night, I took a hammer out of the wagon tool box, placed my small rock on the iron tire of the wagon. A light tap broke off a piece of pure metal. A much harder tap from the hammer broke it into very fine bits and pieces—no smearing. It was quite a disappointment at first. I remembered what my mother counseled me when something didn't turn out as planned. "There will always be other fish to fry." It wasn't really all that important.

The camp tender brought me supplies on Friday, with a large round steak to cook for dinner. The sheep were grazing on a slope facing the wagon and needed little care. The sun would be down behind Mt. Borah in a couple of hours. I was trying to decide whether to get supper now or wait an hour and eat after the sheep had been bedded down, when I heard the clink of a horseshoe on rock. Sound traveled a long way at 6,000-foot elevation. As the horse came closer, I could see a brown Stetson, red shirt, Levis, riding boots, and a bedroll. When the horse pulled up and stopped, I could see beautiful, fiery-red hair. Pinky.

Periodically, for over a year, I had been having dreams. Someone told me that the phase of the moon determines the frequency. A beautiful, auburn-haired girl would snuggle up in bed with me and I would wake up wet and sticky. But this was not a dream; it was real. The beautiful face was framed with bright auburn hair. Her wide-set, candid gray eyes looked at me mischeviously. The best description of her long-limbed, lovely body was by my brother Farrell: "I like the way her bones are covered." She was the reply to my letter.

I wished that I had a box of Agnes, Mabel, and Becky rubbers in their usual aluminum can. In spite of that, it would be wonderful to have her for a night.

"Gee, Pinky, I'm glad to see you!"

"I'm glad to see you, too, Virg." We hugged, kissed, and held each other tight. Pinky felt the almost instantaneous swelling in my pants and said, "We have all night for that. What are we having for dinner?"

"There is a steak and the camp tender brought me new peas and potatoes. I baked an apple pie today." I put my arm around her and kissed her again.

She said, "Control yourself. If you help me shell the peas and pound the steak thin so I can cut it in strips and fry it quickly, it will be ready by the time you bring the sheep in."

In the meantime, we had unsaddled her horse, taken off the bedroll, and hobbled the horse so that it could graze. I called Doug and Sam and started to round up the sheep that were scattered over a half-mile on the hillside. The swelling in my pants never really went down. I thought about my father and mother's counseling on sex: "If you want to stay out of trouble, keep it in your pants until you are married. If you do have sex, remember this girl is putting her future in your hands and you are to take no chances of getting her in trouble. When a girl gets into trouble she is ostracized and looked down upon for the rest of her life. Under no circumstances are you to tell anyone, because people can't keep secrets. Also, remember she is just as nice and

44

respectable as she was before you had sex."

Finger steaks, creamed new potatoes, and peas, gravy on Mrs. Smith's homemade bread with apple pie for dessert—what a feast!

"Pinky, why did your folks let you get away for a night?"

"They didn't. Because it rained and there was no fire danger, Dad could take a few days leave and they went to Boise. I stayed home so I could visit you."

A sheep wagon was the first camper. Everything was in place, and there was just enough room for a small stove, bed, cupboards, racks, and shelves with a small fold-down table to eat on. It was wonderful sitting side by side, touching hip to hip and leg to leg. Washing the dishes didn't take much time, but it seemed a long time to me.

Pinky said, "Come on, we are going to sleep outside." We gathered up a thick layer of pine needles and spread Pinky's bedroll, a tarp, two blankets, and a pillow. She said, "Clear a space and build a small fire." With such a beautiful full moon directly overhead, I couldn't see the need for a fire. It was well started when Pinky said, "Let's go to bed. I'll undress you and you can undress me."

I thought, "She is experienced, just like Mirth and Wilma. They were only 11 and 13. I guess women are born experienced." When my shorts came off, Pinky said that I was ready. I thought, "How does she know?" We immediately lay down on the bed, facing each other, kissing.

Pinky said, "I just finished my period and I probably couldn't get pregnant, but just to be sure we'll use this rubber that I snitched from under my mother's matress. It is a Trojan, one of the best. Do you know how to put it on?"

"I never have."

"I'll do it for you. You have to leave some slack in the end or it might break." She reached over, pushed the foreskin back and was squirted with a stream of milky fluid. She laughed. I laughed. Before the evening was over, I found that she was even more experienced than Wilma. The rubber did break in the morning while she was putting it on after the fourth careful washing. I was in love. She said she would try to get back the next week, as her father would be at a district meeting in Twin Falls. I gave her a letter to mail to Farrell asking him to buy a dozen Trojans, put them in a package and give them to Riley Smith to send up by the camp tender.

Pinky arrived early the next Friday night and stayed until Monday. We were in love. We talked about everything, walking hand in hand while herding the sheep, shutting out the rest of the world with our fantasies. I gave her another letter to mail to Farrell. When she arrived the next Friday, I went to meet her, all aglow with anticipation. Her father rode up and said, "Get on your horse. We are going home." That ended that for the summer. I thought it would be fun when school

45

started, and I would be able to see her again.

I had seen bear tracks, but none near the camp. I told the camp tender and he gave me a model 97 Winchester shotgun and a box of buckshot shells. That evening the dogs were uneasy, walking around and sniffing the wind. Barney was also jittery. I thought it must be a change in the weather. I had been sitting up reading *Moby Dick* by the kerosene lantern when Barney screamed, the dogs were cowering and barking under the wagon. There was growling and the sheep were making distressed noises. I grabbed the shotgun and was out the door in seconds. The sheep were crowded up and in their midst was a bear biting and ripping them with his claws. I couldn't get nearer than about 50 feet to the bear because of the sheep. I pumped three shots into the bear as fast as I could. The bear squealed after each shot and started to run. When he cleared the sheep, I emptied the gun at him. With ropes I tied up the seven wounded sheep. They needed to be sewn up and protected from flies.

I cut off a foot-long section of hemp rope, unraveled the strands to single stout sisal threads, put them in a strong solution of sheep dip in a bucket. There was a package of darning needles in the wagon for darning socks. With sharp shears I clipped the wool away from the wounds. Using a pair of pliers to push the needle through, I put stitches half an inch apart. I applied sheep dip to the sutures and to the smaller wounds to prevent flies from laying eggs and causing maggots. I had to refill the lantern, as it took all of the night and part of the morning to take care of the wounded. Riley Smith arrived as I finished sewing up the last casualty. He praised me for the job I had done and said he would give me a bonus.

"Riley, school will start September 3rd, and I would like to have a few days off first."

"How about August 28th, that will give you three full months of pay. The camp tender will bring a herder in the morning and you can ride Barney home."

Believe it or not, Barney had never been saddled. Because he had not been ridden for three months, he bucked and I almost hit the ground, but managed to grab the saddle horn as I fell and stayed on my feet. I remounted and Barney only crowhopped, so we started the 70 miles back to Gooding. Riley Smith had come early, saying he would look after the sheep until the camp tender brought the new herder in.

Barney was fat and soft. The alternate trotting, walking, and galloping was making him tired. Apparently he did not like carrying the the heavy load, because when I stopped to open a gate, 10 miles into the journey, Barney did not stand as he was trained to do when the reins were put down. When I approached him, he started down the trail-like road ahead of me. When I ran to catch up with him, he ran just a little faster. After futilely trying to catch him for a mile or so, I gave up. I cut a long willow switch and took after Barney, hitting him on the rump and telling him to "Git." This was fine with Barney, but he had to run with his head to the side to avoid stepping on the reins. I was in the peak of condition because I had been running every day, chinning myself, and exercising. I had a grudge to pay back in football. Barney started to lag after being chased for over 2 miles. He stopped at a creek and let me walk up and take the reins and mount.

I knew that I couldn't make it back in one day, so I stopped at Art Dallen's place and helped him milk for supper and breakfast.

The Smith ranch was a mile south of Gooding. I had a heavy black, bushy face—an accumulation of three months of not shaving. My heavy dark hair was a mess. It had been cut twice with sheep shears by the camp tender, who used a bowl over the head for a guide. Jesse Crow, the barber, said, "I'll have to charge you 75¢ for a haircut and shave." When Jesse finished, the combed back, wavy hair looked very sharp. The white exposed skin contrasted with the dark tanned skin that had not been covered by beard.

When we reached the Smith ranch, Barney did not even roll. He just took a drink of water and laid down. He was completely tuckered out.

Being home, able to sleep in my own bed, to sit down to breakfast and have someone to talk to besides the dogs, was really a wonderful feeling of contentment. Slim whinneyed and came galloping to meet me when I helped milk in the morning. Dad was really glad to see me, as the threshing machine would be there before noon.

Barley was the only crop that would mature in the short dry season. Many farmers had planted wheat only to cut it for hay. I was given a place on the stack forking barley bundles into the hungry maw of the threshing machine, fed by an endless belt. Barley beards were scratchy and you had to change clothes completely after work. There was much to do before school started in four days.

Clem, Herb, and I were not eligible for football because of Latin. Miss Erb had given us a final quiz which consisted of part of speech declination, conjunctions, and so forth. We were put on probation, which consisted of translating Ceasar's *Gallic Wars* and reading a chapter of her choosing. I hadn't touched a book. I knew Herb would have the translation. That evening I rode Slim over to Herb's and borrowed a copy of his translation. It took several hours to copy in a loose leaf notebook.

The next task was buying clothes. The check for $150 for three months' herding, plus a $10 bonus, was really a lot of money, as a clerk in the bank made only $40 a month. Clothes were an item. I had gained at least 30 pounds and 2 inches to reach 172 pounds and 6 feet, which made me one of the biggest boys out for football. My shirts had to be 16 and shoes size 11. The navy blue Hart Shafner and Marx suit

47

was my first suit, costly at $22.50. Harry Levy, the proprietor, tailored it to fit my 42-32 body. Black dress Florsheim shoes were $5. A heavy, all wool sweater was $10, and when I had everything added up it came to $65. Harry threw in a tie and a leather belt. I had deposited $50 in the family checking account because I knew they would be short of cash. This left about $30 in my bank account. If I worked at odd jobs, I would have enough money to get through the school year.

Monday was registration day. Herb had contacted Miss Erb and we were to take our Latin test at 2 o'clock in the afternoon. I was first. She looked over my notebook and translations and said, "That is good. Now read or translate this chapter for me." When I rattled off the translations of the chapter, her comment was, "Virg, you surely have studied hard. I should give you a B, but since you failed the first test I'll give you a C+."

I replied, "It took a lot of time to get it right." When I took Latin, I thought it was to learn to read and write it, which I learned to do very easily.

Father said to me, "You seem to be walking on air. How did school go?"

"Wonderful, Dad. There are four new teachers from the University of Idaho and Dwight Kuhns is the new coach. Ikard is going to teach only chemistry and physics. I will have to take chemistry under him for college requirements."

"I know you don't like him and he seems to have a grudge against Crosses. That doesn't keep you from learning all you can from him or from any other person you do not like."

Dwight Kuhns was a direct contrast to Ikard, who acted as if he were God himself and players were just slaves to be ordered around. The first practice was drills and calesthenics to get into shape. The squad had only 23 or 24 players and coaches were allowed to take 18 men on a trip. Coach Kuhns was going to medical school the next year. He was aware that the team would be thin in substitutes so he spent considerable time the first two weeks on conditioning and showing us how to protect ourselves by falling properly and how to take a hit. In the first drills everyone was short of breath and gasping after windsprints, with the exception of John Arkoosh and myself. We both had herded sheep at over 6,000-feet altitude. In fact, we had been only 10 miles apart all summer. The conversation between Fenton Prince and John went something like this:

"John, did you have a good summer?"

"I sure did. She visited me several times at the sheep camp. I got to fish a lot in the beaver dams."

I knew that it had to be Pinky who had visited him. I decided then and there that that was the end of any relationship other than casual. I acted as if I had never heard the conversation, and never repeated it because I thought Pinky should be protected. I couldn't understand why the boys bragged about their sexual exploits, why they talked about girls the way they did. Last, but not least, why they bragged about going to the whorehouse in Shoshone and paying $2.50 for something that lasted only a few minutes. The $2.50 was a whole day's work pitching hay. When Chink Bryan and Billy Boyle got the clapp and braggingly told everybody about it, I remembered the sex education class from when I was a junior. It was a one-period class. Boys were in one section and girls in another. Dr. Cromwell warned the boys about getting diseases from promiscuous sex with prostitutes. The Reverend Miller, also President of Gooding College, lectured them on the carnal sin of masturbating and admonished them that it damaged their brain and if they continued to do it they would become idiots.

My father quite often asked, "What did you learn today?" trying to instill in his children to go to class with the thought, "What can I learn today?" It just happened that he asked me that question on the day of the sex education session. I informed him of Dr. Cromwell's warning, and what the Reverend Miller said.

My father laughed and said, "Son, if that were so, the whole world would be full of idiots. Masturbating is a natural outlet for unmarried people and is not harmful, if not done in excess."

This was somewhat of a relief to me.

FOOTBALL

I was looking forward to football all summer. There was no question that I was bigger, stronger, and faster than the year before. My mother's cooking had added another 6 pounds to my weight in two weeks, and the coach had measured my height at 6 feet flatfooted. In the drills I didn't go all out because of the danger of injuring someone. During the second week of school, a game was scheduled for the following Friday with Shoshone.

Clem was solid in a starting guard position, but his mother was drowned in a fishing mishap that week, so I filled in for him. Shoshone had a huge, 190-pound player called Butch Angelo. His prowress and strength were the talk of the high school football league, and his ability to overpower the opposing lineman and get to the ball carrier was known by every coach.

Coach Kuhns said to me, "Virg, I know you want to play center and linebacker, but you will have to fill in for Clem. John and I (John was the assistant coach) believe you are the only man that can handle Angelo." This conference really fired me up. I was going to play, and to start a game!

Shoshone, the starting point for early-day mining in the Sawtooths, was a railroad terminal and was larger than Gooding.

No one in the football squadron trained more religiously than I did. A breakfast of two poached eggs on toast, a slice of ham, and a generous helping of hash-brown potatoes downed with two glasses of milk satisfied my hunger. No school that day after 10 o'clock. In the dressing room the air was filled with excitement. There was considerable talk as to how big the Shoshone players were, and how mean they played. Butch Angelo was also a focal point of conversation. Gooding had won only one game under coach Ikard the year before. I thought they expected to get beaten again and were rationalizing ahead of time. The 20-man squad had lunch at the U.S. Cafe. In the dressing room, Coach Kuhns told us that this was our first game and if we each did our part we could win. He went over the duties of each position and a lot of stress was put on me.

On the kickoff, I, being one of the fastest men on the team, got to the ball carrier first. He was carrying the ball like a watermelon, away from the body, so I tackled the ball which squirted backwards and Herb fell on it for a touchdown. Shoshone was famous for running the ball through the line with big Butch opening the holes. They tried three successive times with Butch leading and gained only 3 yards. Before the day was over, I realized that I was faster and stronger. Gooding won by 25 points.

The next game was with Caldwell, a much larger school. That week, Herb's father was working under a binder and the team moved up, killing him. I was playing guard again, but not very spectacularly. We were going to play Boise the next game. This meant staying overnight at the Idanha Hotel and eating in restaurants. We ate at the Mechanafe which served the food on a moving belt. You could take anything you wanted for one dollar. That was really a treat. The proprietor told the coach not to bring us back because he lost money.

The crowd of two thousand, the band, the wonderful atmosphere excited me so much that I could hardly sit still. Andy Fredrickson started at center. Herb and Clem were back, and I was sitting on the bench. Gooding won the toss of the coin and received. Cliff Toone, the sprinter, and Nick Asquena had made good gains to the Boise 20-yard line. Leon Pagoda, Boise's huge Basque center, was All-State and he was just simply running over Andy and anihilating him. Andy had been keeping him out of the backfield, but was getting badly mauled. On the next down Andy went out with a badly sprained ankle. I went in and on the first play was knocked flat by a blow to the neck. On the next play the same thing happened, and the only difference on the third play was that I got a handful of dirt thrown in my eyes. Pagoda would tell me every down that he was going to lay me out. Fortunately, Toone scored on an end run and Boise had the ball.

On the first down, I brought the edge of my palm down on the back of Pagoda's neck. I didn't floor him, but brought out a warning, "I'll kill you for that." Luckily Boise had a long drive with several downs. I continued to deal out punishment. Pagoda became erratic in passing the ball back to the ball carrier in a Notre Dame box formation. They fumbled but recovered. He became so erratic the coach put in a substitute who played in a sportsmanlike manner. With Pagoda out, I could concentrate on the ball carrier. Higgs was a sprinter and he just bulled his way up and down the field. The way he ran, he was all feet and knees. Tackling in those days was supposed to be shoe-top or ankle. It was cowardly to tackle any other way. Coach Kuhns called a timeout to try to stop Higgs. Gooding was a touchdown ahead at that time. I said, "Coach, if you will let me play 5 or 6 yards back of the line instead of 2 yards, I can get a run toward the line and meet him as he comes through. If I tackle him high and hit him in the ribs, it will slow him down.

"All right, Virg, we will try it. Clem, you and Herb leave a larger gap between you to invite Higgs to run through. I believe Virg can plug that hole."

It worked on the next play, as Higgs took the ball 4 or 5 yards

51

behind the line of scrimmage and headed for the hole between the two guards. I was at full speed when Higgs got to the line of scrimmage. I was slightly to his left and gave him a hard shot into the ribs with my right shoulder. When the referee picked up the ball, Higgs was down with the wind knocked out of him. The substitute back lasted three downs before succumbing to the same tactic. I suddenly discovered that if you hit the hardest, you get hurt the least. Higgs went back in and again in the second down had the wind knocked out of him. By this time I was really pumped up and it seemed that no one could stop me. The Idaho Statesman, in its review of the game, credited me with 14 tackles, recovering two fumbles, and blocking a punt. In the dressing room, the team all gathered around me and patted me on the back. The crowning incident of the day was when Coach Kuhns introduced me to Sib Kleffner of the University of Idaho coaching staff. Kleffner said, "Congratulations on the great game you had today." This was a great surprise to me because I thought the Toones, Princes, and Rosenbaums were the best players and the stars. Here I was, getting the honors. Gooding won all the rest of its games, playing some of the largest schools in the state. During the rest of the season, because of the hard, bruising tackles that often ended up in injuries, I got the reputation of being the dirty Cross kid. I sometimes got booed and heckled.

I was busy after football season. The new teachers were an inspiration to me, so I decided to take part in school activities. To my surprise, I made the debate team in spite of the efforts of what I thought of as "the brain trust." I was on the negative side of the subject, "Should the U.S. join the League of Nations?" At first it seemed hopeless. I told my father, "I've put my foot in my mouth again."

"What did you do?"

"I got on the wrong side of the debate. I made the team. We flipped a coin and our side lost."

"Virg, if you have the best argument, you can win even though you think you are on the wrong side."

"Dad, what points should we stress?"

"You should bring out the past history of each of the countries in regard to their relationship to the other countries. For instance, France has always been a quarrelsome trouble-maker. Germans are a race of arrogant, overbearing people and will try again for world domination. People of Spanish descent tend to be erratic and explosive. If you scratch a Russian, you scratch a Tartar. They are suspicious, perhaps due to the blood left by Tartar and Hun invasions. Sweden and Norway will not fight. England, Canada, and Australia will stand fast with the U.S."

My teammates, Ted Miller and Ruth Bevington, based our debate on the fact that there were many different ideologies and backgrounds, it would be ridiculous to think the European nations would stay with their agreement and ratification if it conflicted with their interests. As a team we were undefeated. Time proved that Woodrow Wilson's dream that a League of Nations would settle international problems was a complete failure.

I was surprised to get a minor part in the senior play.

I could always run fast. All summer I had been running in the hills. The previous year I was just an also-ran in the 100-yard dash and quarter-mile. My teammates gave me the name of "Idle Boy." Idle Boy was a local racehorse who ran a mile or more and was very successful. Idle Boy always seemed to drop back to last or nearly so until about halfway in the race. At that point he stretched out and started to pass the horses ahead of him. When he raced neck and neck with the lead horses, he would put on an extra burst of speed and win the race. At our first triangular track meet, a runner named Fred Pitts of Wendell was the prior year's district quarter-mile champion. Everyone thought he would repeat. I led at the 100-yard mark, but my lungs were not getting enough oxygen and the field passed me. I couldn't drive, so I ran long-legged. About the 200-yard mark the tight bands around my chest started to loosen and suddenly I felt strong and full of oxygen. Like Idle Boy, I passed the other runners one after the other and finally nosed out Pitts. This happened in the next three races. When I came back from the district track meet, I met my father and Farrell at the barn.

Dad asked, "How did you do?"

"I got third in the 100-yard dash at 10.1. Timm and Toone tied and I could reach out and touch them. I ran off and left them in the quarter-mile."

Dad said, "I'll race you through the pasture to the house. You had better take off your shoes. Your brother will start us."

My father beat me by a step. I said, "Mother, Dad beat me in a foot race."

My mother got up, went to a trunk, opened it, brought out a newspaper clipping and handed it to me to read. It said: "AL CROSS TIES WORLD RECORD IN EXHIBITION RACE AT WORLD'S FAIR IN ST. LOUIS."

At the state meet, Coach Kuhns told me to put a new pair of shoestrings in my track shoes. Since I had put in a new pair a few days before, I didn't do it. I was 5 yards ahead of Fred Pitts, 50 yards from the finish, when a worn eyelet cut the shoestring and the shoe came off. Pitts and one other runner passed me and set a new state 440 record. My failure to change those shoestrings has haunted me the rest of my life.

I liked Emily. She was very pretty, very big, very fat, and very nice. She was my partner, not date, on the senior sleigh ride. We snuggled down in the clean straw, held hands, and kissed a little.

Near the end of the school year, there was a women's day, ending with an assembly. The girls had voted by secret ballot on the boys in high school in 10 different categories, such as Best Dressed, Most Polite, Meanest, Most Handsome, Best Built, Nicest Smile, Smartest, etc. I was not surprised when I was called to the stage to receive the ribbon for Meanest. I was surprised when I also received the ribbons for Best Built and Most Handsome boy in high school. Emily gave me a big wink. I was really embarrassed and red in the face as I walked back to my seat. My teammates really gave me the raspberry cheer.

Actually, I didn't deserve the Meanest award as I was always polite. Girls often stopped and talked to me in the halls about coming events, such as box socials, dances, and school picnics. Emily told me later that they were trying to date me.

TRAVELING

It was Buford Kuhns, the Vocational Ag teacher, who urged me to go to the University of Idaho. I protested that my grades were terrible. He said, "You are smart enough and will have no trouble making it. You have been wanting to be a county extension agent. If you take Ag and Vocational Education minor, you can be an agent in five years."

Clem Ault had been on his own through most of the last year. The district had gotten into financial trouble due to the drought and drop in revenue, so school was let out in April instead of the usual May. Clem and I had been talking about the University of Idaho and about visiting the Gooding boys who were now attending as soon as school was out. Mr. Kuhns had us write and arrange a date to take prep tests. We graduated from high school on Friday evening, April 20, 1925. Saturday we were in a box car enroute to Moscow. We had sent our suitcases ahead. I didn't feel too badly about leaving my father short-handed, as the crops were in and it would be two months before the first cutting of hay. Clem stayed over Friday night with us and Father drove us to the depot in the Model T on Saturday morning. He said, "Virg, I hope you'll be back by haying time. You may be meeting some tough customers. It would be best if you hid part of your money."

"I'll be careful, Dad. I'll try to be back before June 1st. I'd like to look around."

Clem told my father, "I want to thank you and Mrs. Cross for taking me in and feeding me so many times."

We had to wait a little more than an hour for a freight to pull in. We climbed into an empty box car. A warm coat, wool shirt, Levis, and a stout pair of workshoes kept us reasonably warm. By the time we reached Pocatello, the constant clicking of the wheels over the rail joints, the swaying, and wind with smoke and cinders had put doubts in both our minds.

"Virg, maybe we should have stayed home and worked."

"Clem, we can't turn back now. Our clothes are in Moscow. Mr. Kuhns said we should take our achievement tests."

"Neither of us will have enough money to join a fraternity or stay in a hall. We should look over private places to stay."

"Clem, Marshall wrote Stan Smith and he said that he and Frank Coyle would show us around and put us up for a few days."

We cleaned up at the railroad beanery. Two hamburgers and

glasses of milk cost 25¢ each and filled us up. There were other railroad bums in the Pocatello terminal who answered our questions as to what trains went to Montana. A huge Malley Compound with eight drivewheels on the side was making pounding, thumping, and hissing noises. We stopped and stared in awe at the eight large drivewheels. A man in striped overalls and cap was squirting oil on slides and bearings with a big oil can that had a spout several feet long. He greeted us as we approached, "Hi, fellows. Are you looking for a ride?"

Clem said, "We want to go to Spokane."

"Well, fellows, all the box cars are loaded and it is going to be cold in an open car. How would you like to ride in the cab?"

Would we ever! We were elated. He told us to climb up, as they were ready to start, and showed us where to stand or sit to be out of the way. It did not occur to us that the big young Irish fireman had a method to his madness. For the first hour we sat listening to the pounding of the drivers and wheels and watched the countryside. The big fireman was steadily, but not hurridly, shoveling fine coal into the hot firing door. The relatively flat plain with grass and sagebrush turned into hills and forest. Instead of 50 miles an hour, it was a huffing, puffing 20. Coal had to be shoveled into the fire box without any let-up. In a short time I was up on the coal bunker shoveling or pushing it down closer to the door. Mick, the big fireman, became wringing wet with sweat. For the next 5 hours we worked the coal down and spelled the fireman. It was nearly midnight when we reached Monida, which is the nearly 7,000-foot summit of the pass. Water and coal were taken on. Mick showed us where to clean up, as we were covered with coal dust.

"If you want to stay over, there is a freight out of here about 9:30 tomorrow that will take you to Spokane. The sand house is where they store sand for sanding slick tracks, and it is warm sand. You can curl up and sleep there, and be warm." We shook hands with him and thanked him for his help. He added a last word of warning, "Look out for Roscoe, the railroad bull. He is a mean one and I have heard he robs hoboes if they have any money. He also likes to beat people up."

We climbed the wooden ladder up to the window of the sand house. It did not take us long to discover that the trick to sleeping on sand is to dig holes to fit the contour of your body. We slept soundly until about 7 o'clock, and awoke cheerful, hungry, and very stiff. Push-ups, windmilling arms, and stretching soon restored our young muscles to normal tone. Clem looked at his dollar Ingersoll watch and said, "We have 2 hours before the freight is due. Let's clean up and eat."

A gravelly voice asked, "Did you come in on the freight last night?"

"We did." We knew he was the railroad bull. He was large, heavy-set, with a mean face.

"Did you pay for it?"

"We shoveled coal."

"That doesn't pay for it." He pulled out a pistol from his belt and said to me, "Let me see your billfold." All I could do was hand it over. There was a dollar bill in it, which he took out and put in his shirt pocket, saying, "That will pay the railroad for your ride." I was standing facing his right side. He demanded Clem's billfold, and removed the $10 bill from it and put his gun in his belt. When he reached out to return Clem's wallet, he was leaning out and foreward. I swung my right hand and buried it in a flabby solar plexus. He screamed, grunted, and fell, writhing in pain on the ground. We held him down, took his gun and sap, and handcuffed him. We retrieved my dollar and Clem's $10.

"We won't touch his money. That would be stealing and make us as low as he is."

Roscoe was lying on his side, swearing at us. "Undo the handcuffs, give me my gun and I'll let you go free."

"Roscoe, we are free. You are the one that is in trouble." Clem winked at me.

"The easiest thing to do is take him back in the woods, hold the gun tightly against his head to cut down the noise, and pull the trigger."

"Clem, that is a good idea. No one has seen us, and we can be long gone before they find him." I cocked the gun and held it on him while we herded him back into the trees. Clem undid the handcuffs and relocked them after putting his arms around a small tree. Roscoe was whimpering and snarling.

"Virg, we'll need a shovel. I'll hold the gun on him while you get one." That really got him begging. We moved out of earshot.

"Virg, we can't turn him loose because we would be in big trouble. He can swear out a warrant saying we attacked and robbed him. No one would take our word over his and we would end up in jail! If we go to jail we are marked for life and it would mean no university. That isn't all, Virg. They could beat the hell out of us and even leave us badly crippled. Too bad the railroad is the only way out of here."

"I wonder who hires him, the railroad or the town?" Looking at the 20 or so buildings in the town, he said, "It isn't big enough to be a city, but it could have a mayor and he could tell us what to do. You are biggest and a smooth-talker, so you should do the talking. You go, and I'll stay and watch him."

I walked the two blocks to a general store. A short, heavy-set man with a pleasant broad face and a pleasing appearance was unlocking the door. He said, "What can I do for you?" The sign above the door said Reed Baines General Store.

"Mr. Baines, the railroad bull tried to rob us of our money and pointed a gun at us as he took it. We are hoping the mayor might help us."

Baines scowled and said, "He is a dirty, mean bastard. It's a wonder someone hasn't killed him. I am the mayor, but I have no control over him as he is paid by the railroad and the station master hires and fires railroad policemen and watchmen. You will have to see the station agent to get your money back."

"We have our money back and he is handcuffed to a tree."

"How did you do that? And what is your problem?"

I told him how we clobbered the bull, took our money back, and handcuffed him. I also told him that my friend Clem had the revolver. Storekeeper Baines had a good laugh, but he soon sobered up.

"You fellows are in big trouble. The railroad people will do their darnedest to see you won't get away with this. In fact, you could be killed and hidden and no one would ever know what happened to you."

"What can we do? We can't turn him loose."

"That's right. You'll have to use the station master and he doesn't open up until 8:30. The passenger train stops here for water and coal at 8:45. It will pass the freight train that is waiting on the siding and will leave right after the passenger train."

"What can I tell the agent?"

"You can tell him what you have told me. He'll act like he is in sympathy with you, but he's just waiting for a chance to get you. Where do you have Roscoe, the bull?"

"We have him handcuffed to a tree in the woods on the far side of the sand house."

"Tell the station master you have Roscoe handcuffed and you'll give him the gun and keys as the freight pulls out. He'll figure that by being friendly he will stop you from being careful. All he has to do is wire up ahead and there will be a whole gang of men with pickhandles surrounding the train when it stops at Anaconda to drop off ore cars at the smelter. Tell the engineer about what you did and ask if he'll slow down about a mile from the depot so you can jump off the train."

The station agent was a cranky old man who was probably being pensioned off in that out-of-the-way place. It took some convincing to get him used to the idea that we would give him the gun, sap, and keys to the handcuffs as the freight pulled out, and then we would tell him where the handcuffed bull would be. Finally, he agreed to the plan. I thought he had a sneaky smile on his face. I walked in the opposite direction from the sand house and water tank, turned left into the woods and walked back to Clem, who was really glad to see me after spending an hour of uncertainty. We left the fuming Roscoe telling us all the things they would do to us. Among other things, he said he'd smash our balls.

The station agent had already told the engineer and fireman. The fireman asked, "Where is Roscoe?"

"You will find Roscoe handcuffed to a tree right up the hill above the water tank. I am sure he will be glad to see the agent."

They laughed. The engineer said, "All aboard." I handed the station agent the key and sap. Clem handed him the gun. He immediately opened the gun, and seeing it was empty, put it in his pocket. Clem had the shells in his pocket.

The fireman and engineer seemed very much in sympathy with us. They agreed that we should not be on the train when it stopped at Anaconda. The engineer said it would be no problem to slow the train so we could jump off. During the conversation they told us that we could always find a job at the smelter. Union pay was $5 a day and board and room at the smelter beanery was a dollar a day. We thought that with those wages we could make enough during the summer to go to college for a year by doing some outside work.

Sure enough, about 2 miles from Anaconda, the engineer pulled the throttle back and the coasting train slowed down rapidly.

"When you jump, hang down from the steps with your feet close to the ground and push out and away. Stay flat on the ground until the caboose goes by, as we don't know about the brakeman. We will not give you away, but he might."

Both of us pushed off, Clem going first and I right after without falling down. We lay down on the ground until the train went past. I said, "Let's get off of the railroad right-of-way and out of their jurisdiction."

We were walking down the road that paralleled the tracks a half-mile away when a white carryall drawn by a team of matched sorrels pulled up beside us and stopped.

"Would you like a ride to town?"

What we saw holding the reins was a huge woman. She wasn't fat, she was big. In fact, the carryall would seat three ordinary-sized people in each of the two seats. There was just enough room left in the front seat for my 31-inch bottom.

The team trotted briskly and soon we caught up to the caboose of the train. The road had turned toward the track and it was only two blocks away. Sure enough, there were about a dozen men with pickhandles on each side of the train. They were looking in and under the cars, with some standing at intervals away from the train to catch anyone that was flushed out. Clem and I grinned at each other.

Our hostess, on hearing that we wanted to apply for work at the smelter, drove us up to the smelter's hotel and beanery for the single workers. We thanked her for her generosity and help, and watched her drive off in a slight cloud of dust. Clem said, "She surely was nice and big."

"If she had a switch, a grizzly bear wouldn't have a chance."

We checked in at the lodging house and beanery. When the manager found out we wanted work, he said, "If you get on at the smelter, you won't have to pay. I'll call the employment office and see if they can use you." We heard him say, "I have a couple of husky young fellows just off the freight. Can you use them? What time?" He hung up the phone, and told us we should report to the employment office at 7:00 a.m.

"Will we need other clothes?"

"No, they will furnish your clothes and gloves."

We were exuberant after a hearty meal that included the choice of three kinds of meat and four kinds of pie for dessert. Five dollars a day and only one dollar for board and room! That was a lot better than pitching hay 10 hours a day for $2, and lunch and dinner.

We noticed the tall smelter smokestack, several hundred feet high. In spite of this, the vegetation was dead or stunted for miles around.

We were 10 minutes early reporting for work. Almost immediately, a large, heavy-set man asked, "Are you the two new fellows from the bunkhouse? Come with me."

We entered a room where four other men were putting on white coveralls, white caps, and short, white rubber boots. The foreman brought us similar outfits which included not only the coveralls and a tight-fitting cap, but socks and underwear. The gloves were fitted over the coverall sleeves and were kept tight with elastic. Pant legs were held tight on the legs also by elastic. It was then we learned that we would be shoveling powdered arsenic down openings in the flue of the smelter. He warned us never to raise any dust, because some of it would get through our masks and goggles. Under no circumstances were we to work up a sweat. The job was boring to us because we had to move so slowly and exert ourselves so little. During the lunch break, we learned that the oldest man on the job had been there only two weeks and the job was a killer. On Saturday night we drew our pay. Sunday morning we caught a freight going to Spokane.

It was nearly noon the next day when we arrived in Moscow. After cleaning up as well as we could in a service station, we went to the post office to retrieve our suitcases. Clem said, "Let's get a room, clean up, and put on some decent clothes before we meet the Gooding boys." I agreed.

Three of the Gooding boys were batching with two other students. They had rented a house. Dan Warren cooked; Frank Coyle worked in the dairy building and furnished ice cream, cheese, and butter. Chet Mink worked at the hay barn and he furnished feed for the 10 laying hens and cockerels they were fattening. Stan Smith, Marshal's brother, worked in the horticultural department and was able to supply them with vegetables and fruit. Ralph Strecki worked at the dairy barn and was entitled to a gallon of milk a day. They were getting by on $15 dollars a month. All were seniors.

Clem and I were very grateful for their help in getting us lined up for the entrance tests. We both passed, but I was low in English and math. I decided that it would be best if I stayed out a year and saved my money, because it would be difficult for me to make my grades if I had to work. I decided to move on. Clem got a job at the dairy barn and since he had no family left in Gooding, he also would save his money and start school a year later.

It was nearly 2 o'clock when four other hoboes and I got off the freight train at Spokane. The jungle was close by in some trees by a stream. There were remnants of many cooking fires over the years. Forked sticks were in the ground with iron bars across to hold pots for hot water, stews or coffee. In this camp there were large, clean cans with bails for cooking and clean small cans for serving soup and stew. One of the older hoboes took over and organized the group to put together a stew. He asked if anyone had any money. I said I had 15¢.

"O.K., you buy 5¢ worth of salt pork and 10¢ worth of coffee beans." He delegated the getting of meat (preferably chicken), vegetables and punk (day-old bakery goods). Another young fellow and I were assigned to get the punk. At two different bakeries we got two loaves of bread, a half-dozen rolls and a stale apple pie. This took less than an hour. To our surprise, two chickens had been scalded, plucked, cut up, and were now boiling in a 5-gallon can half filled with water. Another 5-gallon can was full of water for dishwashing. When the chickens were partially cooked, turnips, potatoes, onions, and carrots were added, as well as the salt pork. We exchanged stories about how we had acquired our contributions.

Everyone had his own spoon. A willow branch was attached to a tin can for a dipper. Each man served himself, careful to take only one piece of chicken per helping.The talk was friendly during the meal with gossip about work in different places, railroad bulls, and places you could get a handout from housewives and restaurants.

I asked, "How do you know you can get a meal?"

"Sometimes the gates, posts or doorways are marked. If it is a cross, you might get fed. If it is an X, forget it."

The five hoboes cleaned up all of the stew and pie, leaving only a half-loaf of bread. It could have been because we were the youngest, the other fellow my age and I were assigned the task of rinsing and scalding the cooking cans and the tomato eating cans. The other three cleaned up the camp and replenished the wood supply for the next travelers.

I had sent my good clothes and suitcase back home, and was now wearing my school clothes. The small bag I carried contained an extra pair of underwear, socks, shirt, toothbrush, and razor. It was spring.

61

Everything was new and green. Winter snows had cleansed the earth and air. I felt the urge to travel and see things. Other hoboes had told me there were jobs working on the powerline from Hoover Dam to Bakersfield, California. My mother's sister, Aunt Laura, lived in Los Angeles. I mailed a card to my folks saying I was well and was going to visit Aunt Laura and would hitchhike instead of riding freight trains.

Hitchhiking was fun. People in their Models A and T were glad to pick up a young fellow with a presentable appearance. The older people appreciated having some help in driving. Often they would buy my lunch or dinner. Following the advice of my father, I kept part of my money under the insole of my right shoe. My belt had a slip-in compartment in which I kept a $20 bill. Only a dollar and some small change were kept in a small purse in my pocket. To conserve money, I checked fence markings and dwellings, asking for a meal in exchange for work. I cut wood, mowed lawns, fixed gates and fences, in each instance doing a good and thorough job. Quite often they gave me a place to sleep. Twice the housewives washed my clothes for me.

San Francisco was a wonder place for a boy from a small farm in the country. I was fascinated by my first view of the ocean. I spent a whole day at the waterfront. Ships of all sizes were loading and unloading freight. Passengers were disembarking from a huge, immaculate, four-stacked liner returned from Hong Kong. I promised myself that I would also travel on a steamship someday.

I watched a banana boat from South America unloading. To me, bananas were yellow. These were bright green. Two lines of men were doing the unloading, one line carrying crated bunches of bananas and the other line returning. A man supervising asked me, "Do you want a job unloading bananas at 50¢ an hour?"

"I'll try it."

"Report here at 7 o'clock."

When I asked him where I might find a place to stay, he advised me to go to a skid row on Geary Street. The small room had a cot, chair and a battered dresser for 25¢ a day. The place was clean but smelled of creosote disinfectant. I ate at an adjoining restaurant. A hearty meal of hamburger, potatoes, gravy, bread, and canned peas was 20¢.

The work the next day was tiresome, without a break except for lunch. During a conversation with another laborer, I learned that someone had figured they would walk about 12 miles a day carrying a 60-pound load. The other thing was to watch for tarantulas, as they often hid in the bunches. Sure enough, one dropped out on my arm and I flipped it off with my gloved hand. That day we finished unloading. Sleep came early that night. The money belt was buckled around my body and my shoes were under the covers for their safety.

Transferring from a street car on Geary Street to one on Market

Street and going across the ferry to Berkeley was another new experience. The sun was shining in Berkeley and it was warm. There was no cold fog. To me it was wonderful to see all the subtropical trees, shrubs, and flowers. My impression of San Francisco was that it was full of wonders to see. I promised myself that someday I would get to know San Francisco. Little did I know how this would be fulfilled in its entirety.

The 500 miles to Los Angeles were taken in leisurely steps, as I was fascinated by the newness of the country, especially everything that grew. One of my rides stopped at a winery a few miles from Modesto. There I sampled my second drink of wine. I left that car on the outskirts of Modesto, as the couple took a side road toward their destination.

I had checked gates on the edge of town without finding any with crosses on them. The somewhat poor houses became larger, well-kept residences, with groomed lawns and trimmed trees. A woman was trying to mow a lawn that had been neglected and the grass was high. She pushed the mower with difficulty. As I approached, she stopped and looked at me.

"Hello, ma'am. I am hungry. Do you have any work I can do for a meal?"

"Boy, am I glad to see you. When you finish mowing, I'll have something for you to eat."

When I was through, the lawn was smoothly and evenly mowed. The grass was put in a compost bin. There was a pair of grass shears in the shed, and I trimmed the edges and corners.

It was a different person who brought out a plate of delicious sandwiches and a glass of milk. Her face was no longer sweaty with a streak of grease and strands of hair hanging down. Here was a very good-looking, well-groomed woman in her thirties. She said, "You have done a very good job...." and hesitated.

"My name is Virgil. Virgil Cross."

"I am Marie Hanson. I am a widow. I have only been in this place a few days."

"The sandwiches are delicious. Do you have a hammer and some nails? Some of the slats are loose on the fence. There are also some screws missing from the hinges on the front gate."

"There is a box of my husband's tools in the shed; there may be nails and screws there."

In addition to nails and screws, there were brushes and a full bucket of white paint. By the time I had finished nailing loose slats, replacing screws in the gate hinges and repairing the latch, it was nearly evening—a few minutes after five by my Ingersoll watch. Marie had several conversations with me, mostly about my background. I thought this would be a good place to stay overnight and I would bet, based on the sandwiches, that she would be a good cook. After putting the tools away, I knocked on the back door.

She came to the door and said, "What is it, Virgil?"

"I've finished the fence and gate, Mrs. Hanson. I want to thank you for the good lunch. I found almost 2 gallons of white paint in the garage and you should get someone to paint the fence. Thanks again, and goodbye."

"Don't go now. You have done such a good job. I have cooked supper for both of us. Come in and wash up. I have something to discuss with you."

The home-cooked meal of hamburger steak, with creamed new potatoes and peas, was delicious. After a super piece of apple pie, she said, "I've been thinking. There are several things that need to be done besides painting the fence. The garden needs to be weeded and the trees need to be trimmed and pruned. I would be glad to hire you if you would stay over. There is a cot in the garage and I'll give you some blankets and quilts." Since it was what I planned to do, I said I would be glad to stay over a day.

The next morning I was up and dressed at nearly 7 o'clock and needed to go to the bathroom. She came out the back door and on seeing me, said, "Come on in and wash up for breakfast." It was a very good breakfast of hot cakes and bacon.

There was a lot of fence to paint. The day was comfortable, a balmy spring day. It was pleasant painting, wearing just pants, no shoes or shirt. In the middle of the afternoon the temperature was up to 90 degrees and she brought me lemonade and cookies, for which I thanked her heartily. When she patted me lightly on the back and complimented me, I began to wonder. I thought, she is kind of old, but she is downright nice, pretty, and has a terrific figure. But you had better play it cool. You might end up finding another place to sleep.

She was a combination of nervousness and gaiety during the evening meal. "Virg, there is more work you can do to help me. Why don't you stay for a few more days."

"Well, ma'am..."

"Call me Marie."

"Well, Marie, I have things to see and I'm running short of time so I should go to my aunt by tomorrow."

"Virg, you will want clean clothes. Leave your clothes outside your door when you take a bath—and you really need a bath. You can sleep in the spare bedroom tonight."

I brought my bag from the garage, took out my dirty clothes. My pants, shirt, and undershirt were added to the pile outside my door. Wearing only my shorts, I slipped bashfully down the hall into the bathroom. It was sheer pleasure to lather and soak the grime and dust away in hot water. One of the things I noticed was no latch on the bathroom door. Just as I was starting to get out of the tub, the door opened and Marie came in.

"Virg, you didn't put your shorts out to wash. I might as well wash your back."

And she did. There would be no clothes dry until morning, and I crawled into sweet-smelling, crackling sheets and turned out the lights. Wide awake, I listened for footsteps. I heard them coming almost quietly down the hall. Pretending to be asleep, I heard the turning of the doorknob and the click of the bolt. There was the rustle of clothes, and the soft slither of falling silky garments. When the warm body snuggled up to me, I instinctively put an arm around her, held her close and we kissed.

"Virg, you are a louse. You were not asleep. Pretending to be asleep, lying there hoping and expecting I would come to bed with you."

It was different than it had been with Pinky. She made me take my time. It bothered me that I didn't have a rubber, and I told her about it. The answer was, "Forget it—I'll take care of it."

I had never been kissed like that. I decided that older, experienced women were more fun. Three times I smelled Lysol, and heard the toilet flush before I went into a deep sleep.

Marie awakened me when she brought in my clothes and gave me a kiss. Breakfast was rather quiet between us. She implored me to stay. I wanted to stay, but I was afraid I might become involved and the longer I stayed the more difficult it would be to leave. I refused the $5 she offered, as I felt guilty taking it. She insisted until I took it, but I promised I would come back that way. I thought this might be real love and what it's all about. "Too bad she is so old and I'm only 18," I thought.

A ride in a new Willys Knight, a car with sleeve valves, driven by a Norwegian carpenter named Knute, was a long one. Knute was a terrible driver. He had bought the new car a few hours before and had driven it around the sales lot with the salesman giving him instruction that had been his only driving experience. The traffic was becoming more congested.

"Knute, would you like to have me drive for a while?"

"Yah, I vud!" He pulled over to the side and we exchanged places, to the great relief of both of us.

"Ve vill get there yet!"

Knute worked for a construction company and was on his way to a building the company had contracted for. It would be constructing storage buildings for contractors who were building power lines to the new Hoover Dam. Headquarters for the company was in Bakersfield. He told me, "The boss likes me and vill giff you a yob." Knute was right. The next day I went to work with the crew constructing the towers for the 2-inch power cables. They started work at two in the morning and quit at 9 o'clock because the desert sun made the metal in the beams and the tools too hot to handle. It was hard, heavy work, but that really never bothered me. What did bother me was the daytime heat in the company's bunkhouse. Fans and water evaporator coolers helped to combat the 115 degrees-in-the-shade midday heat. Two weeks was all that I could stand. After drawing my pay and sending home a money order for $50, I took a Greyhound bus to Los Angeles. Bus rides were miserable, as there were no toilet facilities and electric fans were only good for blowing other people's smoke out. At the bus stops the passengers flocked to the rest rooms that stank with the smells of human waste. Some were downright dirty. I thought this would be a good place to get the crabs and when I have a chance to take a bath I'd really scrub clean with soap. During football season, I had a very heavy infestation of crabs due to my heavy, thick body hair. In fact, the whole team got the crabs. Gene Broyles was the culprit. Rumor was that he got them from a high school girl who had gotten them from a sheepherder. Gene never had a towel and he constantly sneaked in to use other people's towels. All of the team members were infected. Coach Kuhns brought a half-gallon of blue ointment to the dressing room and it soon cured the infestation. When playing Buhl, Rosy Rosenbaum, the quarterback, said "Scratch, scratch" instead of "Hike, hike" and the backfield in the Notre Dame box scratched their crotches in unison. The Buhl players knew about the crabs and started to laugh. I centered the ball to Fat Toone and caught them off guard. He ran 80 yards for a touchdown.

It was confusing to get three transfers on a street car from the bus station. It was nearly suppertime when Aunt Laura answered my knock on the door. I said, "You are my Aunt Laura, and I am Virgil." She gave me a hug.

"I am so glad to see you. Harvey, come here. This is our nephew, Virgil, Ora's boy. The Fannings had never seen me, and Aunt Laura had seen her sister, my mother, only once in the last 20 years. We talked until nearly midnight.

Uncle Harvey had a black Maxwell, all shiny and spotless. The next day, Sunday, was a tour of beaches, LeBrea tar pits, museums, all new to me. To me, Los Angeles was beautiful with its wonderful subtropical plants and flowering plants. Away from the center of town the air was scented with the bloom of orange trees, other fruit trees, and flowers. The clear, clean air brought the mountains in the background close to the viewer. Aunt Laura told me that my father's sister, Aunt Nell, lived in Hollywood. She had been an actress in the silent movies and married a millionaire named Henry Flagg.

"Why don't you call her this evening, Virgil? Harvey and I have to work tomorrow and it will give you something to do."

"My father hasn't seen her in 25 years. I don't really have any good clothes."

Uncle Harvey left and returned with a good, neatly-pressed blue serge suit which had been left at his cleaning shop and not called for. It fit better than my one good suit at home. I called the Flagg residence and identified myself to the butler who answered the phone. Mrs. Flagg came on and said, "Hello, Virgil. We are anxious to meet you and hear about my brother Al and his family. Could you come about 2 o'clock this afternoon and plan to stay overnight with us?"

I said I could. Uncle Harvey drove me over in the new Maxwell. The mansion in Beverly Hills looked huge as I walked up a long, curving walk that was lined by well-groomed trees and shrubs, with formal landscaping and flowers.

The butler at the door took my bag. I had heard about butlers, read about butlers, and even played one in the school play. It was the combination of the mansion, the butler, and the rich furnishings that made me aware of the wealth of my aunt. A beautiful, middle-aged woman was smiling at me at I walked across the very thick carpet in the living room. She was tall, straight, black-haired, and looked strikingly like my handsome father.

She took my arm and said, "Sit down with me and tell me about your family. You know, I haven't seen my brother in 25 years."

We talked constantly until nearly 6 o'clock. I learned that I had a cousin, Eleanor, who was in France studying ballet at the Sorbonne. Uncle Henry was almost quiet the whole period. He was a large, handsome, grey-haired man. When he asked me where I was going, without thinking and to legitimize my traveling on, I said, "Corpus Christi. It was a place where I lived when I was really young. I would like to see it again."

"How are you going to get there?"

"I'm fed up with riding the rails. I thought I would hitchhike."

Dinner was served in courses by the maid. My mother's training in manners really paid off, and I got through the meal without using the wrong fork. After dinner, it was the reception on the long-horned radio that fascinated me. It came in clearly and the Two Black Crows were hysterically funny. I had heard the faint reception of the Kansas City Jayhawks, which could be received only in the evening with earphones in Cady's garage in Gooding.

To me the bed and bedroom were huge, with a dresser, chairs, table, and a complete bathroom adjoining. I tried to realize how people could get so much money, but could not come up with answers. After breakfast, I was preparing to leave to return to Aunt Laura's when Uncle Henry handed me $50, saying, "I'll give you this only on condition that you buy a train ticket to Corpus Christi."

It really flustered me and I stammered, "Thank you, I will."

Actually, I had forgotten about going to Corpus Christi, as I never really intended to in the first place. I thought, "I've put my whole foot into my mouth!"

Aunt Laura fixed a basket of food for me to take on the train trip, saying that diner food was extremely expensive—at least $2.50 a meal.

My cousin Stanley was a ticket agent for the railroad and he fixed me up with a special rate, slightly over $20. At first the train ride was interesting, but soon my enthusiasm vanished. The red plush seat got harder and harder. If I opened the window, I got smoke and cinders in my eyes. If I kept it closed, the desert heat and smoke got to me. A combination of clicking of the wheels on the rail joints and swaying of the car became extremely monotonous. The toilets were closed at the station and were not opened until a mile from the station. They were emptied on the fly on the ties. When I first used it, the flushing brought a gust of wind on my bare bottom that really made me jump. All this, combined with a diet of sandwiches, made a monotonous three-day ride into Corpus Christi. I did manage to get a *Saturday Evening Post* and read it from cover to cover.

Corpus Christi was really a disappointment. I thought I had located the house where we had lived. Originally, it was 2 miles from town. Now it was surrounded by houses. An oak tree with a hollowed limb still stood in the backyard. When I was five I climbed it to look at an owl's nest and fell, cutting my lip badly on my lower front teeth. The harbor had been enlarged, and I couldn't find the pier where I had stepped on the catfish. What had been a town of only a few blocks with horses and buggies was now a city with street cars and automobiles.

It seemed to me that I was at the end of the world and Idaho was a million miles away. I felt guilty about being away from home so long and leaving my father to do all the work. I enquired at the railroad office and found that the fare to Gooding would be $42. I had only $30 and some change. I had been warned against trying to ride freights because the Texas railroads would beat and jail hoboes. They were trying to prevent illegal entry of Mexican nationals. The employment office told me there were no jobs available in Corpus Christi, but there were plenty of well-paying jobs in the north toward Oklahoma in the oil fields.

The manager said, "Newton, which is 400 miles north of here, would be a good place to go as a boom is going on there. They are paying $7 1/2 to $10 a day for common labor. Ten dollars for a ticket, three changes of trains, and 30 hours later, I was in Newton. It was a town consisting of mostly unpainted buildings and shacks. Everybody seemed to be doing something. There were whole trainloads of pipe, steel for oil rigs and supplies being trucked across the flat prairie in all directions. It was the end of the railroad line.

My seat mate turned out to be an oil driller on his way back from a family wedding. He told me, "I'll show you where to stay and take you into the office and they will give you a job."

We went directly to the company boarding house. It was rough but clean and smelled of disinfectant. There was no plumbing. Outhouses and a bucket of water and a basin were the toilet facilities. My newfound friend was right about the job. The office manager asked, "How old are you?" I had been coached to say 20, as they might not want to hire an 18-year-old.

"Can you drive?"

"Yes, sir. I've driven Ford trucks and a Reo truck on milk routes hauling 10-gallon milk cans."

"Son, do you mind hauling nitroglycerine?"

"I don't mind, sir." I didn't even ask about the pay.

Sleep came easily and I set my mind on waking up at 5:30. By the time I had gone to the outhouse and washed, it was nearly six. There was an abundance of food to choose from. A breakfast of ham and eggs and hotcakes filled me up. I arrived at the office 15 minutes early, before it was open. I watched with interest two men loading 5-gallon cans that were covered with thick felt and a flap of felt to cover the top. I didn't understand why the men moved so carefully and slowly as they loaded the cans into tight-fitting compartments on the back of a Reo pickup. They surely are lazy, I thought. My dad would say they are moving like dead lice are dropping off of them. Suddenly, it dawned on me that they were loading nitroglycerine—then I remembered that nitroglycerine was used as a heart medicine and when it was mixed with fine sawdust, it was dynamite, invented by a Swede named Nobel. Then I noticed they were wearing felt boots and white cotton gloves. There were signs that said "Danger. High Explosives. No Smoking."

The office was opened by a big, grey-haired man with piercing eyes and a square chin. There was no doubt by his mien that he was head man.

"Are you the new driver?"

"I guess I am."

"Are you aware you are going to haul nitroglycerine?"

"I am now."

"You are to drive that Reo pickup up that road 30 miles to a shack and drill rig that has a large sign saying 'Apex Oil Company.' Whether you get there depends on how you drive."

"It looks like an easy drive in flat country."

"Son, nitro is very tricky stuff and a bad jar or bump could set it off. You'll wear these (a pair of felt boots). No sparks from shoe nails. The 30 miles will take nearly 3 hours. If you make it in 2 1/2 hours,

69

you are going too fast. There is a 5-gallon can of water in jugs on the front seat. Stop and sprinkle to wet down the felt cover over the 25 gallons of nitro every hour. Do not drive over 15 miles an hour and mostly around 10. If you see a chuck hole, ease in and ease out. See that the iron chain doesn't fall off, as it is there to arrest any sparks. If you follow these instructions, you will have no trouble. You will bring back a load of empty cans and you can drive back at a safe speed. They will give you your lunch and you will be through for the day at 1 o'clock. Now give me your folks' address in case they have to be notified."

I thought I was in for it, but if I were careful it will be perfectly safe.

The terrain was mostly flat grassland with scattered mesquite and scrub oak. Heavy rains had washed small gulleys in places. When the road became too rutted, travel moved over. In some places the road had been moved three or four times. The new Reo pickup ran smoothly and to maintain a low enough speed, I had to run in second gear with braking and shifting to low over bad ruts and bumps. Part of the time I didn't go fast enough to keep up with the strong tail wind and the dirt kept up with me. A wet handkerchief over the nose helped. After nearly 3 1/2 hours of anxious, tedious driving, I came to a big shack, a huge pile of pipe, blacksmith shop, and stacks of dull shanks and bits. The sign said "Apex Oil Co."

The man in the office laughed at me, with my eyes peering out from a muddy, dust-covered face.

"Boy, you look like you crawled down the road with your nose! You can wash up and get something to eat at the cook house." He pointed to a large, unpainted shack. I dusted off my pants, beat my shirt against the side of the building by the wash stand. When I looked in the mirror, I saw two red eyes looking out of a very mud-covered face. There was actually mud on my teeth. I was hungry. The meal was good except for the flies that were numerous in spite of the screened door and windows. When I got a piece of raisin pie, the cook said, "If it moves, it ain't a raisin."

I didn't want to seem ignorant by asking what they were going to do with the nitro. Two men sitting across from me were talking about a well that was just completed and during their conversation one of them said, "That nitro really brought it in. The boss said he didn't think it would do any good, that it was a dry hole. You never can tell about oil drilling."

The ride back to Newton took less than half the time, and the dust didn't bother me.

Evenings were dull at Newton unless you patronized the saloon, and I didn't drink. The men joked about the cat houses. To patronize one never entered my head. I played checkers in the bunkhouse. It rained or had rained lightly for the next four trips, and the dust was not a problem. Moisture made the road softer. Saturday was my sixth trip. I wondered why the foreman was so solicitous and concerned when he advised me to be very careful about bumps and said you couldn't trust nitro. About 6 or 7 miles from Apex, I found out. Usually the road was straight. At the bottom of a draw there was a dip in the road and if you were not careful, the car would bump and jar. When I came to the dip, I had to drive around a huge hole. After going around it, I stopped and walked back. There were fragments of metal scattered over a large area. A battered heel of a boot in the debris really shook me up. It was difficult to start the car and drive on to Apex. "To bad it is too far from anywhere for me to get out and walk," I thought. "To hell with this damn job!" With fear and trepidation, I started the car and kept it in low gear as I crawled the 7 miles to Apex. No one knew why the load had blown up. All they did know was that it was difficult to find enough of the driver to bury.

When I arrived at Apex, the office manager said I looked as if I had seen a ghost. I just nodded. I was still shaking. It was a waste of time for me to chew my food—it only delayed my departure. After hurridly shifting into high gear, the rough bouncy swaying ride of 30 miles took less than an hour. Walking into the Newton office, I said "I quit."

The office manager said, "I don't blame you, son." The check for $60 was cashed at the saloon where I had a Coke. A mixed train of freight and passenger cars was coming back from turning around on the Y, as Newton was the end of the line. Two blasts of the whistle as I was climbing up the steps signaled the train to start. It was time to go home and help my father.

Four days and five transfers to different railroad lines later, I arrived in Gooding on a Union Pacific chair car. It was May 21 and I had been away from home seven weeks. The shortest way home was along the railroad tracks. My mother saw me coming across the field toward the house. She called to my father, "Al, Virg is coming!"

"How do you know?"

"I can see him walking."

Slim whinnied and put his head over the rail fence to be petted. Ten-year-old Rover, the ever-ready guardian, went to meet the intruder and changed the tone of his bark when he saw who it was. My sister Evelyn gave me a kiss, which surprised me. Boys just didn't kiss their sisters. My parents greeted me at the door joyfully. To be safe in my own home, among my own people, in my own bed and no longer feeling guilty about not being able to contribute to the family fortune took a big load off my shoulders.

Trying to make up for my absence, I insisted on doing the milking and feeding of the stock. At dinner that night, I answered many questions and told them of my adventures on the jaunt. Chicken was usually served on Sunday and it was delicious. During breakfast the next morning, I said, "You folks need a break. Why don't you take a couple of days off and go to Hagerman Valley to camp and fish? I will do the irrigating and chores." Within an hour, I was alone for two days.

I told my parents that I wanted to take post-graduate courses in English, algebra, and agriculture. These three classes would all be in the morning. If I had a good project I could probably win the $100 Union Pacific scholarship. My father suggested that I could rent the 40 acres that Hoodenpyle had farmed. It took only a short visit to Schmidt and Whipkey Realtors, the owners, to rent the property.

The summer was a busy one with haying, irrigating, cultivating, cutting, and shocking grain, allowing very little time for recreation. August was unusually hot and dry. Forest fires were numerous, and it was difficult for the Forest Service to get enough help to keep them under control. Pay was $3 a day and board. Silva's threshing machine was not due for two weeks and the only crop to be irrigated was hay and pasture. The Forest Service had put an appeal for fire fighters in the *Idaho Daily Statesman*, Boise's leading newspaper. Dad said, "You can help them for 10 days if you like." A call to my old friend, Ranger Ed Miller, was all it took. I reported to the Fairfield Ranger Headquarters at noon the next day.

I and seven other high school and college volunteers rode a truck 40 miles to the Cape Horn area to another camp. Breakfast was at daybreak. A dispatch came in saying that lightning had started a fire on a mountain peak in an isolated area. Ed Miller issued pulaskas, a combination axe and hoe, to six men and an axe and crosscut saw to the other two. In our packs we had items of food. The ranger told us it appeared to be a small spot fire in a sparsely timbered area on a high, rocky ridge. We might have to stay overnight, so he said to take our coats to sleep in.

A truck took us within 8 miles of the fire. The terrain was rough. Walking in a straight line was out of the question, as we had to detour around rocks, trees, and downed timber. Feet became tired and sore after 3 hours of steady walking. It was almost noon when the ranger called a halt by a small, clear mountain stream. During the brief lunch period, he had us wash and dry our feet and change socks. Smoke was going straight up on the peak above us, only a little over a mile away. It was a good break that there was no wind. We took the last hour's climb in easy stages. The ranger stopped 50 yards from the fire, telling us to wait while he walked around to assess what needed to be done. It turned out to be an easy fire to control. Lightning had hit a tall dead pine. The rocky terrain and sparse vegetation had kept it from spreading.

Part of the crew dug a trench around it, scraping back the needles and burnable material. We sawed down the big snag, beating out sparks and covering smouldering material with dirt. Everything was going smoothly and under control when the wind came up from the west, the direction we had come from. As it started to blow, Ed Miller said, "We will have to stay all night because the wind will fan the fire and we have to be sure it is out." I saw him looking more and more to the west. A dark cloud was gathering, with rumbles of thunder, flashes of lightning. Smoke started to reach us. The ranger called us together.

"Fellows, we are in trouble. You are to follow me. Leave your tools, but take your food and coats. Virg will bring up the rear. The fire will be here in an hour or less. We will have to travel about 5 miles east of here, where I think we will be safe. We might try to get around it, but if we could not, we would be had. There is no use taking a chance."

The wind increased to almost a gale, blowing bits of twigs, leaves, and some dust, as the unusually long drought had left everything bone-dry. Even the green pines would burn. The destination the ranger selected was a mountain meadow that had beaver dams in it. Most of the way was downhill. Ed Miller led the way with his crew strung out 20 feet apart. We were to follow his footsteps. He set off in a fast walk. He was a tall man with a long stride that made it difficult for the shorter members of the crew to keep up. At the end of half an hour, he gave us a 5-minute rest break.

A dark cloud of smoke was gaining on us. The pace was increased with alternate walking and trotting. Some of the crew were getting very tired and could keep up only with difficulty. The ranger had us stop every 15 minutes for a drink from our canteens.

Ashes began to be carried by the wind and settle on everything, including us. Smoke was getting heavier and beginning to affect our breathing. The timber was thick, tall, and heavy, with almost complete shade. The ranger said we had only a quarter of a mile to go. I couldn't see anything but trees. Everybody was panting and coughing from the smoke. The roar of the fire could be heard. Suddenly, we came to the open meadow with a beaver dam and houses in the center of a pond. Following the ranger, we waded out into the center of the pond. He instructed us to wet our coats, wring them out and cover our heads with the wet cloth. When it became too hot or smoky, we were to duck under the water and wet the coats, wring them out above our heads, and come up under them. We practiced this move under his guidance. Fortunately, the water was not chilling due to the shallowness of the pond and the preceding hot days. A hotter, smokier, searing blast made us duck under the water as a tree exploded with a shattering, screaming burst of flame a quarter of a mile ahead of the fire.

It seemed an eternity for me of ducking under water and coming up under the wringing wet coat. Actually, we were in the water a little over an hour. After the fire had passed over us, it was a relief to get out on the scorched grass in the meadow and wring out our wet clothes. The forest was burning on all sides around and behind us. The water in the pond was warm. We were all filthy, blackened, and tired while we waited for the fire to burn itself out so we could travel. We could hear thunder and see lightning in the distance.

Nine completely exhausted men huddled together for warmth on the grass. Each had been issued a spoon. The canned beans, tomatoes, and little sausages tasted delicious. The ranger rationed the food as he said it would take us two days to get back to headquarters.

With wet clothes, cold and miserable, I fell asleep almost immediately, leaning against a bank. When I awoke, I thought at first that I had wet my pants. It was a little after midnight. It was raining. Mr. Miller said, "I hope it pours!" Someone must have heard him, as immediately the gentle rain turned into a gully washer. The rain came down in sheets. All we could do was sit, wait and be miserable under a partially burned tree. The cloudburst covered a large area and completely drowned the fire.

At daybreak the ranger led his cold, wet crew back up the mountain the way we had come, with me bringing up the rear and wondering why we were going back the same route when it would be easier to go around the high ridge where we had first fought the fire. Five hours later we arrived at our original stopping point. Here we rested and had our first meal of the day. Several times during our climb we saw a small Forest Service biplane that seemed to be searching the area. Our blackened clothes and features blended with the blackened tree trunks, making us invisible.

That afternoon my father picked the *Idaho Daily Statesman* from the mailbox. It carried the story of the fire and how the heavy rain had miraculously prevented a huge area of timber from being burned. It carried a sub-caption, "Crew is missing," with an account of the plane search which had been unable to find us. It said that the crew was under Ed Miller, one of the most experienced rangers, and he probably had led the crew to safety. My father didn't take the paper into the house. He didn't want Mother to worry. She sensed something was wrong because my father was so silent at dinner. She tried to find out what was bothering him, but received a noncommital answer. That night he tossed and turned. He was up before daylight to change the irrigation water and milk the cows. Impatiently he waited for breakfast. When Mother went out to feed the chickens, he called the ranger station headquarters. With hope and fear he waited for the answer to his call. When the phone rang, a voice said, "This is the Sawtooth Ranger Station."

"Have you heard anything from Ed Miller's crew?"

"Sorry, Mr. Cross, we haven't heard a word. Ranger Miller is the best and we expect him to bring them out this afternoon. Give us your phone number and we will call you."

The *Idaho Statesman* headlined the missing fire fighters. It was lunch time when he carried the paper into the house. He would have to tell Mother right after lunch, before she read it in the paper. Just then the phone rang. I said, "Hello, Dad."

He was speechless for a moment. "Are you all right?"

"I'm fine, but tired. We just got in. I've had a bath and been fed. I need a ride. Can you come and get me?"

"I'm on my way!"

COLLEGE

A month before it was time to leave for college, I went to see the school superintendent, Mr. Doane, and requested that he send my grades to the university. He said my grades were so low that I might do better in some sort of manual labor, such as digging ditches or farm work.

"Nevertheless, I want you to send my grades."

"I will send them, but remember what I said."

Although the heavy farm work, haying, and threshing, was over, I hated the thought of leaving my father without help and told him so. We were sitting on the rail fence looking at two young fillies.

My father said, "Son, you have to go on and fill your destiny. Do not worry about your mother and me. We will survive. You have been a very good son."

It was to be the last close talk between us before I left and we both knew it.

"The Lord blessed you. You are very handsome, your body is unusually strong, and you are intelligent. I know you have been disappointed in not being better accepted in high school. All you have to do is be honest, work hard, and be considerate of others at all times. Eventually your professors and classmates will respect and appreciate you, and you will have a pleasant, rewarding time in college. You are going to be short of money all four years. You will meet many wonderful people. In every society, especially schools, you are going to meet some snobs. Just forgive them because they are either ignorant or trying to hide their breeding. Some of your high school classmates will be in fraternities or sororities and may avoid you. In the long run, you will be more successful and well-liked than they are.

"You probably are going to meet your future wife in college. You see those two fillies? One is a gorgeous, almost red bay with white mane, tail, and stockings. The other is grey with a neat head and neck blending into her shoulders. Her chest is deep, and her legs thin. She moves gracefully with spirit and she comes to you with affection. She will bite if you slap her, but she will love you for kindness. You can count on her taking you there and bringing you back. We know her sire and dam and both are good, reliable horses. Her brother is also a very nice horse. Her colts will be like her. Now that bay is a beautiful horse, but you are never sure as to what she will do. She actually takes after her dam and her sister. One time they are all affection and obedient. The next time they fight you all through the ride. You can get run under a limb or even nipped. We are selling her—some sucker will pay a high price for her."

I never forgot the parable of the grey filly.

There were tears when I hugged and kissed my mother goodbye, and sadness when I hugged my father and shook hands before boarding the train for Moscow. My trunk with clothes and bedding was in the baggage car. The conductor waved his arm and the train gave two short blasts of the whistle as it began to roll. I was on my way.

The red plush seats smelled of tobacco. If you opened the window, smoke and cinders got in your eyes. I could see my mother waving a white dish towel from our porch. Memories of growing up kaleidoscoped in my mind as the train crossed the tracks where I had herded cows with Wilma and Mirth. Big Wood River where I had fished and trapped. Hagerman Valley. There was sadness in my heart to be saying goodbye to my youth. Now I was a man on my own.

I explored the train by wandering back through the dining car with its gleaming silver and white linen. I was surprised that a number of women smiled at me. I was impressed with the jewelry and clothes of the pullman passengers. It must be wonderful to be able to afford pullman cars, diners, and clothes. Someday, I will be able to do these things, I thought.

After eating my lunch of fried chicken, cookies, an apple, and bread and butter, I fell asleep, emotionally exhausted. The conductor woke me to exchange trains at Wallula. I had written Wilfred Coon, whom I thought was a close friend, that I was coming. When the train stopped at Moscow, he was not there. Two Gooding boys who were seniors when I was a freshman in high school were there to meet me. Fred Judevine was a big wheel, a star basketball player. Gene Beebe was Cadet Captain of R.O.T.C. and Vice President of the student body. Wilfred had told them that I expected him to meet me and acted as if I were some inferior person.

Fred and Gene took me to their fraternity house to spend the night so they could talk about my joining the fraternity. I wanted to join, but knew that I would not be able to afford it. They found a place called Smith House on Sixth Street where 15 other boys stayed. It just happened that Smitty and Clem were staying there also.

I checked with the registrar and found that my credits had not been sent. I called my father and told him about Superintendent Doane, also asked him to contact Captain Dunham of the National Guard for verification of my service. My three years in the National Guard would keep me out of R.O.T.C., which I hated with a passion. If I had liked the Army, I would have accepted Senator Thomas' offer of an appointment to West Point.

My father went to see Superintendent Doane who had said he thought it was a waste of time to send my credits because he didn't think I would go to college. Father waited while his secretary made a transcript. Then he told Doane, "You are going down to the post office with me and mail this. I may have to drag you, but you will mail it like you should have without all the snide remarks about my son's ability." Doane mailed the letter.

Because I had made the grade of sergeant in the National Guard, I was squad leader with eight freshmen to drill. In two weeks the squads were all to be brought back together and drilled as a unit. In a week my papers were due and I would be freed from R.O.T.C. I drilled the squad, but added some commands that were not in the manual. Master Sergeant Lonnie Woods had been downright arrogant and nasty when I told him that I had three years in National Guard. He said I would drill those men whether I liked it or not. The day before the deadline, I received my release from R.O.T.C. I stayed out of Woods' way. He had said publicly that he wished he could get that Cross jerk in the R.O.T.C.

The football coach, Erb, gave me a $20 scholarship for opening and closing the doors of the girls' gymnasium. I had arrived a week early and started football drill immediately.

Freshmen were cannon fodder for the Varsity. It became apparent that 3 hours of scrimmage left me too tired to study. I told the coach I was quitting. He told me to change courses from agriculture to physical education, saying that the chemistry, math, and zoology were too hard for athletes to take because they didn't have enough time. In phys ed course all I would have to do was to attend class. I had to drop football because I was on probation and had to have a 2.2 grade average at the end of the 9-week period or be dropped.

During the first chemistry class, Dr. Van Ende lined us up and told us to look right and left, because every other one of us would fail. To my surprise, chemistry was not difficult as long as I spent a lot of time studying. With the shadow of flunking out hanging over me, I spent most of my time studying during the week. Rooming with Clem was fun; we started to attend Saturday afternoon dance classes at the women's gym where school dance bands took turns practicing.

I soon became aware that the girls were the cream of the high school crop. It was difficult for me to get used to the fact that they were cordial and respectful and interested in me.

At the Saturday afternoon dances, I soon became very popular. When the girls asked me where I was staying and I answered, "Smith House," some immediately lost interest. A very pretty and cute freshman girl said, "I wish you were in a fraternity." I asked why. She said, "We pledges are not allowed to date barbs."

In English class, Lou Ann sat on my right. To me she was simply gorgeous. I couldn't help stealing a look at her shapely knees that short skirts displayed. When she sat down, her greeting of hello and a smile made my day. I wished I could date this very popular freshman girl. Next year she could date me if she would.

Mid-term grades were 2.4 and with it a letter from Ella Olsen, the registrar, stating that I had been removed from probation. When my mother received her copy of the letter, she greeted Father when he came in for lunch: "I knew he could do it!"

"I hoped he could, but I wasn't sure because of his low high school grades."

It was when I went home for Christmas vacation that I really began to realize and appreciate the advantages and training that my parents had given me. It made me aware that I had very unusual parents.

My mother, Ora Farrell, was a great-great-granddaughter of Samuel Adams. Her father, an officer in the Civil War, was a farmer. He died early, as he never recovered from three years of hardship in the Civil War. Ora was a very good-looking, fiery, red-headed woman with a driving ambition to better herself. The day after she received her eighth-grade diploma, she packed her small valise and boarded the train for the Illinois State Normal School 60 miles away. Her mother was dead. Her two sisters and brothers were in foster homes. The $7 she had saved doing field and housework was down to $5 and some small change. She was lucky to get a job doing housework for board and room. The family was cooperative. She enrolled in summer school at the college and received her certificate to teach grade school. She continued to teach and go to summer school. Twelve years later she received her degree from the Illinois State Normal School. The first years of teaching were rough, living with a different family every month for board and room. Pay was $15 a month at first. Some of the pupils were as old as she was. Ora married Alvin Cross in 1900.

Alvin Wesley Cross was the son of Wesley Cross, who was also a Civil War veteran. He had been reared on the Mississippi River and had worked his way up to second mate on a riverboat. When he was drafted, he thought because of his experience they would keep him on the river or assign him to the navy, but after shooting 10 rounds in the first target practice, he was assigned to a sharpshooting company. He went through four years of the fiercest fighting without a scratch. After the war, he returned to the river as a steamboat captain. My mother heard gossip in the area that he ran aground on his second run and was banned from the river. He became a farmer, and married Evaline Bruener right after the war. She was tall, with black hair, very light skinned with classical features that indicated Indian blood. She was the second generation Cherokee-German cross. She died when my father was born. Father was reared by the second wife, a Clanton from the Ozarks.

79

Al was a very handsome man with coal-black hair to match his widely-set brown eyes. If you knew he had Indian ancestry, you would recognize it in his features. He was blessed with a powerful 6-foot, 175-pound body, broad shoulders, and narrow hips. His most remarkable talent was a photographic memory. Sometimes he would read a newspaper column and repeat it word for word to us when we were children. He was an avid reader, and fortunately a minister encouraged him to read the classics. He could discuss and recall quotes from Shakespeare, the Bible, Homer, Tennyson, Plato, etc. He studied philosophy and logic. We children did not fully appreciate all of this until we were nearly adults. He was sought after for talks at political and church meetings, judged debates, was on grand juries. To these parents I was born early in the morning on July 22, 1906, at St. Louis, Missouri.

Father was a street car conductor. He took this job to bide time until he could find something that would lead to better things. They had several thousand dollars in savings due to Al's having purchased a magic lantern which showed scenes on a screen. It was powered by an acetylene light and powerful lenses. There were a hundred slides such as the Battleship Maine, Nigara Falls, Old Faithful, etc. Motion pictures came in and stopped the enterprise. A boyhood friend went into partnership with him and they bought options on $2,000 acres of oil land in Oklahoma. Standard Oil offered them enough to make them rich. They thought they should have a million. The Panic of 1907 hit. They could not renew their option and walked off broke. In 1908, the family moved to Corpus Christi, Texas, where father found a job as a realtor.

The man who returned home for Christmas vacation was quite a different person from the scared and apprehensive freshman. It was a triumphant return. I was accepted, respected, and popular with the students and faculty at the university. There was no question that I could make my grades and eventually become a county extension agent of the university. The Crosses went to town on Monday. My mother took my arm and proudly walked down Main Street. She introduced me to a couple of new acquaintences as her son Virgil from the University of Idaho. She went into a dress shop saying, "We will be ready to go home in an hour."

I was on my way to Jeffries Drugstore where everybody drank Cokes and talked. A tall, well-built girl was walking toward me. As she came closer, I could see she was downright beautiful. She was smiling at me. I couldn't believe it was Emily until she said, "Hello, Virg."

"Emily, you are beautiful, gorgeous, and just terrific! How about a Coke?"

"I'd love that, Virg."

We sat by the marbletop table in the rear of the drugstore and informed each other as to what had happened during the 18-month separation. Her aunt had enrolled her in a famous women's college in the East. The Physical Education Department put her through a program of losing weight and she now weighed 130 pounds on a 5-foot, 7-inch frame, which was 40 pounds less than her weight in high school. I asked if she would like to go to the homecoming dance Saturday night, and she squeezed my hand and said, "I'd love to!"

"I can dance a lot better than I used to, Emily."

"I can dance better, too."

Wednesday she called and asked if I would like to have dinner with her family before going to the dance. The dinner was a typical Scandinavian meal. I thought it was no wonder Emily had been overweight. Her parents were very polite and appeared pleased that Emily and I were going together. After dinner Emily excused herself to go dress. Her dark red dress complimented her fair complexion and light brown hair perfectly. When I helped her into her coat, I whispered into her ear, "You are beautiful!"

We were a strikingly tall, handsome couple. When we entered the dance hall, there was a lot of whispering as to who we were and how we looked.

The first dance was a waltz. It was as if our two bodies flowed together as one. I tried the new variations I had learned in dance classes. Emily followed me perfectly. She put her lips against my ear and whispered, "You are terrific."

I answered, "You are better."

"Virg, I want to dance only with the boys that danced with me before. Let's dance mostly together. It would be a shame to waste dances on someone else."

Couples flocked around us, but we stayed with our plan and Emily had her revenge. We started kissing as soon as we were seated in the Model T. It was cold, but the side curtains kept the wind out and a blanket kept the cold seat from touching us. The radiator was covered with a blanket. Emily put her foot on the starter and I cranked to get the motor started.

Emily was going to visit her grandparents in Boise, and I didn't expect to see her until our date the next Saturday, but on Friday she called me and in a half-whisper said, "The folks are going to Twin Falls early Saturday and won't be back until about milking time. Why don't you come over in the morning?"

There was no doubt in my mind as to what would happen when we were alone in the house. I stopped at the drugstore, waited until Proctor was free. Proctor didn't scold as proprietor Jeffries did and try to shame us with a lecture about our sisters, etc. Proctor slipped me the dozen Trojans and I was on my way. I suddenly realized I was driving recklessly down a rutted gravel road and pulled the lever on the steering wheel back to a sensible 20 miles an hour. I parked the car in the cleared space in the yard and covered the radiator with the quilt.

Emily helped me remove my coat. The house seemed unusually warm and I noted the door to her bedroom was wide open. The covers were turned down as if to invite a body to sleep. Our embrace was a long one heightened emotionally by a long, tongue-touching kiss.

What followed was mutually unfastening buttons.

"Take it easy, Virg, and don't hurt me."

"I'll be very careful." The entry was surprisingly easy. Emily said she had been deflowered by a 14-year-old cousin when she was 12. We exhausted the pent-up passion of two very healthy young lovers. Between sessions we talked about the future. Emily wanted to get married the next summer.

I said, "It is out of the question now. I can barely support myself to go through school. Who knows, I might flunk out and then where would we be?"

"If we got married, my rich maiden aunt would put us through college."

"Emily, time will soon pass and you have two and a half years to graduation. I have three and a half."

Shortly after one o'clock, Emily said, "Virg, you are like a young ram. I am completely exhausted. We are going to take a long nap or we will not be able to dance tonight, and it is our last dance for nearly six months. We had better put our clothes on in case the folks come home early."

The barking of the collie warned us. We hurridly made the bed. Our clothes weren't wrinkled, as we had not been wearing them, and this apparently allayed the suspicions of Emily's mother.

"Have you been here long, Virgil?"

Emily answered for me, "Not very long, Mother."

At the dance we did almost no exchanging and danced slowly and close together, not saying anything, enjoying the warm glow of being together. When we arrived at Emily's house, she took off her shoes and tiptoed upstairs, listened to her parents' snoring, and silently crept back down. After a tearful parting, I left at 2:30 a.m. I would not get any sleep, as my ride in the Model T would pick me up at 5 o'clock for the 24 hour trip back to Moscow.

We wrote letters to each other weekly. In April, Emily's letters had a subtly different tone, and I sensed something had changed or was in the process of changing. My last letter had said I was anxious to see her in June. The reply was a "Dear John" letter. She was going to marry a young professor in July. It shook me up for a short while. Clem told me it wasn't meant to be and there are literally thousands of wonderful girls that would make good wives.

The first time I came home, my mother asked, "What are the girls like?"

"They are nicer, more polite, better dressed, and more intelligent than most of the high school girls, with the exception of three or four. They are ladylike and do not act forward in any way. So you don't try to get forward with them. You don't want to offend them."

"It is to be expected that they act that way because they are cream of the crop of high school graduates—just like you." That remark boosted my timid ego.

My father asked, "Are there any grey fillies?"

"There are a lot of them, but they all seem to be going steady. There are also plenty of gorgeous bay fillies. I am dating a little, but studying is taking almost all of my time. For the first time I am really studying."

Dean Permeal French was a large, well-built woman close to 70 years old. She had been Dean of Women almost since the university was founded. Scuttlebutt was that she had been a madam during the mining boom at Hailey, Idaho. Anyway, she knew all the answers. Her rules were strict. She said, "If I keep the girls penned up, you boys will not be able to do what you are thinking about." Losing dating privileges and being confined to the house except for classes were common punishments. Some offenses brought automatic expulsion. Of course, there were a lot of infractions that were never caught. Girls had to be in their dorm or sorority house by 12 o'clock on Saturday night or be locked out. Freshmen and sophomores could go to the library but had to check in by 8:30. Dates walked to dances and school functions. Girls were scared to death about breaking a rule because of the consequences. The university officials had the theory that if girls were unavailable men could not defile the little darlings. Transgressions of a serious nature by men brought them before the Academic Council which met every two weeks.

The university Dairy Department liked to have their majors work in the industry during summer vacation. They placed me in the Gooding Creamery. The manager had fired two men and said, "We can work the devil out of the college boy and save money," and he did. I felt I had to make good because the university had placed me. As a result, I worked 12 hours a day instead of 9 with no extra pay. I went from 178 to 155 pounds, which spoiled my chances to play football after I had made the team in spring practice.

The next summer, having quit the Dairy Department and my milking job, I had to do farm work and help my father. I earned enough to register, pay a month's board and room, and buy books, leaving me with less than $10. The Animal Husbandry Department head, Dr. Hickman, welcomed my change of major and gave me a job at the sheep barn. I received a late Union Pacific scholarship of $100;

this, with sporadic poker playing and a student loan of $75, got me by.

It was apparent that if I went home for Christmas I would not have enough money to register for the second semester and buy books. Professor Hickman of the Animal Husbandry Department asked if I would feed the university hogs for three weeks starting the week before Christmas vacation. The actual care took 6 hours a day and by getting up at 4 o'clock the first week, I cared for them while going to school. The weather was nice the first 10 days, then it started to snow and it got deeper and deeper. I had to shovel more and more to get the troughs clean and get the hogs well bedded.

Clem had no home to go to and his fraternity house was closed, so he was staying at Herb Clark's apartment. Herb and his wife had gone to Gooding for Christmas. I stayed with Clem for company.

The grocery stores were delivering by sleigh during the snowy weather. Their teams were trained to stand while they carried the groceries to the house door. About five in the afternoon I was returning from the hog barn when I had to stop and let a grocery sleigh go by. The horses were galloping wildly with froth coming from their mouths and nostrils. As they swung around the corner, Christmas orders in clothes baskets spilled out into the street as the sled turned over. The basket I saved from scavengers and looters was a heavy one. When Clem and I unpacked it, we found a complete Christmas dinner. Clem said, "We will never eat it all in a week. I'll bet there are some students left in the halls who couldn't go home for Christmas."

"What a wonderful idea. If we can get some girls, I'll bet they would do most of the cooking and work." Phone calls found three girls and one boy who were staying over and would be glad to have dinner with us. The girls said they would come over Christmas morning and help prepare the dinner.

There was a 2-pound package of rice in the basket. Clem decided he would like some rice for dinner and would make it in the morning. About 10 o'clock, the phone rang at the barn. When I answered, it was Clem. He had cooked all of the rice and run out of pots to put it in. I told him to try the garbage can, and hung up.

Everyone pitched in and the dinner was a success—turkey, corn and oysters, yams, cranberries, mince pie, and all. When we were seated at the table, we held hands, bowed our heads, and I gave the blessing and thanks. The six homesick students forgot their longings. One of the girls played the piano and we sang for hours. Clem's try to get the girls to stay overnight met with a polite but positive, "No, thank you."

The day after Christmas it rained and melted all of the snow. The hog pens were a mess of water and mud. I was working at least 10 to 12 hours a day trying to clean up and dig out the muddy troughs and get the hogs bedded out of the water. Most of the time I was wet and cold. I became so sick I went to the school doctor and he put me into the infirmary. After three days, mostly spent sleeping, I felt good but weak. Professor Hickman and his assistant had to feed the hogs until the herdsman came back four days later. They told everyone what a terribly hard job it was. The $75 I earned would get me through the year if I could borrow another $50 dollars.

Paul Hutchinson was a football player who was taking pre-med. I had tutored him in organic chemistry on classes he missed due to games. He called and said there was a big poker game going on at the old Beta House, and there were a lot of pigeons flush with their Christmas money. I could afford to lose $10. Fortunately, I had several good hands at first and was able to build up a good taw. The pigeons played recklessly and even stupidly, and I really plucked them. I won $150 cash and a $50 check from Fred Cromwell, who gave me his coonskin coat as security. I wore it for a month before he redeemed it. I could get by without scrimping for the rest of the year.

Judging teams in Animal Husbandry, Dairy Cattle, Dairy Products, and Grain Grading and Plant Identification were important to an Ag student. Making one was prestigious and meant you were among the elite intelligencia. It also meant spending five days at the Portland International Livestock Show. For a farm boy to ride on a Pullman car, stay at the most prestigious Multnomah Hotel and be allowed $7.50 a day for meals was a dream trip. Practice judging was in sessions of one hour three times a week and 3 hours twice a week. On Sundays we took out-of-town trips, one to the state prison at Walla Walla. The four prisoners holding the cows were all lifers in for murder. They were polite and seemed just like normal people. The three of us that made the judging team were all juniors. All of us had switched our majors from dairying to another field. No matter what you did, dairying was an everyday, tedious job. Because you had to deal with farmers, the pay would be low and the hours long, so I changed my major.

Professor Atchenson was a small, cocky New Englander. It really burned him up when we beat out the three senior dairy majors that he had held back to insure winning that year. Because of our scores, he had to take us. We heard him tell the other coaching professors he should have used his own brains and left us at home and he expected us to get last. Ed Waggoner said, "I know how we can fix him."

Atchenson took us to the arena in a taxi. He advised us to give concise reasons to the judges as to why we placed the classes and to think about our reasoning ahead of time. In fact, he was red in the face and very short. Evans said, "He acts like he is mad because we are judging."

I asked, "Prof, what average score will win?"

"Eighty-seven and one half percent, and you will have quite a time reaching that with your record."

Judging the eight classes of four animals each took most of the day. We had to wait our turn to give reasons. When we compared our cards, we were almost identical in our placing with an average of 90-plus.

Ed said, "Here comes Prof. Give him our placings backwards." He kept getting redder and redder in the face and chewing his cigar. Finally, he walked away muttering to himself.

Only the judges knew the winning teams and they were to be announced at the awards banquet that evening. Professor Atchenson had really moaned to the other Idaho team coaches, saying we were complete washouts and he could have done better with three freshmen. He wouldn't sit with us at the banquet. Professor Hulbert said, "They were grinning and acting like they were the best. Knowing Ed Waggoner and Virg Cross, I might have known."

The toastmaster announced the high man in Holsteins was Muller of the University of California, Davis, and high team University of California. High man for Guernsey was Virgil Cross, University of Idaho, and high team, University of Idaho. We went to the podium to get our cups. Prof sat up and started chewing on his cigar. Next was high man in Ayreshire, Ed Waggoner, University of Idaho, and high team, University of Idaho. Again we walked up to receive our congratulations and trophies. When we sneaked a look at Prof, he was really chomping on his unlit cigar and looking bewildered. The last was Jersey judging. First was Ralph Magnussen and high team, University of Idaho. The winning team with the all-time high score was the University of Idaho. They asked the team and coach to come up and receive their trophy and have their pictures taken. Prof joined us for the picture, red in the face and speechless. The other Idaho professors knew he had been taken and really gave him a bad time. He didn't say anything in the cab ride to the hotel. As we parted in the lobby, he said, "I am taking you dirty, sneaking little bastards to the Millionaires Club tomorrow night for dinner." His was the only winning team in the Idaho contingent.

My friend Ken Richardson, who lived at Burke and worked during the summer in the lead and silver mines, said I could get a job at $5 a day and get board and room at the company bunkhouse for one dollar a day. It was better than the seasonal farm jobs at $2 to $3 a day, and more steady. He was right. The manager at the employment office sent me to the Tamarack Mine, high on a mountain. I started to walk the 7 miles, carrying my suitcase. A short distance from town, I was picked up by a miner driving a Model A Ford. Upon reporting to the office, I was assigned a bunk in the bunkhouse and told to report to Fred Rachees at the 800-foot level. He advised me to buy a pair of short boots, a miner's cap, and carbide lamp that fitted on it. The company store had everything and I was able to charge it.

I thought the dinner that night must be a special occasion, with three kinds of meat, vegetables, milk, tea or coffee, and five kinds of pie, but found it was standard. I filled out a slip for what I wanted in my lunch pail. When I walked out past the door after breakfast, I was handed a pail with a brass tag numbered 22, the date of my birth.

We were high on the mountain, but still had to walk up a 200-foot hill to the mine entrance. We had to walk one-fourth of a mile into the tunnel to get on the main hoist and get off at the 800-foot level. The shift boss was waiting. He showed me where and how to sort ore from slag and dump the ore into a chute that would empty into cars another 400 hundred feet down, which would travel in that tunnel, emerging lower down the mountain and empty into railroad cars to be taken to the smelter. My miner drilled 10 to 12 6-foot holes on the face of the vertical vein. Levels were at 200-foot intervals. When the vein ended at the present level, you started back at the beginning and mined out another 8-foot high section of the drift. The ceiling was shored up by timbermen to protect workers from falling rocks.

The 6- to 8-foot holes were filled with dynamite with fuses of different lengths to ensure a clean break and straight walls. My last job was to stand at the end of the drift and repeat the miner's "Fire in the Hole" warning and not let anyone in until the miner left with me. The air was unusually good, as there was circulation from the bottom to the top. It was not too hot or too cold. It was comfortable to wear a coat at lunch break. The work was easy—I could have done it in 4 hours, but being underground did bother me a bit.

One morning I helped my miner set his bar for his waterliner drill and helped lift the drill in place. He started the hammering, stuttering drill. In a few minutes he stopped, climbed down over the muck I was working on and sat down. He was white and shaking. With trembling hands he lit a cigarette.

"Virg, get the shift boss and hurry."

I didn't have to go very far down the tunnel when I met the shift boss and told him to come quickly. The miner had not moved. He pointed to some soft yellow material oozing out around his drill bit. It was part of the seven dynamite sticks from the previous shift that had not exploded, and he had drilled into it. Why it didn't go off with the pounding of the drill bit was a miracle. Both Phil and I were saved by the fickle finger of fate. Louie disconnected the air hose and helped take down the drill. He told Phil to leave the mine now and come back at the end of the day and shoot the charge just before quitting time. The more I thought about it, the more scared I became.

There was a poker game almost every evening in the bunkhouse. It was stopped at 11 sharp, company rules. It was a big game, especially Saturday night (pay day). I was playing very conservatively and the $10 I kept out of my paycheck usually lasted me all week. After each session, I sent my winnings home by money order from the company store. Two players seemed to have won most of the money by the end of the week. They were very hard to catch as losers in most of the pots. Dorr Holloway, a student in mining engineering at Oregon State University, discussed this with me. Louie Horne, the shift boss, was a knowledgable old-timer, so we decided to ask him.

"If you never repeat what I say, I'll tell you what I think is happening. They are using a factory-marked deck supposedly for magicians and trick artists. The deck is called Big Diamond. Starting at the top on the right-hand side, if the first diamond is slightly larger, it is an ace. If the second is larger, it is a king, and so on until it is a nine."

"How can you beat them?"

"You can order decks called Shades, but you have to have excellent eyesight to read them."

Dorr tore up a couple of cards during the next session and we fished them out of the wastebasket later. Sure enough, after practice we could see the big diamonds and our playing improved some, but poor light often prevented reading them.

The Fourth of July was a big event, as all mining operations shut down for the two-day holiday. Louie Horne gave Dorr and me a ride to Wallace. I was in great shape from running up the hill to the mine entrance every day and decided to enter the 100-yard dash. Running on pavement is different from running on a cinder track. My basketball shoes felt comfortable on the pavement on Main Street. Most of the contestants were from colleges and at least a dozen were entered. They knew each other and kidded about who was going to win. I am sure some of them had been drinking beer and maybe hard liquor. When I won by inches, they asked where did I go to school, and I said, "Idaho."

"Why don't you go out for track?"

"You all run the hundred under 10 flat, which is my best time. You just don't know how to run on pavement."

Louie warned me to be careful at the dance that night, as it always ended up in a big fight and the police would come in and stop it. I didn't know that I would help trigger it. The tall girl was a good dancer and we were swinging it up when we bumped into another couple. I turned my head and said, "I beg your pardon." A clout behind my ear sent me tumbling to the floor. I was so woozy that I couldn't stand, so I crawled off to the seats on the side of the gymnasium. I grabbed a folding chair just in case someone came after me. Everybody was swinging at everybody else and the women were up on the seats or going out the door. Dorr, who was Pacific Coast light-heavyweight champion, was standing in the center jump circle and would conk anyone that challenged him. He went down when a little runt sneaked up behind him and clobbered him with a looping right back of the ear. The dance was over and it wasn't even midnight. Dorr and I joined four that had been drinking and were singing as they wobbled up the street. Someone in the group thought our singing was so good that we ought to serenade. Since there were no sororities or women's dorms, the only women available to serenade were at the cathouses. The madam finally objected, saying we were making too much noise and bothering her customers. We paid no attention to her and continued singing "The Sweetheart of Sigma Chi" even after the police arrived. We all ended up in jail and were let out the next morning with no charge.

Miners of the area, except maintenance men, were called out to fight a huge forest fire west of Wallace toward the Montana border. When the men from the Tamarack were assembled at the embarking point, rangers asked if any had previous experience. I was put in charge of a crew of eight men, six pulaskas, and two saws. We were assigned to control the fire on the windward side where it was slowly burning upwind. The vegetation was scattered with bushes, trees, and grass. The crew followed me a half-mile up hill to the fire. For an hour we were trenching, sawing down burning or smouldering trees and stumps and had about a half-mile under control. The wind shifted and started to blow in our faces. The wind-borne sparks started fires back of our trenches. I hurriedly led the crew a half-mile downhill and across a wide shallow stream to a road that bordered a sparcely covered hill. It was just in time, as the fire picked up with much greater intensity. We moved back up the hill and watched it burn, hoping it would not cross the river. You could hear the hoarse squall, almost human, agonizing scream of the porcupines. They climbed up to the top of the trees to escape the fire. Deer and coyotes were trotting side by side down the road and not paying any attention to each other.

They moved us that evening to patrol another area high up on a slope facing the fire. We could see for miles the carbide lights of the 2,000 miner fire fighters trying to control this mammoth blaze. The Forest Service men were surprisingly efficient in getting food and water to us with pack animals. Food was mostly sandwiches and canned goods, which we heated. They left us up there for a total of 62 hours patrolling the area. Smoke was hiding the sun. The smoke actually hid a big black cloud that opened up with a pouring, beating rain that undoubtedly saved thousands of acres of timber.

I figured I needed $400 to get by the next school year. It looked as if I would have to work until school started in September. By this time I dreaded going underground because of the dynamite incident with Phil, and another narrow escape. Louie had me help the powder monkey load the powder and deliver the fuses for the miners' shots. We would push a car with the powder (dynamite) in boxes down the track to the different hoists to be hauled up to the miners. Shorty, the powder monkey, was 15 minutes behind on his last delivery. Powder and fuses were not supposed to be hoisted together because of safety. On the skip that is hauled by compressed air, he had three boxes of dynamite and a coil of capped fuses. I said, "That is not right."

He said, "It won't make any difference," and started the load upward. Somewhere about 400 feet it stuck and refused to go any farther. He backed it down a way and put on full air pressure. The cable went slack and the next thing I knew, I had run around a curve into the blank end of a tunnel. My lamp fell off my head and went out. Searching around on my hands and knees, I finally got it alight and back on my cap. Shorty was just sitting numb, looking at some smashed and broken dynamite boxes. The cable had snapped.

Our six decks of blue diamonds and a like amount of red ones arrived from the card company. Dorr and I went out in the woods. At first, even with the key, we couldn't tell anything. It was a good thing we both had better than 20-20 vision. After 10 days we could play solitaire with the backs of the cards up.

Pay day and the big game was the day to make our killing. That afternoon the game was in full swing and the two crooks were playing. Dorr accidentally broke a corner of a card, causing a blue deck to be discarded. I scruffed a couple of cards with readily detected scratch marks. One of the slickers said, "Since you ruined the cards, you two punks go to the store and buy two new decks."

We went to the store and bought the cards, but threw them off into the canyon and brought our decks in to the game. I had a run of good cards, and the slickers also had good cards, but mine were better. At 9:30 I counted what I had sent home and what I had in front of me, and it came to over $400.

I quit, drew my time at the office, sent a money order home, packed my suitcase, and started to walk the 7 miles down the hill to Wallace. It was between shifts and no one was traveling at that time of night. The 7 miles took 2 1/2 hours.

The early morning bus arrived in Spokane around 10 o'clock. The fair was on and I knew university stock and people would be there. It was gratifying to be among friends again. I had kept $20 in my billfold for bus fare home. The few silver dollars in my pocket were for jingling. For once I wasn't careful and put my billfold in my hip pocket, and had it picked sometime before noon. I arrived at home two days later after hitchhiking and sleeping in straw stacks.

It was a pleasant surprise for my folks. I had two weeks to help with haying and threshing. My father told me they were going to leave the farm and go to San Francisco, as he was tired of bucking the uncertain water supply. I was to meet them in Pendleton at Christmas time and help drive them to San Francisco where my brother Farrell was working for Ford Motor Company.

I was anticipating my senior year. Marshall Smith had reserved a steam-heated room close to the campus. There was enough money to get through the school year if I was careful and got a part-time job. We were able to buy a Model T that was altered to look like a racer. It even had a fish tail. The doctor's son had lost his registration money in a poker game. He had to be desperate to sell the car for $65. It was souped up with an Atwater-Kent ignition and different carburetor, and could do 50 miles an hour, which was 10 miles above the legal limit. We concluded, after replacing two sets of bearings each costing $10 besides our labor, that babbet bearings would tolerate only 40 miles an hour.

The day before registration we met with our faculty advisors and major professors. To my surprise, there was a note on the bulletin board, "Virgil Cross, please call Mabel Gill." She was the administrator of a university loan fund and had granted me a $100 loan the year before, to be paid back after I graduated. Surely she didn't want me to pay back the loan now, as that was out of the question. I looked forward to seeing this very striking, kindly person. She was the widow of the former head of the Law Department. She opened the door soon after I rang the doorbell.

"Come in, Virgil, and have a chair."

"Thank you. I have your note."

"How would you like to live with Mother and me this school year? We need someone to clean the furnace, bring in the coal and wood, wash the car and even drive it for me sometimes. In other words, make yourself handy. You would also help Mother with the dishes."

Her offer overwhelmed me. I think I stammered, "I'll be glad to, and I'll try to be very helpful. If you can put up with the early mistakes I'm bound to make."

"You can move in today."

Back at the room I told Smitty that I hated to leave him, as we had so much fun and had done so many things together.

He said, "We will see each other every day anyway."

"Smitty, you will have to look after the bug, as there is no parking at Mrs. Gill's."

I dated Helen a few times at the beginning of the semester. Dwight Engle (who later became a world famous cancer researcher) had his brother's car for the weekend. He was in trouble, broke with no money for gas. He wanted to take his girl to Spokane to see Al Jolson in Sonny Boy, one of the first talking movies. We said we would buy the gas and the tickets, total outlay of about $5. Another problem, two of the girls lived at the hall and there was no way we could get them back by the curfew. The six of us had a conference. We really enjoyed the show. It was about 12:30 when we parked a block away from the back side of Forney Hall. We quietly walked up to the rear of the building. The girls in turn said, "Turn your back," handed up their dresses, and went down the coal chute.

Now I was living right in the midst of the campus. The Blue Bucket Inn, owned by Permeal French, was just across the street and sorority houses were on both sides and across the street. To get my board and room in a pretentious home and be treated like a son by my very kindly, caring, intelligent hostess was wonderful. I even had money for a new suit. No longer did I have to tell my date at intermission refreshment time that I have 25¢ and how shall we spend it. Actually, the girls had never seemed to mind. I guess they were hard up for money, too.

Mrs. Gill had been getting students to stay and help her and her mother for years. At her request they would plant a garden, starting early in the spring, only to have it turn to weeds after they left at the end of the school term. That fall it was overgrown with weeds which I cleaned up and burned. We discussed what to do with it.

"Virgil, do you know anything about flowers?"

"Not much. I can tell a petunia from a begonia. We have the whole Horticultural Department with which to consult. Why not let them give us a planting plan for a 20- x 30-foot garden?" When I told them it was for the very popular Mrs. Gill, they came up with a simple, flexible plan.

She asked, "What about weeds after you leave?"

"If I keep them weeded every week, there will be few weeds that sprout later on."

Because of her kindness and her unbelievable help, I wanted to try to do something special. Hauling manure from the dairy barn and spading it in took considerable time in the fall. It was a gratifying change to use my muscles and work outdoors. That fall I planted the bulbs, daffodil, tulip, crocus, etc., placing the colors in solid plots rather than scattered helter-skelter.

Mrs. Gill, her mother, and I got along very smoothly. We tried to coincide with each other's schedules. It was fun driving her to Spokane and her friends to club meetings on some weekends. Keeping the car spotless and the rest of the chores really took very little time. My study habits had improved each year, and grades were no problem. Dr. Gildow, the school veterinarian, asked me to assist him with the university stock and that supplemented my income.

Ken Richardson, a friend since Smith House, said, "My sister, Mil, is a freshman at Forney Hall, and asked me if I knew of a nice guy who is a good dancer. She hasn't a date for the first house dance. Would you do me a favor and take her to the dance? She is a good-looking chick." She was a tall blonde with above-standard equipment. Her face had a pixie look, with slightly slanted blue eyes and somewhat pug nose, and a wide mouth with upturned corners. We enjoyed the date. I thought Mil would not have any trouble getting dates. I met and danced with her roommates, Carolyn Schmidt and Ethel Tobey. They were also attractive and Toby, as they called her, seemed special.

I was surprised at the invitations I was receiving for dances, some of them a month in advance. Carolyn asked me for a date a few weeks ahead for another house dance. The three roommates had two dances with me on my card. Toby and I must have had that certain charisma for each other, for we talked and held hands and laughed. She said, "It is my turn for the next house dance in November."

I was also getting invited to dances by the untouchable Kappas and Phi seniors whom I had met at dances in the past. I never realized until afterward that the senior girls were shopping for the outstanding seniors for the future. They were fun, but I couldn't classify any of them as a true grey filly. My date with Toby was coming up and we started talking over the phone. I learned a lot of things about her, not only from her but from her roommates. She was a B+ student, a member of the winning intramural basketball and softball teams and the ranking women's tennis player. She had auburn hair, green eyes, and a beautifully coordinated 5-foot, 7-inch, 125-pound figure, with long legs. She was listed as one of the fairest of the Vandals. After our date, she notified her roommates that I was her private property. Actually, we were going steady, but occasionally dated other people.

When a card bearing my name appeared on the bulletin board ordering me to meet with the Academic Council the following Saturday, it caused a lot of gossip among the Ag students, as everybody read all the cards. It perturbed me, but I was sure they would only reprimand me and not expel me.

It happened like this: Studying by reading silently was not too effective, but if I heard something I could recall it. After realizing this, I decided that the dairy building, where I worked and had a key for, would be a good place to study by reading out loud. This enabled me to get my studies done in half the time. It occurred to me that Ethel, Mil, and Carla might want a half-gallon of ice cream. I called and got Ethel on the phone. She said a bucket of strawberry ice cream would be heavenly. Forney Hall was not out of the way home. With the bucket in a sack, I walked up the sidewalk toward the hall. Mil was watching. There was a long, slit-like window about 6 feet above the walk. She said, "Hurry," as she reached down and took the ice cream. Then she said, "Give me your hands," and reached down, pulled me up, and kissed me. She was a big, muscular, well-built athlete of nearly 6 feet. She dropped me down and said goodnight. There was another couple walking down the steps across the street. The kiss must have given me some pep, as I ran almost all out the two blocks down to the Nest Cafe. I could hear the clop clop of some heavy person running behind me. A yell from him caused me to stop. He was really puffing and said, "Dean Kirsey wants to see you."

I said, "O.K., but I am going to make a phone call first." I told Ethel what happened and for them to hide the ice cream, get into bed and pretend they were asleep. We walked back to the Dean.

She said, "Mr. Cross, what were you doing in front of the dormitory window and who was the girl?"

Fighting for time to fabricate a story, I told her about my having to study at the dairy building and that I was taking a box of ice cream home to my roommate. Then I told her as I was walking by, a voice in the shadows said, "What do you have there, little boy?" When I told her it was ice cream, she said, "My roommates are starving because the food is so awful. Please keep us from dying of hunger." I reached up to give her the ice cream and she grabbed my hands and pulled me up and kissed me.

"Who was the girl?"

"I don't think I ever saw her before. The light was bad."

Dean Kirsey was furious and said, "You are going before the discipline committee." She wasn't just talking. A few days later, I received a note from Dean Iddings. I was to appear before the committee. The time, 10:15 on Saturday morning.

The five members of the committee sat facing me. To my surprise, Professor Don R. Theophilus was the chairman. Don R. was one of my favorite people. In fact, he gave me my first job at the university. He acted very formal. His first question was, "What did you do in front of Forney Hall about 10 o'clock last Wednesday evening?"

The seven days had given me time to think about what to say. I repeated the story that I had told Dean Kirsey, but added that I struggled and tried hard to get away, but the girl had kissed me in spite of my efforts. Dean Kirsey asked again, "Who was the girl?"

"She was in the shadows and I did not get a clear look at her face."

"She kissed you, didn't she?"

"Yes, but I closed my eyes while being kissed."

Don R. was getting redder and redder in the face, because of his struggle to keep from laughing. After a whispered conference, he told me that this was a serious breach of campus rules and I would hear of the board's decision shortly. The only reference to their decision was a few days later. Don R. said to me as I passed him in the hall, "You should be in the movies!"

I had made the Animal Husbandry judging team and was an alternate on the Dairy Products team coached by Don R. Theophilus who would be the future President of the University. On the Pullman, Smitty and I had adjoining bunks in the same car with the four teams from neighboring Washington State. The schedule was to leave

Moscow about 7:00 a.m. Sunday and arrive in Portland at the same time Monday. We had been told by students who had made the trip previously that it was customary to leave your shoes by your berth for the porter to shine. In the morning a hat was passed and for his all-night efforts he would get over $20. Clem, Smitty, and I decided it would be a good idea to trade shoes. First we traded with each other. Clem went one way and I went the other, trading shoes back and forth across the aisle. The switch was discovered early in the morning when Smitty yelled, "Some bastard has switched my shoes!" Clem and I joined in the confusion and indignation. We were never blamed. The train was just pulling into Portland when Professor Atchinson traded a size 12 shoe to Austin Summers for a size 7.

Again we were in the Multnomah Hotel and given the magnificent sum of $7.50 a day for meals. A complete T-bone dinner was $2.50 to $3.00 at the best restaurant in town.

Our livestock judging team was next to last. My placing was fifth in the contest. Judging horses was my downfall.

Because I was an alternate on the Dairy Products team, I was supposed to visit creameries on Wednesday. I thought that was superfluous, as I was no longer a Dairy major and had visited creameries the year before. Busses carried the student judging team members and professors to visit the various creameries to study their operation and management practices. I was contemplating an out in the form of ditching the group and going on my own sight-seeing trip. I pointed out a sign to Wes Boice that read, "To the Battleship Oregon." We agreed to go see it. We walked toward the creamery very slowly until everyone passed before turning around and walking away.

The battleship was fascinating. The gun turrets with 10- or 12-inch rifles, as the sailor called them, were huge. Everything about it, from the many boilers to the crew quarters and mess halls, was new and very interesting, as I had never been on a boat bigger than a two-man row boat. It was anchored in the Williamette River that had just been dredged out to accommodate deep water ships. We saw a large number of people talking by the entrance of a building. Some were entering the building. When we inquired what was going on, we were told that the city of Portland was holding a banquet to celebrate the event. This was the celebration party with the Mayor and Governor the speakers.

"Wes, are you hungry?"

"Very. I'm starved. Let's see if we can crash the party and get a free meal."

Both of us were dressed in our blue serge suits with collar and ties. When a man at the door asked us who we were with, Wes said we were with the Governor's party, giving his full name. I had never heard of the Governor. The man waved us in, and we endured the speeches and ate the fillet mignon.

95

When we were back in our room at the hotel, Wes answered a knock at the door. It was Professor Don R. Theophilus. He asked what happened. I didn't see any reason not to tell it like it was. I added that since we were no longer interested in having a career in dairying, it was a waste of time to visit creameries. If we had asked him for permission, he would have had to make a decision. It was easier just to do it and take the consequences. He laughed and said, "Virg, not being able to lie is one of your better assets. Frankly, I wish I could have been with you."

The city of Portland gave all of the team members tickets to a burlesque show in the city's largest theater. There was a chorus of 10 girls for the first show. The grace and precision of the beautiful girls really held our attention. There was a short intermission, and everyone commented on their features and dancing. Someone said to Clem, who was sitting beside me, "How would you like to have a date with one of them?"

Clem really put me on the spot, as I am sure he meant to do, when he replied, "Virg could get a date without any trouble."

To get the monkey back on his back, I stated, "Clem and I could date two of them for dinner with no trouble." We had put our feet into our mouths.

"You want to bet?"

"We'll bet, but we have to have 20-to-1 odds." I told Clem to shut up, but he persisted. They offered 2-to-1 odds. I didn't want to be involved. They finally offered 6-to-1. Clem urged me to take it, saying that if we put up $2 each, we would have $24, which would give us $12 after buying the girls' dinners.

"Clem, what makes you think they will go with us?"

"I have read that chorus girls are always hungry and they even eat violets." We each gave $2 to Professor Hulbert to hold. We were to bring the girls back and they were to say they were going to dinner with us. Half an hour later we gave the doorkeeper 50¢ and asked to see Lucille Lind who had the lead in the chorus. He brought her out and we introduced ourselves. I said, "We are in big trouble and you are the only one who can help us."

"What is your problem?"

Hurridly, I explained what had taken place and if they came down the theater aisle to the fellows so we could get the $24, they could order anything they wanted for dinner. She laughed. "I'll be right back."

Clem said, "I think we are in the money!"

Lucille returned with another striking brunette who was smiling. "This is Betty. Let's go get the money." In triumph we walked from back of the stage.

Lucille said, "Hello, fellows. Thank you for the dinner!"

Clem and I followed them backstage and waited outside the door while they changed. They knew of a place where you dined and danced. They were nice people and we had a most enjoyable time. I heard that Lucille sang in the Met years later. The next day our teammates asked us a lot of questions. They seemed to think that chorus girls were loose and easy, but these two were fun to be with and didn't allow any liberties—although we tried.

The Vocational Ag teacher at Twin Falls resigned in February to go into private industry. Substitute teachers from the Vocational Ag students at the University of Idaho were offered $150 and train fare for a month. It was a bonanza. When Ethel learned that I was going to be in Twin Falls, she wrote her parents and I had an invitation to dinner. They were really nice and cultured people. There was no way I could miss the intent of their questions. Apparently, I passed with flying colors. A letter from Ethel said they were really impressed with me.

The teaching was very pleasant, as there had never been any discipline problems in my other practice teaching. It is surprising how a silent pause to get the class' attention and a smile can set the tempo for the day. Everything was going smoothly until I was quarantined. Spinal meningitis had broken out in the high school. Cultures were taken of everyone in the building. It would take a week for the cultures to be read. The private home where I lived on Blue Lakes Boulevard had a sign on the door. Six teachers were confined to the house. Five of these were young women teaching in grade school and one substitute Vocational Ag teacher. One man and five young women made quite a situation. We played all kinds of games including a strip poker party. Too bad I didn't have additional male company.

We got supplies by phoning friends. It was a relief when the quarantine was lifted. A cook of the noon lunch turned out to be the carrier. Helen Welch was to practice teach in Home Ec in high school. On my last day in Twin Falls we had dinner together. When I asked her if I could go to her room with her, she said it would be fun. We were on the steps in the Perrine Hotel when the manager stopped us and asked where we were going. I said, "I was seeing the lady to her door."

"Forget it. We don't allow carrying on in this hotel." The sanctimonious s.o.b. probably saved me from a mess that I might have had trouble getting out of. In the past I had almost asked Helen to marry me. She just was not a grey filly.

When I returned from teaching practice at Twin Falls on April 1, the daffodils and tulips were starting to bloom. Their tender loving care and the planting plan made a spectacular flower garden in the backyard. I persuaded Mrs. Gill to take bouquets to the annual flower show. She won seven blue ribbons on eight entries.

Freshmen from the nearby sororities started asking for flowers for parties. Mrs. Gill told them they would have to see her gardener, as he was in complete charge of the flower department. The following became standard practice and the freshmen girls got used to it and didn't seem to mind it one iota.

"Mrs. Gill said to ask you if we could have some flowers for our house party."

"You can have two dozen, but you have to pay for them."

"Pay? How much?"

"One kiss per dozen and not over two. The kisses must be whole-hearted, vigorous kisses and not just pecks."

It was surprising how many dozen bouquets I sold. Mrs. Gill would watch from the kitchen window, and she and her mother got quite a kick out of the transactions. After one sale she said, "Don't you think you over-charged that girl? In fact, I think you have been over-charging from the beginning!"

To my surprise, the professors didn't ask me to make up the classes that I had missed. I had over $100 for spending money for April and May until school was out! I called Ethel to find out what color corsage she would want for the Junior Prom. To take the most beautiful girl to the Junior Prom made me very proud. She looked absolutely breathtaking. At her request we had every other dance together, because we had a lot to catch up on. She told me again how much I had impressed her parents. She didn't dance; she floated to the music. It was like I was in a beautiful dream or trance. Dean French allowed an extra half-hour after the dance was over. We walked hand-in-hand in the moonlight on the edge of the school's arboretum. A clarinet started to play Hoagy Carmichael's "Stardust." Soon a trumpet and cornet joined in playing the haunting tune. We held each other and kissed. There was no question that our emotion was at a high pitch. I asked her to marry me. She gave me a long kiss and said, "I'll marry you if you will wait until I get through school long enough to get my grade school teaching certificate."

The moon was full, the spring was balmy, and we were in love. I spread my coat on the ground and we sat down and continued to pet. Things were getting out of hand and she said, "Please stop right where we are. I don't want to mess up things between us. We will have plenty of time in the future." Actually, it was a relief to have her refuse to have sex with me. If she refused under those circumstances, she was not likely to be promiscuous with anyone else.

My grades were good enough that I was taken into Alpha Zeta honorary for grades and leadership. To my surprise, my professors exempted me from all of the final exams. That week was actually a lonesome one, as everybody else was so busy that they didn't have time to do anything but study.

Five dollars for the cap and gown rental and one dollar for a tassel seemed to be outrageous. Like many other things, the merchants of Moscow seemed to have divided up the business concerning the students so that each had his own monopoly.

The long-awaited graduation day of June 8th, 1930, was one of mixed emotion, first, one of sadness to think this was the end of the good times and wonderful events that I had enjoyed during the past four years. There was a feeling of relief as the four-year battle to stay in school was over and I would no longer have to make the sacrifices and put up with some jobs that were menial and unpleasant. There was also a feeling of elation and triumph. I remembered my conversation with Dean Iddings a few days before. He greeted me with, "What do you know, Virgil?"

"Dean, I know that what I know is very small compared to what I could learn in the future."

"Good. Now you are beginning to learn."

I heard part of the graduation speech. Most of the 3 hours I was in deep thought. My attitude of "what can I learn today" had given me a good start in basic principles for fundamental reasoning. Now I had the tools to make a living other than with a pick and shovel. These tools would help me to continue to learn and progress the rest of my life. The speaker said, "What you have learned and accomplished here cannot be taken away from you."

By the time it was my turn to walk up and receive my diploma, I was confident and at peace with myself. "If anyone can make a go of it, I can," I thought.

ABERDEEN

My love for fishing and hunting, which I had been missing while going to college, influenced my selecting Aberdeen from the five schools offering a position as Vocational Ag teacher. The Depression was being felt throughout the country. Jobs were scarce, and wages were being cut drastically. Vocational Agriculture was subsidized by the government, and the $1,800 per year salary was in the high-income bracket.

Aberdeen was a small, prosperous farming community close to American Falls Reservoir where wildlife and fish were abundant. It had been settled by Russian Menonites of German descent. There were seven different branches of the church. Each had their own church. The Scharts and the Weibe families were the sole members of one branch and had their own tiny church. One Sunday Mr. Weibe preached and the next Sunday Mr. Scharts preached. They were opposed to dancing and drinking, and promiscuous fornication was a sure expulsion. There was a dance hall in town, but Albert Funke, School Board Chairman, bought it and nailed the doors and windows shut.

In Aberdeen, everything I did went wrong. Starting to work on July 1 with a new school building, a good salary and a used but good Dodge Fast Four costing $300, the world seemed rosy. In the past everything I did had turned out right. I thought there was no way anything could go wrong. I was visiting students' agricultural projects and suddenly came to a small pile of gravel left by a road crew. The steering arm broke. The car rolled over completely and landed back on its wheels. The top caved in. The windshield shattered, cutting a tendon in my right hand. My index finger was in a splint for six weeks.

The Future Farmers Boys' Club had scheduled a trip into Stanley Basin to catch salmon in July. It was well-planned, with at least three boys in each tent who would cook for themselves. I called a meeting after supper the first evening. We were camped in the national forest. A discussion was held, with all taking part, about preventing forest fires. It was emphasized how necessary it was to put out all fires when leaving camp. This included feeling in the ashes after they were watered down to see if there were any live coals. For two days everything went smoothly. The boys really had fun chasing salmon in the shallow stream. Every night a meeting was held with Frank

Howard, President of the chapter, presiding. Frank did a good job and everybody cooperated well. The camp was kept clean and neat. In fact, the forest ranger attended the evening meeting and complimented them on the camp and their conduct.

Four students from Aberdeen High School moved in and camped close to the F.F.A. camp on the third evening. I met an elderly prospector who had claims in the area. He wanted me to look at his claims located a couple of miles downstream. The road was two deep ruts. In fact, it was like driving down two troughs. On the way back we picked up a hitchhiker. He rode in the middle of the front seat. Somewhere on the way he tried to get the prospector to slow down, as he was afraid of the deep ruts. The driver lifted up the detachable steering wheel, which he had added in order to have a larger steering wheel, and handed it to the hitchhiker, saying, "You drive." The hitchhiker said, "No, No!" and handed it back to the driver who put it back on the steering column. The hitchhiker was silent from then on.

About a half-mile from camp the prospector pointed and said, "There is a fire!" Smoke was spreading up in the direction of the camp. Sure enough, it was from the camp. It had started from a fire left by the four new arrivals. The boys had it under control, but it had burned an area nearly 100 feet in diameter. Only two small trees were affected, as the area was mostly grass. Only a few wisps of smoke were visible when the Forest Ranger drove up. I explained that it was not my responsibility, as the other boys were not in my group, but had come there on their own. The Ranger said, "They are from the same high school and you are a teacher and are responsible. I am arresting you and taking you to Challis where you can tell it to the judge." The judge sided with the ranger and advised me to plead guilty, be fined $15 and $3 court cost and that would be the end of it. Being inexperienced, I fell for the solution.

When I returned to Aberdeen, I was asked to explain what happened. My explanation was all right with everyone but Chairman Funke whose son was partially responsible for the fire. I had never met his son, Ronald. Chairman Funke said I was a high school teacher and was partially responsible for the conduct of the high school students. His motive was to take the heat off his own son who hadn't taken proper precautions in putting out his campfire.

I was popular with the students. Discipline was no problem once I had established I was fair but firm. I enjoyed the class work and the supervision of the students' agriculture projects of crops and animals. There were six first-year teachers in the faculty. Card parties, dinners, and some dancing in the L.D.S. Church were the main diversions from the regular routine. I was busy hunting and fishing in my leisure time.

Early in November I received a very disturbing letter. It was from Helen Welch. We had gone together the first semester of last year.

When I visited her family and saw her brothers and sisters, I was reminded of my father's remarks about the grey filly and the beautiful sorrel. Helen was a very nice person and I was still fond of her. Helen was in trouble. She was almost two months pregnant. She was engaged to a football player from the east. When he heard she was pregnant, he just dropped out of school and disappeared. She didn't want her folks to know so she asked me if I could lend her $200 so she could have an abortion performed in Spokane. I had no idea how the consequences from this letter would disrupt my life for the next few years. I answered her letter in the next mail saying that I didn't have the $200 but would get it. I also said that I would call her on Saturday evening about 7 o'clock and she could tell me of the arrangements and how she wanted the money sent. The two phone calls turned out to be a mistake. Wilma Mann, a senior, was the night telephone operator at the Moscow exchange. She had a grudge and a chance to get even. I had gone with her for several months during her sophomore year. It had been a close, fun relationship. I had tutored a pre-med football player at the Beta House in bacteriology during football season. It was 10 o'clock and Paul and I had finished the catch-up work. I started to leave, opening the door slightly. Paul said something to me and I stopped. I heard very light footsteps coming down the hall. Curiosity caused me to close the door, leaving a small opening to see through. To my surprise, there was Wilma slipping down the hall. I closed the door, turned to Paul and asked, "What is Wilma Mann doing here?"

Paul said, "She comes to see a couple of the fellows regularly."

Wilma called me after two weeks' silence and asked why I hadn't called. I said, "You know why," and hung up.

Bill Clegg, my roommate, loaned me $50 and I sent Helen the $200. The abortion was carried out quietly.

Wilma, now a senior, became engaged to Ward Mink, a graduate student and a favorite of Dean Iddings. The Iddings had no children and Ward had lived with them for most of his college years and they were very close. Wilma told Ward about me getting a girl in trouble and about my paying for the abortion. She knew only that the girl's name was Helen. Ward told the Dean the gossip at the dinner table. Mrs. Iddings was hell on wheels about sex. To her, illicit sex was a sin punishable by death. This gave her something about which to hound the Dean. William Kerr, head of the Vocational Agriculture Department, was in close contact with the Dean, who told him that I should be fired for immoral conduct.

Kerr said that I was doing a good job and he didn't have enough evidence to fire me.

That Christmas holiday I visited Ethel in Twin Falls when she came home for the holidays. We went to a homecoming ball and the charisma of being together returned. I asked her to marry me, and she said, "When I get through school." We had been corresponding almost every week. One thing bothered me. She had two spells of crying and wouldn't tell me what was the matter. Finally, crying, she said, "I have been raped."

She was crying while she told me about the act. The man was a senior in high school when she was a freshman. She had a few dates with him. He made attempts to have sex, but didn't insist when she said no. He knocked on her door about 2 o'clock one afternoon. She opened the door and was surprised to see him. It had been four years since their last meeting. He had moved to Washington and was visiting friends for a few days.

She invited him to come in. He sat in the big arm chair and she sat on the davenport. Their conversation at first was light and fun as they recalled their high school days. It never occurred to her that this was anything but a friendly visit. He got out of his chair and sat down beside her. When he put his arms around her and pulled her over toward him, she tried to resist. He was big and powerful and in spite of everything she could do, he was on top of her and taking her underthings off. He did not use a condom. When he finally let her up, she grabbed an andiron from the fireplace and managed to hit a glancing blow that scraped his ear and hurt her hand as he tried to ward it off. She said, "I was trying to kill him, but he got out of the house in a hurry. I hope the soap suds douche works, as there wasn't any Lysol in the house. I am no longer a virgin."

"Why didn't you tell your folks?"

"My father would have hunted him down and killed him."

"Where is he staying? I want to take care of him."

"I don't know. He just said he was staying with friends." I could not help believing her, as we had been on picnics and places where we did considerable petting. She had left no doubt that she was not going to get intimate no matter how much she cared. All I could do to console her was to tell her that she was just as nice a person as she ever was, and not to feel ashamed.

"After all, it was not your fault. I still love you, as much or more because you confided in me. And I am going to marry you someday—that is, if you will still have me."

A month later I got a letter from her. She was almost hysterical as she had missed her period for the first time in her life. She didn't know what to do if she missed the next one. The last thing was she didn't want her folks to know. I wrote back that a doctor in Spokane would perform the abortion for $200. I would find out his name. A phone call to Helen solved that.

Her next letter confirmed her predicament. She called the doctor in Spokane and had an appointment for a Saturday afternoon. Her letter said she didn't know where she could get $200. I said to myself as I mailed the money order, "Here we go again!"

The doctor wouldn't perform the operation without parental consent, so her folks had to know about it after all. They asked her who was paying for it and she said, "He is paying for it." She apparently did not realize that they would assume that I was the guilty party, so they never discussed the incident when she came home from school in the spring. The $400 took a big bite out of my income for two abortions that were not my fault.

I missed the good feminine company that I had experienced in college. The single women available were not on a par with the girls I had been associating with. Bill Clegg, my roommate and high school coach, remarked about the situation that "the only reason to go with them is sex." I knew that high school girls were just pushovers for older men, especially if they had good jobs during the Depression. With the poor start and the way things were going wrong, I was just plain gun shy and knew it would be easy to wreck a career by dating a high school girl you had no intention of marrying.

Early in the spring, Bill Clegg and Wells Smith started to double date with two pretty high school seniors. Why they were so careless as to get them both pregnant, I could not comprehend. Bill approached me.

"Virg, I'm in big trouble."

"Don't tell me you have Nancy in trouble?"

"She missed her period. I don't want to marry her. Can you help me?"

"Bill, I'll see if I can get some ergot apial and find out the dosage."

My mother was Supervisor of Nurses at the Emergency Department of the City and County Hospital in San Francisco. I wrote her a letter stating the situation and assuring her that it was not for me. A week later the well-wrapped package contained a bottle and printed instructions and nothing else. In the meantime, Wells said he had Mary M. pregnant. They both used the bottle and, fortunately, it worked.

Ronald Funke, one of the group that started the forest fire, was a big, fat, incorrigible freshman. His father was the town's richest man, as well as the Chairman of the School Board. I was conducting a discussion in class and Ronald got up and started toward the other side of the room. I said, "Where are you going?"

"I want to talk to Fred." He kept on going.

I grabbed him by the collar, flipped him over the desk and proceeded to blister his fat rear end with my hand. Ronald howled, blubbered, and tried to leave the room, but I shoved him down in a seat and he stayed there. I told Superintendent Weston about it after school. His comment was, "Good, but his father will raise hell with me." I then told him that I had applied at Blackfoot for the Vocational Agricultural teaching job there and the school would send me a contract after they met early in June. Weston said, "You've done a good job here and we will miss you. I don't blame you for wanting to move, as this is a difficult community to live in."

"You have been simply super with me and I'm going to miss you."

"You should write me a letter stating you are resigning."

I wrote a short letter and handed it to him.

School was out a week later. I wanted to visit my folks in San Francisco and my aunt in Los Angeles and to see Ethel in Hollywood. She and I had corresponded regularly. We had kept each other informed of our activities, she giving detailed accounts of her comings and goings in school. Late in February, she said she didn't want to be engaged, as it was binding and two years was a long time. This did not end our steady correspondence.

School let out the first week in May, and I took off in the Dodge Fast Four for California. It was 1931. Gas was 13¢ a gallon, Cokes a nickel, and cheese burgers 15¢.

I drove down Market Street to the ferry and took Highway 101 to Los Angeles. I rested a day at Aunt Laura's. Friday I called Ethel and said I would see her Saturday afternoon. The Tobeys were living in a court on Lexington Avenue. I parked in front of a well-kept duplex in the court. I started to walk up the steps to the door and Ethel's father, Guy Tobey, came out. His greeting was, "You are not welcome here. You have caused enough trouble."

"It was not my fault."

"That's what they all say. Get in your car and don't come back or I'll use a shotgun on you." Stunned and perplexed, I got in my car and started back to Idaho.

My landlady had placed my mail in a neat pile on my desk. On top was a letter from the Blackfoot School District. Instead of a contract was a letter stating they were not hiring me. There was no explanation for the refusal.

There was also a long letter from Ethel. It had never occurred to her that her folks would assume that I was the guilty party since they respected and thought highly of me. She told her father that I was not guilty but had come to her rescue. She had called Aunt Laura, but I had left for Idaho.

I went immediately to the school house and contacted Superintendent Weston, who said he thought there would be no trouble about reinstating me and the board would meet the next Monday. The board met with Superintendent Weston and he recommended that I be rehired. Chairman Funke said that he would vote against me, as I had caused a lot of controversy and needed to get a new start. The other board members were in favor of rehiring me, but Funke stood firm on his position, stating, "We agreed it had to be unanimous." The result was I was out of a job.

I contacted the Oakley School Board members individually. They all assured me they would hire me at their next board meeting in July. I received another letter of refusal instead. I couldn't understand what was happening, as my credentials and performance were very good.

I contacted William Kerr, Director of Vocational Agriculture.

"Mr. Kerr, what is happening? I get promised a job and get a letter of refusal each time."

"Dean Iddings ordered me not to place you because you had gotten a girl in trouble. His word is law and he is very strict about sex."

"Mr. Kerr, I never got anyone in trouble. I had not seen her for a year. All I did was try to help." I told him about Helen.

"I'm sorry, Virg. I wish I had known this earlier. Due to the Depression, we had to drop eight departments and there are no openings. I'll talk to the Dean. It would clear things up if the girl would talk to Dean Iddings. I'll try to place you in the first opening."

I spent the whole month of July contacting schools for openings on any kind of teaching job, to no avail. The Depression was tightening its grip and the economy had come to a screeching halt. I ran out of money and had to turn back my car for lack of payments.

I stayed at Uncle Jack's in Hagerman Valley. The ranch bordered Upper Salmon Falls, where Morrison-Knudsen was putting in a dam and power plant for Idaho Power. I worked there, drilling holes 6-feet deep with a jackhammer. Eight hours of holding the pounding, jarring, deafening jackhammer was very tiring. This was not a union job and if you were low man for three days in the number of your allotted holes, you were dismissed. There was a long list of applicants for the $5-a-day job.

There was a meeting of Aunt Alpha's women's club and the home agent told them how to cook the abundant fresh water clams in Snake River. What she didn't know was that Twin Falls had been dumping raw sewage into Snake River for years. This was evidenced by the condoms caught on the set lines of the sturgeon fishermen. I was infected with a bug, probably giardia, causing a violent, painful intestinal disorder. I tried to work and could not, so I reported in sick. Four days later when I tried to report for work, I was informed that there were no openings.

I stayed at Uncle Jack's, helping with milking, irrigating, and selling melons. For the first time in my life I was depressed to the point where there was little hope for the future except farm work at a dollar a day.

NORTH DAKOTA

One morning on the way to the two-holer, I picked up yesterday's newspaper just in case the Sears-Roebuck catalog had run out. While seated on the throne, I read, "Heyburn High School is going to be a four-year school and hire three new teachers." Heyburn was only 3 miles from Burley.

In half an hour I was out on the highway, washed, shaved, and wearing my good dark blue suit, trying to hitch a ride. The paper said the board would meet that day. It was 9 o'clock. I had a suitcase just in case I had to stay overnight. A shiny new red Buick roadster with a rumble seat drove by. I waved at the two girls and they waved back and drove on for almost half a mile. Evidently, I made an impression on them, for they stopped, turned around and drove back. After a couple more passes to look me over, they stopped and asked where I was going. When I explained where I was going and why, they said, "Get in and we'll take you there."

It turned out they were from North Dakota. Mary was driving her graduation present. It was an hour and a half of exchanging information. There was considerable laughter. It was almost 11 o'clock when I walked into the Heyburn schoolhouse after reluctantly bidding the girls goodbye. I thought the two tall girls, blonde Mary and brunette Ruth, were good-looking, nice, and desirable.

I introduced myself and gave Superintendent Weston as a reference. The board was impressed. Chairman Croft called Aberdeen and luckily Weston was in his office and gave me a good recommendation, stating I had no trouble with discipline. The board discussed whether I was large enough to handle some of the big, tough boys that had been troublemakers. Chairman Croft filled out the contract for $135 a month for nine months, and all signed it. We shook hands and I left.

To my surprise, the girls were sitting in the red convertible waiting for me, grins on their faces. They had an idea.

"We are going through Yellowstone and Teton National Parks. We have a tent and some cooking utensils in the trunk and occupying part of the rumble seat. Do you know of another nice boy that could or would spend a week going through the parks with us?"

"There is a chance that Ross Lowry could go. He finished school last year and teaches in Burley High School."

Ross was walking in the driveway as we drove up. There was a lot

107

of laughter for nearly a half-hour. Ross and I were about the same size, and Ross put in extra traveling clothes for me. It took considerable rearranging and tying on. Ross put in two fishing poles and some extra bedding. He told the girls, "We have to stop in Burley."

The stop was the Rexall Drug. I whispered "two dozen" and Ross grinned and nodded. He returned quickly with a small sack which he put in his bag.

Mary said, "What did you buy?"

"I'll whisper it to you. Two dozen Trojans."

Mary laughed and Ruth said, "What did he buy?" Mary whispered to her and she said "Goody."

The girls had never seen such spectacular mountains as the Grand Tetons loomed larger and larger. As we neared the high altitude of the park, we could see there had been a touch of frost. The quaking aspen were tinged with gold and bright yellows. Maples showed tinges of red. All were overwhelmed by the beauty of the forest and the swift flowing and sparkling streams. We pitched the 8x8-foot tent under a big pine tree, close to Old Faithful Geyser. A grill and picnic table were in front of our tent.

That night I cooked finger steaks, baked potatoes, and corn on the cob. Old Faithful was beautiful in the full moon. Bears roamed around but didn't bother us, as we had put all the food in the car's trunk.

After cleaning up the supper, we joined the group around the campfire and listened to the ranger give the history of Yellowstone. To our surprise, we heard that President Roosevelt had declared and set aside the area for posterity. The ranger told of Colter, who was the first white man to see the park, and Colter's unbelievable escape from the Indians. Naked in the dead of winter, he ran the gauntlet and got through. He killed the Indian that was far ahead of the other runners, taking his moccasins, buckskin trousers, and fur jacket. When he came to a beaver pond, he dived in and swam up inside a beaver's house. It was lined with grass and twigs. Exhausted, he slept for 12 hours. With the Indian's knife and a piece of obsidian, he was able to start a fire and build shelter for the night by cutting small trees and putting them up under a larger tree. He dug a trench in the pine needles down into the dirt. When the fire had burned down to coals, he covered it with dirt and pine needles. This was his bed. It was over 76 miles to Fort Hall. The snow gradually became shallower. He was almost starved when he stumbled on a partially eaten deer. He built a shelter, cooked and ate, rested one day and staggered into Fort Hall on the evening of the third day. The tips of his nose and ears were peeling. It was several weeks before he could walk on his frost-bitten feet. It was no wonder he died an old man at 37.

There was considerable hesitation and uncertainty when we wandered hand-in-hand back to the tent. No one seemed to want to make the first move. I realized there was a lot of difference in talking about getting intimate together and actually doing it. It appeared that all of the foursome had become aware of this. Ruth broke the ice, bringing out a bottle of Canadian Club.

"Everybody is so stiff and tongue-tied, and this will loosen us up." She poured a full three fingers in two glasses and the two coffee cups and diluted it with orange juice. None of us were used to drinking. I had never had a drink in college, and very few after. It turned us into a laughing, giggling foursome.

Ruth said, "Mary and I will go to bed first. We will call you when it is decent. When we entered the tent, there were two long, giggling mounds in one bed. Ross and I had hoped there would be one in each bed. After we were in bed, Ross whispered to me, "Think of something."

I said, "O.K., Ruth, I'll trade Ross for Mary."

There was a spontaneous eruption of laughter in the tent. Ruth asked, "What will you give me to boot?"

"I'll give you a good breakfast."

"Mary and I will hold a conference."

After a few minutes, Mary kicked Ross and said, "Get out of my bed."

On the sixth day we broke camp at beautiful Jenny's Lake at the foot of the majestic Grand Tetons. The girls wanted us to go with them through Glacier National Park at Banff. This was impossible, as both of us were going to have to start teaching the next week. The ride back to Burley was rather quiet and subdued. Each was engrossed in his or her own thoughts and the reluctance of ending a wonderful interlude in our lives. The parting at Burley was a sad one with hugs and kisses. We agreed to write each other. I promised Mary that I would visit her over the Christmas holidays at her home in Lancaster, North Dakota. We corresponded almost every week.

Helen, who was teaching school in Coeur d'Alene, sent me a check for $200.

To get to Lancaster, which was near the Canadian border, was a long, tedious bus ride with several changes of busses. Mary was waiting at the bus depot with the engine running in a snow-encrusted Cadillac. It was cold. The thermometer outside the bus station said 12 degrees. The snow was over a foot deep on the level, but the roads had been plowed and were well packed. The wind was so cold, it felt like a knife cutting into my face. I immediately put my hand over my nose. When I complained about the cold, Mary said, "It has warmed up a lot—almost 15 degrees." It was a joyful reunion, without any hesitation on either part.

Mary had told me she was an only child and her father had a cattle ranch. She didn't tell me that it covered almost 10,000 acres and had over a thousand head of cattle. I found out about the cattle operation during the 10-mile ride from the stage depot.

Her mother was a large, tall, and very good-looking woman with the brightest blue eyes I had ever seen. After she greeted me warmly, she told Mary to show me to my room. There was a fire flickering through the isinglass windows of a cast iron wood stove, giving the room a cozy, warm glow. It was then I realized why the large rambling house had so many chimneys.

"Dinner is always ready at 6:00, not 6:01 or 6:02, because that's the way Daddy has it." I thought Daddy must be the head honcho in this house, and further events proved this point.

After bathing and shaving in the bathroom across the hall, I changed into clean casual clothes. Mary had slipped into my room, bringing sheets and pillows and snatching a few kisses each time. I asked where her room was.

"It is down the hall quite a ways."

"Mary, what is quite a ways?"

"It is far down the hall from yours. In fact, it is next to yours. You are so excited that you didn't notice anything. That is a connecting door," she said, pointing to another door in my room.

"What about your folks?"

"Well, Daddy won't notice about the rooms. Mother is a Swede and this sort of thing has gone on in Sweden for hundreds of years. Besides, I told her I intended to marry you, so she is well aware of the situation."

I said, "The room arrangement is going to be super. In fact, it will be out of this world."

I knew when her father, J.D., arrived home by the noisy stomping to get the snow off his feet on the back porch. When he walked through the living room on his way to wash up, we shook hands and he said, "So you are the man that Mary has been talking about so much." He turned on his heels and went down the hall to the bathroom. It was 5:45. Mary and her mother were busy in the kitchen. The table was set and they started to put food on it. At 5:59 the big, tall, vigorous, bushy-headed man with a full, short, grey beard walked into the room and sat down at the table. We bowed our heads and he gave the short blessing in a deep, rumbling voice.

It had taken over two and almost three days to get there due to bad connections on stage schedules. Snacks, sandwiches and meals hastily eaten from second- or third-rate cooks in stage depots are not too palatable or filling. I was starved for a good meal. I had visions of a big steak or prime rib roast and gravy, hot bisquits, etc., but was surprised by a pork loin roast and sauerkraut. She had also made some beautiful golden brown dumplings in the remainder of a beef stew. The hot apple pie with a big slice of melted sharp cheddar cheese had the most inviting aroma and tasted even better. Most of the conversation was "Please pass this or that." J.D. did ask a few short questions such as, "Where were you raised? What are you teaching?"

It was after the meal when I was alone with him in the living room while the women were doing the dishes that I was interrogated and he pulled no punches. We were facing the big fireplace, watching flames. He lit his pipe, took a couple of puffs, and asked, "What do you know about cattle?"

"Well, J.D. (he had told me to call him J.D.), I have a lot to learn about cattle. I'll never live long enough to know it all. I was reared on a farm. We had cattle and a few sheep. I graduated with an Animal Husbandry major. I worked at the university beef barn feeding and helping take care of their purebred herd. I believe I have a practical, workable knowledge in feed and feeding for Idaho conditions. I have book learning for range cattle ranching and raising cattle for feeders, but little practical experience."

He asked about Idaho range. Having herded sheep, I was intimately acquainted with Idaho range plants. Somewhere during the hour of conversation with him it was brought out that I had been trained in selecting registered herd bulls and was high in beef judging at the Portland International Livestock Show.

The surprise was when he said, "Virg, the Depression has all cattlemen losing their shirts. I can weather it. At least I think I can. Under the government program to purchase cattle to get rid of the surplus, I have really culled my herd, not only to get cash but to keep only the best. Much of the culling has been old cows, bulls, and undesirable she stock. I know you and Mary want to spend time together, but tomorrow I need your help. There is a bull sale. It is the biggest bull sale in the state and there will be some very good herd bulls for sale."

I thought, "You old bastard. Your motives are as clear as a pane of glass. You are really going to check out a possible future son-in-law. I don't know what you are going to do, but I have my fingers crossed."

Mary objected to no avail. J.D. said he would get me home in time for supper and we wouldn't miss the homecoming dance.

We looked at several pens of bulls. They were good but not outstanding. J.D. stopped at a pen and pointed. "Now there is a very good herd bull."

"Ah ha," I thought, "the old fox is trying to trap me. I'll fix him good." The 2-year-old bull seemed to have everything. His back was broad and straight, the head and neck fitted in well with the rest of the body. Straight legs, a deep round, and a straight underline. The bull was so symetrically proportioned that he was a picture of perfection. I knew or felt something was wrong and J.D. was trying to trap me.

"What do you think of him?" he asked.

111

I hedged and said, "I would like to look at him some more." The panel fence was small and I gently prodded the bull until he had his side against the wood panel. I started at his tail and, using my hands, spanned off his body length. Then I spanned his depth. The span of my size 11 hands is exactly 9 inches. J.D. was impatient for an answer.

"J.D., you are not going to buy this bull. He is perfectly proportioned; in fact, he is beautiful. In spite of that, you know and I know you wouldn't touch him with a 10-foot pole. Comparing his measurements with the young herd sire the university bought, he is almost a foot shorter and almost that much less in depth. You are selling weight, bone and hide. The herdsman would call this a chuffy bull. That is his definition for a beautifully-built small bull that will sire similar progeny."

His small grin was my reward.

Very little was said until we came to a pen of three bulls. They were all large for their age with plenty of width, depth, and length. It was true there were a few minor defects. These would sire big, fast-growing calves.

"What do you think, Virg?"

"These will do the job."

He laughed and bought the three and arranged for a trucker to haul them home. On the way home I knew I was in when he patted me on the shoulder and said, "We have had a good day."

At the dinner table Mary asked J.D how the day went.

"Mary, we had a great day. I bought three good bulls at a very low price. Virg did a great job in helping me pick out the bulls."

The family and I were seated at a card table playing pinochle in the living room, when a knock came at the door. The woman was the wife of one of the ranch hands, coming to report that her husband and his brother were both sick with the flu. J.D. said, "Dammit. They have been feeding the herd here at the ranch and the cattle have to be fed. Virg, can you pitch hay?"

"I've pitched a lot of hay."

"It looks like it will be up to us to feed the cattle in the morning. It is going to be a hard day. You had better get to bed early, as we have breakfast at 6 o'clock."

Going to bed early was what I had been looking forward to. Getting up at 6 o'clock in the morning was not. I could keep up with anyone pitching hay when I was in shape, which I wasn't.

It was a delightful, busy night. Mary got up at 2:30 to go to the bathroom and told me I had to get some sleep. She went back to her room and closed the door. To me it was only minutes before J.D. pounded on the door and bellowed, "Time for breakfast." It was 5:45. Washing my face with the cold water, two cups of black coffee, and a breakfast of pancakes and sausage did a lot to restore me. Fortunately, I had always been able to sleep and had done a lot of sleeping on the bus. Actually, I felt just a little cocky. "I'll show that big rancher I can keep up with him." We harnessed the huge matched grey percherons and hitched them to the big sled with a large hay rack. The weather had moderated. The thermometer beside the barn door read 20 degrees. White vapor condensed in the air as the horses trotted slowly to the first stack of alfalfa and brome grass. I wasn't going to pitch the hay any slower or faster than he did. It was going to be a long, hard day. J.D. worked at a moderate, steady pace. After getting a slight sweat even though I was wearing a light jacket, I started to feel good so I stepped up the pace. We drove out into the field to the cattle. They were hungry and let us know by their constant bellowing. J.D. tied up the lines and let the team take their own route at a slow walk. We stood back-to-back pitching off hay on each side.

The second load was unloaded just in time for lunch. Lack of sleep and activities of the night before were definitely taking its toll. I no longer set the pace. I was just trying to keep up. Lunch helped and I managed to get a 15-minute nap. Due to stiffness in my arms, back, and shoulders, it was almost painful to hitch up the team. The first dozen forkfuls of hay caused me to grit my teeth. Slowly my muscles warmed and with difficulty I kept up with the perpetual motion of J.D. He had said when we started, "We feed them three loads of hay."

At 3 o'clock we had finished unloading the third load. I was completely exhausted or at least I thought I was. Instead of driving to the barn, he drove up to a granary. There we loaded 100-pound sacks of ground grain and cottonseed meal. J.D. said, "These are the breeding stock and they need extra protein to have big healthy calves."

I lifted the heavier and heavier 100-pound sacks onto the sled and he stacked. The last sack barely made it up. Putting the grain in feed troughs was easy, as we poured it from the sled. Through at last at 4:30, I staggered into the house. Mary's mother said, "I filled the tub with hot water for you." Soaking in that tub was sheer pleasure. What a relief for fatigue and sore muscles! With a change of clothes, I flopped on the bed. Mary woke me at 5:50 for dinner. It was a sumptious meal of prime rib roast. Actually, I ate sparingly—too tired to lift my fork.

Shortly after 7 o'clock J.D. said, "Virg, we have another long day tomorrow. Better get to bed early." My clothes were left scattered on the floor by my bed. It seemed that Mary said something to me and I think I muttered something back. I had gone to bed dreading the morrow. The next thing I knew, Mary was shaking me and saying, "It is time to get up, sleepyhead."

"What time is it?"

"Time to get up. It is 8:30."

"What happened?"

"The Larson brothers had a remarkable recovery from the flu."

I thought, "You old bastard—you planned all of this."

When we first arrived at the ranch, I thought being married to Mary, working on and eventually taking over the management of the ranch and being independent with no school boards was very tempting. A little doubt was entering my thinking. J.D. left me to Mary the remaining four days and they were pleasant. I had first thought Mary was really the grey filly. The grey was beginning to have a little tinge of sorrel. Mary was a little spoiled. When she didn't get her way she pouted a little. I thought she could have been a little more helpful in the kitchen when I helped do dishes and cleaned up. We had talked about children and she said, "I don't like kids and one will be enough."

As for J.D., he was going to be completely in charge for many years. He would make all of the decisions. It was wonderful to be with Mary, but I didn't propose even after the family showed I was the fair-haired boy. On the long bus ride home I did a lot of thinking, pro and con. I thought of Ethel and comparisons began to enter my mind.

When I went through my mail there was a nice, affectionate letter from Ethel and a package with her picture in it. I realized how beautiful she was and how she fitted the image of the grey filly. Mary and I corresponded regularly. Near the end of the school year Mary wrote saying she had been going with a nice fellow. Her parents preferred me and she did, too. "Virg, you have to fish or cut bait."

I reluctantly wrote back that I wasn't ready to marry. That was the end of that chapter in my life.

HEYBURN

I was hired to teach sciences, chemistry, biology, general science, and two classes in applied agriculture at Heyburn. Shortly after school started the high school coach was fired for messing around with one of his students. I became the girls' and boys' basketball coach with no warning. My basketball experience was limited to playing outlaw ball on the Aberdeen Krazy Kats. This left me uncertain and leery of the assignment. My protest to Superintendent Wynn fell on deaf ears. Bill Clegg, the Aberdeen coach, loaned me two books, one by Phog Allen of Kansas and Ruby of Illinois with pictures and diagrams of all of the drills and fundamentals. He advised me to spend the first month on fundamentals. The players and I learned together. Neither of the Heyburn teams had won many games in the past few years. As the season progressed, the young teams improved enough that they were respectable. Crowds began to pack the small, narrow 70-foot gymnasium. In those days every school had a different sized gym. The ceiling was low and often the ball would bounce off it. It wasn't until the third year when the Brower brothers joined the team that Heyburn became a power in their B-class league.

There was no discipline problem. I put the following items on the board for discussion at the first meeting of each class:

> *Students*:
> You are here to learn; to prepare for life.
> Do nothing to hinder others from learning.
> Do not embarrass me.
> How can we improve the room?
> Be fair and polite.
> *Teacher*:
> I am here to help you and guide you in learning. I will be fair and polite.
> To see that learning and study conditions are all right.
> Make classes as pleasant and interesting as possible.
> I will try not to embarrass you.
> How can we improve our place of study?

The first classes in each course were spent by leading the students to discuss each item. The items were left on the board for several days. When it was suggested that we should have curtains to cover up the bare blinds and flower boxes in the windows, the home ec. girls volunteered to make the curtains. The manual training class made the flower boxes.

Why the school board selected Shelly Wynn to be superintendent, I'll never know. He was bald, short, with uneasy, piercing eyes. Unfortunately, he had a very short fuse and this, combined with a belligerant, dictatorial manner made him very unpopular with the students and they gave him lots of trouble in the two classes he taught. Having power had gone to his head. Because I was so popular and had no trouble with discipline, Wynn just couldn't stand it and began to find fault over insignificant things, sometimes before the faculty and students. It finally became almost unbearable. I had to remain polite and subserviant to the superintendent because his word was law. The final straw was when he was observing my chemistry class. Chemistry in those days was really primitive compared to what it is now. I was demonstrating safety in handling chemicals when transferring or combining them. In some experiments in the lab book, chemicals had to be ground in a porcelain mortar with a porcelain pestle. Trying to emphasize the importance of having the pestle and mortar absolutely clean for safety and to get the desired result, I picked up a mortar and put a small pinch of potassium chlorate in it.

"We want to grind this into a fine powder so that we can mix it easily. You will note that I have the mortar tilted away from me to protect my face and eyes. Grinding should be slow and gentle."

Making the first stroke resulted in a flash like a tiny firecracker. Wynn left the room. The students did not know I had put in a very small pinch of ferrocyanide and the combination formed a very unstable explosive substance. I thought I had given a good demonstration on safety.

Shortly after that Wynn told the school board that I was conducting dangerous experiments in chemistry lab; he was there when it happened and he thought I should be fired. Lew Sabin, chairman of the school board, questioned his son and daughter about my abilities as a teacher and they evidently gave me good marks. In fact, his son was in the chemistry class and told him the explosion was no big deal. Evidently it bothered Sabin, as he contacted me at the end of a school day and asked me about it.

I said, "Mr. Sabin, come with me and I will show you what I did." Taking the bottles of potassium chlorate and ferrocyanide from a locked drawer in my desk, I repeated the demonstration.

His comment was, "That should teach them to be careful."

It was a small matter that put the lid on the pot. Wynn and two board members visited my biology class. It was a good class with order and lots of student participation. I was sitting at my desk putting papers in order for the next day. When they left the room, Wynn was

116

first. He switched the lights off. To me he was showing off his authority to the school board and maybe indicating my lack of responsibility.

Keeping my head under stress had always been one of my assets. After a few minutes I went up to his office. The board members and students had left. When I entered his office I turned the lock on the door. Then I proceeded to tell him how little, overbearing, and ignorant he was. If he bothered me in any way I was going to beat the living hell out of him. I had decided that rather than submit to all that harrassment, I would find another occupation. When I told the other teachers about it, they were sure I would be fired, and I was, too. The board members were all L.D.S. and Wynn was an active churchgoer. When it came to a confrontation between a gentile and a Mormon, they were duty-bound to take their church member's side.

The school board meeting was for hiring teachers for the next year. When it came to rehiring me, Wynn told the board that if Cross was rehired he would resign. Sabin said, "From what I can gather from the students, Cross is the best teacher they ever had. I make a motion that we rehire him with a $10 raise." It was seconded and passed. Then Sabin said to Wynn, "And we accept your resignation." I was rewarded and pleased. The rest of the month was like living with a nasty, surly, wounded bear. It had been a good year. To find out I could hold my own in my profession and do a good job was very gratifying.

J. M. Whiting, principal of Burley High School, was hired as superintendent of schools and he met with each of us separately. He encouraged me to go to Berkeley for summer school graduate work. I decided to do that and go to see Ethel in Hollywood after finishing the summer school.

It was the end of the first year of teaching at Heyburn. The Depression was on with its W.P.A., where people were working on all levels of projects—in the forest, fields, road building, and many other assignments. Soup kitchens were in all of the cities. Bank clerks were making $35 to $40 a month. Farm workers, if they were lucky, got $1 a day and dinner. I decided to go to my parents in San Francisco. My father, through study, had become a landscape gardener for the city of San Francisco. My mother, who started as a practical nurse four years before, had become an R.N. and was the supervisor of the night emergency ward. Father took me to meet Frank Tanaka, a Japanese graduate of the University of California at Davis and supervisor of the City and County Hospital grounds. He gave me a job as gardener for the city of San Francisco. My bailiwick was the showplace, the isolation ward with locks, fences, and gates. The pay was $40 a month with board, room, and medical attention. There would not be a room available for a week.

117

My parents were saving to return to Idaho when they retired. They had a tiny economical apartment close to their work. There was no room for me to sleep except on the floor. Mother mentioned this to Susie Wong, one of her nurses. Susie said, "I work nights and he works days. He could sleep at my place." Her apartment was tastefully furnished with a blend of Chinese and American. I was almost afraid to touch anything as it was so spotless. The fear of leaving a spot on anything caused me to take personal articles and shave and shower in the hospital's restrooms. I started sleeping there on Sunday night. After work on Monday I gathered a small but beautiful bouquet of flowers and left it on her table, with a note saying: "This is a small thank you for sharing your beautiful apartment with me. I hope my imposition for a week is not unbearable. You are very generous."

The note on the pillow Tuesday night said: "Thank you for the beautiful flowers.—Susie W."

Every day there were fresh flowers and an exchange of notes. In one note I said: "You have to be beautiful inside and out to have such a lovely apartment. I would like to meet you."

The reply was: "Are you trying to romance me? Your mother showed me your picture and I know you are tall and handsome. She was subtle in warning me about you. I am curious."

Thursday her note caused some thought. It read: "Saturday night is my night off. What do you suggest about sleeping arrangements?"

I wrote, "I'll call for you at 6 o'clock Saturday night and we will discuss this weighty problem over dinner at the Sir Francis Drake and while we dance. If this is not acceptable, leave a 'No' note on your doorknob and I'll not even knock." All morning Saturday I worked feverishly among the flowers and shrubs. Frank Tanaka was watching me and said, "Virg, there is always tomorrow." Just before quitting I cut six beautiful roses of different colors. The rest of the afternoon was spent getting my suit pressed, shaving, bathing, shining shoes, and anticipating the big meeting.

There was no note on the doorknob. I knocked softly, and the door opened, and a soft, musical voice said, "Come in, Virgil. I am so glad to see you."

I was speechless from what I saw. She held out her hand. I kissed it. Finally, I said, "You are beautiful!" I saw a tall, slim girl with a light yellow dress, yellow topaz earrings, a yellow necklace. Her bobbed hair was long. She was close to my 6-foot height and could not have weighed over 115 pounds. The large, slightly almond-shaped eyes, a slightly pugged nose, combined with a mouth upturned at the corners to give her a pixie look. She was enjoying my discomfort while trying to put me at ease. She thanked me for the roses.

I asked, "Where shall we go for dinner?"

"The Sir Francis Drake will be great, but isn't it too expensive?"

I had not touched my last paycheck. "Due to the seriousness of the problem confronting us, the best will be none too good."

She smiled and handed me a rather heavy, dark wooly coat. It was needed, as the fog was in and the air was cold. The street car ride down Market Street didn't take long.

The doorman took one look at us, bowed, smiled, and opened the door, receiving a thank you and a quarter. We decided on the five-course dinner, which included wine, clam chowder, shrimp cocktail, crab salad, fillet of sole, and a miniature loaf of hot bread. The total bill was $5 including a 50¢ tip. We danced fast fox-trots and two-steps together. We had almost finished our meal and were sipping the wine when the orchestra started playing the slow Stardust of Hoagy Carmichael. We became almost a single, compact body following the music in slow, graceful, swaying movements. Up until this dance, we had been somewhat reserved. I had not wanted to do anything to break the enchantment. We returned to our table, holding hands and smiling at each other.

It had taken us almost 3 hours to finish the meal. We were curious about each other's family life and childhood. Susie was the eldest of five unwanted daughters of a well-to-do Manchurian merchant. She started to be trained to please men and be a Chinese wife at the age of 10. Fortunately, they were able to actually receive a sum of money from a rich Chinese merchant in San Francisco, and she was sent at the age of 12 to be his bride. If she had been still single by the age of 14, she would have been sold to a house-of-joy proprietor. Her 5-foot, 10-inch height was a drawback. The old Chinese merchant died of a heart attack on his wedding night. Apparently, he had no heirs. Susie became the ward of the Chinese Council and the city of San Francisco. She had been sent to dancing schools but never dated in high school. She attended Berkeley and became an R.N. She loved Berkeley and had dated and lived in a sorority there.

My family life and especially the herding of sheep interested her very much. In the street on the way back to her apartment, we held hands and talked about the dinner, music, and how well we danced together. Nothing was said about the sleeping arrangement problem. I opened her door with her spare key, let her in, and stepped in to help her with her coat. When I hung up my topcoat, she was still standing by the rack. We spontaneously reached for each other and had our first long kiss.

Finally, I said, "We were to discuss sleeping arrangements."

"This is a wide bed and will sleep two easily."

"Susie, you know what will happen if we sleep together."

"Yes, I know what is going to happen, Virg. I hope I can please you."

"Susie, it is not to please me. It is something for us to share. What

119

worries me is I didn't bring any rubbers. I really didn't expect this to happen, but I confess I hoped it would."

"Virg, we Chinese women have used sponges for hundreds of years."

I was amazed by her versatility in bed. She had been trained by experts. We told each other how wonderful it was. It was nearly 10 o'clock when we awoke. Susie prepared breakfast. During the meal she called me "my hairy bear." I had hair on my chest, stomach, back, as well as pubic hair.

I said, "You don't have one hair on your body."

"Very few Chinese have any hair on their bodies. Hair hides fleas. Fleas spread typhus, so over thousands of years the people with the least hair survived."

"Why is it that the Japanese have pubic hair?"

"Because Japan is a nation with a cold or cool climate which fleas do not like."

The Friday night date each week became ritual for us. I repeatedly asked her to marry me. She kept saying she couldn't decide, as there was much to think about and it had so many problems. A week before I had to leave for Idaho, she replied to my urgings, "I'll tell you my decision on our last date next week."

We were quiet on the last date. I was very apprehensive and Susie appeared to be sad.

"Virg, I would never fit in with your life in Idaho. Our children would be ostracized and looked down upon."

"I will get my master's degree and come back to California."

"Virg, you would never be happy in the city. As Kipling said, 'East is east and west is west, and never the twain shall meet.'" Our parting was tearful and painful. I wrote several letters but they were never answered. My first communication was an announcement of her marriage to a Chinese doctor in May.

Ethel and I had corresponded regularly about once a month after my visit to Hollywood. She asked me to visit her and I wrote back that I didn't want to get shot. Her next letter said she had told her father I wasn't the culprit and I would be welcome. I said I would plan on visiting her next summer. She wrote back and said that that would be a long time. She was enthusiastic about the course in accounting she was taking at U.C.L.A.

The school year went smoothly. Four men teachers rented a house and hired a housekeeper and cook for lunch and dinner.

It happened I fell in love. A roommate of one of the teachers came down for homecoming. Peg asked me to take Betty to the dance. I was completely dazzled by a beautiful, witty, good-humored person whose components were perfectly assembled. For two months I either went to American Falls to visit her or she came down to visit me. I noticed that

I said, "You'll fish it. Just follow me."

When we walked up behind the man, he said, "I am fishing here. You will have to go find another hole."

"Can you swim?" I asked.

"I can't."

"You are going to learn real quick." I handed my jacket to the doctor.

The man got out of the way, saying, "Mr. Grey isn't going to like this!"

"Piss on Mr. Grey!" said the dentist bravely. He waded out to hip-deep and started to make short casts. I sat on a rock to one side away from his backcast. It was so pleasant and tranquil sitting in the warm sun watching a truly expert fly-fisherman casting with unbelievable precision. He cast toward a submerged rock that made a riffle. The fly floated over the rock, the line tightened, and the raised rod hooked him. The aerial acrobat on the end of the line was out of the water in a series of jumps followed by long runs.

While he was fighting the fish, he said, "I've got to be careful, as I have only a 5-pound test leader." When he beached the fish, I flopped it up on the bank. He said, "Let's take a break." He took a thermos out of his pack and we smoked and had a cup of coffee. When we were through, he said, "One more to go. The limit is two."

The next fish didn't come easy. Two got away after fighting several minutes. Finally, he landed a fish that he guessed weighed 15 pounds. On the way back he told me about Zane Grey.

Grey was the exact opposite of a true sportsman. He was an egotistical game hog. When the author fished for bill fish in New Zealand, he would hire three charter boats. They would fish three abreast about a quarter of a mile apart. When a fish was hooked, Grey would jump into a motor boat and go over and land the fish. He held world records that should not have been allowed.

My next stop was at The Dalles, where I watched the construction of the high dam, and saw the Indians netting salmon while they were tied to poles way out in the powerful, swirling current of the mighty river.

My ride from Cascade was a nightmare. The road was blasted on the side of the canyon. It was narrow and crooked. Many times the side toward the river had no shoulder and it would be hundreds of feet straight down. The elderly, bearded driver had thick lenses in his glasses, and it was apparent that he didn't see too well. Most of the time he drove down the center of the road, just barely turning out to let the honking oncoming driver get past. I was about to ask him to let me out, when he stopped at a service station. I walked on and waved him by later when he passed me.

My mail box was full when I returned to Heyburn. It was good to

she would start to breathe more rapidly after being kissed and became very affectionate. We became engaged. I let her wear my Alpha Zeta pin until I could afford a diamond. I wasn't walking on air—I was just tiptoeing, barely touching the clouds.

Idaho was going to play the Southern Branch at Pocatello. I asked Betty if she would like to see the game and spend the weekend. I would pick her up after school Friday and we would return on Sunday. We registered at the Bannock Hotel as Mr. and Mrs. Ross. We had just enough time to eat and get ready for the dance. I didn't care about going to the dance, as I figured there was something more entertaining to do. In fact, I told her so and she said, "There will be all night for that." She danced beautifully and I met a lot of old acquaintances.

Betty insisted that we take a bath in the tub together. After an hour of furious contact, I was sure she would be satisfied and we would say goodnight and go to sleep. It was fun the first two times after an hour's sleep, but from then on it became less and less.

It was a fine, clear autumn day for the game, with no wind, which is unusual for Pocatello. It was dusk when we came back to the hotel. Betty met an old schoolmate. She stopped to talk and I said, "I'm going up to the room and take a nap."

She said, "I'll be up soon."

She woke me up 2 hours later when she opened the door. She looked a little disheveled and I thought that was normal after attending a football game. The activities of Friday night were repeated. By Sunday morning we had used 10 Trojans. It was a relief when we checked out of the hotel.

Five weeks later we went to her homecoming at Albion Normal and we repeated our frequent lovemaking. My roommate, Ross Freer, knew her at Albion. Sometime during the next week we were talking about Betty and he let it slip out when he said, "She can't help being a nympho. When she gets hot, she will screw anything."

I couldn't go home to San Francisco for the holidays because there was a basketball game scheduled for January 3rd.

I had written Ethel that I was engaged. Her letter in reply said she also was engaged. She thanked me for the good times we had together and since we were both engaged this letter was goodbye, as it wouldn't be fair to our fiances to carry on any further correspondence. We agreed to send each other wedding announcements.

My brother had sent me an over-sized hot water bottle filled with grain alcohol. There had been a heist of alcohol from a government warehouse in San Francisco. He traded a radio for a 5-gallon can of it. Ross and two other coaches decided we should have a New Year's party. We planned to go to the dance and have a steak dinner afterward. We filled a large cut glass bowl with fruit juice and added a long pint of alcohol to it. It was agreed that we would each have one drink before the dance. We were in L.D.S. territory and drinking was a sure way to get fired. School teaching vacancies were nonexistent.

When we arrived home, Haggerty Hult said, "I think the punch is too weak." He added another pint. We ate the steaks, rolled back the rugs, and danced to the radio. Sometime later on, one of the girls passed out. Her partner said she never could hold her liquor. Ross had to be put to bed a few minutes later. I remember going to the bathroom. It was daylight when I woke up and discovered I was without any clothes. There was someone in bed with me and she didn't have any clothes either. It was Peg, Ross' girl friend. We didn't like each other. She woke up and said, "You!" and I said, "You!" She brought her knees up and kicked me out on the floor. We were the only two awake. Betty and Haggerty were on the davenport and her panties were on the floor beside her. That ended our engagement. She was definitely not a grey filly.

A month or so after the big holiday party that caused me to break off the engagement to Betty, I received a letter from Ethel. We had not written to each other for months because we were engaged. It started with: "Hello, darling. I haven't received a wedding announcement." It told of her activities and Culbertson's new system in contract bridge.

My reply was: "I haven't received any wedding announcement from you either. You didn't get an announcement because I am no longer engaged. You still haunt me and seem to stay between me and other women! Besides, she isn't a grey filly."

She wrote back: "I also am no longer engaged, and I feel about other people the same as you do. You mentioned something about a grey filly before. What is the score?" The P.S. on her letter was: "Give up. I'll get you anyway."

When school was out, I decided to attend the summer session at Berkeley. It was like getting into a different world compared to San Francisco. I hung my topcoat and stocking cap in a locker and went around with a light jacket. The well-kept grounds were almost tropical with all kinds of plants and flowers in harmony as only a professional landscaper could do. I was in awe not only of the size of the University of California, but of the quality of the professors. My three courses were vocational guidance, a course in logic (what is right and what is wrong) and adolescent psychology. For six weeks these courses kept me busy studying, eating, and sleeping and going to and from. There were so many brilliant students in the class that I was in awe of their intelligence. When Dr. Lee, a visiting Harvard professor, read my solution for putting violin playing in the simplest and most logical terms, I was very surprised and pleased. My answer was, "Stretched horse hair drawn across dried cat's bowels, creating harmonious sound."

No one cheated at Berkeley. If someone looked at another's paper, they started to tap their pencil and didn't look up and the rest of the class joined in. I was on the street car on the way back to the ferry when I discovered that in my haste to catch the car, I had left my watch and lifetime Shaeffer pen on the desk in the library where I was studying. When I told my seatmate (another student), he said, "Don't worry. They will be there in the morning." Sure enough, they were. At noon everyone seemed to lunch outdoors. Each seemed to have a favorite spot. Each spot had its own rabbits and squirrels that came out and shared lunch with them.

I called the Tobeys in California. The person who answered the phone said they had moved and she didn't know where they went.

After attending graduate school at Berkeley, there were a few days left before school started in Heyburn. The cheapest and most interesting way to get back to Idaho was to hitchhike. In the '30s, everybody picked up hitchhikers if they had room. A crime by a hitchhiker was almost unheard of. The route up the coast to Portland, then up the Columbia to Idaho would be scenic. My brother Farrell took me to the edge of San Francisco. I was carrying a bag with basic necessities; my suitcase had been mailed to Idaho. Fortunately, my first ride was a long one to Eureka. The elderly couple was glad to have me ride and bought my lunch. Two more rides took me to Crescent City where I spent the night. Two women picked me up at Crescent City. They were going inland to Grants Pass. It was there my route was changed. I was resting, watching large fish dimpling in the Umpqua River, when a car pulled off the road close to me, and the driver said, "Do you want a ride?"

"You are going the wrong way. I was just resting and watching those huge trout feeding."

"Those are steelhead. I am going to fish for them." This was a chance that I didn't want to miss. I asked him if I could watch. He said, "I would be glad to have your company."

A mile later he turned off on a dirt road and stopped at the end. I watched him put his rod together, thread the line through the guides, and attach a long leader with a big fly on it. He waddled in his waders ahead of me through the willows to the river. When he walked into the open, he started to swear. A man was fishing in the only advantageous spot. It was an unwritten law if someone was fishing a steelhead hole, you either moved on or fished in a less desirable spot.

He said, "That fellow isn't fishing. He is just holding the pole and letting the line drift in the water." We watched the man slowly fill his pipe and puff on it. My friend said, "He is hired by that son-of-a-bitch, Zane Grey. He hires three men to hog the holes for him, as he fishes upstream toward them. I'll have to find another hole. He is bigger than I am." My friend, a young dentist, wasn't over 5-feet, 6-inches tall and weighed about 125 pounds.

be back in my own room. There was a large envelope with Ethel's handwriting on it, containing a portrait of her. The only pictures I had were snapshots taken at college. I had forgotten how beautiful and charming she was. It was hard to believe that the Tobeys had moved back to Twin Falls on August 20th. She had been there for five days. Her father had taken a job as manager of the used car lot for the Ford agency. There was a second letter which gave me her address in Twin Falls and said they would have a phone soon. To say I was excited would be a vast understatement. It had been three years since her father had ordered me off the place because he thought I was responsible for getting her in trouble.

The bus ride from Burley to Twin Falls took an hour. The bus driver let me off in front of the house. I was just walking up the top step when she greeted me with open arms. Her mother finally stepped out and said, "You two can continue in the house. The neighbors are going to talk." Seeing Ethel made me glad that I hadn't gotten myself entangled or messed up in any situation. We were sitting on the davenport holding each other. Her mother said she had to get groceries. We had so much to catch up on. They had bought a house. Her father was so happy to get away from the noise and crowding in Los Angeles.

Ethel lacked three semesters to finish her accounting course. That night we played bridge with her parents. The Culbertson system was the ultimate in contract bridge. Thank goodness they went to bed early. Her mother, being a smart woman, moved a cot for Ethel into their bedroom and I slept in Ethel's room.

The next day we went swimming at Durkey's Lake. There was no question she was a grey filly. I'd have married her then, but it was out of the question. My school loans had all been paid off. I had helped my sister, Evelyn, a junior at the university. Summer school was costly and I had not had a check since the 15th of April. Except for $30-odd, I was broke. I was ashamed to tell her that, so I didn't commit myself other than to say I would see her when I returned from visiting Uncle Jack in Hagerman.

There was little to do at Uncle Jack's and it gave me a lot of time to think. I knew that a marriage had to be open and based on truth. Saturday I would ask her to marry me and wait until I had enough saved up to start housekeeping.

Saturday evening we were walking home from a show. She stopped and said, "You asked me a question the night of the prom. I said yes, and you said you would wait. We both have waited."

We were passing the park. I said, "This isn't the place for proposals. Girls don't propose to men. It isn't ladylike." Taking her arm, I led her to a park bench and told her to sit down. Then I got down on my knees, held her hand, and asked, "Darling, will you

125

marry me?"

She hugged me and said, tearfully, "I've waited so long for this. I was afraid I would lose you." When I told her I had gone with other people but things just didn't seem right and the thought of her turned everything off, she said she had similar experiences. It was after we got back to her house and were sitting on the swing on the porch that I told her of my financial situation. I needed to have about $400 to have enough to buy a car and set up housekeeping. My folks had bought sagebrush farm land and since water was now available, I would get paid for clearing the land, fencing it, and planting. My teaching contract was for eight months at $115 a month. After a lot of conversation and figuring, we decided the only solution was to wait until August 8. This would give us three weeks before school started to have a honeymoon in California and get settled in Idaho. She asked, "Have you told my father about us becoming engaged? I think he would appreciate that."

Dad Tobey was a happy man. He smiled and patted me on the shoulder when I told him of our plans.

Shortly after we became engaged, Ethel said, "You promised to tell me about this grey filly bit." After I told her about my father's remarks while we were sitting on the corral fence, she looked at me and said, "This implies you are comparing me with a horse and are marrying me for breeding purposes." My denial was a frustrated one. She laughed and said, "Honey, it is all right. I also thought you would father beautiful and wonderful children. I can't say what you will be because I don't know what kind of horse you are."

In November the bottom fell out for the Guy Tobey family. He was out of work. The bank refused to extend the company's loan and the company declared bankruptcy. For a month he tried to find work while working for the county on W.P.A. (Works Progress Administration), one of Roosevelt's many programs to create jobs. The Tobeys had rented the house and were all packed and ready to move when I visited that weekend. A friend was going to truck their furniture down to California.

That night Ethel slept on the davenport. Sometime in the night she slipped into bed with me and whispered, "I thought we should have something to think about while we are apart. It will help us to remember." There was nothing else to do but agree vigorously.

On the way to Los Angeles they dropped me at Heyburn. It was "Dad" Tobey now. He got out after Ethel and I had our goodbye, and he handed me a cased shotgun, saying, "Since you and Babe are engaged, I will not need this anymore." I had a good Ithaca which I prized, but I didn't say anything about it and thanked him. Actually, it never occurred to me that the new gun could be anywhere near as good as my own. Two days later, when I took the gun out of the case, it was a Crown Grade L. C. Smith with all the trimmings and engraving in silver and gold. The gun is still in the family after 50 years and is worth many thousands of dollars.

I was 27 and had found no difficulty in holding a job. Getting married to a beautiful, wonderful girl and having a life together was an incentive to save. Saving $50 a month wasn't easy, but at the end of the school year my bank account was a little over $400. School let out at noon on Friday. Ross and I went to the bank and cashed our last checks, and I drew out all my savings and put the money into my bank book in the inner pocket of my coat. We decided to splurge at Pete's barber shop and spend a dollar for a haircut, shave, and massage. Several people came in to wait their turn, but left saying they didn't want to wait. I got out of the chair, put on my coat, and reached into my pocket to pay the barber. My bank book was gone. Frantically, I searched all my pockets and looked near the coatrack, but there was nothing. Ross and I tried to find the people who had been in the barber shop, but they had vanished. It was as if the world had come to an end. On the way back to the lodging I just sat until Ross said, "We are here." All my plans had been blown to pieces.

The only possible solution was my father. I hated to be dependent on anyone. Waiting to make a call until he was home from work, 6 o'clock their time and 7 my time, went slowly, long minute by minute. When my father came on the line, I told him that I was going to the new land at Gooding the next day and had made arrangements to board and room at a deaf couple's place. A neighbor would rent me a team of horses for $40 for the summer and feed them. Our plan had been for me to deposit my money in the Gooding bank and pay the expenses out of it, then Father would reimburse me and pay me wages for the four months of work. There was nothing to do but tell him the whole story.

He said, "You go right ahead with your plans to get married. We have enough in savings to take care of everything. I will have a check deposited to your account in the Gooding First National Bank." The world was tilted back on its axis again.

It must have been around 7 o'clock when I hitched the team to a walking plow, locally called a foot burner. Of the 50 acres of tillable land, about half was cleared of sagebrush and the grass could be plowed under. The other half was grass and sagebrush which would burn off clean after the grass died in a couple of weeks. The grassland would be planted first, leaving the drying grass and brush land to be plowed after it was burned off. People had been pasturing stock on it and that had to stop to allow the grass to grow tall enough to burn. If it were fenced before burning, there would be danger of burning the fence posts.

In order to get the first furrow straight, you drove to a marker that you could see between the horses. My furrow was almost as straight as a string. While I was admiring it, a herd of cattle started grazing on the luxurious grass in the fertile soil in the unburned area. They were being driven by a short, stubby man riding a pinto. It was Hickory Jones. Hickory was bad news—in fact, he was pure poison. He was the bully in the eighth grade. Even the high school boys left him alone. When he got mad, he roared like an animal, and it took a lot of force to subdue him. He was kicked out of school from the eighth grade at the age of 16. Probably 5-feet, 2-inches and weighing 145 pounds, all muscle. I was sure I could take him, as I was 35 pounds heavier and had at least a foot longer reach, but I wanted no part of him. The summer before, my father had told him not to pasture that land anymore. Hickory knew he was dealing with an elderly man. He told Dad that he had always used the land for pasture and since it was not fenced, he would continue to do so, and there wasn't a damn thing Dad could do about it. This remark was still rankling in my mind. I walked up to him and said, "Hello, Hickory."

He said, "Hello" in a grudging, surly manner.

"I want this grass to grow so I can burn it and the brush off. I don't want it pastured anymore. It is O.K. to use it today, but don't come back tomorrow," I warned.

"I told your old man and I'll tell you. I've always pastured this and it isn't fenced and you can't do anything about it." Apparently he saw the same skinny kid that always ran from him to keep from getting beaten up.

"Don't come back tomorrow."

I stopped plowing and spent the rest of the day putting up a three-barbed-wire fence. The soil was deep and moist and post holes went in easily. The gate was three barbed wires attached to a pole and fastened with a bar and a loop. The fence posts were all in a line, as I had carefully sighted them in.

The next morning I closed the gate and hitched up the team and started to plow. Looking back on the back furrow, I saw cattle were walking through the opened gate and there was Hickory. It never occurred to me to have him arrested for trespassing. I told myself to stay cool and keep my head, because he was going to get wild.

I walked up to him and said, "Hickory, you are up early. That is a nice-looking horse you have." I reached over with my left hand to pat the horse, and simultaneously grabbed Hickory by the shoulder and jerked him out of the saddle, slamming him hard to the ground.

That should have been enough to finish off anyone but Hickory. He came up roaring like an animal, charging with his arms flailing wildly. It was easy to step aside and land a long, looping right hand to his mouth, breaking teeth and bringing blood. It was a good thing I had heavy leather gloves on. Time after time he went down after being hit with all my power. He tried to get a rock, but I kicked it out of his

128

hand. Hitting him in the stomach did very little to slow him down. He was getting tired and so was I. My hands were so bruised from hitting his hard head that it was painful to punch. It occurred to me that if I could get behind him and hit him on the liver, it would fix him. It took some maneuvering, but I finally got a clear shot at his right side for kidney and liver damage. He doubled over in pain and just to make sure, I hit him on the other side. That finished it. He was helpless. I slapped him and told him that if he ever set foot on my land I would kill him. I helped him on his horse and drove the cattle out and headed them for home.

When I took off my shirt and washed away the blood, I saw that Hickory had landed more blows than I had realized. One of my eyes was almost closed. My nose was bruised and bleeding, but not broken. My mouth was a mess of cuts. It was a fight for my life. Hickory never showed up again, but I kept a loaded rifle ready.

Marshall Smith probably knew me better than anyone except my parents. He said, "Virg is a chicken at heart. He will do almost anything to keep from fighting. If you crowd him, you are in big trouble, as he will find a way to beat the hell out of you."

By working long hours seven days a week, I was able to get the land seeded in clover and alfalfa. The ditches were all in and setting the irrigation water only took an hour night and morning. The Smiths hired me to help in the second cutting of hay in July. Riley Smith asked me if I would take three cars of lambs back to Chicago. Sheep tended to bunch up toward the rear of the car after they were first loaded. My job was to see and unpack any overcrowding. Livestock had to be fed and watered within 24 hours after loading. Checking to see that they were loaded back into the right numbered cars at these stops would be part of my duties. We loaded at Ketchum and straightened out the piling at the stop in Shoshone. There was no piling up or sheep hurt when we stopped at Laramie for feed and to rest them for 10 hours. Because there were four other men doing the same thing for other sheep outfits, the railroad put on a passenger coach instead of a caboose. Three of them were Basques and their use of English was very limited. The fifth, Bob Foster, was about my age. He was clean-cut and from his conversation I could tell he was educated. The Basques wanted to play poker. It was a penny-ante game. Before going to bed that night, we each had won $7 or $8. We complimented each other on our poker skill.

The sheep were unloaded at 10 o'clock in Laramie for a rest stop. After seeing that they were fed and watered, we decided to see the town. We had lunch in a cafe pool hall near the tracks. While we were eating, a noisy poker game was going on. Most of it was in singsong Chinese. There were three Chinese and two white men playing. The Chinese were losing slowly but steadily. Bob said, "The three are

129

playing against the white men." Luck changed and the two white men left. Bob said we would play, but we had to go to the rest room first. He grabbed my arm and we went into the rest room. He said, "They are telling each other what they have and will bet a poor hand just to get you into the pot."

"How do you know that?"

"My folks were missionaries and I was raised in China. I learned to speak Chinese before I could speak English. I'll signal you with my fingers as to what their hole cards are. I will use the thumb as a marker and I can signal the denominations of the first ten high cards."

It didn't always work, but by 5 o'clock that evening we were nearly a $100 ahead. We cashed our chips in. Bob walked back toward the poker table where the Chinese were really carrying on about our winning. Their mouths dropped open when he began talking fluently to them in Chinese. One said, "Ah, so." The rest were quiet.

"What did you say to them?"

"I told them it was not honorable for them to cheat a poor, stupid white devil, and from now on they will have bad luck if they do it again." The Chinese started chattering to each other.

"What are they saying, Bob?"

"They decided that I signalled you with my hands."

The next day we unloaded in Kansas City. Swift and Company bought the lambs. There was just enough time to shave and shower and change from dirty sheep-smelling clothes to clean ones from my suitcase and catch the Portland Rose back to Gooding.

Diane Marie was a black and white Lewellen Setter with brown on her nose and ears. She was two months old. My superintendent of schools, J. M. Whiting, owned her mother and he charged me $2.50 for her. The people I lived with had a fenced backyard and liked dogs. She ended up in the house, sleeping beside my bed. I had never had a bird dog and it never occurred to me that you had to train one. All I ever did was talk to her and she seemed to understand. When pheasant season opened that fall, she was almost seven months old. I didn't know you never did very much in training a dog until six or eight months and didn't shoot over the dog until it was at least a year old. She was small and would tire out easily, so I put her in a game bag with her head sticking out, and walked out into the field. When I put her down in the scrubby beet field, she started tracking back and forth. I thought, "She knows how to hunt." Suddenly, she stopped, stretched out with her tail level and pointed toward a tumble weed a few feet away. I kicked the weed and a small young rooster flew out. It fell at my shot and Diane ran toward it and tried to pick it up, but it was too heavy. She found two more birds and I brought her back sitting on top of them in the game bag. It was only after her death when I had another setter that I realized how remarkable she was.

Of course, I took her to Gooding when I was putting the new land into cultivation. She spent almost all day stalking rock chucks on the far side where Little Wood River bounded the farm. She would come at once for a whistle. She was going to come in heat again early in August. John Kaneaster had a kennel of bird dogs which he trained and sold. He would furnish the male for the choice of the litter. He insisted that he would have to try her out in the field to see if she was good enough for his field trial champion to breed. I thought, "I hope *HE* is good enough." John wanted to take the dogs in individual cages and hunt them separately on the opening day of the sage hen season.

It just happened that a doctor and a dentist from Shoshone were hunting with him. They must have been impressed. Diane had been back with me for 10 days. I was going to leave the next week for California to be married. Diane would stay at Kaneaster's kennel and I would pick her up on the way back from California.

Two men drove up in a Buick, introduced themselves, and petted Diane. She was friendly with them.

"How much do you want for your dog?"

"She isn't for sale." To the $100 offer I just shook my head. When they offered $200, a lot of thoughts went through my mind. This, combined with the nearly $200 I had made in poker games and taking four cars of lambs back to Kansas City, really fired up my finances. So after a lot of soul searching, I said, "You can have her." Each gave me a check for $100, which I put in the button pocket of my bib overalls.

I wasn't happy. It was as if I had let down a friend who trusted me. For the next three days I regretted the decision. On the evening of the third day after her departure, a gust of wind blew off my straw hat as I was checking over the irrigation water for the last time. It started whirling over and over with me chasing it. When I ran out of breath, I stopped and watched it stop against a bush a block or so away. A dirty black and white dog picked it up and limped slowly toward me. I ran to meet her and hugged her. There was no way to keep us both from crying. Her feet were raw. She was thin and dirty. She had traveled 50 miles to get back to me. I had a sandwich left and fed it to her bite by bite. It wasn't long before the red Buick drove up. They said they had tracked her all the way here. I took the two checks from my bib pocket and handed them back. Then I said, "Diane, let's go home."

When I told Ethel about Diane's long trek back to me, she said, "If you had let them take her back, I would not marry you."

There was only a week left until my trip to California. The neighbor would finish irrigating. John Kaneaster would keep Diane until Ethel and I returned. With what Smith paid me for helping with haying and shipping lambs, I had about $225. This, with what my father paid for my work, would get us by until the first paycheck in October.

The deaf couple that I lived with did not have a radio. The Max Baer-Jim Braddock fight was scheduled for the next Saturday night. I left the field early to go to town. There was a good crowd listening to the preliminary fights. A big man walked into the pool hall. I said, "Does anyone want to bet on Braddock?" No one did.

"Braddock doesn't have a chance. Baer is too big and too powerful. Braddock will be lucky to go three rounds, let alone 12."

The man next to me said, "Braddock does have a chance, and a good chance." He had seen him fight in St. Louis a couple of years ago and thought he was in excellent condition, almost as big as Baer, and faster. I had seen Max Baer win a 12-round decision over Paulino Uscudun in Las Vegas two years before. Baer won the fight by hitting the shorter and almost punchless Uscudun at will. Baer showed Las Vegas was getting to him. He was getting overweight around the middle. The last three rounds he clowned to hide his being tired. Sometimes you get a hunch, and one came to me. I said to the big Baer fan, "I'll bet on Braddock to win the fight."

"How much will you bet?"

"Five dollars. I have to have big odds." The crowd was getting interested.

"What odds do you want?"

"I know it would just be like throwing money away to bet against Baer, but I like long shots, so I'll bet $5 against $100 on Braddock." He did not like it, wanted 5-to-1, but I would not bite. Baer staggered Braddock early in the first round, but Braddock had come back strong at the end. At the end of the round the man said, "Do you still want to bet the five against a hundred?"

I said, "Put the money on the bar." The barkeeper put the $105 on the top of the cash register. Baer had a slight edge for the next few rounds. Braddock was gaining as the fight wore on. Baer was so weary it was all he could do to last out the last three rounds. A new champion was crowned on a unanimous decision. I tucked the bills into the bib of my overalls and buttoned it. It was 8 o'clock and time to go home because tomorrow would be a busy day.

When I stood up, a big, tall man walked toward me and said, "Hello, Virg." It was high school coach Frank Knight. We shook hands.

"Virg, there is a good poker game going at Mahoney's. We will make seven. You should do all right, as there are at least three pigeons in the game."

"Frank, counting me that makes four."

It was an easy game to beat, as some of the players were playing loosely and making wild bets on nothing. All that was needed was to be patient and wait until you had a good hand. Around 10 o'clock my stack of chips totaled $95 more than my $20 buy-in.

132

I said, "I wish I could stay, but I have to set my irrigation water."

Frank said, "You are going to set it at night?"

"Yes, Frank, I have a gasoline lantern."

As I rode my horse the 3 miles back to the ranch, my hand kept reaching up to check the bills in my pocket and see that it was buttoned.

WE MARRY

It took 10¢ on a car going up Market Street, transferring to Mission and I got off in front of my folks' front door. My mother opened the door and we had a hugging reunion, for it had been over a year since we had seen each other. When my father came home, it was another joyful reunion, for we had a close relationship. In fact, I always felt free to discuss anything with him when I was quite young.

That evening, Ethel answered the phone when I called. Her first words were, "Where are you?"

"I am at my folks' house in San Francisco."

"It's about time I heard from you. Do you know it's been a month since I heard from you? Mother was getting ready to call off the arrangements for the wedding if you didn't call up soon. I am so glad to hear from you and know you are safe." She agreed with my plans to get a car in San Francisco, drive to Aunt Laura's where I would visit one day, and drive over to her house early on the morning of the wedding.

When my father heard of the improvements on his land, he was very pleased. Pointing to the scar on my left eyebrow, I said, "Hickory Jones gave me that."

"What did you give him?"

"He was in the hospital for four days."

After hearing the details, he said, "You could have been killed!"

My father went with me to buy a car. Brother Farrell had told him the Chevrolet company was reliable and guaranteed their used cars. After inquiring as to what I preferred, he said, "We have a 1930 with low mileage that you might be interested in. It belonged to two school teachers who split up." He guaranteed that the 10,000 miles on the odometer was the true mileage. The car was immaculate. It ran like a watch as I drove to Aunt Laura's the next day.

My mother's sister and Uncle Harvey were glad to see me. A cousin Stanley that I had never seen before came over for a short visit. Aunt Laura helped me hang up my clothes and said they needed to be cleaned and pressed. Uncle Harvey took them to his dry cleaning shop the next day. They had 2 acres in the Watts area. It was filling up very fast. They said land prices were going up and they had been offered $500 for a 75-foot lot, but had turned it down.

Ethel insisted that I come over and stay the night before the 11 o'clock wedding, saying, "After all, I haven't seen you for six months and we should get acquainted. If you drove up in the morning and we went to the chapel and got married, we'd be standing before the minister wondering what was going on."

Our greeting embrace was a long one. Ethel said, "We have a lot to talk over. First, how much we can spend on the honeymoon and have enough left to get by until the first payday?"

Fortunately, there was a swing in the backyard where we could talk privately. If we took five days for the honeymoon somewhere down the coast, lodging would cost about $25. Meals would be about $30 with gas another $30. That would leave $100 after we got back to Idaho. I was surprised by the confident, sensible manner in which she was treating our forthcoming marriage. In the past she had been on the quiet side, especially around her mother. Sometimes I was a little annoyed by her mother answering a question that Ethel would have answered if she had been given the opportunity. The wedding rings we would pick up when the jeweler's shop opened at nine in the morning. We had allowed $50 for the rings. The reception and lunch would be at her folks' at one o'clock. If we could get away gracefully by three, we would have 3 hours to find a place to stay. We had our arms around each other, laughing and talking, when she suddenly stopped laughing and said, "We have made certain definite commitments to each other concerning this marriage. Do you remember the ones you made to me?" She added that in a course she had taken on family relationships the commitments made prior to the marriage were more apt to be kept than those made after the ceremony.

"I will provide a steady, comfortable income. I am not marrying you to wash my dirty clothes, cook, and do dishes, raise kids, and change diapers, because that is what our marriage isn't going to be. It is to be one of caring and sharing. I expect to help with household chores, sometimes more than others. We both want children, and I will also help wash and change diapers and help feed them. If walking the floor at night is called for, we will share equally or more so. It will be necessary that we do many things together."

We agreed that we should accept each as we are, and the past is past. We can only give and share the future. We are to be open and truthful at all times in our discussion of problems and finances. I promised not to be critical or harp on mistakes, figuring we did the best we could with what we had to work with. I wanted us to do as many things together as we could.

She said, "I believe you will keep those commitments. When we were in college at Forney Hall, Milly and Carla said you would make the best husband. If we both keep these things in mind, we can make the adjustments without friction."

Suddenly marriage became a more serious business than just wine and roses and riding off into the sunset on a white horse.

Sleeping arrangements were the same as usual—she on the davenport and I in her bed. I went to the bathroom, changed to pajamas and went to bed. Almost immediately she was snuggling up against me, saying, "Phooey on the davenport." I flipped the small elastic band around her waist and said, "Honey, is this what I think it is?"

"Yes. I have always been regular as a clock and I counted the days and I am one day off. I wanted us to have a safe week. Don't worry, it will all clear up and be gone by the wedding tomorrow."

We were up first and went to pick up the rings before breakfast. Her mother had a sumptuous breakfast which we were too nervous and excited to enjoy. Finally to the wedding chapel at 10:30. The bride was radiant and startlingly beautiful. The groom was serious and worried. She said to me, "It isn't the end of the world, darling. It is just the beginning."

I whispered into her ear, "I just can't tell you how beautiful you are."

The ceremony went smoothly with no fumbling or dropping of rings, and it was wonderful to realize this delightful person was my wife to share my life with. When it was over and people were shaking hands and congratulating us, I walked up to Dad Tobey, shook hands with him and said, "I'll take care of my bride as long as I live and see to her well being and happiness."

He had tears in his eyes when he said, "I'm sure you will." Little did I know that he would remind me of my promise in the future.

It seemed like hours and hours before the reception was over. Actually, it was over in 2 hours. After changing into casual clothes, we were on our way to find a suitable place to spend five days before we left for Idaho. We kept checking motels along the beach and the prices were outrageous or at least it seemed so to us. Any place that looked pleasant and comfortable was at least $7.50 a night. The same type of motel 2 miles from the beach would be no more than $2.50.

I said, "Let's stay here. I'm tired of asking about prices."

"We can't afford to pay that much. Let's try Newport. It is just starting to grow." There was no way that she would let me drive in the city. She said I was great on the hills and mountains but a dropout in traffic. We stopped at a motel in Newport. It had been open for business only a few days. I got out of the car and walked into the office. A man with the nicest smile and a warm, pleasant voice greeted me. "How can I help you?"

My nervousness must have been very obvious when I told him, "We would like to stay five days. How much will it cost?"

"You are just married?"

"Yes."

He laughed and said, "We have a special rate for newlyweds. I'll talk to my wife about it." In a few minutes he came back smiling and

136

said, "How about $12.50?"

"A night?"

"Oh, no. For five days." His wife came back with him and she was very friendly, solicitous about our comfort. They were from Iowa. In 1929, he had sold his large Iowa farm for a good price. They were in their early fifties and soon found out it was too early to retire. They had fallen in love with Southern California. In looking for land, they were able to buy the plot big enough for 10 cabins on good-sized lots for a fraction of what they would have cost before the crash. They appeared to be lonesome for company, as he asked, "Do you want to play pinochle?"

His wife said, "They don't want to play cards tonight." They laughed and so did we.

Two days of eating, sleeping, swimming, or just lying in the sun was heavenly after the grind I had been put through during the summer. My weight was down to 155 from my normal 180 pounds. It must be that people in love are lucky because Ethel wanted to play Bingo. Tickets were a quarter, and on the first ticket she bingoed in a hurry. California prohibited cash prizes—what she won was 10 cartons of Camels. We didn't smoke. Then the caller of the bingo game pointed to a stand across the pier and said, "He will give you $1.50 a carton for them." The stand gave us $15 and did we feel good!

We danced one night at a place where you bought tickets for 10¢ a dance. The second day we decided to fish for anything that would bite from the pier. Pole, line, and bait cost $1.50. Other people were fishing with little luck, as they were catching mostly sand perch. While we were getting started to fish, a gabby woman said she had seen a big halibut caught right off from where we were fishing. When asked, "When was that?" she said, "Last spring."

I told Ethel, "When it comes to fishing it is always some other day, time or place the fish are biting."

Small minnows like anchovies were used for bait. Like a greenhorn, I put three or four on a rather large hook. A bystander said, "You'll never catch anything on that bait. It is too big." Paying no attention, I cast it out about 50 yards from the pier. Just to be safe and not lose the $5 deposit on the pole, I tied it with a string to hold it propped up against the rail. Ethel went to buy our lunch. She came back with three cheeseburgers and a couple of Cokes. Her first remark was, "They surely know how to charge. Thirty cents for cheeseburgers and 10¢ for a coke." The extra cheeseburger was for me, as she said I looked like a scarecrow in my suit.

We were leaning back relaxing sleepily when the reel clicked. I listened—it clicked again. Then the pole began bobbing up and down. Something was chewing on the bait. I said, "It isn't hooked because the line isn't moving." I checked the drag to see if it was loose enough, and started to reel slowly. The uneven pressure on the line indicated that it was a halibut because they swim in a flap-like motion. Someone yelled, "He has a big fish on!"

The crowd gathered and a dock attendant kept moving them back to give me room. The fish, somewhere between 30 or 40 pounds, was 40 feet below the pier and could not be pulled up by the relatively light line. Another fisherman came over with a three-prong grappling hook on a heavy line which he let down into the fish's large, gaping mouth and we lifted him up by hand over hand. It was the biggest halibut caught from the pier for some time. A reporter took pictures of us holding it between us. The Tobeys saw it in the newspaper the next day and saved the clipping for us. The paper said it weighed about 50 pounds. What to do with it? Ethel said her folks would like some and it would help if we had a refrigerator. Carrying the fish to the cabin in a burlap sack, we stopped to weigh it at a grocery store. The 30 to 40 pound fish now weighed 23 pounds. Proudly we displayed the fish to our host and asked what shall we do with it.

His wife said, "That is easy. The four of us will have part of it for dinner tonight and we will play pinochle."

Ethel said, "You can have it all except enough for four people for us to take to my parents."

"No problem. I'll freeze a package for you." Ray and Martha Wheaton had us for dinner and cards on the evening of our last day. For many years after, we would visit them when we went to California.

We took the frozen fish back to Ethel's parents. They gave us a table, two chairs, kitchen utensils, and a mattress from storage. We tied all this on top of the car with ropes running through the windows that had to be untied in order for us to get out of the car, and took off for Idaho. When we reached Gooding, we added the dog and Marshall Smith's mother gave us a chicken.

Heyburn had two stores, a post office, and a garage. There were 120 students in the high school. Taxes from the railroad, elevators, and power substation made it a rich little school district that paid in cash, not warrants like the larger neighboring schools. Suitable housing was a problem. We had trouble finding a decent place to live. Ethel was very cooperative and said, "This place is only temporary. Would you move the pump for water into the house and put in a sink?" It was a cold seat that winter on the outside two-holer. Ethel had never cooked on a coal or wood stove, and the Smith's chicken was a rubbery disaster. Later we bought a pump-up gas stove at Sears and a refrigerator on time. For a few years that followed we were in debt to our credit limit. We mutually agreed that it was better than camping.

We enjoyed each other's company very much as we swam, danced, played tennis, and worked together in improving our living conditions. The house had been redone inside—new paint, curtains, and shades at our expense. By the end of November, a modern house was for rent at $17.50 a month and we moved.

LEO HANDY

Dorothy and Leo Handy lived next door and became our very close friends. I fished and hunted with Leo for over 40 years. He was a big man in all ways, probably the most honest and responsible person I have been privileged to know. These characteristics allowed him to grow from operator of one milk truck to owner of a fleet of 30 trucks—the Handy Truck Line.

There was nothing spectacular about Leo, but he was always there and you could count on him to do the right thing. I enjoyed and treasured his company.

Dorothy and Ethel were very close. After the Handy's son, Donald, was born, Dorothy started to have heart attacks. Usually they were of short duration. Leo smoked cigarettes at home, but didn't smoke cigars in the house because Dorothy hated them.

Dorothy went to Los Angeles to visit her mother. A few days later Leo came to our house and said her mother had called to say that Dorothy was in the hospital with a bad heart attack, and the doctor did not think she would live very long. We had a new Chevrolet coupe, just broken in. Ethel wanted to visit her mother, who also lived in Los Angeles. We decided that Leo should take the Chevrolet and by 10 o'clock that morning Ethel, Dallas, and Leo were on their way. Eight days later they returned with a healthy, smiling Dorothy, much to my surprise and delight.

Dorothy had picked a bouquet of flowers that had been sprayed with Blackleaf 40 (nicotine sulphate) and had not washed her hands until several hours later when she started to prepare dinner. In the night she developed severe pain. Fortunately, a young intern from Stanford ran allergy tests and found that she was extremely sensitive to nicotine. She could relate her previous heart attacks to cigar smoke. Leo stopped smoking at home and 40 years later Dorothy had never suffered another heart attack.

Leo and I changed from bait fishermen to fly-fishing specialists over the years. We fished most of the major fly-fishing streams in Montana, Idaho, and Wyoming. We were fishing the North Fork of the Snake River below Mack's Inn, close to Yellowstone Park. It was August and the deer flies were thick. The slow-moving stream was lined with a scattering of pines and a few aspen. A moose snorted, pawed, and splashed water on the other side of the river. We moved back into the timber, walked about a quarter of a mile and started

140

fishing again.

"Leo, what was bothering that moose?"

"His horns are in the velvet and are very tender, as the blood vessels are close to the surface. The deer flies are driving him crazy. He is just mad at the world and we were the handiest to take out his anger on."

The stream was narrower and deeper. We started fishing close to the bank. In a short time the moose was snorting and threatening to come after us. Leo picked up a rock about the size of a tennis ball and threw it, hitting him squarely on the right antler. It must have been painful, as the moose went to his knees and with angry noises started to swim across toward us. We shucked off our waders in a hurry and climbed up two big pines that had almost parallel branches. It was a good thing that we climbed high enough, because the moose not only butted the tree trunks but reared up as high as he could. After 20 minutes or so, he wandered off through the brush, shaking his head in the willows to get rid of the flies.

One of the prices that one has to pay for being big is that some smaller man gets drunk and the resentment of being small comes out, and his drink has given him courage to pick a fight with a larger man. Leo and I were fishing Big Lost River, lost because it disappeared into the big lava flow that was part of the Craters of the Moon area which erupted 1,000 to 1,400 years ago. Mackay was a typical gone-to-seed Western mining town. We were at the bar enjoying a drink, when a medium-sized man sat down by Leo. It was apparent that he had a snoot full. Leo tried to joke with him, but he took offense and challenged Leo to a fight.

"Friend, you don't want to fight him, you want to fight me."

"Virg, he had better fight me. Remember how you broke three ribs on the fellow you fought in Hailey."

"Leo, you shouldn't fight him. You broke the fellow's jaw in Ketchum." We kept naming the places and victims and the injuries we had inflicted on them. The man got up to leave. Leo put his hand on his shoulder.

"Don't be impatient. Virg and I are going to the can and when we come back one of us will fight you and we promise we will take you to the hospital." We went to the sandbox and when we returned, the bartender was laughing. He poured us a drink on the house because the drunkard had quietly slipped out the door.

1934

Ethel was elected president of the L.D.S. Cultural and Literary Society which met once a week. I accepted a Sunday job of teaching a Mutual class. For a while the community thought we were good Mormons.

When pheasant season opened, there was only the 12-gauge, too heavy for Ethel to shoot. She went with Diane and me on opening day. Pheasants were plentiful and we could start hunting within a quarter of a mile of our house. I cleaned the birds. After the delicious young pheasant dinner that evening, Ethel said she wanted a light shotgun. I recalled that she had been on the women's rifle team in college. The local hock shop had a single-shot 410 for $7.50. I brought it home with a box of shells. A few days later when I came home from school, Ethel was radiant and smiling smugly. She was full of surprises. Not only was she a super cook, she could sew. She was so cheerful, I knew that she had something going and was going to surprise me. The smells from the kitchen were very appetizing. She had taken Diane hunting and killed two pheasants which were being cooked for dinner. After that I always asked her if she wanted to go hunting with me.

The first Christmas of our marriage our car tires were worn so we decided not to go to Hollywood to visit her folks. Byron and Ione Lowry, two grade school teachers, were going to Los Angeles to visit friends. Byron came from a wealthy family and had a new Plymouth coupe. He also had an exalted opinion of himself. In fact, he was an obnoxious, spoiled brat at times. He was not conservative about his money, just plain tight and almost miserly. He knew Ethel was from Hollywood and asked if we wanted to go with them and pay for the gas and oil. With gas at 15¢ a gallon it would not cost over $30. When Ethel heard of the offer, she was enthusiastic about spending Christmas with her parents. Byron agreed that I would just give him $30 for the trip and each of us would pay our meals and lodging. Since the car was a coupe, someone had to sit on someone's lap. We thought the Lowrys would trade off driving and sitting on laps. Not so. Byron drove all the way to Las Vegas while Ethel sat on my lap. Every so often we stopped for gas, rest stops, and lunch. We stayed at a hotel with a casino. Our room was No. 11 and theirs was No. 14. After dinner the girls played a dollar in the slot machines, and Ethel won a $5 jackpot on the nickel machine. They left us playing blackjack to go to bed. An hour or so later I was a few dollars ahead and Byron lost the last of $5, and we went to bed.

The hallway was dimly lit. I found No. 11. Byron said, "I can find my room easy—just count three doors down and it is No. 14." What we country boys did not know was that hotels do not have room No. 13. It was late when he found this out. The next day he told me what happened. Not wanting to wake Ione, he undressed in the dark and crawled into bed naked. Her back was toward him and she was also nude. She mumbled something and he patted her. Her backside was enticing. When he entered, she rolled over and said furiously, "You're not my husband!"

He explained what happened while pulling on his pants and gathering up the rest of his clothes, and bolted out the door. We both had a good laugh.

Somewhere enroute, Ione bought a Los Angeles paper which said the fleet would be in over the holidays. Byron said he would like to see it, and wondered if it would be possible to go and get on one of the warships. Ethel said, "I'm sure you can. I've visited the fleet." We were arriving on a Sunday and they would pick us up on Wednesday morning to visit the fleet. Both of them tried to impress us with the high status and importance of the people they were visiting. It would not be possible for them to take us anywhere except to visit the fleet.

On Wednesday Ethel gave Byron the directions to the piers where small boats took passengers out to the battleships anchored in the harbor. We stopped close to a ticket booth. Byron got out and walked to the ticket booth. In a short time he returned, really riled. He said, "They want $3 each for the trip and we'll have to wait 2 hours." While he and Ione discussed pros and cons, Ethel was standing by the car, saying nothing. A naval officer was approaching.

Ethel walked up to him and said, "I want to see someone on the heavy cruiser Salt Lake City."

"Who do you want to see?"

"My uncle, Commander Rome Jondreau."

He blew a whistle and a sailor came trotting up. "Call the captain's gig. These people want to visit the Salt Lake City."

The sailor saluted and said, "Be ready to board in 15 minutes." We were the only passengers in the gig. The Lowrys were almost speechless when we were piped aboard. We had tiffin in the captain's cabin, as he was in command of the ship. Byron did ask some intelligent questions. One was about the vulnerability of warships to airplanes.

Commander Jondreau's answer was, "I cannot comment to civilians about defense. At present we are installing anti-aircraft guns and I would like to see plenty of them mounted on the decks."

Civilian workers from Dad Tobey's firm were covering the decks with linoleum-like floor covering. It was a very lucrative contract for the firm. To show the inefficiency and waste of government spending, these deck installations all had to be removed later because they were flammable.

On the morning we left Los Angeles, I told Byron I wanted to stop and call a friend, Dr. Stauffer, who was a famous brain surgeon from Salt Lake. He was also a very good artist and had pictures exhibited in many top art galleries in the west. We became acquainted when he exhibited pictures for years at the Heyburn art exhibit. At my invitation he came down from Salt Lake and hunted pheasants with me and Diane on two occasions. Once he brought Mrs. Stauffer with him and they had a pheasant dinner with us. Ethel was a super cook. They were going to retire and had bought a home in Santa Barbara and asked us to visit them, as they wanted to repay us for the wonderful pheasant dinners they had at our house.

Byron reluctantly stopped to let me make a phone call. Mrs. Stauffer answered the phone and seemed delighted to hear from us. She insisted that we stop and visit with them.

She said, "Dr. Stauffer wants to talk to you." He was very insistent that we have dinner with them and stay overnight, and said they had plenty of room for the other couple and they would be welcome.

The Stauffer house was really a mansion among similar imposing dwellings. I could not help but wonder how people got so wealthy. It was an indescribably beautiful area with blocks and blocks of houses that only the very wealthy could have. The carefully manicured lawns, shrubbery and plants were a riot of color.

The Stauffers greeted us warmly and after a drink Dr. Stauffer showed us his new paintings. They were even better than the ones he had done when he was practicing medicine.

Byron, the money conscious, asked, "Do you sell them?"

"Sometimes. I paint for my own pleasure. If I painted for money that would be work. I retired to keep from working."

His wife said, "He can sell all he wants to paint."

Dr. Stauffer offered to take us on a tour of the city, and we gladly accepted. The weather was a contrast to the 10 inches of snow we had left in Idaho. It was bright and balmy, with fresh, pure air and an occasional clean smell of the ocean. We were seeing another facet of living in the United States. It was hard to comprehend the magnitude of wealth and beauty of the town. When we arrived back at the house, Dr. Stauffer looked at his watch and said, "We have time to see the last art class."

Mrs. Stauffer said, "You girls don't want to see this. It's for dirty old men only." They got out of the car and we drove to an imposing building that said "Art Gallery." We each paid a dollar to sit in the drawing class. Posing on an upraised platform was a beautiful, young nude model. Thirty or more elderly men with easels were supposedly sketching. One was playing tick-tac-toe. The doctor explained that the models were movie starlets and they posed for one hour at a time to get eating money. Every week the proprietor brought in a new set of models for the six daily art classes.

On the way back to Idaho the Lowrys had an entirely different attitude toward us. We took turns in changing seats. After we got home they told everybody what a wonderful time they had visiting the fleet and Santa Barbara. They invited us to go to dinner and dances with them, but Ethel made polite excuses. She said, "They are snobs and I will not forgive them for their attitude toward us on the way down and changing it when they thought it would enhance their social prestige."

In spite of the poor housing and living conditions, we enjoyed our first year in Heyburn. Before we were married we had decided not to have any children for at least two years for a get-acquainted period and to enjoy doing things together. In addition to attending school functions and dances, there were card and dinner parties. Ethel fly-fished with me on Wood River and Silver Creek. Her father had given her a complete fishing outfit, rod, reel, and waders. She would often take Diane and hunt by herself.

1935

Minidoka Forest was open to deer hunting for the first time in years. We put in for the drawing of 2,000 permits. Ethel drew and I didn't. We borrowed Leo Handy's rifle with a telescope, which she had tried out, hitting a gallon can at 100 yards. It was no wonder she had been on the rifle team in college.

We had slowly hunted a long ridge bordering the road, as we didn't want to carry a deer uphill. We had seen several deer, but they were all too far away. Every so often we could hear the boom of a gun in the distance. We took a break at around 11 o'clock. The air was warm and balmy on a typical clear, windless autumn day. We were hungry. We sat down with our backs against a log and ate our cold chicken and finished off our Coke bottles.

"I'm not used to all this walking. Why don't we take a nap?" We used our coats for pillows and curled up together. Some time later we awakened. We became affectionate with each other. I was insisting this was as good a place as any. She said, "Someone will see us."

"Phooey, do you see anyone?"

She reached over and picked up the rifle. Looking through the scope at a thicket about 200 yards away, she put the gun down and waved.

"Who are you waving at?"

"The two men that are watching us through field glasses. You take a look." Sure enough, they had been watching us. She rested the gun over my shoulder and said, "Sit still." She cocked the gun, drew a deep breath and the gun bucked. It was then I saw a young buck stagger and fall. We enjoyed the venison for most of the winter.

The next spring Ethel was going to stay with her folks for two months while I helped the renter get my parents' place planted. Having a car and staying at the Smiths' was a lot different from the year before. My old friend Proctor was the manager of the town baseball team and he asked me to play shortstop. Playing once a week and practicing two nights a week was fun.

About the middle of June we were playing Buhl. There were two outs, two men on base, and my turn to bat. The limping, tall, grey-haired man with the kindly eyes walked up to me as I was picking up my bat. It was William Kerr, Director of Vocational Agriculture.

"I want to speak to you, Virg."

"You will have to wait until I hit a double and drive two runs in to

146

win the game."

"Good luck."

Twice this pitcher had fooled me with a very slow curve ball. He got two strikes and two balls on me. His next pitch was a slow curve over the outside corner and I popped it over the second baseman for a double.

Mr. Kerr was laughing and he said, "Do you always come through in a pinch?"

"I try."

"What I want to talk to you about is that your agricultural work in the high school is so good we would like to put in a new department there."

"Mr. Kerr, that would be wonderful. When do I start?"

"July 1st, because you will need time to get reference books, bulletins, and other special equipment to meet government requirements for a classroom." From his briefcase he gave me a folder with all of the requirements and instructions.

This changed the whole picture. I was on my way again toward my goal of being a county agent and getting on the university staff. In addition, instead of $125 a month for nine months I would receive $135 for 12 months. One could raise a family and even buy a house on that salary. There was no way to tell Ethel the good news as she was on a bus on her way to Idaho.

It was nearly 6 o'clock when the bus pulled up to its stop at the Overland Hotel. To see my beautiful, wonderful wife after two month's absence was delightful.

"Honey, I'm tired and hungry."

"O.K. Let's eat in the dining room."

"I have to go to the bathroom."

"Why don't we stay here tonight. It only costs $2.50."

We registered and went up to the room. It was there I told her the wonderful turn of events. She was ecstatic and said, "We can start a family."

"Now?"

"No, it isn't two years yet." Needless to say, we had dinner somewhat later.

147

1936

It was early in February. The house was snug and warm. A blizzard with heavy, blinding, wind-swept snow was blocking all the roads. We were snuggled up together in bed and Ethel whispered, "This would be a good time to start a baby. It would be a Libra."

"The time is just great. But why a Libra?"

"They are balanced people, in harmony with the rest of the world."

Ethel and I were both Presbyterians. In Heyburn there was only one church, L.D.S., which we attended in order to become a part of the community. Ethel was elected to an office in the Relief Society. I coached the Mutual basketball team, which became runners-up in the state tournament. On this team were two high school drop-outs, Paul, 16, and Dean Browers, 18, both excellent ball players. I tried every means of persuasion to get them to go back to high school, to no avail.

I read in *The Burley Herald* that they and Ned Sorenson had been arrested for stealing three horses and selling them at the sale yard in Twin Falls. They were to appear for sentencing the next Friday afternoon. I had an idea. J. M. Whiting, the school superintendent, went along with it. I contacted the judge and discussed the plan. He sentenced the boys to one year in the reform school. He would put them on probation providing they returned to high school. If their grades were failing, or they were absent without just cause, they would go to St. Anthony Reform School to serve the sentence. They were also to practice basketball with the high school team. Every week they had to report to the probation officer (me) who would report their progress to the court.

From the results it was a complete success. They starred on the high school team which won the sub-district championship, but lost the district tournament to Twin Falls which had 1,000 students compared to Heyburn's 120. All three became successful, responsible citizens.

It was difficult to teach in Heyburn because of the wide variation in ability of the students. Most of them you taught as best you could, accepted their performance as being the best they were capable of, and passed them. There were a few families with children of exceptional ability and they required special projects to keep them interested and busy. Also there were trouble-makers. Amos Jordan was undoubtedly the worst. He wanted to quit school but his father wouldn't let him. Amos had moved to Heyburn from Burley at the beginning of his sophomore year, resentfully leaving his many friends in Burley and a school building and classrooms which were much newer and nicer than Heyburn's.

In the classes of the men teachers he didn't dare misbehave too much, but in the women's classes he was incorrigible. He disrupted the class so much that they said they couldn't continue to have him in class. We knew that he was intelligent. Superintendent Whiting and I thought we could save him.

"If you take him in your biology class and I take him in my geometry class, he will be on schedule with his credits."

Amos was surly and uncooperative in class, but he did his school work. I made him responsible for roll-taking and checking class excuses. He did these jobs accurately and without prompting, but there was no change in his behavior.

I was walking to the store and met Amos at the corner.

"Hello, Amos. Diane and I are going bird hunting tomorrow. Would you like to go with us?"

"No, I won't."

"Amos, Diane is a very special dog. She finds the bird, sets and holds it until we flush it. She marks where it falls and brings it back to you. She just doesn't hunt with everybody and is very choosey as to whom she asks."

Amos didn't say anything and continued walking until he turned the corner. Then he turned around and said, "What time are you going hunting?"

"Two o'clock. Bring your gun and a game bag, as we'll get birds."

He knocked at my door a little before 2 o'clock. While we were walking out to the field, I told him about hunting ettiquette.

"Hunting, like everything else, has rules. First, you never run up to Diane when she is set on a bird. You walk slowly with your gun loaded and the barrel pointed up. We take turns on the shots. You get only one shot. If you miss, you can't shoot again. Your hunting partner gets the next shot. There are certain rules of safety to follow and we never break them. You probably know all of these, but we will go through them together." We came to a fence.

"Amos, hand me your gun." He did so.

"Amos, you go through the fence first." When Amos was through, he was told to lay down his gun, and I handed mine to him and climbed through the fence. I held the wire up for Diane to go under.

"Amos, many hunters are killed each year going through fences carrying a gun. If you are alone, do not leave your gun leaning on a wire or a post. It can fall and go off." Amos followed the safety precautions perfectly.

"You take the first shot. Remember, you only get one shot. If the bird falls, do not run. Reload, put your gun on safety. Diane will bring the bird back to you."

Diane went on point about 50 yards ahead. Amos started to run, but stopped when I reminded him. The rooster flushed in a startling, explosive flurry, feathers flew and he crumpled in midair. Upon command, Diane retrieved the bird in a burst of speed. I told Amos to pat her and tell her what a good dog she was. Birds were plentiful and the hunt was successful. Amos became quite talkative and acted as if he were having a great time. I treated him as an equal partner, and did not mention his negative behavior.

We hunted together most of the fall. In the later hunts we talked about his problems and plans for the future. He began to ask about education and possible occupations. Fortunately I had taken graduate work in vocational guidance at Berkeley. He revealed a desire to go to West Point.

"Amos, it will be a long, hard road to get there. You will have to make straight A's from now on. Grades aren't everything. Officers have to have leadership qualities, which means that you will have to take part in school affairs and be elected to student office, preferably Student Body President. If you want to enough, you can make it."

"But don't you have to be appointed by a senator?"

"Yes. Senator Henry Dworshak is a personal friend of mine. I have been writing editorials for *The Burley Herald* for five years. I am sure that he would appoint you on my request. You will have to make a plan or program to follow the next three years. I would suggest that you write this program on paper. I will be glad to go over it with you if you feel that you need help."

Amos came up with a program that needed very little change and posted it in his bedroom. There was a marked change as he blossomed into a pleasant, cooperative, and friendly student. When he graduated, he had held every honor that was possible. After graduation, he spent a year at the University of Idaho, four years at West Point, was a Rhodes scholar, and retired as Colonel Amos Jordan, Advisor to the President.

In order to visit the students' projects and take them on field trips, it was necessary to have more room than the Chevrolet coupe. We traded it in on a new Chevrolet two-door sedan. They allowed us $250 on the coupe, leaving $457 to be paid in installments of $25 a month. We kept it waxed and dusted, as we were so proud to have a brand new car.

About the middle of March Ethel said she was sure she was pregnant. A visit to the doctor confirmed it. We enrolled in a class for young parents held in the evenings at Burley. I put diapers on dolls, learned about burping, diets, and child care. Shortly after she felt the first sign of life, she started to croon and talk to the baby. That baby was talked to for six months. A psychologist who had been one of her teachers in college had a theory that a child knew whether it was

150

wanted before birth. Children who were love babies were much more secure all the rest of their lives and their chance of success was over 40 percent greater than an unwanted child, whose chance of getting into trouble was much greater. His study of people in corrective institutions substantiated this theory.

The baby started kicking in the first few months and never stopped, sometimes waking Ethel at night. Late in the pregnancy we were listening to music on the radio, and she said, "He is kicking in time, so he is going to be musical like my father."

She was healthy as a tick all through the pregnancy and went fly-fishing with me until August, when the doctor told her to stop.

She started having pains about 8 o'clock one evening, and the doctor said to bring her to the hospital at 10. When he examined her, he said it would be several hours and left instructions for the nurse to call him when any change occurred. It was then that I learned that there were two firsts—Ethel's first child and the doctor's first delivery since graduating from medical school.

I sat holding her hand. You can't help being anxious when the life of your loved one is in danger.

Dallas Guy Cross came into the world at 5:00 a.m. on October 28, 1936. He missed the Libra target date and was a Scorpio. According to Ethel, Scorpios were sometimes difficult to get along with. It turned out she was so right.

I went to morning classes. The 5-mile drive to Rupert at noon to take her a bouquet of roses took only minutes. She was sitting up nursing the 22 1/2-inch, 8-pound boy. She said, "He is a greedy little pig, but I am a good Holstein. Now I know why cows want to be milked!" Before they left the hospital, Ethel had the nurse supervise me in changing diapers and bathing Dallas.

Watching babies develop day by day is very interesting. You catch yourself tiptoeing to look into the crib to see that the baby is still breathing. We were lucky, as he was unbelievably healthy and in three months slept from seven to seven.

151

SHELLEY

When Dallas was two months old, we moved to Shelley for a better life. An opening occurred in the Vocational Agriculture Department there and Mr. Kerr offered it to me. I was delighted to accept.

Dallas's favorite act, around nine months old, was to put the pablum bowl on his head before it was empty. I was looking after him while Ethel took a break and went to a movie. He put the bowl over his head and laughed. I kept the bowl on and smeared the pablum over his face. Then I got a mirror and made him look. He howled, but that ended the pablum stunt.

After Dallas learned to walk, Ethel had to have a harness and leash to keep him under control when she traveled. Diane became his guardian dog. When we went fishing, she would stay between him and the water. We took a picture of her holding him by the seat of the pants at the curb, with an approaching car in the background. He liked to sneak out without Diane. All Ethel had to do was turn Diane loose and say, "Find the baby!" She would circle the house and in a short time would have him located, and she would sit by the door if he was in a house. One day Diane charged our door, barking frantically, and when Ethel came to the door, she took off running. Ethel followed. There was Dallas playing in the railroad tracks and the passenger train was due in minutes. Ethel broke a switch off a bush and switched Dallas all the way home. Then she told him about all the trouble he had caused. That night when she bathed him she cried about the red switch marks. It did cure the running away. After that he always asked if he could go somewhere.

Dallas had seen me wring a chicken's neck. He opened the gate on the neighbor's chicken pen and sent Diane in to fetch. Diane brought back a half-grown pullet. He tried to wring its neck and ended up braining it with a short cane he carried. He was in the third act when the neighbor caught him. A laying hen was only a dollar, but these were special—I paid $2.50 each for them. We didn't spank, but put sanctions on him.

Leo Handy moved our furniture from Heyburn to a nice three-bedroom home in Shelley that had central heat. What pleased Ethel most was trading our gas cookstove to Idaho Power for an electric range. They gave us $50 for the gas stove and threw it in the river. When Ethel learned about that, she said, "What a waste!"

"Not to them," I replied. "They don't want it used."

We were lucky that our house was only a few blocks from the schoolhouse and in the nicer part of town. Stull Wright, the owner, had been transferred to a bank in another town and didn't want to sell the house for sentimental reasons.

Shelley was a small, well-to-do town located between Idaho Falls and Blackfoot. It was a rich farming community settled mostly by people of German and Scandanavian descent. The railroad, sugar beet factories, and potato warehouses made it one of the richest school districts in the state. The school house was new. What pleased me the most was the intelligence level of the students. Heyburn was an old L.D.S. community and everybody was related to everybody else. Very few of the students had IQs of over 110. There were a considerable number of students with misplaced features and extra toes. Shelley's school board members were all Protestant or Catholic.

The elite had a dinner and bridge club that met every two weeks. Ethel wanted to join, as she was an excellent bridge player. In fact, she and her mother won the Invitational Biltmore Bridge Tournament in Los Angeles. Dr. Dyer, a dentist, and his wife were members of the club. Neil Sage, a prominent potato dealer, was also a member. I learned that they liked to hunt, but both had had their bird dogs poisoned. I invited them to hunt with Diane and me. In 2 hours we had our limit of four birds each. Doc Dyer and Neil were amazed at how good Diane was. On the way back they kept talking about how she returned when they each knocked down a bird as a flock flew up. She had each bird marked perfectly.

"I'm going to hunt tomorrow. Would you like to join me?"

"I thought you'd never ask!" This was the start of a close, friendly relationship with the two school board members.

When I let Dick Dyer off at his house, Mrs. Dyer was in the yard and she came over to the car to see the birds. Dick said, "Come into the house for a drink."

"Thank you, but Ethel and I always have a drink only when we are together."

"Go get her and bring her over."

The two Ethels really hit it off well together. They were both bridge enthusiasts and had a lot to discuss with each other. Ethel Dyer invited us to the bridge dinner party coming up that Friday, as one of the couples was on vacation. Ethel must have made a good impression because when a vacancy occurred a month later, we were invited in.

Our turn to entertain the bridge club was two months away. Ethel sent to her mother for Chinese things such as napkins, back scratchers, fortune cookies, some Chinese food items, and Chinese prizes. The Chinese food she cooked was superb and everyone commented how good and unusual the party was.

Dallas was still nursing and was fussing while his mother was

153

trying to get the dinner served. Madge Sage handed Ethel a Vodka Collins and told her to drink it and then nurse Dallas. He never woke up until 7 o'clock the next morning.

Shelley High School Vocational Agriculture Department was an ideal place to make an outstanding showing with achievements. It was like a coach having excellent material, good facilities, and ample finances. I realized that if I could make it an outstanding, if not the most outstanding Future Farmers Chapter in the state, it would almost assure me a good chance of being picked by the university for extension service. Active participation and cooperation by the students was the only way this could be accomplished. Giving a student responsibility, praising, encouraging him, and seeing that he got recognition really brought results.

Within a year the chapter had a loan fund set up so students could apply for a loan to purchase either an animal or feed or supplies to be paid back in a nine-month period. The loan committee was composed of one member from each of the four grades, with the vocational instructor as advisor. The loan fund was raised by the chapter's participation in fair booths, raffles, school carnivals, prizes at the Annual Idaho Spud Show at Shelley, and bounties from Fish and Game Association for magpie heads to help game bird population. The judging teams won state and regional contests. Activities such as the Ag Ball, when the gymnasium was decorated with bails of straw for seating, pumpkins, and corn shocks, with overalls and gingham for the dress code, were so popular that sale of tickets had to be limited to 200 because of the size of the gym. Home Economics girls served doughnuts and cider.

The annual Father and Son Banquet was really a fun enterprise from start to finish. First we had to get enough pheasants for 120 people. This was accomplished by having 10 hunters keep in line and walk slowly to cover the field. Some of the boys just blasted holes in the sky. Others were good shots so we spaced them apart. Out of the 40 birds shot the first Saturday, I would guess I killed 20. The school board was always invited to these banquets. I saw to it that there was a speaker from the university. The first year it was William Kerr, Director of Vocational Agriculture. The next year it was Warren Barker, county agent leader, and the third year it was Dean Iddings of the College of Agriculture.

There was a deliberate plan in my selection. The year before, Dean Iddings had been scheduled to speak at the Shelley Spud Show. Due to poor connections he had to arrive in Shelley the day before the meeting. I had to meet him in Pocatello. Ethel told me to invite him to dinner and she would fix something special.

I had not seen the Dean for several years. He had aged and was nearing retirement. When I introduced the Dean to Ethel, she remarked,

"I'll bet you are tired."

"Ethel, I have been on a speaking circuit for two weeks and I am tired."

"Would you like a drink of scotch? And since it is 2 hours until dinner time, take a nap in the back bedroom, and we will call you." (I had heard the Dean liked scotch, so I had purchased a bottle of White Horse.)

When Ethel called him to an excellent dinner, he was somewhat rested and his usual effervescent self. He really complimented Ethel on the dinner and gave her a hug when he left to go to his hotel. It was really gratifying to hear him say that very good reports on my work had been coming in to him.

There was only one church in Heyburn, L.D.S., and being Protestant, Dallas had not been baptized. When the Halls decided to have little Bill baptized in the Methodist Church in Shelley, we arranged for Dallas to be baptized on the same Sunday. Dallas was four years old and could really raise hell on occasion. To ensure his being quiet and behaving during the ceremony, I promised to take him fishing where he could catch perch in a barrow pit. He was a very good boy during the baptism and I was very proud of him. I looked at Ethel and she was beaming and looking so pleased. I took Dallas' hand and we were walking back down the aisle to our seats when he said, "Virg, let's go fishing now." The congregation laughed, and the minister joined in. Dallas' parents were red-faced.

The three years at Shelley were very pleasant. There were many activities that we could share together. Three other faculty couples, the Hawks, Halls, and Haddocks, each had one child. The four couples got together at least once a month. It was really something to be secure with a good salary and pleasant surroundings during the Depression. In fact, we scarcely knew a Depression was going on. Ethel's parents visited us in the summer and we spent Christmas with them in California.

My relationship with a very knowledgable, understanding superintendent, Hiram Grady Garard, was close and cooperative. It was during the annual district teachers' conference in Idaho Falls that was held just before school started that I became really acquainted with him. On the second day I had put my waders and fly rod in the trunk of the car. The 2:30 p.m. recess on that Saturday afternoon saw me stay in the rest room until the meeting convened. Then I stepped out a side door and drove to Snake River in the vicinity of Ririe which was famous for its super fly-fishing. It was nearly 4 o'clock, just about time for a big bug hatch at the 5,000-foot elevation. Some days it is just wonderful to be alive. This was one of those lazy, hazy days of early September. The beautiful, clear, rippling stream framed by steep canyon walls decorated with early fall colors of red, yellow, green, and

155

orange made me stop to enjoy the beauty. I wished that Ethel could be fishing with me, and promised myself to bring her there next Sunday.

To my surprise, there was a lone fisherman about a quarter of a mile below me. I started casting, seeking out the likely spots in the current. There was not an insect in the air or a ripple of a feeding fish in the water for nearly an hour. About 5 o'clock a few dimples of feeding fish occurred. There was a big splash by a rock about 50 feet away. After a couple of casts for distance, the fly hit the rock and bounced into the water. The big swirl of the striking fish and setting the hook was almost instantaneous. It was a big trout over 20 inches long. I let out a yell as the rainbow gyrated with its runs and high leaps out of the water. Finally, the fish tired and I was leading it toward the shallow bank when a voice said, "I'll net him for you."

Hiram Grady netted the fish. We shook hands.

"Why didn't you tell me you were going fishing? I would have gone with you. The afternoon meetings are just a hash-over anyway."

It was by accident or merely by chance that I had my first contact with the F.B.I. This resulted in numerous incidents during the war and shortly thereafter.

The Future Farmers of America was an organization of each chapter of vocational agriculture. State and regional contests were held in agronomy. One of the contests was to be able to identify 50 plants and their seeds from a list of 200 plants which included cultivated crops and weeds. The grading and identification of different grains was also part of the contest. To be able to compete, a large number of specimens showing all stages of growth were necessary for students to learn.

Reed Lewis, Ag instructor at Firth, cooperated with me in gathering specimens. We were traveling down a dirt road on the edge of the Meacham project. I was driving.

"Virg, stop. What is that growing in that corn field? Corn fields are supposed to have nothing but corn. There is something other than corn in this one."

We stopped, got out of the car, crawled through the fence and started to walk across a narrow strip of grain that bordered the corn field. A short, squat Japanese man stepped out of the corn and pointed a double-barreled shotgun at us. He hissed in broken English, "Get out of here. No trespass!"

"We only wanted to get a sample of that plant." This remark only agitated the man with the thick glasses. He cocked his hammers, and we left hurridly.

"Why didn't he want us to look at that plant?"

"That is easy to guess. He is growing marijuana. I am pissed off and I am going to call the F.B.I. in Pocatello."

When I called, a voice said, "Bannister speaking." I told him what had happened and said I thought the plants were marijuana.

"Will you meet me at Firth High School at 9 o'clock in the morning and show me where the field is?"

The handshake of the tall, athletic man was firm and his greeting friendly. He was traveling in a car with U.S. license plates on it, and suggested that we drive my car to the field. When we stopped in the road bordering the field, he took out his field glasses. They were partially hidden as he rested them on my shoulder to prevent blurring. It could have been only a few seconds when he put his glasses down.

"Let's get out of here before someone gets suspicious. It is marijuana."

A few days later the newspaper reported a huge marijuana bust. There was nearly a half-acre growing in the corn field.

Reed and I did get our specimens of marijuana. Part of my duties was to visit and surpervise the farm projects of the students. While visiting a project, I noticed tall, strange plants growing among the willows on a canal bank adjacent to the beet field. There were large numbers of the plants scattered along in open spots among the willows, with no weeds growing closer than 6 inches around the roots.

Investigation revealed that Mexican field workers were thinning the beets and they planted marijuana seeds in the fertile, moist canal bank in spots cleared of plant growth. They came back twice to hoe out the weeds in the beet field. During those times they tended the marijuana plants. In the fall they topped the beets and harvested their drug crop at night. Eventually county officials checked canals and ditches. To my knowledge there was never a Mexican arrested for growing it.

The specimens that I collected didn't do much good, as they kept getting smaller and smaller when they were handled by the students, and finally disappeared altogether.

Ethel and I tried smoking it after dinner one night. It really made the world a carefree, wonderful place. It scared both of us, as it could easily become a habit and we never tried it again.

DRIGGS

On November 15, 1939, the phone rang at the Cross residence. Ethel answered, and the operator said. "I have a long distance call for Virgil Cross." Ethel handed the phone to me.

The voice at the other end of the line said, "This is Warren Barber, county agent leader. Would you like to go to Teton County as county agent?" Wow! I finally made it!

"I surely would." County agent job openings were very scarce during the Depression, only one or two occurred in a year. The salary of $2,400 a year and car expense would put us almost in the luxury class.

"I have cleared it with William Kerr, Director of Vocational Agriculture, and you can start work on December 1. I will stop in Shelley next Sunday night and drive you up to Driggs on Monday morning to meet the county commissioners."

We started out at 8 o'clock in the morning. Due to the heavy snowfall the first part of the way, it was slow going. Then the snowfall stopped, the sun was shining brightly, making the snow sparkle as far as you could see. Barber stopped the car.

"This is your county, Virgil. The people here are your people. Teton County is a poor county. These people can be helped to improve their living conditions. You are the leader. You must use the best people to plan your programs. Remember, you are not paid for guessing; never be afraid to say 'I don't know' or 'I am not sure, but I will find out.' You have the specialists and the research departments only a phone call away. As long as you are in the University Extension you will be trained, and you must never stop learning."

We were on a hill looking down into a flat basin with the winding Teton River meandering through it. It was horseshoe-shaped with mountains and hills bordering the sides and the toe. The heel opened up to flat and rolling green fields. The early trappers called it "Pierre's Hole." They met there annually for several years to sell their furs and buy supplies. These meetings were boisterous, and in many instances, violent. It was an unfriendly place. When Indian tribes met there, they usually fought. On the east it was bordered by the Grand Teton Mountains. The highest Grand Teton was called "Big Nipple" by the French. The second highest was named Mount Wister for a man who spent considerable time writing in the Tetons. The Teton River flowed with gently rounding bends through willows and poplar trees. It was a sparkling clear stream that joined the Snake River to the north.

Barber said, "See those dimples? They are made by trout feeding. Now let's go meet the county commissioners."

The meeting went smoothly. Chairman Jim Kunz, who was a patriarch of the L.D.S. Church, said, "We would like you to meet with us every month and go over your progress."

"I am going to need the help and guidance of the county commissioners, and when you meet, call me when you are able to see me."

After leaving the meeting Barber told me I had made a good impression. We met with several of the leaders of the community. Claude Dalley and Jim Breckenridge impressed me as leaders and if properly approached would be a great help in developing programs to improve the living conditions in the valley.

The first winter in Teton County was a long, hard one. Snow covered the pastures a month early. The low point in the valley was over 6,000 feet above sea level. On the 15th of March snow was almost 4 feet on the level. The condition of the roads made it almost impossible to get into and out of the valley on trucks. Snow slides had blocked the railroad. Many of the ranchers were running out of feed. The farmers that had hay were selling it for $40 and $50 a ton. In the fall hay had sold for $15 a ton. I had been busy trying to locate the people who had surplus feed for the growers that were out. I had just called a farmer named Little, who said he had 40 tons of hay for $50 a ton.

"That is going to hurt people."

He said, "They can take it or leave it."

Jim Breckenridge was sitting in my office and heard the call.

"Virg, we have not been able to use all our hay for years and have not had enough cattle to feed it to. We talked about selling some every year but never got around to it. We will sell it at $20 a ton. They can also have a load of straw. They can have only one load at a time. If we find out they have feed on hand, we will haul ours home and theirs, too."

I thanked Jim and commended him and his brother for their humanitarian attitude. Another fellow who was also in my office said, "People had better believe the part about hauling the hay home." The Breckenridge offer ended the high prices and the scarcity of feed.

The Breckenridge brothers, Pret (called "Tiny"), Jim, and Bill, were big, strong men, handsome in a rugged way. Their grandfather had settled in Teton Basin. Their parents had died young. Bill was married and had a family. Jim and Tiny were bachelors and lived together. They were the most respected and influential family in the county. This was unusual, as they were gentiles in a county that was almost entirely L.D.S.

159

Claude Dalley told me that a Breckenridge word was his bond and he also expected you to keep your word.

During the winter the members of the Cattlemen's Association met to discuss how to improve their situation. They asked me what I could do to help them control heel flies. I did not know, but promised to find out. I consulted the new extension entomologist who informed me that heel flies could be completely controlled by spraying the cattle with rotenone, and promised to have a meeting with the cattlemen the following Friday. Heel flies drive cattle crazy with their buzzing as they try to lay eggs on their heels and legs. The cattle lick them off and the eggs hatch into grubs in the stomach, which work their way through the flesh of the back. They form a big, thumb-sized warble. It takes them nearly a month to eat a hole in the skin and drop out. Infected cattle would stay in shade and not eat enough, causing them to lose weight in addition to damage to flesh and hide.

The meeting was a success. The cattlemen bought a spray outfit, trailer, a 250-gallon tank, high-pressure pump, and gas engine. I was to supervise the spraying with the help of men to run the outfit. There were four cattle ranches that almost joined each other and the Breckenridge ranch had the best corrals for holding and small chutes for spraying.

Tiny Breckenridge called me one evening and asked, "Virg, have you read *The Children of God* by Vardis Fisher?"

"Tiny, it just happens that I am reading it now."

"Read again the part where the apostle said that Porter Rockwell had been badly injured in an altercation with a renegade blacksmith. After much discussion Brigham Young decided to let the blacksmith leave in peace. Rockwell was a gunman and Brigham's enforcer. Rockwell lingered on for almost a year before dying, according to the diary of the apostle. You will be here three days for the cattle spraying and I'll let you read a diary during the noon hour. You can take notes."

I told Ethel about the phone call and she said, "I'll bet the renegade blacksmith was a relative of the Breckenridges." She was right—he was their grandfather.

During the lunch hour Tiny handed me the diary, saying, "We guard this with our lives." The diary was a large, thick, cloth-bound ledger. The pages were yellow. The words were printed, the E's like 3s. The entries were irregular and very brief. The first page heading read, "This is the diary of John Breckenridge, age 21." The weight was in stones, transposed to 250 pounds, and his height over 6 feet. He had started the diary when he was converted to Mormonism. The diary was a priceless account of the conversion of an English blacksmith and wagon builder who joined the church and arrived just in time to join the wagon train as it left Missouri to trek across the plains. I had only 15 minutes each day to read it, and I asked Tiny if I might come over some Sunday and study it more thoroughl\ invited me to come the following Sunday and bring my wife to dir..ier. "The ladies can talk while you read."

The diary began by telling how the Mormon missionary persuaded him to join the church and leave England. He felt because of the English caste society there was no chance of being anything other than a blacksmith. Here was a possibility of an idyllic society and a new way of life. An entry stated he was taking his tools and leaving the anvil and forge. A short entry about the voyage said, "It is a good thing I am not married. It was hard on the women."

The diary didn't say he had a complete shop on the wagon. However, there were constant entries on repairs of oxen yokes, spokes, tires, shoeing of oxen. It told of flies, dust, heat. It related to faith, devotion, and obedience to Brigham. It told of Indians following the wagon train. Brigham Young ordered toys and clothing from wagons that had been quarantined with measles to be left on the trail. Six or seven days later the Indians stopped following.

He had been in Salt Lake only a short time when the entries began to show some doubts about the religion. He was dissatisfied with polygamy. It appeared to him the higher the church officials, the more and better land and opportunities. He wanted to get married, but it seemed to him that by the time a girl was 16 she was already promised to an elder. His entry concerning the Mountain Meadow Massacre by the L.D.S. when all gentile men, women, and older children were killed, with the exception of small children who were too young to remember, read as follows:

"In church on Sunday a small boy pointed to a woman and said, 'She is wearing my mother's dress.' The boy was grabbed and taken outside. He was never seen again."

Another entry:

"The Indians and Brigham Young are very friendly. They permitted only one high church official, Thomas Rhodes, to supervise mining of gold in their territory. Rumors were a large quantity of gold was found. It was supposed to be used in church buildings. There was no public accounting and church leaders, especially the apostles, were getting very prosperous in their businesses."

The next entry was brief:

"I told Brigham Young that I have lost faith and I am going to leave.

"Brigham said, 'Brother Breckenridge, you cannot leave. You are needed here and you know too much.'

"I said that I was going to leave anyway, and I turned my back and walked away."

His next entry was the one Tiny Breckenridge had referred to where the apostle told of the renegade blacksmith leaving. It was the longest of all entries:

"I was in the blacksmith shop carrying tools to load my wagon as I was getting ready to leave. Rockwell, Brigham Young's enforcer, shot me in the back with a pistol, after sneaking up to a window. It was lucky I was wearing a buffalo hide apron to keep my clothes clean. The bullet hit where the straps crossed in the back through both layers of buffalo hide and didn't enter very deep in my flesh. My rath rose up and I decided to kill him. I ran him down and was somewhat cooled off so I threw him through the boards of the blacksmith shop door and left him lying there unconscious."

Tiny showed me two 41-caliber pistols and holsters. I said, "That is an unusual caliber."

Tiny replied, "They are English. He was marshall of Fort Dodge for a while before moving to Teton County. When we were kids, Grandpa told us that he might not have been as fast as some, but he could pack more lead."

Claude Dalley was my friend and hunting partner. We also raised seed potatoes together. Although Claude was not a large man, about 5 feet, 9 inches tall and 175 pounds, his strength and stamina were unbelievable. He was center on his high school basketball team in the days of jump ball. His team won the state championship. The valley was snowed in at the time of the tournament and the team had to make the 35-mile trip to the railroad in Ashton by dog sled.

Claude was a pleasant, kindly man who didn't know how to lie if he tried. We spent many happy hours together. He could dry-track an elk.

During my second year in the valley, Claude and I were sitting against a log on a hillside watching a herd of elk slowly feeding down the opposite side of the draw toward us. We hoped they would get in range.

"Claude, I have heard that someone is supposed to have found gold in the basin. Is there any truth to these stories?"

Claude whispered, "I know there is. My uncle found it."

I was so surprised that I blurted out, "What happened?"

"Shush. He couldn't find it again."

The railroad from Ashton was completed at the turn of the century. His uncle, who worked for the railroad in Ogden, used his railroad pass to visit his brother (Claude's father) in the basin. Claude's father lived with his two wives on the Wyoming side of the state line. His farm was across the road. Idaho did not permit polygamy. Wyoming was still a territory. It was late in October. The sun was bright, the air crisp, the hills were red from sumac patches, the leaves of maples and birches were yellow and red. During lunch the uncle said, "Let's go up the creek (Teton Creek ran by the house) and shoot some grouse."

Claude's father said, "Martha needs some things from town. You go ahead and we'll have grouse for supper." Uncle Ed took the double-barrel shotgun, called the hound dog to help flush the grouse, and walked up the creek on the right-hand side of the stream. He thought it was nearly a mile upstream that he flushed a covey of grouse. He shot two of them and the flock flew off to the right into a cover of very thick, tall lodge-pole pines, which were located on a large, almost flat plateau. A small cloud darkened the sun and it was difficult to determine in what direction he was going. He didn't pay much attention to where he was going, as he was following the flight of the birds. Every so often he was able to get another shot. The bag was heavy with birds. He was not sure of where he was, but knew that if he went downhill he would come out into open farm land. He started angling downhill, trying to go in a straight line by lining the trees ahead of him. A bird flushed and he shot it. It was hit but flew on a short distance and fell in a thick patch of berry bushes. In searching for the bird he stumbled over a pile of loose rock and rolled into a hole several feet deep and about 10 feet across. He sat there trying to get back the wind that was knocked out of him. Looking around, it was plainly evident that someone had been digging there. The hole had been man-made. He saw what appeared to be a vein of green quartz. He picked up a small piece. It was laced with small, yellow wire-like metal. He took out his knife blade and pressed a spot of the yellow. It was soft gold.

He tried to mark it by cutting slashes on trees and bushes as he went downhill. It began to snow and blow, and he could see only a few feet ahead. Luckily he came to the creek and followed it down to the house.

Next morning the snow was over a foot deep. He said he could walk right to it but he would have to wait until spring. The next spring he looked for it. To make a long story short, he looked for it for three different summers. He finally gave up after losing his job and impoverishing his family.

Amosy Clark had an agency that certified titles and made appraisals. He was medium-sized, thin, very energetic. He never had very many close friends and did very little associating. Someone remarked, "Amosy isn't close-mouthed. He just don't open it." He called on me to help classify soil on a land appraisal and we became good friends. The Clark house was three houses down the block from ours. Most of the county agent's work in the summer was farm visits. I noticed Amosy's car parked on the Idaho-Wyoming line on weekends over a period of nearly four years. When I inquired, "What is Amosy doing parked here on weekends?" the answer was, "He is looking for the lost gold."

The county agent was appointed chairman of civilian defense. The

163

main purpose was to organize and train a group of volunteers for duty such as fighting fires, locate Japanese fire balloons (two of which landed in the county), conduct scrap metal drives, and watch out for sabateurs in regard to power plants, bridges, etc.

About 10 o'clock on a late September evening, I heard a knock on the door. It was Amosy's wife who was worried because Amosy had not come home. She had tried to call the sheriff, but he was out of town. It took a little while to call five civilian defense members for a meeting. Plans were made for search operations. Equipped with flashlights and a gasoline lantern, the two carloads of searchers easily found his abandoned car parked in the usual place. They honked the horns in case he had lost his way. The flashlights picked out a distinct trail that his travels over the years had made. They followed it until it became indistinct. Three teams of two each were spread out within signaling distance—the signal, two shots close together. It did seem futile, stumbling in the dark, calling to each other, listening, following a compass. It was slow, rough going. The search had started after 12 o'clock. On the sweep-back after covering about a mile and a half, it had begun to get light. We decided to go home, get something to eat, and return with more help. As we came out of the timber, there was Amosy sitting slumped against the front wheel of his car. Within 15 minutes he was in the hospital. Dr. Olsen was there helping with a delivery. By noon Amosy was sitting up, alert and eating soup. Digitalis, oxygen, and heated blankets had done wonders toward his recovery. He had found the gold, had a heart attack, passed out within a quarter-mile of his car. He had heard the searchers pass by but was too weak to answer loud enough to be heard. He was finally able to stagger to the car, but didn't have enough strength left to open the door.

The next day he was sitting up, really bright and cheerful. He said, "I finally found it. Actually, I didn't find it—I fell into it. I have it marked so I can go right back to it." He had a piece of green quartz with yellow flecks showing all over it.

Amosy was coughing a little due to lying on the cold ground many hours. The next day he had pneumonia and two days later he died, never telling anyone where to find the gold.

Fred Durtchi had to be around 60 years old. His parents were Swiss immigrants who had settled in the valley as L.D.S. converts in the early 1880s. We were waiting for the train to come back from Victor so we could load the hogs. It was cold—below zero. We had a fire and kept warming backs and fronts alternately. Just to make conversation, I said, "Fred, you are an old-timer. What do you know about gold in the Tetons? Is it just another tall tale?"

"There is gold in the Tetons. I know for sure there is."

"How can you be so sure?"

164

Fred said, "A tall, spry, grey-haired man arrived in Driggs and asked if he could hire someone with a buggy to drive him around. I just happened to hear the conversation, so I volunteered to drive him around for a week. The $20 was a lot of money to a 19-year-old."

The elderly man told Fred that he must not tell anyone what they were doing. If they found what they were looking for, he would give Fred 10 percent of it and it might make him rich. Four days they drove up as far as they could along Teton Creek and then searched into the woods to the south. The old man could not locate his old camp site. In 50 years the stream had changed channels many times due to beaver dams and floods. Forest fires had burned off the area and the growth was different.

The fifth day Mr. Johnson bought a shovel and had him drive to Bitch Creek. There was a road and a crossing now instead of a trail. He asked Fred to look for four big trees that were close together, forming a square. The big trees had been cut down for lumber. The area had been burned off several times. They found only one big stump, and dug around it for two days. On the last day on the way back, he told Fred that the three of them, Fred, Jed, and he (Rafe Johnson), were looking for gold. They were on their way to Idaho where they heard gold was being found. They had spent the winter with some friendly Indians in Wyoming, being welcome for their ability to shoot game. One of their Indian friends said to them, "Much gold in Pierre's hole." They were excited and questioned him. He gave them a good description: "Over mountain [pointing south] one stream, two stream, three stream [pointing east] up to tree, beaver dams, go [Pointing south and east]." He held up 20 fingers, then imitated the shooting of an arrow. A distance roughly of a mile and a half. "Tall tree, showing it partly burned by lightning. Close by green rocks— gold." With his hands he showed the outcrop was only a little way above the ground. With a twig he drew a map of Teton Valley in the dirt.

The three heavily-bearded men were riding their excellent horses, with a heavily-laden pack horse. They went over the Teton pass. First there was Spring Creek, then Darby Creek, and the third, Teton Creek. They followed Spring Creek down the west slope. Near the bottom of the slope, hills and grassland with scattered trees replaced the forest. It was in this area that they saw smoke rising across the valley to the west. They made their way carefully to remain unseen. They left Spring Creek, crossed Darby Creek, and late in the afternoon found Teton Creek. The beaver dams were only a mile upstream. Here they made camp and a pole corral for the horses that were to graze hobbled during the day. The next morning they started to search for the green rock. They spread out about 50 yards apart, angling south and east. They kept a straight line by sighting on trees and rocks ahead, blazing a tree now and then. They had been searching less than an hour when Jed stopped and called to the others, "Come look at this tree." It was the remnant of a huge tree trunk, split and charred by fire. It belonged to another age compared to the present growth. It had survived fires that others did not until lightning struck it. The surrounding area was mostly grass and light brush, due to recent burnings. Fred stumbled over the outcrop of greenish rock. There was gold in it—not just flecks but wire-like bands and threads. The quartz was somewhat broken up because there had been a great deal of slipping of the rock up and down in the Teton ledge. Most of the rocky cliffs were of shattered rock.

Because of the danger of Indians, they did not dare to build a fire during the day. They could only make a fire at night and that a small, shielded one. They would have liked to have been able to make charcoal and use the cast iron skillet as a melting pot.

They decided to use the horses to pack the ore down to the camp. One man was to stay in camp to watch the camp and horse. They made ore sacks out of the canvas tent. They had been there several months. Several hundred pounds of very high-grade ore had been pounded out on a deerskin to catch small flakes of gold. The larger and heavier pieces were set aside in sacks to be packed to an area where they could work it safely. The small pieces of rock and gold particles were collected on the deerskin and panned by Fred because he was short and could squat and stoop more easily. They figured that they had nearly 20 pounds of gold dust and nuggets.

Johnson said, "Let's make this the last trip to the diggins. Tomorrow we'll load up the horses and walk them to where we can work the rock over." It was so agreed. Rafe and Jed started for the diggings, riding their horses. There was the boom of a gun in the direction of the camp. Because of the trees and brush, they could only trot their horses back. Fred with his rifle greeted them.

"Two Indians came. They got the pack horse. I went to check on the horses and one Indian had a rope on Nig and the other was trying to cut the hobbles on the other horse. I took a bead on the one leading the horse. He moved. I hit him in the hip. He went down, but got up. The other Indian jumped on the pack horse, helped the wounded one up, and they rode away."

They could see the bobbing of the Indians on Nig nearly a mile away. It took only a few minutes to load the high-grade ore on the three horses, along with a few necessities including a pick and a shovel. Leading the horses, they trotted westward and north down hill at an angle to the large stream now called Bitch Creek, 10 miles away. It was going to be close, because there was no way they could travel any faster. The two Indians had to get back to camp, about 7 miles, and then go 18 more miles to overtake them.

In a short time the timber thinned out and gave way to brush and grassland. They realized that the Indians knew the only way they could go and what they would do. Only a short stop to get a drink of water slowed their escape. At the top of Bitch Creek Canyon, they looked back down the long, grassy slope behind them. Nothing was in sight. Jed climbed a tree, then climbed back down in a hurry. "They are about 4 miles back—say about half an hour!

Hurriedly, they decided to bury the ore and come back for it later. Rafe, the taller and better runner, was to stay at the top with two rifles in strategic cover while they buried the ore. He would fire both rifles, being sure to hit either horses or men to make the Indians scatter and take cover. It worked. He downed two horses and ran down the steep canyon, jumping over trees and rocks. The ore was buried and covered with dirt and a layer of pine needles. The horses were ready and they rode up out of the canyon. Before them lay a comparatively open country with mostly grass and sparse bushes and trees. The dozen or so Indians gave up, as their horses were no match for the better mounts of the miners.

When they camped, Rafe asked, "How did you mark where you buried it?"

"There were four large pine trees, 2 feet or more across, bigger than any other in the bottom. They were located in a square shape. We buried the ore in the exact center of the square. We also blazed the trees so we can find it easily."

They continued on to Fort Hall. While they were resting and restocking, a wagon train stopped on its way to Oregon. It was short-handed because of an Indian attack 50 miles out of Salt Lake. They decided to take the free ride to Oregon, and arrived in Portland without any trouble. In Portland they got haircuts, beard trims, baths, bought new clothes. They exchanged their 20 pounds of gold for money and put it in money belts for safekeeping.

It had been nearly a week. The nightlife, new clothes, good food, and liquor had been fun. It was getting tiresome. Fred said, "Let's go back and get the gold. I want to buy a farm or settle on land in the Boise, Idaho region." It was agreed to start soon.

That night while they were eating at a restaurant, they became friendly with three good-looking women seated at the next table. Rafe said, "They really had us panting." The women said they were new in town and were looking for a good time, and revealed that they were staying at the Oxbow Hotel where the miners also were staying.

Fred said, "Come on, I'll buy us all a round of drinks."

The girl he had picked out was a large redhead named Gertie, who said, "Don't waste money at the bar. We have plenty of liquor in our rooms."

In their room they brought out two bottles of whiskey. Gertie poured three drinks out of a partly full bottle for the miners, saying,

"Please wait for us." Then she opened the other bottle and poured three drinks for the girls.

"Bottoms up." So they drank them down.

Rafe said, "I woke up, the floor was rocking. I was sick with a terrible headache. We had been robbed, shanghied, and on board a ship with furs and lumber to China. Our money was gone. I decided to make the best of it in spite of the abuse by the second mate. He knocked Jed down for no reason. Jed came up with a knife only to get beaned with a belaying pin. We were in Hong Kong for a week unloading and loading when Fred took cholera and died in a few days. There was a clipper bound for New Orleans. I jumped ship and went around the horn to New Orleans. I was nearly broke. Got a job on a fishing boat. The captain and owner had a daughter. We fell in love, married, had a family. Eventually I had a boat of my own. It was a good living. After over 40 years I never got over wanting to go back and dig up that gold. Here I am and I can't find it."

Knowing Fred Durtchi, I don't believe he could possibly have made up this story. I do believe that there is gold buried in Bitch Creek canyon. It could be anywhere in a 5-mile length. The dam for the power plant may have caused the area to be under water.

MAN'S BEST FRIEND

Stull Wright, my ex-landlord, was looking around in the bare garage when I walked by the house where we had lived in Shelley. The house had the look of a vacant place—no curtains, no glimpses of furniture as you walked by the windows. Stull had moved all right.

I knew how he felt by the droop of his broad shoulders and the sag of the short, heavy body. The usual cheerful smile was missing from his broad, pleasant face. This had been the only house he and Nancy had lived in since she came out from Kansas to be his bride 25 years ago. The bank which he helped start was now a part of a big chain. He was to be vice-president of a larger bank in a bigger town.

When he saw me, we shook hands and said in a half-apologetic manner, "I was just looking around for the last time to see if we had missed anything."

Just then his gaze became fixed upon an object high up on the opposite wall. He walked over and took an odd-looking brass key from the wall.

"Do you know what this is?" he asked, handing the key to me. I didn't have the least idea so he explained it was a Presto Lite key to the gas tank for lights on a car. The car was his first and the one he and his bride drove through Yellowstone Park on their honeymoon. We talked about old cars for a short time. Then I got around to the purpose of my visit.

"Stull, up in Teton County there is the best bear hunting in the West. Why don't you come up for a weekend?"

"Virg, as well as I like to hunt big game, I could never shoot a bear. After all, I feel that bears are man's best friend." A big grin spread over his face. My surprised look must have prompted his next remark.

"If you have time, let's sit on the bench by the outdoor fireplace and I'll tell you the reason why. It's a story I've never told anyone before."

It was one of those bright, lazy autumn days with just enough warmth to be comfortable. Stull filled his short briar pipe and started his story.

When he finished college, he worked two years in a bank in Kansas. An uncle died, leaving him $10,000. Through a college classmate who was living in Idaho, he met Mr. Evans who wanted to start a bank in Idaho. They pooled their capital. It totaled $25,000, just

169

the bare minimum required by law in those days to start a bank. Stull and Nancy were engaged, but they decided to wait a year until the bank was on its feet and going smoothly. His salary as vice-president and cashier just got him by. At the end of the first year, it was apparent the bank would be a definite success. So by correspondence he and Nancy made arrangements to be married in Idaho on July 1st. As a complete surprise, he made careful plans for a honeymoon in Yellowstone Park. Stull arranged everything down to the finest detail. They were going to camp out. He secured an 8-by-8 tent with a canvas floor, a camp stove, bedding, utensils, checking off each item from a list that he had been compiling for months.

The date was set. His vacation was arranged for, and Nancy was to come out from Kansas the day before the wedding. They were to leave immediately after the ceremony for the park. Finally the day arrived. He went down to the depot an hour ahead of time. The train arrived on schedule and Nancy was the first passenger off.

"Gee, she looked beautiful. I hadn't seen her for a year. She was just as glad to see me."

Finally he noticed someone else trying to talk to him. It was Nancy's mother. She explained, "I just couldn't let my little girl come all the way to Idaho by herself to get married. I'm going home right after the ceremony and leave you two to yourselves."

When he first saw her, he thought the bottom had dropped out of everything, but when she explained that she was going right back home it was like sunshine after a storm. It was such a relief and to show his appreciation before his prospective bride, he really poured it on thick to have her stay awhile. They drove over to a friend's house where Nancy was to stay and the wedding was to take place. There he told Nancy of the surprise—the honeymoon in Yellowstone Park.

He was feeling magnanimous in knowing his mother-in-law-to-be wasn't going to make the park trip with them. Then it happened. His mother-in-law said, "I've been thinking, it would be a shame to miss seeing the park after coming this far and being so close to it. You have been so nice and insistent on my staying. I believe I will go with you. I am small and will not take up much room. If you think it will be all right, I surely would like to go!"

Stull's mind went numb. He didn't want to start things on the wrong foot and say what he really was thinking. He blurted out, "That will be great."

The worst part of it was that in his anxiety, he said it so forcefully she took it for true enthusiasm. The die was cast.

A short time later when he and Nancy were alone, she whispered to him, "You big chump. If you had stalled until I could talk to her, she would not go. We will have to take her now."

He said, "Honey, I was trying to think of a solution with a head so

170

full of gloom it just would not function."

She cuddled up to him, trying to ease the situation and said, "Darling, it will be all right. She won't be here long and we can take another honeymoon in the park next year all by ourselves."

There was nothing to do but go through with it. His finances were rock bottom. He had borrowed to the limit for the new house and car. The bank examiner wasn't due for four or five months and his partner, Mr. Evans, said, "The bank should be solvent again by that time."

Staying at the lodges and hotels was just out of the question. They would have to camp out. He started out to find another tent and more bedding. The only clear thoughts that entered his mind centered around poison, drowning, shooting, and how it could be done legally. He thought no jury in the world would commit a man for what he wanted to do.

The first call yielded bedding and a tarpaulin. Tents were not to be borrowed, bought or stolen.

Early the next morning he packed the car, tied the extra bed roll on the spare tire, turned off the water and electricity in the house, and drove slowly to the place of the wedding. He even looked in the sky for clouds for the possible chance of lightning. The sky was clear from horizon to horizon.

The bride was radiant and lovely, her mother tearful, the groom jittery. The ceremony by the old, experienced minister was one of his best performances.

At 10:05 the three were in the front seat of the car headed for Yellowstone Park, 119 miles away. He and Nancy just sat not saying much, squeezing each other's hand now and then. It wasn't as if they were by themselves even though Nancy's mother said, "Now don't mind me. I just won't see or hear anything." At one o'clock they stopped at Ashton for lunch and were entering the beautiful Targhee Forest. Neither of the women had been in a forest before. Nancy's delight and enchantment in the scenery made Stull glow with pleasure. Her mother was enraptured but not enough to be spellbound, as she constantly bubbled over with enthusiasm. She repeatedly said how wonderful it was that they invited her to come along.

To Stull the trees never seemed so tall, the grass so green, or the wild flowers so gorgeous. These grew in profusion mile on mile by the roadside. Sometimes they were mixed, often in small solid fields with blues, reds, and yellows blending into each other.

It seemed like the drive to the west entrance of the park didn't consume much time. Actually it was 4 o'clock. The park attendant registered them, gave them a receipt, a map, and park regulations and a thorough warning about feeding bears. He concluded this lecture by saying, "Bears will eat right out of your hand up to your elbow."

"Bears!" exclaimed his mother-in-law.

"You'll see lots of them before you get through the park," replied the ranger. "There are three people in the hospital at Mammoth Hot Springs because of injuries by bears. Just don't get too close to them and they won't bother you. Be sure to keep your food in the trunk of your car and be careful about your bacon. Bears are just crazy about bacon."

Stull remembered that they didn't have any.

Old Faithful, the first overnight stop on Stull's carefully planned itinerary, was a scant hour's drive away. Their road meandered along the lazy Madison River with its wide open meadows of grass and flowers bordered by trees. Mountains near and far blended into the panorama, making it a wonderland. Soon they turned south and followed up the busy Firehole River with its falls, rapids, and steep cliffs. They didn't stop because Stull wanted to get the camp set up before dark. About halfway to their destination, Nancy exclaimed, "There's one. It's a bear. Stop, Stull!" Sure enough, there was a bear off to the side of the road about 50 feet. When the car stopped, the bear started to shuffle toward them for a handout. His mother-in-law shrieked, "Stull, get out of here!" The engine was running, so he just put it in gear and drove on. They arrived at the camp grounds at 5 o'clock. The park wasn't crowded 25 years ago as it is now. There were only a few other cars scattered around. They pitched their tent on a nice, level grassy spot under a big tree in the far corner of the camp grounds. It seemed small when it was staked out and smaller still when the two beds were made inside.

He and Nancy had fun gathering wood while her mother started to prepare supper, which she graciously insisted on doing. They had gathered quite a pile when she said, "Why don't you stop over and see Old Faithful erupt? Be back in an hour because dinner will be ready by then, and it will be almost dark. I don't want to be alone after dark with all the bears around."

They strolled over to Old Faithful hand in hand. It gushed its awesome, stately column of water and steam the minute it was supposed to and for their special benefit it gave an almost record performance which pleased them greatly.

Mother had a marvelous dinner awaiting them—steak and hot bisquits. She had done wonders with the camp oven. Nancy and Stull did the dishes. He did the drying, thinking this is all right for the trip and maybe even sometimes at home, but thought he could find something else to do most of the time.

"Would you folks like to hear the ranger naturalist talk at 7:30?" inquired Stull. They would.

"We need bacon for breakfast. I'll run over to the store, get the bacon and catch up with you. It is almost time for the lecture to start. The store is nearly a quarter of a mile in the opposite direction."

He asked the clerk for 2 pounds of bacon, to be wrapped in two packages. It was 50¢ a pound and only 25¢ at home. The clerk raised an eyebrow about the two packages, but made no comment. Stull guessed they expected anything from dudes. When he took the bacon back to camp, there was a big bear sniffing around the ground where they had eaten. It was lucky they had taken precautions to put all of the food in the car trunk. The bear took off with a burst of speed when showered with a handful of pebbles.

"I hope he comes back tonight," muttered Stull as the bear ambled through the trees. With the bacon safe in the trunk of the car he found his bride and mother-in-law on the logs that were being used for seats. They sat facing a huge camp fire. A handsome young ranger led them in singing. The ranger naturalist gave a most interesting talk on bears.

The moon was full, big, yellow, and bright as they made their way back to camp, a fairyland of light and shadows. Just as they reached camp Nancy's mother got behind Stull.

"There he is!" The same big bear was nosing around the camp. When Stull showered him from long range with rocks, he lumbered reluctantly off into the trees. It wasn't time to go to bed so they built a big fire and sat on the log and talked. Finally, Nancy's mother yawned and said, "Nancy, will you go with me to the washroom? I am completely worn out and am going to bed immediately. You two can stay up all night if you want."

They sat side by side on the log watching the fire.

"It's just too wonderful. The park is the most beautiful place I have ever seen," whispered Nancy. "Maybe Mother won't want to stay the whole 10 days."

"I hope not," whispered Stull back. The fire died down into glowing embers and the moon was touching the trees in the west. His bride softly told him she would go to bed first. Stull waited for what he thought was a decent interval, undressed outside the tent and entered carrying his clothes. The mother-in-law was snoring. She really is fagged out, thought Stull.

He dreamed that he was back in Kansas with its volunteer fire department's alarm blaring. When he finally woke up it was to the screaming of his mother-in-law. Finally, the completely terrified woman was able to gasp out, "It was a bear! He was rooting under the canvas floor of the tent. He was actually rolling me around, grunting and sniffing. I could hear him licking his chops."

Stull slipped on his pants, looked around outside, but evidently Mother's screams had routed bruin back into the woods. After considerable reassurance that it probably wouldn't happen again, it became all quiet inside the tent.

The next time he woke up it was Mother again calling, "Stull! Stull! Stull!" in rising crescendo. Stull pulled on his pants again and went outside. No bear in sight. Next morning all three were tired and red-eyed. The bear had paid another visit.

"I just can't understand why the bear wanted to root under my bed," the elderly lady kept repeating.

"There must be something about you that attracts them," ventured Stull.

"Well, whatever attracts them will not be here tonight because you are taking me to the train right after breakfast. And don't you try to talk me out of it!"

Stull helped with the breakfast, cleaning up, and the dishes.

"We'll leave the tent just as it is because it rushes us to make the train at West Yellowstone. Nancy, help your mother pack and I'll get the car ready."

The Buick really did its stuff and they made it with 20 minutes to spare.

When Stull told about the rest of the park trip, he really got eloquent. He concluded the story, "You see why bears are man's best friend?"

"Stull, you haven't told me why the bear kept rooting under the tent."

With the biggest grin, he said, "He was after the extra pound of bacon."

TRIGGER

In the late 1870s and early 1880s, stockmen had an almost unlimited area to graze their herds. Photographs and tintypes showed bunch grass reaching above the stirrups on a horse. Large herds of antelope still grazed on it even after the buffalo were gone. Cattle could winter on the bunch grass when it was dry. The dry grass hindered the eating of the green grass growing in it. The stockmen burned off large areas every year. Bunch grass requires two years of growth before reseeding. Sage brush grew mostly on rocky knolls. When the bunch grass became thinner, the unpalatable sage brush took over.

There were many of the pioneer sheepmen left in the second generation. They resented the settling of the more fertile farm land. The problem of sheep being grazed on winter wheat land in the spring was a sore spot to the wheat growers of Teton County. While it didn't happen every day, the sporadic stealing of feed was common.

During the spring drive to summer range, wheat growers might find a large acreage of their crops eaten, destroyed by a flock of 1,000 ewes and 1,500 lambs. The crop was gone. The sheep were gone. What could they do?

In Gooding County, the Goodings and the Thomases owned the banks and set the price of hay by making a loan due in September, forcing the farmer to sell his hay cheap in order to pay. Basque herders were brought from Spain. They in turn became sheepmen. These ambitious people became our bankers, lawyers, and doctors.

Eventually sheepmen were alloted grazing permits on forest lands for early spring and summer grazing. Their trespassing on cultivated lands occurred during the drives to and from the grazing areas.

The two leading sheepmen in Teton County were in their late sixties or early seventies. These large men were domineering, as if they owned the world. Dry farmers and grain growers in Teton County had tried for years to catch them trespassing and eating the early tender grain crop when the head was in the boot. This resulted in the grain being unable to head out.

Most of the dry farmers lived in town and their large acreages were not fenced. The trespassing would take place usually on a moonlit night. There was vacant land designated as bedground. The sheep would be bedded down hungry. Sometime in the night they were herded down the road and pushed out into a field away from the road. This resulted in a gain of weight worth from $150 to $200—a lot of

175

money in those days.

Charlie Ard was really angry when he came into my office. Sheep had eaten off nearly 40 acres of his winter wheat.

"Charlie, you have a lot of ground squirrels. We have oats poisoned with strychnine. You put it out in handfuls, because if you scatter it, the squirrel will eat just a few grains, get sick, and never eat another oat."

His face lit up with a big grin.

"I'll take 500 pounds, as some of my neighbors have a lot of ground squirrels, too!"

"Remember, Charlie, if you put out squirrel poison on unfenced land, it must be posted."

Evidently the Basque herder couldn't read English, as a sheepman lost nearly a hundred head in a wheat field. Also, the owner of the sheep had to pay for damage to the crop. After that the farmers just put up signs.

My third altercation or confrontation with sheepmen was like my first. It was over a big white Lewellen setter named Trigger. She was given to me when I lost Diane to poison in Shelley. The owner said, "I can't teach her anything and maybe you can make something out of her." She had been kept in a small pen and almost never got to exercise. A neighbor hunted once with the owner and said that all he did was yell and beat her. From the way she cringed and cowered, it was evident that she had been abused.

With tender loving care and never raising my voice to her, she became a happy, affectionate dog. She assumed that Dallas was her responsibility. After two sessions with a leash and collar, she would heel, sit, and stay. In fact, all you had to do was give commands in a low voice and she would obey.   She learned to pull Dallas on the sled and to respond to Gee, Haw and Whoa. She was an important part of the family.

Claude and I were loading two loads of lambs for the lamb pool. Trigger had been helping load for two years. We would load the top deck first, remove the ramp while one of us stood in the door of the upper deck. Then we would load the lower deck and close and fasten the car door. Trigger just loved to bark at the sheep and nip them to keep them moving.

We had finished loading one car when Claude's oldest son ran up and said, "Dad, the threshers are at our place."

Claude had to go, so I told him, "Go ahead, I'll get the brakeman to help load the last car."

The brakeman had gone to get a sandwich at the restaurant a few blocks away. A sheepman was busy culling lambs a few pens away and they wouldn't spare a man. There wasn't anything left to do but try to load the lambs with Trigger's help. The ramp was heavy, but I could manage to put it up. There was no difficulty in loading the upper deck. There was a problem, as the car door was in one piece and someone had to guard the upper part of the door while the lower deck was being loaded. It had to be either Trigger or me. I closed the door while we moved the sheep from the holding pen to the loading pen. Trigger followed me up the ramp, watched me open the door and climb up and stand on the edge of the upper deck.

"Trigger, put the sheep in the car." With a wave of the hand I repeated, "Put them in the car."

She ran to the rear of the sheep and began to bark and nip. In a matter of minutes she had them in the car and I closed the door.

Two men had been watching from outside the fence. I hooked the leash on Trigger's collar and walked out the gate. The large, elderly sheep baron grabbed the leash and said, "I'm going to buy your dog. I'll give you $50 for the dog." Indignation and resentment of his domineering, aggressive attitude made me boil.

"You are not going to buy that dog. She isn't for sale." I grabbed the leash back.

"I'll give you a hundred for the dog."

"The dog isn't for sale."

He pulled out two one hundred dollar bills and tried to shove them into my pocket, saying, "No dog is worth that much," and again grabbed Trigger's leash. I gave him a hard shove and his head bounced against the upper rail of the fence. A blow from the rear on the side of my head really dazed me and made my head ring. As I staggered forward, I swung my long, heavy prod pole in a backward swing. There was a cry of pain and his son was holding his wrist and moaning. I shoved the elder against the fence and slapped his face, as I didn't dare punch him. I told him that if he stole my dog I would kill him.

The powerful Trigger just loved to pull Dallas on his Flexible Flyer sled. Dog teams were used to deliver mail. Dog sled races were popular. The street in front of our house was a popular route for these teams to practice on. Dallas would wait until a team was even with him and race them. You could tell a team was coming a long way off by the barking. Trigger just could not stand to be beaten. Pulling almost no weight, she would run low as if she were chasing a rabbit. Dallas taught her the word "Mush" by touching her lightly with a slim willow branch. When he said "Mush," she put out an extra effort.

The annual chariot sled racing day in Driggs had in addition dog sled races of several miles. There were also races for kids with single dogs, in two-year age groups up to 17-18, with a final championship race for the winners. We entered Dallas in the 6- to 7-years-olds category. I had led Trigger hitched to the sled over the quarter-mile course. Ethel greeted her at the finish line. When the starter shot the pistol and Dallas yelled "Mush," Trigger was going away.

I purposely lined Dallas up on the outside for the championship race. When they started, a big Irish setter lead dog cut across toward Trigger. I yelled "Whoa." Trigger stopped off to the side to keep from getting hit by the sled, which turned over, spilling Dallas. I grabbed Dallas and put him face down on the sled. Trigger seemed to be hopelessly behind. Dallas was crying and yelling "Mush." Trigger picked up speed as if she were closing in on a rabbit. Ethel was at the finish line urging Trigger to come on. About 50 feet from the finish line her head was even with the big red dog team leader. She put on a burst of speed and won by a dog's nose. Dallas crawled off the sled and put his arm around her neck and his mother snapped the picture. Twenty-five dollars was a lot of prize money for anyone in 1940, let alone a 6-year-old.

A year later I told Trigger to stay on the edge of the sidewalk while I went into the drugstore. I heard a cry of pain and howling. Someone had driven over the flat sidewalk and broken her back and she had to be put out of her misery. Dr. Ole Hoffman had seen it, but he would never tell me who did it. He said he did not want me to kill someone.

In the winter the roads in Teton County were often long, narrow ditches with banks of snow 4- to 6-feet high. In order to pass another car, you had to slow down, pull over and often scrape the side of the bank to get by. The elderly heads of two big sheep companies would get drunk every so often. Then they would drive down the center of the road at high speed, forcing any oncoming car into the ditch. It seemed that no traffic officers were assigned to the area and the sheepmen had been getting away with this behavior for years. After I had to take to the snow bank and spend an hour shoveling out, I was more than furious. When I told Claude about the incident, he said, "Eventually they will meet each other and the whole valley will celebrate."

About 11 o'clock on New Year's morning I was shoveling 12 inches of new snow from my walk to the car when Claude drove up. We wished each other a happy new year. There was a loud crash and a car horn started to honk continuously.

Claude said, "Somebody is hurt bad. Maybe we can help."

I got into his pickup and we were just behind the police chief. Two pickups had met head on. Their total length was that of one pickup. Both of the elder sheepmen were dead. We turned around and drove back home. It took 2 hours with a cutting torch to get the bodies out. Many people in the valley celebrated the accident.

Our neighbor, Shelby Atchley, was the prosecuting attorney. He was a rabid republican and the only republican to hold office in the county. The reason for his election was that he was the only attorney in Teton County. To my knowledge there was never a trial during my six-year stay. His salary was a mere pittance, but it gave him free office space with lights and telephone, which made his practice profitable. He settled estates and made will contracts. For three months he worked on income taxes, and when he learned that Ethel had training in accounting and typing, he hired her to help him one or two days a week. In a short time she could complete most tax forms and he would call on her when work piled up. She enjoyed being able to use her bookkeeping and typing training.

"It is nice to have my own spending money," she said. "It makes me feel independent."

"Please don't account for your money to me." This netted me a hug and kiss.

SILVER

One of the most important jobs of a county extension agent is to organize and conduct a 4-H program. The 4-H Club motto is "Head, Heart, Health, and Hands." Projects carried by 4-H Club members included all kinds of clubs. In a county there might be clubs in livestock, crops, rural electricity, clothing, foods, room improvement, and many others. The Teton County agent was busy in the spring contacting local people to persuade them to lead the various clubs. I was recruiting leaders in Kunzville. The northeast area of the valley had been settled in the 1860s by Aaron Kunz, who was a polygamist. His many progeny and their in-laws settled in this area, which the locals called Kunzville. The descendants of these German immigrants were big, blond, and thrifty. I had just recruited three club leaders and felt very pleased with myself. As a matter of good relationship, I decided to pay a call on County Commissioner Jim Kunz. Jim was in his garden. I told him there would be a meeting on getting rural electrification into the county on Monday night and asked if he would attend. He said that he would and invited me to lunch. While we were waiting in the living room for Mrs. Kunz to announce lunch, I noticed a shining piece of rock on the mantle of the fireplace.

"Jim, this is galena, a high-grade silver lead ore. Where did it come from?"

"That is what a lot of people have been trying to find out for the past 70 years."

During and after lunch, Jim told the following story:

"My father saw a ragged, tattered man staggering up the lane toward the house. The man recovered in a week or two and left for Fort Hall a hundred miles away, carrying a small sack of food and his rifle. He told us that he had trapped all winter on the Gros Ventre River in Jackson Hole. It was in July when he found the place to winter and trap. He deepened a cut bank, made a lean-to with logs, covered them with dirt. A lean-to was built to shelter his two pack horses from the weather. Feed during the summer was no problem. The hobbled horses grew fat on the abundant grass. In the winter it would be almost impossible for the horses to survive without extra feed. He almost wore out his big hunting knife cutting willow branches. The pile was as high as he could toss them and more than 15 feet across. The bunch grass was as tall as a horse's belly. He tied bundles of grass and stacked them so they would shed water when it rained. There was a warm spring a few steps from the lean-to and watering the horses would be no problem. The problem was how to ration the feed to keep them alive through the winter.

"Trapping had been very good. The beaver and marten pelts and his gear would make heavy loads for the horses. They had made it through to grass but were very gaunt. It would take a month on grass for them to have sufficient strength to carry the load to Fort Hall. It was a late spring and the grass was short. He planned to leave in two more weeks. One evening he climbed the ridge above the camp to see if he could kill an elk or a deer. In the valley a mile or two below there was smoke rising. Indians. He had to get out of there quickly. The closest place for safety was Teton Basin where, he had heard, there were some settlers.

"Most of his gear had to be left so he buried it in the floor of the house lean-to. In a short time the horses were packed. They made good time during the daylight hours, as they were going downhill toward Snake River. The moon was full and they continued on during the night. When they reached Snake River, they camped. The horses needed rest in order to have strength to ford the river. His plan was to cross the river and travel to the foot of the mountains about 8 to 10 miles away, where he would rest the horses for the rest of the day for the 8-mile climb to the top.

"Crossing the river was difficult, he had to lead each horse separately. It was slow going, winding up in and around trees and fallen rocks. Starting at daybreak, it had taken them almost 10 hours to go 8 miles. The horses had to rest, and on a level spot just over the top he made camp. The horses drank from pools of snow water and tried to eat brush. It would be an easy 10 miles to the basin, and not having seen any Indians, he took his time about leaving.

"Just to make sure, he took his rifle and climbed up a knoll a short distance away to look at his backtrack. When he looked at his camp, there were several Indians holding his horses and opening his packs. It was a long shot. It missed. They did not scare as he had hoped, but came for him. He ran. There was a little spring at the top that ran down into Teton Valley, with fewer trees. The Indians couldn't follow him with horses, so they chased him on foot. When he came to a wide open meadow, he crossed it and waited. One Indian was ahead of the others and he shot him in the leg.

"The trapper ran on. He said he was 2 or 3 miles below the top when he stopped to rest. There was a shiny crystalized metallic rock which he picked up and put in his pocket. When we questioned him about where he found it, he said, 'It came from the bottom of a rocky ledge on the right side coming down. I would guess about halfway from the top.'

"People have been looking up Spring Creek for the past 70 years."

I said, "If all those people have been looking for it up Spring Creek and couldn't find it, he must have come down another stream."

Jim said, "It could have been covered by a snow slide."

Elmer Bowles, who lived on the Darby Creek drainage, showed me a piece of galena that he had found 2 or 3 miles up the creek. I told him of the trapper finding it nearly 70 years ago. We went looking for the source. There was no outcrop of ore where he found the specimen.

"It must have been carried down by a snowslide."

"Elmer, it could not fall uphill."

It could not have been more than a half-mile when we came upon an outcrop that had been uncovered by a snowslide. A tip of galena was exposed and promised to get much wider deeper down. We could trace the ridge of mineral-bearing rock nearly a mile. We filed our claims in Jackson Hole, but we had to get permission to mine it because it was in Teton National Park. Because of the need for metal, we thought there would be no trouble to get permission. It would be easy to mine as the ore could be trammed in cable cars, the loaded cars furnishing the power.

Not so. Our application was turned down. I had an appointment with Senator Thomas of Gooding to get assistance. Nothing was written down, but it was understood that he would get an interest.

This didn't work. The geologist of Guggenheim Foundation looked at the claims. He offered $1,000,000 down and a graduated royalty. This was providing we could get the easement. We were turned down. The mystery was solved. The seekers had looked up the wrong creek. The vein is still untouched.

PAUL HENRY

The horseshoe shape at the north end of Teton Valley opened up to gently rolling hills, then to flat land. The mountains curved back sharply to the right. To the left were wide open spaces which had been Indian hunting grounds. Patches of scraggly pines and quaking aspen were widely scattered through the area. Buffalo and elk in abundance had used the area for summer grazing. The curved road south to Ashton divided the area called Felt. The perpetually snow-capped Teton mountains that were heavily timbered rose steeply about 2 miles east. Numerous small creeks from the snow in the hills and mountains crossed the road on their westward way to the Teton River. The soil was good, grain could be grown profitably with few lean years due to lack of moisture.

Paul Henry, called "Pete" by everybody, was one of the veterans from a small North Carolina community who each homesteaded 360 acres on the Felt tract right after World War I, when a congressional act opened it to homesteaders. Under the Homestead Act they had to live on the land at least two years and at least half of the land had to be under profitable cultivation. Six of the eight homesteaders had their land proven up within the five year time limit. They were all bachelors and soon became tired of their own cooking. At the first annual meeting in the fall with the federal supervisor, one of the settlers said to him, "We need wives. The Mormon girls act like we are trash when we talk with them. When we ask them to dance, they say, 'I have this one.' We are all Southern Baptist."

The supervisor thought for a few moments, laughed and said, "Why don't you put an advertisement in a North Carolina newspaper? I am sure there are a lot of North Carolina girls that want to get married if they have a chance. You will get a lot of letters; sort out the most promising. You will have to do a lot of writing. You can exchange photographs. This will give you something to do."

After considerable laughter and arguments, they pooled money for an ad in one of the largest North Carolina newspapers. Replies were to be sent to one box. In a month they had actual piles of letters from interested women. They held a meeting, went over all of the letters and decided to pick out 40 of the most desirable prospects. This took three nights. The first night someone brought a jug of moonshine which resulted in great hilarity and little progress was made in the selection. They decided that as this was serious business, no liquor for the next night's meeting. They finally agreed on the 40 possible wives-to-be. These letters were put into a sack and shaken. Each homesteader drew one letter at a time until all 40 were drawn. When someone asked, "Now what do we do?" the chairman replied, "We answer them."

"That is a lot of writing to do. What should we write?"

"We can send the same letter to all of them. All we have to do is copy it and change the name!" The discussion as to what to write ended with a decision to tell it like it was, with no glowing terms, because the women might take a look at the reality and take the next train home.

A committee of three composed the letter, which was to include a photograph. They described the temporary log house, land, country. They also said they were successful in their farming operation and with the help of a good wife who was willing to stand hardships and hard work, there would be a new house and financial security.

They were busy all winter answering letters. Some of the correspondents reached a decision quickly, others dragged on. It was early spring before all arrangements were made for the prospective brides to meet in North Carolina, get on the same train and arrive at the same time. When the L.D.S. women heard that there would be families in the Felt area instead of bachelors, they decided that these would be possible converts for the church. They arranged for each of the prospective brides to stay in a home for a week in order to become acquainted with the groom. They arranged to have a dance and party for the couples the day after the ladies arrived. At the end of the week there would be a group wedding with the Bishop conducting the ceremony.

The party and dance were a great success. However, two couples traded mates-to-be at the dance and party. There were no divorces afterward, and all but two of the settlers became prosperous. Of the more successful were Pete Henry and his wife, Martha.

I was working in my office at the courthouse at eight in the morning when the phone rang.

"This is your county agent. How can I help you?"

"I am Pete Henry out at Felt. Our milk cow has milk fever."

"I can get there in an hour. Put a blanket on her and straw under and around her to keep her warm. I am out of calcium glucanate and will have to wait until the drugstore opens at 8:30. Have a kettle of hot water ready."

Pete met me at Felt with a horse and sled because of the deep snow. The family cow was a Jersey. Her head was against her flank. This was a typical symptom of milk fever where there is not enough blood going to the hind quarters due to the loss of blood during calving and blood going to the udder. The hind quarters become paralyzed. When I touched the hind quarters with the needle, the cow did not flinch. Pete brought the kettle of hot water from the kitchen and I put the bottle of glucanate in it to warm it. Then I attached one end of a rubber hose to the bottle. I put a finger of my left hand on the large vein in the cow's neck just below the jaw, causing the vein to swell so I could insert the needle, checked the hose for air bubbles, and attached it to the needle. This procedure took about 15 minutes.

"In a few minutes her hind quarters will begin to tremble as the blood returns to them. We can get her up in about 15 minutes, but you will have to be careful for a few days and only milk her enough to ease her udder. Get some bone meal and mix it with salt, but not over one tablespoonful to a pound of bone meal."

A short time later I pricked the cow's hind quarters with the needle. She staggered to her feet and started wobbling toward the creek, walking more steadily with each step. She took a drink at the creek, went to the rick and started to eat hay.

Pete said, "I'll be damned. We never had a case of milk fever before. You surely know your stuff."

"When I was a kid they used to pump the udder full of air and tie off the teats with caps."

"How much do I owe you?"

"You pay for the county agent's services with taxes. However, you owe my petty cash fund $2.25 for the medicine."

Martha had watched the whole operation and was beside herself with joy. She invited me to come in and have a cup of coffee and a piece of cake, but I had to decline because I had another emergency call in Kunzville, 20 miles away. This was the first contact of the Cross family with the Henrys. It led to a long, close, and pleasant association.

The annual sportsmen's jamboree, held in the high school gymnasium, was one of the big events in the valley. A barbequed elk and smoked whitefish were furnished by the County Fish and Game Commission. Everyone brought a dish. It started at 6 o'clock, they ate until 8 o'clock, and then danced until the wee hours of the morning. I saw the Henrys enter the hall and asked Ethel to come with me to meet a nice couple. After we had exchanged greetings, Ethel asked Martha to eat with us. We exchanged dances, and the tall, good-looking Henry couple were surprisingly good dancers. The association of the two families gradually became quite close—dances, pinochle, dinners together. There were shopping trips to Idaho Falls, 60 miles away. Pete and I hunted and fished together.

It was after one of the dinners, with the dishes cleaned up and put away, that Ethel asked Martha, "How did you two get together?"

Martha looked at Pete and laughed. "I was a mail-order bride. I am one of the eight North Carolina mail-order brides that settled in Felt."

Ethel had heard of the mail-order brides but never associated the Henrys with the action. They were such a devoted, affectionate, and considerate couple.

"Martha, you had never seen him before?"

"Only his picture. I didn't even know how tall he was or whether he had any hair or teeth. His mouth was closed and he wore a cap in the picture. When I stepped out of the car onto the steps I looked at the eight men lined up to greet us. They had name tags and we had name tags. I saw the tall, good-looking man and said to myself, 'Please Lord, let it be Pete Henry.' He walked up to me and said, 'You are Martha.' I said, 'You are Pete.' He tried to put his arm around me and I shook hands with him. He acted dumbfounded.

"Mrs. Sheets, the lady I would stay with, came up. 'Pete, Martha is tired after the week's train ride. You come after lunch tomorrow. You two can get acquainted then.' She took my arm. Pete loaded my trunk and suitcase in the buggy, and we drove off and left Pete standing there."

I asked Pete, "What did you think when you first saw her?"

"She looked calm, cool, collected, and tall. There were not any of the other seven that could come close to comparing with her. I was too excited and thrilled when we got together. I tried to hug her, but she gave me a warm, firm handshake.

"I'd had a good crop the previous fall. I joined the army at 18, didn't smoke or drink, sold my cigarettes blackmarket and sent my money home. I really had saved quite a stake in the few years. Being able to buy six good work horses when I arrived allowed me to plow a lot of land and get it ready to plant the first spring. I drove up to the Sheets' home in a new buggy with red wheels that were spattered with mud. I helped Martha into the buggy, tucked the lap robe around us. I asked her what she would like to see. 'I want to see the farm.' She did not say 'our farm.' She let me hold her hand but had her mittens on."

Pete's first house was a log cabin, one room. It was long and wide. When he found out he might get a wife, he added another room, replaced the sod roof with shingles, ran water into the house by gravity and had a sink. The two-holer was on the hill behind. A neighbor woman helped him with curtains. The view looked out over the rolling prairie with the Tetons rising majestically beyond it. He had left enough pine trees to shelter the house and barn from the prevailing west winds.

"When we drove up into the yard and tied the team up, we went inside. We talked—mostly I talked. Once in a while she would ask a question: 'You are not smoking or chewing?' 'No, I don't.' She looked the kitchen over first and said, 'It will be nice to have water in the house. I have always had to carry it. Your house is clean for a bachelor. A lot can be done to make it better.'

"When we opened the bedroom door and looked at the bed, I thought 'Oh boy.'

"I had bought a big brass bed that came across the plains in a covered wagon, a big dresser with matching chairs. I was proud of it. The walls were papered. She said, 'Only one bed.'

"There isn't room for any more."

"Her next words were, 'I would like to see your barn.'

"After she looked over the barn, corrals, and the Jersey milk cow, it was time to go back and get ready for the party and dance. The party and dance were fun. I was so proud of this beautiful, wonderful girl that I hoped would be my wife. We danced very well together, held hands at intermission. I kissed her goodnight. Wasn't much of a return kiss.

"During the rest of the week we drove around the country looking at sights to see. We also took three more trips to the ranch. We drove and walked over all of it. She remarked that if it were fenced properly, I could run several head of cattle on the wasteland and the stubble in the fall. She kept asking questions about what I thought about this and that. What future plans did I have. How did I think children should be raised. One question was, 'What do you think a wife's place should be in the home?' I tried to answer as best I could. Guess I must have made some of the right answers. Anyway, Friday, two days before the group wedding, I asked her if she would marry me.

"She said, 'Pete, I will marry you but under certain conditions. I left North Carolina because I didn't want to be a slave to some hillbilly and have a whole batch of kids. So until I am sure, I will not sleep with you. I will fold a sheet back and you can sleep on the other side.'

"Boy, did I feel like the bottom had dropped out of the world. She said, 'After all, we are not really acquainted. I am a good cook and housekeeper. When you are working in the field, I will milk the cow. I didn't come to Idaho to sit in a cabin all the time. We are going to parties, dances, and visit neighbors.'

"The change of coming in from the field all hot, dusty, and tired to find the chores done, a clean house, and a good meal was pure heaven. I guess it was about two weeks after the wedding and things were going nicely. She even kissed me goodnight. She was walking in the garden when I unfolded the sheet between us. In the morning I woke up proud and reached over for her. She awoke, gave me a push, got dressed, and went out the door. I didn't get any breakfast. When I came in for lunch, she wasn't there. I cursed myself for being a darned fool. When I came in from work, there she was in the kitchen cooking supper. You can't imagine how elated my feelings were. By the first of June the crops were all in and prospects were good for an excellent harvest.

"One Saturday night we drove to Driggs for the dance in the church house. We had a good time. She danced close to me and even gave me a kiss. On the way home we kissed a couple of times. She always undressed first and got into bed. When I undressed down to my long johns and got into bed, the sheet was not folded. Brownie was late getting milked the next day."

Ethel asked Martha, "Is that the way it was?"

"Ethel, he left out one part of it. On the way to the dance that night he said, 'We should start planning a new house with a flush toilet and more bedrooms, as we might need them.' What he didn't know was I almost told him on the way home from the dance that we might need extra bedrooms especially for a crib because of the way I was feeling about him. I wanted to surprise him when we got home and into bed."

"She did," said Pete.

JAPANESE BALLOONS

As chairman of civilian defense, I and my group were training in fire-fighting and sabotage. Fire-fighting was very important because of the Japanese balloon barrage. The balloons were made of rice paper and loaded with incendiary bombs. They were launched somewhere in Japanese territories and the wind carried them into Oregon, Washington, Idaho, Montana, and even Wyoming. They started fires in the forests of these states, with release time and altitude coordinated with time and place. No news was released on these landings, as it would give information to the Japanese as to their success.

The forest ranger called me and asked for help on a fire reported east of the valley. Within a few minutes, two pickups with eight men and tools were on the way to the area. It was a still day and the smoke rose straight up. The smoke from this fire was first black and turned white or grey. They were about 6 miles from the fire. The road was a slow, narrow, rutted mountain road. They noticed the smoke getting less and less. As they drove around a bend, there it was in a meadow of dry grass. The fire was practically out. They laughed at the two blackened men in their underwear who had taken off their bib overalls, soaked them in water and beat out the fire. The forest service bought them new overalls and gloves.

A Jap balloon had landed in a clump of bush in the meadow and exploded. The Brown brothers just happened to be poaching elk. They said they were looking for a place to fish in some small lakes nearby, but each was carrying a 30-30 carbine.

Claude Dalley and I were marking lambs for the lamb pool. On the way to another farm, Claude said, "Stop! Look! There is a balloon." The road bordered the forest. The balloon was really hard to see, as it was carefully camouflaged. We lost sight of it as it descended slowly into the timber.

"Looks like it is going to land in the Spring Creek area. I have it about marked where it is landing. Let me drive. I know the roads."

The old road had some dead timber that had to be moved and the going was very slow. The road was following a small, meandering creek. Claude yelled, "There it is!"

There it was, with its support lines snarled in a beaver dam in the middle of a small pond in the dammed-up creek. We were laughing.

"It couldn't have landed in a better place." Claude said. "I wish we could send the Japs a picture of it!" He stayed to watch it, while I went to a phone to call Bannister of the FBI in Pocatello. Bannister flew in with a demolition specialist from the Pocatello air base. The balloon was booby-trapped. We all got behind trees when the specialist exploded it. All people seeing the two Jap balloons were sworn to secrecy and there was never any loose talk or publicity about them.

THE BIG SNOW

Teton County was separated from Yellowstone Park by the lofty Teton peaks which were always snow-covered. When a storm came in from the west, the wind was swirled around to the right when it hit the high foothills and mountains. The moisture-bearing clouds could not go over the mountains due to their weight, and stayed until they unloaded their moisture. In 1942, it came early. It was Friday, October 15, that Claude Dalley and I were harvesting the last of our certified seed potato crop. He ran the digger and helped pick. I loaded the 60-pound half-sacks onto a trailer which was pulled by a Ford 6 to a cellar. Ethel picked and managed a crew of 10- to 11-year-old school children. There were no men available to work in the potato harvest because of the war. We gave the students candy bars, cookies, and pop at rest breaks to keep them going. We had been working 12 hours a day for a week and we were tired. We had just finished unloading the last sacks into the cellar and Claude said, "Let's not work tomorrow and start again Monday."

"Claude, last night's radio said there is a big storm coming up the Snake River valley. It could reach here tomorrow. If we are snowed in we would lose about $2,000 or more."

The evening radio news commentator ended his program telling about the big snow storm that was closing roads and main highways. The storm would reach us in about 24 hours. Ethel prepared extra sandwiches. I bought cookies and other goodies at the store. Saturday morning was a beautiful, clear autumn morning. On the way to the potato field we noticed cattle milling and the young horses running and bucking, reacting to the change in the atmosphere. Claude had arrived at the field earlier and had several rows dug.

"There is going to be a big snow storm." He pointed toward the river. Clouds of ducks and geese were coming in from the north, circling and alighting on grain fields. "They have come a long way and are hungry." They often came in a day ahead of a storm.

The pickers filled a bushel wire bucket and dumped it into a sack. Two buckets to the half sack. We were paying them 10¢ a half-sack and they were making between $4 and $5 a day. This was big pay for 10- and 12-year-olds. Everything went along very smoothly and it looked as if we could finish that day. We stopped to eat lunch. Everyone was tired. Ethel pointed to the west and we could see a big cloud appearing over the horizon. We told the pickers we would give them 20¢ a half-sack if they could finish that day. That spurred them

191

on and increased their picking speed. When Claude was ahead with the digging, he picked. I also started picking, figuring we could pick up the sacks in the snow. The blizzard hit with a blast of wind and blinding snow as the pickers were finished and leaving the field. This left three trailer loads to haul to the cellar. We had to hitch the tractor in front of the car to pull it through knee-deep snow. We finished, completely exhausted, at 11 o'clock that night. This was the start of one of the severest winters on record.

The next morning we didn't awaken until 6-year-old Dallas climbed in bed with us complaining that he was hungry. We heard sleigh bells. Travel had changed overnight from gasoline to horse power. Winter was a month early. While we were eating breakfast we heard the barking of dogs and watched a dog team run by. It was Irv Matthews, the mail carrier of the Felt route. His team was an Airedale-bear hound cross, heavy-coated and long-legged. Each dog must have weighed 90 pounds. Matthews was also hired by the government to kill predatory grizzly bears that wandered over from the park and killed cattle and sheep. When they got cattle or sheep, they killed for the love of it.

What followed was snow every few days until it was 3 feet on the level. Early in December a storm blew in from the west. By one o'clock there was no visibility. The teacher had experienced this before and would not let the children in town go home until their parents called for them. The two school busses were traced in their progress by parents calling my office as their children were delivered. I kept a map with pins showing the last reported location of each bus.

It was nearly 4 o'clock when I was free to go to the schoolhouse to take Dallas home. I could not see 20 feet ahead. The snow was coming down as if it were from a gigantic flour sifter. I could not see the street lights a block away. When I walked into Dallas' classroom, there was one child, but no Dallas. The teacher was reading a book.

"Where is Dallas?"

"He's right here." She looked startled. He wasn't. "I told him to stay until you came!" He was not in the building. I cannot describe my sinking feeling of despair. It was only three blocks out to open sagebrush and Teton Creek. A 6-year-old had no chance in the storm. There was nothing else to do but try to find him. I could not see anything, but I started to call, listen, and walk. When I was opposite the church about a block from the schoolhouse, I called again and listened. I thought I heard a faint cry. It could have been my imagination. It seemed to come from the direction of the church. As I walked closer, my call was answered by "Daddy," and he was coming around the end of the church. He ran into my arms crying, "I'm lost!" He told me that when he came to the church he didn't know the way home so he decided to stay there until someone came for him. He said, "Daddy, when you took me hunting, you said if I ever became lost, do not move. Stay there and somebody would find me."

I put him on my shoulder and started toward home. When we paused under the street light, it was only a blur at 30 feet. We finally ran into the garage door that was on the far side of the house. We stopped to thank God for his deliverance. His mother really praised him for his presence of mind, but got a firm promise he would never start out on his own again. Later, Mrs. Minor, the teacher, told us that Dallas, being a Scorpio, was delightful but difficult to handle. If you told him not to do something he would be apt to do it just to show he could. He also resented any questioning. These characteristics were evident all through his adolescent years.

Horses and sleds were the only means of travel in the rural areas. It had turned cold, often never getting above 10 degrees below zero during the day. Horses were breathing freezing air while working. There was an epidemic of distemper. For two weeks I was busy inoculating horses with distemper serum. I was waiting in the Felt store to be picked up by a sled to make the rounds of the community. Grade-school children were arriving at the schoolhouse. The first arrivals were three bundled-up children riding on a sled drawn by four dogs. The teacher unharnessed the dogs and tied them up in the barn. While I was watching I heard a deep bark, more like a baying. It was getting louder and louder. There was a 6-year-old in a sleeping bag on a very wide sled. The teacher tied up a big, long-legged wooly dog. He was a cross between a Great Dane and some long-haired dog.

The teacher said, "He is nine years old and this is the third child of the family that he has carried to school."

The Driggs librarian handed me a small book.

"Mr. Cross, you might be interested in this. You can't check it out, and you will have to read it in my presence. We guard it with our lives."

It was an interesting and revealing history of Teton County. I found out from questioning old-timers that the author had been a small, weaselly person who associated with few people. They said he was always slipping around watching people, not doing anything but looking. In fact, he was a snooper.

He mentioned the shooting of a farmer over a dispute about irrigation water from Darby Creek. He told about an Englishman who settled in the early days in the valley. He wanted to be a big cattleman, but he didn't last long. He thought branding was cruel so to identify his cattle he had their horns painted. Neighboring cattlemen with rustling instincts cut off the horns and applied their own brands. The Englishman was broke in five years and left.

He also mentioned a mysterious disappearance of a young, good-looking black man shortly after World War I. He hinted but didn't mention names, saying that it was because the man had been intimate with a wife or wives, someone had killed him. This was still mentioned when I was in Driggs 20 years later. The young black had a room next to a furnace in a building he looked after. He was very likable and did windows and yard work. Everything was found intact in his room, even his wallet and money were in bureau drawers. Authorities did a lot of checking and no trace of him or any violence was found. Pete Roberts had a very pretty wife and people suspected Pete because it was reported that she and the missing man were very friendly.

The sneaky author mentioned who was carrying on with each other and even hinted at the fathering of some children. When I asked Claude's father about the author, his reaction was, "He was a dirty, sneaking rat. He brought up all of the transgressions of people in the valley. I was on the committee that gave him 24 hours to pack up and leave or he would disappear." He did leave and no one ever heard of him again.

Ethel and I were close friends of Pete and his wife. They were a close, affectionate couple. Pete retired and moved to California a year before I left Driggs.

Byron Nelson and Pete had been inseparable for over 30 years. They fished and hunted together. Byron and I were going elk hunting. I was driving and started to turn into a little road off the main highway.

"Don't go up that road. I will never use that road."

"It is on account of Pete, isn't it?"

"Yes."

"You have kept this secret so long it would be a relief to tell about it and get it off your mind. You know me well enough to know that I will not report what you say."

"Pete is dead now so I suppose it is all right to tell about it. It was late at night when Pete drove up to my house and knocked on my door. My wife was away visiting in the valley and I was alone. He said, 'Come with me.' When I went to his car there was a quilt covering something in the back seat. We drove up that road and stopped where there was a lava outcrop. He said, 'I have a place fixed for him.' We carried the body about 200 feet from the road. There was a hole in the lava about 5-feet deep. We dumped the body in and covered it with rock that Pete had piled up. With shovels we covered the rocks with dirt that was also piled up. It started to snow as we were leaving and continued to snow, which hid all evidence and baffled authorities."

WES

My cousin Wesley (Frog) Wharton was six years younger than me. The Whartons lived in Hagerman Valley on a dairy ranch bordering Snake River and the upper Salmon Falls. We had spent many pleasant hours together fishing, hunting, and gathering arrow heads. The name "Frog" was attached to him when he started to imitate a bullfrog perfectly when he was in the fourth grade. There was no reason for him to be only 5-feet, 6-inches tall and weigh only 135 pounds. His parents were both good-sized. They had brown eyes and dark hair. He had grey eyes and light hair. His mother said, "He is the spittin' image of his grandfather Cross." Wes was downright smart and seemed to learn without any effort. This may be the reason he never extended himself in high school. Evidently it bothered him that he was small, as he never would take any guff from anyone.

I knew that Wes had enlisted for one of those one-year enlistments that came out just before we declared war on Germany. I was surprised to hear his voice on the phone say, "Hello, cuz."

"Where are you? The last time I heard you were in the South learning how to shoot a cannon."

"I'm in Pocatello and need a ride"

"Wes, the roads are bare and I can be there in 2 hours. I'm on my way." I called Ethel and told her we would be home in time for dinner.

Wes had a 10-day furlough before shipping out. It had been eight months since he had seen his folks. They were now in Seattle working in the shipyards. He had already used three days leave and would arrive in Seattle with only a few hours to spend before having to start back. With us he would have four days. He looked very sharp in his Corporal stripes.

The next day in overalls and warm jacket he had fun herding and loading hogs. We shot ducks and he got a goose. We let him sleep in the mornings and just relax.

He complained to Ethel that his father almost never wrote to him and asked Ethel if she would write, as he felt left out when he didn't get any mail. From then on she sent him a letter every two weeks and we received replies from his numerous assignments of duty. His year of enlistment turned into over 300 days under fire in three years. Wes could hit a rock chuck in the eye at a hundred feet with a .22. His captain said that he was a genius with directing artillery fire and could hit and destroy with uncanny accuracy.

The only way I could get Wes to talk about his war experiences

195

was after a couple of drinks. His battery knocked out the first two lead tanks in a Kasserine pass. He said, "We pulled into place at night. The trucks that hauled us left. Our orders were to destroy the enemy or else." This information I learned after the war.

His next stop was the invasion of Sicily. In his letters to Ethel he kept asking her to send him soap. She would send six bars at a time. She asked him what he was doing with all that soap. He wrote, "Cousin Ethel, you can sleep with a whole family in Italy for a bar of soap."

He went into France shortly after D-Day. He wrote that he was tired of drinking wine and asked for a bottle of White Horse Scotch. Our postmistress was a strict Mormon. It was her privilege to inspect all parcels sent to soldiers. She refused to allow any liquor to be sent to soldiers. In fact, she even boasted about it in church. A solution came to me while I was getting a haircut. I asked the barber for a Fitch shampoo bottle that he had just emptied. I had Wes write a letter requesting some Fitch shampoo for a dandruff problem. I washed the bottle and filled it with Scotch, adding some red food coloring to make it look like Fitch shampoo. I wrapped it in cotton doused with a little Coty L'Oregon perfume and took it in its packing and box to the post office. She read his letter, sniffed the bottle, and said it would be O.K. to send it.

When Wes received the package, he and seven others were at a rest camp in France. He said, "That damned cousin Virg has sent me shampoo!" Rolly Powers reached over and took the bottle and unscrewed the lid. He poured a little in his hand and tasted it. "It's Scotch! Get the captain!"

THE PIG PEN

It was during late December of the second year of World War II that FBI Agent Bannister called while I was out treating a cow for milk fever. He told my secretary that he would call me at home at 7 o'clock.

The phone rang at exactly seven. Bannister said, "Someone is making unauthorized wireless transmissions from a powerful long-range transmitter. The calls are originating in Teton Valley. Triangulation places the calls near or on the Heindrick Mueller ranch. We have had operators posing as phone company employees visit the farm, but they could find no evidence of any wireless equipment. It would have to have a tall antenna, but since the calls are made at night it could be retractable."

Heindrick was a prime suspect, as he was a German immigrant just before World War II. He had children and grandchildren, some were in the armed services. I found it hard to believe because he was such a kindly, friendly man. He had called me many times for assistance and I had been invited to lunch with him and his wife.

On my visit to Mueller's a few days later, I looked at the wiring. The farm was unusually well wired. The FBI was sure that the wireless was not in the house. Bannister advised me to look for power lines going somewhere for other than light or heat connections. The hog shed and pens had a light in the low ceiling. That was normal, as it became pitch-dark by 5 o'clock due to the mountain peaks on the east. I reported to Bannister that I couldn't find any evidence. It was hard for me to believe that Mueller was involved in espionage.

The schoolhouse was the meeting place for the Grange. It was relatively close to the Mueller ranch. The Grange lecturer had scheduled me to talk at their Friday meeting about new rationing restrictions. Due to blocked roads I had two choices. One, to drive back to the north on the other side of the river, a distance of about 20 miles. The roads were icy and a rut or a wrong turn of the wheel would leave me stuck in deep snow. The alternative was to drive 2 miles south of Driggs, park my car in Charley Alben's farm yard, put on my snowshoes and snowshoe 2 miles and cross the hard-frozen Teton River. I chose the latter because I thought it would be a surer way of getting home that night.

My half-hour talk was well received and the Grangers took part in a discussion. I stayed for the closing ceremony but skipped the refreshments. It had begun to blizzard and I would have to face a blinding snow. Since I had open country to cross, it would be difficult to find my way. A section fence line that ran east across the river was near Mueller's ranch. I walked my way down the road to the fence. If I followed it, I could not get lost.

There is no way you can cross a fence with snowshoes on. As I was rebuckling my snowshoes after crossing the fence, the lights came on in the farm yard a short block away. The blinding snow shielded me and I moved silently closer. Heindrick was forking off the clear area in the large pig pen.

Hogs, if allowed enough room, are the cleanest of farm animals. They have a place to eat, to sleep, and a place for their toilet. I was against the haystack to avoid making a silhouette. Heindrick opened a trap door and disappeared from sight. A long, thin rod with a ball on top of it slowly emerged. I had seen enough. It was a good thing I had decided on the fence line. It was almost impossible to see more than a few feet ahead.

The coal fire in the heater at home made me appreciate being warm and cozy. Snow is beautiful and we looked forward to it. It left the world bright and clean. Ethel helped me take off my coat.

"Honey, would you like a cup of hot cocoa?"

"Darling, that would be absolutely super."

We sat in the kitchen discussing why someone who had enjoyed the freedom and bounty of the United States and had grandsons in the service would be disloyal.

Ethel said, "People seem to have a strong loyalty to their mother country."

"Honey, I'm dead tired. Let's go to bed."

The next morning at 8 o'clock, I called Bannister from my home, as I did not want anyone to know of my involvement in the case. That morning they took Heindrick to Pocatello. Two days later he was back home. I asked the sheriff, "Why did they turn him loose?"

"His monthly reports were really harmless, as he didn't have any access to damaging information. He isn't really turned loose. They gave him his choice of staying on that side of the river and never coming to town or going to Federal prison. So I have to check on him."

HUNTING

The war had brought on ration cards for food and gas. Red stamps were issued for food. If you were not very careful, you ran out of stamps for meat before the end of the month. Claude had four big sons and a daughter, and he hunted mostly for meat. Sometimes we just hunted for fun and did not shoot anything.

It was early in October. There was no snow. Frost had painted the aspen, ashes, willows, and maples. They were colorful and beautiful interspersed among the green spruce and pine trees. At 7 o'clock in the morning, the sun had not appeared over the high mountain peaks, but by nine it was warm and bright, with no wind. We stopped and sat back against a large pine to rest and eat some of our corned beef sandwiches. We were about a block above a small stream flowing through the mountain meadow. Claude whispered, "I hope nothing comes by today."

I said, "Let's just sit here and see what comes by."

There was a long period of almost absolute stillness, broken occasionally by the call of a Canadian jay, the cawing of a crow, or the hum of a bee belatedly trying to gather honey.

"Bears," whispered Claude, pointing. A mother bear with her twin cubs was coming leisurely down the hill toward us. Fortunately, the wind was blowing toward us and she didn't get our scent. She did stand up and take a hard look at us for several seconds. Satisfied that we were part of the landscape, she started to feed. She broke open rotten logs for grubs. The cubs began to play, wrestling and chasing each other. They would stand up and bat each other as if they were boxers. One climbed up on a short stump and they took turns being king on the mountain. They sneaked up behind the mother and nipped her, trying to get out of the way of her wide swinging paw. They never made it. She was too quick and would send them rolling. Then they would come back whimpering for their hurt feelings, and she would nuzzle and lick their faces. We watched and laughed silently for over an hour. The sow and cubs ambled down the slope into a patch of timber.

Another time we were hunting and stopped under a tree to rest and eat lunch. A twig cracked above us and Claude whispered, "Squirrel." I nodded. Then there was a big crack above us. We jumped to our feet and looked up into the tree. There was a half-grown bear cub with his hind feet straddling the tree trunk, peering down at us with his shiny black eyes.

Claude said, "He is almost too young to live through the winter, and he doesn't want to be a rug." We left a sandwich and an apple for him and went on hunting.

I am most proud of our outsmarting two young bull elk after they had fooled us for three weeks. We were hunting in the east hills of the Tetons about 20 miles from the north end of the valley. There was just enough snow to track. About a mile up the hill we ran across the tracks of two elk. We could see they were in no hurry, as they were nipping and browsing as they walked along.

"Virg, they will probably lie down in the next mile. They will probably circle back about a hundred yards below their tracks and watch their back-track. When we reach their tracks they will run over the top ridge." Claude followed the tracks and I paralleled him, walking about a hundred feet below him. Claude soon came to a sudden halt when there was a crash, crash. They had back-tracked above their tracks rather than below. We knew they were headed for their winter quarters in the game preserve 30 miles away.

The next Sunday we found their tracks about 8 miles farther along the ridge. This time I went on the hill above the tracks and they had back-tracked below. We followed their tracks two more times. If they came to a small open space only a few feet across, they slipped around the opening. Large open spaces were crossed at a dead run. On the other side they would stop in cover and leave when we entered the opening. If we followed them up a trail they would stop behind a tree and watch the trail with part of their heads showing. All we got to see were tracks.

It was the last day of the season. The snow was a foot deep and we were on snowshoes. We found their tracks and sure enough, they were headed for the game refuge only a few miles away.

Claude grinned. "Now we have them. They will circle back toward the refuge. After we jump them they will go over this hill and cut back. If we can travel fast enough, we can run over the hill and wait for them to come by."

You don't really run on snowshoes. It is a fast, shuffling walk. There was just enough time to catch our breath when we saw them coming down the small valley below us.

"We finally fooled them and we have them cold."

"Is your locker full of meat?"

"It won't hold much more."

"They will be bigger next year." He turned on his snow shoes and I followed.

Claude and I had E.S.P. that was manifested in our ability to anticipate what the other would do when we were separated while hunting. As a result, we kept our lockers full of elk and deer meat all through the war years. Claude believed in a hereafter and reincarnation. He remarked more than once that we had known each other in a different time.

We were going hunting in Jackson Hole. While we were driving up the Gros Ventre River, Claude stopped the pickup.

"Have you ever been up this river before?"

"No, this is my first trip."

"Virg, you have been up it before. See that point ahead of us? Close your eyes and tell me what is around the bend." I closed my eyes.

"There is a small stream with a beaver dam. There is a steep bank and a lean-to."

Claude started the pickup. Around the bend was a small stream, an old beaver dam, and the rotten remnants of a log lean-to against a cut bank.

"Virg, we were mountain men and we wintered here."

I didn't know what to think.

THE FAMILY

The six years in Teton County were happy, pleasant years for the Crosses. Ethel and I fly-fished together on the Teton and Snake Rivers. In the 1940s, these were two of the prime fly-fishing streams in the United States. We were wading and fishing abreast on the Madison. I said something about the way she was casting. She paid no attention to my remark. I repeated the statement again. At times Ethel had a short fuse, and this was one of the times.

"I don't need you," she said as she played and netted a 16-inch trout. "Go fish somewhere else."

"All right. I'll leave you alone, but you will be sorry." I waded upstream and was casting for a large trout that was dimpling for mayflies close to a large rock. Ethel yelled and I heard the splash of a big fish. She had hooked a lunker. She handled the series of shaking leaps expertly.

"Virg, honey, you have to help me! Will you net him for me?"

"No way. Quote: I don't need you. Unquote. I said you would be sorry."

Ethel continued to play the 23-inch trout until it was completely worn out, getting madder by the minute. She was afraid that if she tried to net it, she would lose it.

"If you don't net this fish right now, you will really be sorry!"

"How come?"

"How come, you will sleep on the davenport for at least 15 days."

I netted the fish.

In the winter there were weekly dances, card parties, and dinners. Ethel, with her beauty, intelligence, and interesting personality, was very popular. She was an excellent dancer and we enjoyed dancing together very much. Sometimes she would whisper in my ear while we were dancing close together, "I wish we didn't have to trade dances."

In January of 1940, Ethel took Dallas and went to visit her parents in Hollywood for two weeks. One of her friends from Hollywood high school days was in the movies. She had a minor part in a film which was a super production. She invited Ethel to attend the party celebrating successful completion of the film. Ethel was thrilled about meeting the superstars and producers at the party. She thought she really would have some exciting things to tell me when she came home. She did, but not what she thought it would be.

I met her train in Pocatello. I sensed something was wrong from the way she acted. She cried as she rushed into my arms.

"Honey, you must be glad to see me."

"I was never so glad or relieved to see anyone!" She clung close to me and gave me a pat or a squeeze every now and then. We ate at our favorite restaurant in Rexburg on the way home. Dallas was hungry and really stuffed himself. As soon as he settled into the car he fell asleep in his mother's arms.

"It is so good to be home and safe with you," Ethel remarked as we entered and closed the front door. Dallas hardly woke up as we changed him into his sleepers.

We were young and had been nearly a month apart. Our lovemaking was spontaneous. Afterward, she began to cry in my arms. I finally coaxed her into talking about what had happened.

She and Delphine had been invited to the movie party. The dignitaries mixed and there were introductions by Delphine to many actors and personnel.

"The dinner was filet mignon and everything else. I drank only one glass of wine. The dance was fun and I never had to sit out. Delphine was popular also. A couple of handsome, distinguished-looking men of about 40 years came up and asked us for a dance. We both had been asked to go away from the dance floor into rooms. Some were rude and insistent. We were talking about taking a taxi home when these two asked us to dance. My partner was very nice, polite, and a good dancer. I was hot and perspiring after the dance. He said, 'Wait here and I'll bring you a drink.' They brought us drinks. They were good and cold, and we practically gulped them down.

"Almost immediately I felt woozy and said, 'I'm dizzy.' He took my arm and led me into a room that had a huge bed. I could barely sit up on the bed. Right away Delphine joined me. They locked the door and undressed us. I was too numb and woozy to get up. I can remember their laughter as they took turns using us. Sometimes I passed out.

"It was 6 o'clock when I woke up and shook Delphine awake. We took a taxi home and took a douche as soon as possible. The extra week was to see if I was pregnant and it was wonderful when I found out that I was all right. Delphine was not so lucky; she is having an abortion.

"Do anything you want to me, but don't divorce me because I love you so much."

I was silent for some time.

"You could not help what happened and you should not be punished for that. I will not hold it against you and we will never mention it again. However, because you went to the party without your husband or his consent, you will sleep on the davenport for two weeks, so get your pillow and move!" She kissed me and moved to the davenport.

On the second day I noticed a big calendar in the kitchen with two days blotted out in red. Each day she made a dramatic marking out of the day at breakfast time. She was so pretty, nice, and sweet during this period that I was tempted every night to have her come back to bed.

Two weeks later on Friday noon, she asked, "What are you looking so smug and self-satisfied about?"

"Honey, you will soon see. Mrs. Sheets is going to come through that door in about 15 minutes. You will just have time to pack your bag. She will take care of Dallas and we are going to Idaho Falls for the weekend to celebrate." She grabbed me and I kissed her through tears of joy.

The two days alone in Idaho Falls were spent dining, dancing, and just loving. We planned to have our children four years apart so we wouldn't have more than one in college at a time.

Ethel said, "I didn't bring anything. I thought it would be a wonderful time to start a baby." That's how our son Lary was conceived. His birthday was within 11 days of Dallas'.

When our daughter, Susan, was 15, she said to her mother, "I wasn't a love baby like Dallas and Lary."

"You were very much a planned love baby. Shall I tell you about it or would you rather have Daddy do it?"

"Let Daddy do it. He tells the best stories."

"Well, Susan," I said, "it was like this. We thought you would arrive that day. In fact, we had been expecting you for a week because you had been kicking impatiently and vigorously for days. We were having breakfast and looking out the window toward the hospital two blocks away. Your grandmother Tobey with a supposedly weak heart had come up to help. We watched a car drive up to the hospital and Dr. Hoffman emerged, wearing rolled-down hip boots.

"Ethel said, 'I'm feeling great but I hope he doesn't leave town.'

"He is going duck hunting on the river.

"'Well, I hope he doesn't go very far.' She had finished a good breakfast of ham, eggs, and hashbrowns of my making when Dr. Hoffman got into his car and drove off. Ten minutes later she said, 'I have a big pain!' In 15 minutes she had her bag packed and was in the hospital.

"The nurse had gone to Idaho Falls about the same time. Her replacement was due to be there in a few minutes, the cook and cleaning woman told me. The telephone rang, and she answered it. I heard her say, 'Oh, my! Oh, my! The doctor is hunting at Kunz's, the other nurse is gone and Mrs. Cross is in labor!' The nurse had called from Idaho Falls saying that she had car trouble and would be an hour late.

"I jumped into the Chevrolet and took off for the east side of the river. It had been raining and snowing. The dirt road was barely passable. I gunned going through low places, hoping to have enough

204

momentum to reach the knolls. When I came up a slight hill, there was the doctor's car, sunk in mud to the hubcaps, blocking the road. He was not in sight. He did respond to the honking of my horn. It was a relief to see him sloughing through the snow and mud!

"He drove and I pushed to get his car turned around on top of the knoll. (In fact, I got a hernia from that.) He let me off at our house, as I was plastered with mud from pushing while the wheels were spinning. I didn't dare tell my mother-in-law about the situation on account of her weak heart. There was barely time to get washed up and into clean clothes, when the phone rang. Dr. Hoffman asked me to come over as quickly as I could. I ran to the hospital, anticipating the worst. Dr. Hoffman told me, 'Wash up and put on this gown. You are either going to deliver or give the ether.'

"Your mother begged for more ether, saying I was stingy. Fifteen minutes later you arrived, squalling your head off. We washed you in the sink, tied off the cord, diapered, and dressed you. I did much of this while the doctor was attending your mother. You were a beautiful baby with lots of hair and your mother was very happy that you were a girl. When I visited her later, she said that you were an eager eater. She sent me back home to fetch her knitting."

"Daddy, that is a good story about my birthday, but it has nothing to do with my being a love baby."

"O.K. About that. It was on a clear, cold wintery February day. The clock said a few minutes after 11. The phone rang in my office. I picked up the receiver and said, 'County agent's office. How can I help you?' The voice on the other end of the line purred, 'Oh, you can help me all right, darling! I have an idea.'

"Again?"

"Lary is three years old and I think it would be nice to have a baby around the house. This one a daughter and our last one."

"You want me to come home now?"

"No, darling. Wait until noon."

"So I said, 'Get into bed.' I started throwing clothes as soon as I had closed the front door. When we were through, I asked, 'How about lunch?' and Ethel answered, 'You get lunch, dear. I have to keep my hips up on a pillow for at least 20 minutes.'"

"Well, Daddy, I was a love baby after all!"

JAN

Jan was another English setter after Trigger. She always left the house at 5 minutes to 5 o'clock which was the time I left the office. She went to Ernie Weston's service station just across the street from the courthouse. There she waited inside until I came for the car. I noticed that evening she was not there. When I got home, I asked, "Where is Jan?"

"She left here just a few minutes ago to meet you."

I walked the two blocks back to the station and asked Ernie if he had seen her.

"I was busy fixing a car in the shop and I had only one customer around 5 o'clock. I think they were the bigwig speakers for the church conference from Ogden. Bishop Fulmer was talking to his brother when I went back into the shop."

It never occurred to me that the high church official would steal a dog. Besides, I had taken him pheasant hunting on the Blackfoot Indian Reservation and he remembered what a wonderful dog Jan was.

It had been snowing heavily all day and visibility was almost zero. The sheriff was stationed at one end of the valley and Chief of Police Arden Stevens at the other. They were checking cars, looking for a murder suspect. When I asked about cars leaving the valley, they reported they had checked one car between 5 and 6 o'clock and it was the car from Ogden.

I refereed high school basketball games and the coach and his wife were friends of ours. When I told him of the theft, he said, "I'll check the yards of those people when I go to Ogden." He was a Mormon, but he did believe in fair play. A few weeks later, he called on me. He had just returned from a visit to Ogden. He said, "Jan is in the Fulmer's fenced yard." I contacted Atchley, the prosecuting attorney, and he sent a telegraphic warrant to the Ogden sheriff. It was received by a cousin of the thief. The report came back, "There is no dog in his yard."

I was on the lookout for his return to Driggs. Sure enough, on the opening day of fishing, Claude and I saw his car parked just off the road by the Buxton Bridge. It was unlocked. The bridge had no railing. When we started to fish, only the roof of that car was sticking out of the water. It bore a note saying "DOG THIEF." No report was made to the police on the matter. Fulmer never returned to Driggs.

POTATOES

The high altitudes of the upper Snake River counties were almost ideal for growing certified or disease-free seed potatoes for the commercial growers to plant. The cold weather kept down the insect population which spread potato diseases. A diseased potato plant yields less.

Dad was nearly 70, and he and Mother wanted to move back to Idaho away from the smoke, noise, and dirt of the city. His retirement pension from the city would be adequate for them to live on, but they did not have enough, even with selling the small farm, to buy a lot and a decent house in town.Their savings were not very substantial because they helped Farrell to rear his two motherless children and he lived with them. Dad's sister, Nell, who had married the millionaire Flagg, was left almost destitute when he jumped out of the window during the 1929 market crash. Nell was existing in a single room in a cheap rental district of Los Angeles, and she would ask for money to live on. Dad would send her some. This was quite a come-down from the mansion, servants, and three cars they had when I visited them a few years earlier.

Soil will stand only a few crops of potatoes. The yield will drop down so low that it is unprofitable to plant them.

It was time to leave Teton County because it was listed as a training county. Dean Iddings was a tightwad and bragged about about how many with doctor's degrees he had on the staff and how little they were costing the university. I was offered openings but he actually had applicants bid against each other. When Idaho Falls had an opening, he gave me first choice.

"Dean, John Robertson got $2,800 and I am better than he is, but I'll go for $2,800."

"Tommy Chester will go for $2,600. If you will accept that amount, the job is yours." That was only $200 more a year for a larger county and more work.

"Let Tommy have it." Teton County's fishing and hunting was too good to leave for $200 a year. Ethel was eager to get away from Teton County because the Crosses did not fit into the predominately L.D.S. society. Several incidents of prejudice bothered us. The Relief Society was presenting a Christmas pageant. Dallas was to recite "The Night Before Christmas." When Stake President Choules found out that the son of a non-Mormon had the lead, he ordered that Dallas be removed. Five days before the play, the new lead did not know his lines. Dallas said, "I can do it," and was restored. His rendition was perfect. I had worked closely with the church, spending a lot of volunteer time. When my valued dog, Jan, was stolen by a high-ranking church official from Ogden, it left a very sour taste in my mouth.

Claude Dalley and I were planting seed potatoes. Teton County has a short growing season. It was necessary to get the potatoes in as early as possible. Springs were very unpredictable, as you might get snow in June. It was a calm, clear Saturday morning. Claude was driving the tractor and I was making sure the slots were full of the cut potatoes that dropped the cut set into the ground. We were laughing because the first row went diagonally across the field. Claude had lined up on a white rock that was in line with a tip of the Grand Teton towering above everything to the east. Closer scrutiny revealed that the white rock was a white horse grazing from left to right, and Claude had been driving toward it. He sighted on an inanimate object on the return. I could not look up, as I was busy feeding cut potatoes into the slots. When the tractor stopped, there was Bishop Murdock walking toward us.

"I wonder what he wants us to do?"

Claude said, "We are not going to help him until after we finish planting the potatoes."

The bishop said, "Hello," shook hands with brother Dalley and brother Cross. We knew some request for help was coming. He said the church was behind in its Boy Scout contribution to Salt Lake and he wanted us to stop and solicit funds.

"We will finish planting tomorrow. I will take a day of my annual leave on Monday to do it," I told him.

"We want it done now, as it is supposed to be in the mail tonight."

"It is very important that we get these potatoes planted now, as it may storm. This is important to me and the welfare of my family."

"The church comes first ahead of the family."

I saw red. "I have worked very hard for your church. From now on I will do nothing to help and I free myself from any obligation to the church. And you can get the hell out of here before I lose my temper!" The bishop tried to placate me, but Claude, knowing me, told him to leave.

We had just started the next row when we heard a scream. We turned to look and Murdock was rolling on the ground, holding his penis. He had stopped to pee in the fence corner and had hit the wire of our new electric fence. When we reached him, he was lying on his back, holding it and moaning. The electric shock caused him to ejaculate all over himself. What he was holding was long, red, and swollen. After we watched him stagger to his car, Claude said, "No wonder he has had six kids in nine years. I'll bet Mrs. Murdock gets a rest tonight."

"Now he knows how a bull feels when they collect semen with an electric prod."

During the previous two years, Claude and I had raised 20 acres of certified seed potatoes together and we had made money and enjoyed the working partnership. His son, Alvin, wanted to farm with him and we dissolved the friendly partnership. I had bought a John Deere tractor that ran on stove oil. It had been on an irrigation pump. An unexpectedly cold night had frozen and broken the radiator. It would not start. The owner went broke and it had been sitting mired down in a field. I bought it for $200 and had it hauled in to the tractor dealer. He said, "You will have to work on it, as we are full up until May."

I took it apart, checked everything, and ended up putting on a new radiator hose and gaskets. Now I had the power which Claude had previously furnished. There was enough of my share of unsold seed to plant 40 acres. I thought about how to get my father involved so he could make some money and feel that he had earned it. With a suitable piece of land he could irrigate it with my help, and rogue out the diseased plants so that it would pass the rigid inspection of the Idaho Crop Association.

Larry Hatch, who owned a large dry farm, was also a supervisor of the AAA (Agricultural Adjustment Act). Larry had some of his farm land almost due east of Driggs, about 3 miles away. It bordered the Wyoming State line. The foothills of the Grand Tetons started to rise about a half-mile farther east. There was about 40 acres in alfalfa hay that was irrigated. Alfalfa, a soil builder, had been there for nearly 20 years. The soil would be ideal for a potato crop except that it was infested with pocket gophers. You could not step without stepping on a gopher mound. Larry had left it in hay, as the gophers would ruin almost any other crop.

Quite often we went together to meetings in Idaho Falls, Boise, and Pocatello. I really bugged him trying to rent it. Finally, I said in desperation sometime in early February, "Why don't you rent me that land?"

"Virg, you want it real bad. You've asked me how much I will take for rent. The answer is, plenty."

"Larry, actually I'd be doing you a favor. I'd have to kill all of those damn gophers, as they go right down a row and eat all of the roots off. After I've killed the gophers, you will have 40 more acres of prime wheat land."

"Virg, I won't say that you won't get it. I want to think about it. There may be some way that I could use that piece of ground in a better way."

"Larry, you know damned well it is to your advantage to rent that land to me for one year."

He just grinned and said, " It's a long way to planting time." We were both feeling pretty good, as we each had won over $200 in the weekly poker game.

On the way back we stopped at a restaurant in Firth that served super barbequed ribs. There was a 4-5-6 dice game going on in the back room. It was wartime and money flowed like water. I wanted to go on home, but he insisted that we each try $20. Dice were never my forte and I didn't last 10 minutes. Larry couldn't lose. When he threw a 4-5-6 and got the dice, he asked, "Go in with $100 with me and we will be the dealer."

"No. But I will pay and collect while you roll the dice. I'm good at counting and watching and I've got big pockets in my coat to stuff bills in. I'm sure you are going to clean up this bunch of crooks."

Everybody laughed. Larry plunked down $100 in bills for the bank. It was covered immediately and he threw a natural, letting the bank ride. For six straight rolls he won and they had covered his bet each time. He won steadily for over 20 rolls. A player with a $5 bet threw a natural and Larry said, "I'll give you $50 for the dice." The fellow jumped at the chance. I had a pile of twenties, fifties and a few hundreds in front of me. I was also stuffing bills in the pockets of my large sheepskin coat. Finally the big money boys quit or backed off, leaving only the little players betting $20 or less.

I wanted to go home. It was nearly one o'clock in the morning and we had 2 hours of icy roads to cover. I gave him wads of bills which he stuffed into his pockets.

"Larry, we are leaving."

"O.K. There isn't much left here. Virg, you have to drive." He had been drinking and was quite high. He had me turn on the dome light and started to count his winnings. When he was through counting, he exclaimed, "There is over $12,000! What a night!"

"Larry, reach into my pocket." It was crammed with bills. "When you get that pocket counted, you can count the other pocket."

When he finished, he sat there grinning. "This is going to give banker Steve Meikle a pain."

"Why will it bother Steve?"

"This is about the amount I would borrow to finance this year's crop at 10 percent. On top of that, I'm not going to give you one damn cent. You had your chance." He sat there and laughed.

"You tight-fisted, skinflint S.O.B," I thought.

"Virg, you offered me $2,000 for rent for the 40 acres. It would be to my advantage for you to try to clean up the gophers. If you can, I'll let you have it for free. If you tell me when you want it plowed and disced, I'll do it on the day you name, as I will have my spring planting finished." I reached out my right hand for the handshake and I could have kissed him.

I wrote a long letter to my father explaining the situation and said I would need him as a partner to supervise, irrigate, and rogue out diseased plants during the growing season, from April to September. His reply was a joyous response. The county physician, his chess-playing partner, had given him a recommendation for six months at

210

high altitude for his health. He had never missed a day at work and had six month's leave coming.

He arrived on April Fool's Day. The next day he was cutting up carrots into thin, 3-inch long strips. When I came home from work that night, he had nearly 5 gallons of strips. The next day, Saturday, we took them out to the infested field. The carrot strips were lightly dusted with strychnine. We found the gopher tunnels by poking a rod near their mounds, and put three or four poisoned carrot strips in each tunnel.

"Virg, you said the gophers store food in the form of roots for the non-growing season. If they store the carrots, when will it kill them?"

"Dad, they carry the carrots to their storehouses in the pockets on each side of their mouth. They have to bite the sticks in two to get them in their mouths, and that is when the poison gets to them."

"You said to put three to five sticks in each tunnel. Does that kill more than one gopher?"

"They are very antisocial and live alone. Each has his own set of tunnels and storehouse. After they mate they separate and if a female, which is larger, encounters a male, she tries to kill him."

At first it seemed hopeless, as new mounds kept appearing. Every day Dad poisoned and trapped. The boys and I helped on weekends. By the first of May, the 40 acres were almost gopher free. Larry Hatch brought in his seven-gang plow and plowed and disced it in half a day on schedule. Dad had never run a tractor. He practiced running the pufferbilly, as he called the big John Deere. We hooked it up to an eight-section harrow. He was just finishing at noon and he had double harrowed it twice.

"Son, it would take a week with a team of horses!" Planting went along smoothly. Dad did an excellent job of irrigating and roguing. He was happy to be able to work outdoors, free from stress. We enjoyed each other's company, as we could fish once or twice a week, play chess and checkers. It was a pleasure to watch and care for a promising bumper potato crop. Mother joined us in June for her two-month vacation.

"Ora," he said to her, "we may be able to get a break at last. If everything goes well, we may be able to make enough to go back to Idaho next year."

"Al, that would be wonderful!"

Being conservative, I said, "We should get at least $5,000 apiece if we can harvest this crop."

In July the rows were almost touching and it looked to me to be the best certified field in the county. The next week there was unusually hot weather coupled with heavy rain clouds that traveled up the Columbia to the Snake and eastward to the Tetons. It was about 10 o'clock Sunday morning when the big black cloud came in from the west. It started to hail with hailstones nearly an inch across. It was so sudden and so fierce that in half an hour waist-high grain and alfalfa fields were just bits and pieces and stubs. Then came 4 inches of rainfall in an hour. It filled the barrow pits by the roads so deep that for a while only the main highway was open. In 2 hours the sun came out warm and the flood waters had run into the river, leaving the ground almost bare of any vegetation. Battered ground squirrels and gophers were lying dead. I was sick at heart, as it appeared the storm had hit our potato field 3 miles away.

My father was just a born loser. First the oil in Oklahoma, losing his real estate earnings in Texas, the bank going broke at Gooding, and the loss of a big hay crop to the bankrupt alfalfa mill. Again fate had taken away his hope when it seemed that he would have it made.

I was afraid to go look at the field. It was almost 2 o'clock when Dad came over to the house.

"Let's go see if we have to irrigate or if we can fish the rest of the summer."

"Dad, they will come back some. We won't lose any money and we may even make a little." As we drove up the road the 3 miles toward the mountains, there was nothing left of crops on each side of the road. There was just bare ground. I didn't want to turn back to the left and go to our field. We didn't say a word but sat there mutely with hopeless resignation. When we turned to go down into the farm to get to the potato field a quarter of a mile away, I noticed it was very wet. There was damage to the plants, but they were not completely ruined. When we came up over the hill and stopped, there was a very wet potato field but there was not a hole in a leaf. I looked at my father, who said, "I'll be damned!" as he wiped the tears from his eyes.

"Dad, it was bound to hit part of the field. Let's drive down to the far end." There we found that the hail had hit and damaged only about 100 feet across a corner. I could not believe our good fortune.

"Dad, you will not have to irrigate for two weeks. You can fish."

We went home to tell mother. She said she had prayed and she felt everything was going to be all right.

My mother would babysit for us, and Ethel and I were able to get away for a couple of weekends. Teton County is a fairyland in the summer. Everywhere you look is a beautiful scene. The weather is ideal, with cool nights and warm, pleasant days. Ethel's folks came up for two weeks. Dad Tobey had a wonderful time fishing in the Teton and the north fork of the Snake.

About the first week of October, the first frost killed the potato vines so we could dig. Our field had passed the field inspections as disease-free and was in demand. Two large potato growers contracted the crop out of the field at $4.50 per 100-weight which was the Office of Price Administration ceiling. My neighbor, Cliff Wilson, was a retired mining engineer who had spent 20 years in Venezuela oil fields. He was to dig first with his harvesting equipment and then he would dig ours. Because of the war, we had 200 Mexican nationals for farm laborers, which I placed. I could speak Spanish well enough to get by if they spoke slowly, which they didn't. For the first few days things went along smoothly. I dropped by to see when we could expect to harvest.

Cliff said, "Virg, we are going to have trouble. That big Mexican with the blond hair is a labor agitator and he is talking about striking to get more money."

Sure enough, when Cliff had dug enough potatoes for a full day's picking and they were lying on top of the ground, the Mexicans all sat down. They wanted double the money they were getting. The wage for a farm laborer was $5 a day. The Mexicans were making close to $20 a day, and the demand was ridiculous. If the potatoes were not picked that day, they would freeze during the night and be ruined. I tried to get them to pick the field that day and then we could talk about raises, but to no avail. Cliff had driven away in his pickup. When he came back, he pulled out a double-barreled shotgun. The Mexicans were sitting lined along the ditch bank. Cliff cocked the gun and shot down the line just in front of them. Then he told them they would not leave the field until the potatoes were picked and we would talk about raises mañana.

They were housed in good quarters on his ranch and he gave each of the 12 two gallons of milk a day and free vegetables. The next day they came to the field to pick and Cliff said, "Mañana," and shrugged his shoulders. The same process was repeated the following day. In the meantime, I had the agitator pick up his bundle and suitcase and put him on the train in Pocatello with a ticket to El Paso paid for by the Marketing Association. I told the conductor not to let him off under any circumstances until he reached El Paso. He had his wages. I got a call from the Mexican Consul in Salt Lake and the State Department to the effect that I had seriously strained international relations. I called Barber, the county agent leader. He said, "Apologize all over the place verbally and with letters. They can't do a damned thing to you."

Cliff asked the workers to appoint three of their number to speak for them and to meet with him. The result of this parley was if they stayed all through his two weeks' harvesting and did a good job of picking the fields clean, he would give each of them a $50 bonus. I made a similar arrangement for harvesting ours.

Our field was the best-looking field in the county, and when the farmers saw it on the crop tour there were remarks like Golden Johns': "We should have listened more to Virg about raising potatoes." The buyers hauled and weighed the trucks. It was mid-October when we settled up with the buyers.

Dad said, "I have 15 days left on my leave. There is that big trout that I've hooked three times and lost by the Rainey bridge. The city doctor in San Francisco is always bragging about big trout and so far the biggest he has ever caught was only 12 inches. I would like to show him what an Idaho trout looks like. And I want to catch up on my duck hunting for the 20 years I've missed. I have even had dreams about shooting ducks."

He stood by a shock of barley and killed 12 ducks—the limit at that time. He came back all elated.

"What on earth are you going to do with 12 ducks?"

"Son, I'll pick them and dress them and you can put them in your locker." When he had picked four of them, he gave up.

"What can I do with the other eight?"

"You can try to give them to the neighbors." In a short time he came into the house and started to read a book.

"What happened with the other eight ducks?"

"Don't worry about it."

An hour later 8-year-old Dallas came in and said, "I gave them all away. People even thanked me! Where is my $2?" Granddad reached into his pocket and handed over two silver dollars.

Two days later most of the snow had left. The towering Grand Tetons had heavy snow down to their foothills but the valley was almost bare. The weather was warm and pleasant. It was early Friday morning.

Dad said, "I'm leaving tomorrow, much as I hate to. This has been the most wonderful summer of my life."

"As soon as the bank opens, we will go down and settle up. In fact, I'll give you a check for your share." I wrote out a check for a little over $14,000. That much would buy a good 2,000-square foot house in a good neighborhood. He looked at it.

"Is it real?"

"Of course it is real. I'll go to the bank with you and you can cash it."

He endorsed the check and gave it to cashier Merlin Minor, who looked at the signature and said, "How do you want it, Mr. Cross?" Dad still couldn't believe the size of the check.

"I'll take a certified check for $14,000. Give me the remainder in cash, and I would like to have a 100 dollar bill."

On the way back to the house, he said, "This means I can retire next spring, and we can come back to Idaho. It is supposed to be a big secret that you are moving to Jerome the first of January. Evelyn and Norman are there, and we will move there and buy a small acreage. I just can't wait to tell Mama. She will have a hard time believing it!"

Saturday morning I got up at 6 o'clock. We had to leave by eight to get to Pocatello because the Portland Rose left there at 12 and this would give us an hour to spare. While I was cooking hot bisquits and sausage gravy for our breakfast, Dad came out wearing his ragged fishing clothes.

"I thought you would dress in your good clothes. We have to leave at eight to catch the train."

214

"I'm not leaving today. I don't have to leave until Sunday. I don't have to be back on the job until Wednesday. It's a beautiful day and I want to have one last try to catch that big trout."

Ethel said, "There is no use fishing until 10 o'clock when the warmth will cause a late bug hatch." We agreed with her.

When he put his rod together and threaded the line through the guides, I tied on a new silkworm gut leader that had been soaking for 3 hours. The sharpened "County Agent's Special" fly was carefully tied onto the leader. He waded out to a shallow sand bar and cast a few short casts before making a long cast to the far bank with deeper water. The fly hit the bank and bounded off into the water. Immediately there was a big swirl. He set the hook. The big rainbow gyrated in silver leaps followed by long, deep runs. Dad played the lunker perfectly and I netted him after a 15-minute fight. We both exclaimed, "What a fish!" as we admired the 22-inch trout.

"That will really show the doctor what a fish should look like. Let's go home. I want to make a box to keep him iced." I noticed a large swirl about 100 feet downstream.

"Why don't you try for two?"

With the first cast he hooked and landed a twin to his first fish. We put them in a wet burlap sack and headed for home where he dressed the fish and put them in the refrigerator. He made a light-weight box and water-proofed it with an old oil cloth table cover.

Ethel didn't talk a lot but when she did, it really made sense.

"Surely you are going to take the Pullman car. For a dollar or so I'll bet you can get the porter to put the fish in the chef's refrigerator."

"That idea sounds great! For once I'm going first class!"

We got him to the train on time. His next letter said, "The fish reached California in good shape. We are moving to Jerome on July 1st."

MOVING

There were a few minuses for leaving Teton County and going to Jerome as University of Idaho agricultural extension agent (commonly called county agent). I knew I was going to miss Claude Dalley and the wonderful fishing and hunting. On the plus side were a much higher salary, better housing and schools, mild climate, and last but not least, a Presbyterian Church for the family to attend. It was a small, rich farming community. It had been settled right after the very rich Twin Falls area just across the Snake River. An entirely different class of people, mostly from the Midwest, had settled there. The average farmer was well-educated and readily cooperated and sought help from the county agent to improve his farm practices.

A large portion of the rich sedimentary soil in Jerome County was the result of a large dike near Castleford that dammed up the Snake River as it was draining the huge ancient Lake Bonneville, which is now the Great Salt Lake. Wind also deposited rich lava ash soil. Snake River had moved seven times from north to south, a distance of nearly 30 miles. This was caused by the seven lava flows that could be counted in the steep lava walls of Snake River Canyon. Each new eruption would cover the old channel and force the river to find a new channel farther south. The covered channel would not be completely blocked off and as a result there were many underground streams 200 to 400 feet below the surface. These streams came out of the bottom of the cliffs. Many of them, like Blue Lakes, Clear Lakes, Riley Creek, and Thousand Springs, were large enough to be called rivers. The underground aquifers were eventually used for irrigation.

Although Teton County with its hunting, fishing, and lucrative potato seed enterprise was very gratifying, when the offer came for us to move to Jerome, we were ready. Teton County held a big going-away party for us and gave me a jeweled Hamilton railroad watch.

Shortly after Christmas, I visited Jerome. I found a nice three-bedroom house in a desirable location for $7,500. This seemed to be in line with the new $3,000-a-year salary. The $2,500 down payment until we sold the Driggs home came from my poker account. Poker had supplemented my income since college days. I was not an addict, but picked my games based on need. There was a weekly poker game in Driggs during the fall and winter months. The doctor, druggist, county agent, depot agent, and five to six dry farmers usually played. It was a big game, and for me it was an easy game.

Ethel had almost finished an advanced bookkeeping course and would not allow me to mix poker money with the household account, so I had a special poker bank account. She demanded 10 percent of the winnings and none of the losses. I was honest about paying her and she happily deposited her cut in her personal spending account. I had been throwing unopened bank statements in the back of a drawer, and when I went to Jerome and wrote the check for the house, I had only a rough estimate of how much was in the account. On the way home I picked up the latest bank statement. The last one I had looked at was about 60 statements ago.

"Ethel, I wrote a check for $2,500 down payment from my poker account. How much do you think is in it?"

"If you haven't lied to me about your winnings and your losses, I can tell you pretty close." She consulted her ledger. "You should have $4,212." The bank statement showed a balance of a little over $4,000 for the six years of playing. She was pleased with the house.

JEROME

When we moved to Jerome in January, 1945, the war was still going on and farm labor was scarce. Mexican nationals and Jamaicans were brought in to harvest crops. These were housed in segregated quarters on the fairgrounds. There were also 70 German prisoners of war who worked under guard in the fields and were kept in a guarded stockade at night. These prisoners received $1.50 a day. The wage for similar farm work was $4 per day.

As county agent I was in charge of placement of the workers and feeding and housing the Jamaican and Mexican workers. My association with the Jerome County Labor Association went along smoothly. An English-speaking Mexican volunteered and was accepted to supervise the feeding of the Mexicans and two sisters contracted to feed the Jamaicans. The German POWs cooked for themselves.

No one could explain how Pierre and Marie, a displaced couple from Vichy, France, accompanied the German prisoners of war to Jerome County. Marie worked in the Mexican kitchen as a cook. All of the help was warned against using the Mexican toilets because they were infested with crab lice. Apparently, Marie did not heed the warning and she got them. She was acquainted with Dr. Reubel, the veterinarian who worked on stock in the fairgrounds' corrals. It seems that in French rural areas, doctors were scarce and peasants often called on the veterinarians for help. Marie went to Dr. Reubel's office and he asked, "How can I help you?"

Marie said, "I have boogs in the bush." It just happened that there was a heavy infestation of red spider mites on plants in the county. I was conducting a control campaign in newspapers and radio.

"Marie, you don't want to see me. You want to see the county agent." So Marie came to my office.

"How can we help you?" asked my secretary.

"I want to see Mr. Cross about my boogs."

Eleanor ushered her into my office.

"Virg, Marie wants to see you about her boogs."

"What are the bugs like?"

"Mr. Agent, they are like the leetle spidaire."

I, thinking that the boogs were red spiders on Marie's house plants, just happened to have some DDT and lindane in the office. I measured out two heaping teaspoons in a paper sack and told her to mix them with one-half cup of flour, as they were concentrated, and dust on the bush.

Two weeks later when I saw her and asked about the bugs, Marie said, "The boogs are gone from both Pierre and me." Only then did I realize that she had been infected with crabs!

One of the first things Wes Whorton did after he returned home was to visit us in Jerome. He wanted to catch up on all of the hunting that he had been missing. We decided to go deer hunting in the Sawtooths. Our first day of hunting was successful and Wes had killed a buck with a good set of antlers. He said he was tired of camping out, so we rented a cabin on the edge of Sun Valley. When Wes had a few drinks, he ceased to be his quiet, conservative self. He could really spin some wild, embellished tales. We were resting and enjoying an open fire in the fireplace. I rated the following story on a par with Arabian Nights.

He and his driver were in a jeep reconnoitering behind the lines. They stopped to inspect the ruins of a large castle for possible souvenirs. They heard the explosion of bombs. It just happened they were going back in the direction of the explosion. They came upon a truck that had taken a direct hit. The driver and two guards were dead. The scene was littered with $20 bills, much of it in unbroken bundles of $1,000. The payroll truck must have become lost and gone too close to the front.

They had a barracks bag and they hastily stuffed the $1,000 packages into the bottom of the bag and replaced the personal contents on top. There were no other troops visible, so they took off in a hurry. When they were several miles away from the scene, they called in to establish their position well away from the wreckage. The Army found that a large sum of money was missing and did a lot of checking, to no avail. Keeping track and protecting their cache in the barracks took a lot of ingenuity.

The eight remaining members of the original one hundred in the company were in Paris for 10 days rest from the front. Their barracks bag was intact. The first thing they did was to rent a complete 12-room floor of a small hotel. They had agreed not to drink until they were settled in a hotel. They toured several burlesque shows and after considerable bargaining they purchased one show for a week. The manager got $2,000 and each of the girls got $1,000.

The hotel management closed the upper floor. House rules were only one piece of clothing per person after 12 o'clock noon. They were able to order everything from whiskey to steak from the black market. Sometimes they hired small orchestras or combos to play for them to dance. Everything was paid for in cash on the spot. Wes said he was sure they paid as much as $2,000 for one meal.

The morning of the seventh day, they ran out of occupation money and closed shop and moved back to the rest barracks.

"Wes, how much did you spend on that wing-ding?"

"I think $80 to $90 thousand."

I thought his story was full of fantasy and wishful thinking of what might have been.

Some months later I received a request for assistance from Rollie Powers, who was one of the new settlers on the Hunt Project. After we had shaken hands and exchanged greetings, Rollie said, "Virg, I want to thank you for that drink."

"What drink?"

"You are the one that sent Wes a bottle of Scotch in a Fitch shampoo bottle. I was in the same company with Wes all through the war."

"Rollie, you must have been in the party in Paris."

"I was the paymaster."

"Wes said you spent around $90 thousand."

"That figure is low. I know it was closer to $125 thousand. That was a party to end all parties!"

Wes wasn't lying about the party.

Being a county agent in Jerome County was never like work. Everything went along smoothly. It was satisfying to help people and the community while enhancing the worth of the University of Idaho. I was sought after as a speaker and toastmaster. In order to get the information to the people, I had a weekly column in the *North Side News* and a radio program. Tours and schools for different farm practices were well attended. The secret of my success was to get people to take an active part through committees that planned and worked on the programs. For instance, the Granges took over and sponsored the 4-H programs in each community. Twice the county received the award for the best 4-H program in the state. A lot of credit had to be given to my co-worker, Edna Weigen, home demonstration agent. It would be difficult to say how much she contributed to the program. Her work was outstanding.

My sister and her husband, Norman, and children, Earl and Lynda, lived a few blocks away. After my parents retired and moved to Idaho in July, they lived with Evelyn and Norman for a few months until their house was ready. Dallas and Lary always stopped by Grandma's on their way home from school. She always had a glass of milk and a cookie waiting for them.

It was when my father moved to Jerome and was in contact with his three grandsons, Earl Hintze, Lary, and Dallas, that I realized how much he had influenced my own philosophy, conduct, and ethics. His subtle way of teaching the young was to involve them in a discussion by asking questions and guiding and encouraging their thinking. The four were fortunate, as they needed each other. Dad was proud of his healthy, handsome, and intelligent grandsons and enjoyed their company. They would not go fishing, hunting or camping without him. When they camped, he would cook and the boys would do dishes and chores. They also played pinochle with him for nickels and dimes.

He was a master chess player, having won a draw with the national champion when he was in Portland. We all played checkers. Dallas and Lary really studied chess and Lary did beat a careless grandfather once. When Lary was a sixth-grader, he challenged the high school champion and won two straight matches.

I recall my father saying, "You have a think-tank in your head. Your brain has untold millions of cells, each one a storage for a thought or event. Actually, you are born with the ability to reason. Some people are much more gifted than others. You can improve your reasoning by using your think-tank. If you have a problem, try putting it in the think-tank. Eventually you will get the answer." He never seemed to be teaching.

The five of us were sitting on logs around a campfire at Williams Lake. The coyotes were howling to each other in the distance. A great horned owl hooted in a fir tree. Someone remarked, "Those visiting fishermen didn't let anyone get a word in." This was the kind of opening that Granddad liked.

"What did he learn while he was talking?"

Earl said, "How could he learn anything when he was hearing nothing but his own voice?"

"What impression did you have of him?"

"He was a lightweight."

The summary of the discussion was that if you join a group, let someone else do the talking. If you keep a low profile, they will listen when you have something to say. If you ask a question, make it a legitimate quest for useful information and not one you know the answer for.

Lary summed it up: "Don't be a loudmouth."

When Granddad was 87, he said he had never been deer hunting, so he entered the drawing on the South Hills deer hunt and drew a permit. When we tried to get him to use our 257 Remington with a scope sight, he said no. He had borrowed a little 30-30 carbine with open sights. His first shot at a gallon can 50 yards away rolled it and that was his target practice.

It was almost daybreak when we parked the car. Granddad was going to walk around the side of a gently sloped hillside with sparse brush. The two boys and I would circle around a mile or so and sweep back toward him. This could send some deer toward where he would be sitting on an outcrop. The boys downed two of them. I didn't shoot, as there was no way we could use three deer. While we were dressing out the deer to put in the game sacks, we heard a shot. I could see the deer running down the hill across the draw nearly a half-mile away. Then we heard a second shot.

"That has to be Granddad. He got his deer."

Carrying our meat sacks down the hill took considerable time. We left Lary with the game and walked back toward the car. On the way we met Fred Mathews, a conservation officer.

"I met your father and he is something! He had his deer pulled up with pulleys and a rope and had it almost dressed out. When I looked at his patched and faded complimentary license, it gave his birth date as 1873. I asked him what he was going to do with that deer. He said he was going to carry it to the car. I picked up his rifle and one sack to carry to the car. The deer was a big mule deer buck and that sack was heavy. I dropped the sack in the shade by the car and turned to go back and help him with the other. There he was, about 10 steps away. He remarked, 'I'm almost too old for this kind of thing!' He opened the trunk, brought out two cups, poured three fingers of whiskey, topped them off with 7-Up, and handed one to me, saying, 'I hope you like 7-Up.'"

Granddad and the boys would legitimize their jaunts by calling up and saying, "I am with the boys at Hailey," or "We are with Granddad." He often said that he was lucky to be able to live and watch his grandchildren for 20 years. They were the lucky ones.

The boys were doing well in school. Ethel was really enjoying life. She was reared in Hollywood and Twin Falls and had missed a social life in Driggs. While we had enjoyed our stay in Driggs, she said, "It is wonderful to get into a different atmosphere."

She belonged to the supper and bridge clubs. When she was chairman of the Jayceettes, the club won state honors two years in a row. She and two close friends, Iola Tilly and Marian McKnight, were busily enjoying their work in charitable organizations. We were a young couple sharing and caring, raising a delightful family of three healthy, very bright, good-looking children.

When the war ended, the buildings on the Hunt Project 6 miles east of Jerome were still in place. They had been the home of 2,000 Japanese that were interned there for three years during the war. These well-built, 80x20-foot buildings each housed four families of internees. These buildings had to be moved in a hurry, as the land was going to be open for veteran settlers that fall. The government sold them for $400 each. My folks bought one, cut it in two, and moved it to a foundation on a nice lot on the outskirts of Jerome. With the surplus lumber from the second half, they added on and built an attractive home. Norman and I helped my father, who was a good carpenter, finish it in two months, and they happily moved into their first real home.

The government plan was for about one hundred farms to be developed by war veterans on the Hunt Project. The farms varied in size because of the location of fields and their accessability. The veterans had to have farm experience and $1000 to qualify. After their applications were received, their names were put into a big churn. The names were drawn and the order of their selecting a farm. They had only two days to decide what piece of land they wanted to file on.

For the next several years this project was a constant headache. Some of the future settlers had a hard time deciding between farm units. I would be asked to go out with them, look over the two parcels and give my opinion. There was no way they could get me to stick my neck out so they could blame their choice on me if they became dissatisfied later. I pointed out the desirable and undesirable features of each and let them decide.

Less than half the settlers had ever done any irrigating. The Soil Conservation Service surveyed several ditches, but the Extension Service was obligated to help with the application of the water to the field. The farmers were from over 20 different states, varying from Idaho natives to Georgia peanut growers.

To cut down on farm visits, I held schools on various aspects such as irrigation, fertilizers, feeding of livestock, and farm management. The record snowfall in the winter of 1949-1950 blocked all roads for days. The commissioners hired caterpillars with bulldozer blades to clear the roads. The job of managing or determining what roads needed to be plowed on a particular day was my responsibility. The objective was to give everyone a chance to go to town for necessities at least once a week. There were emergency requests to get to medical help. Some calls were actually ridiculous. One woman wanted me to plow out the road because her mother was unhappy and wanted to go back to town. She said her mother was fretting and worrying herself sick. To make her think I was granting her request, I said, "We'll have the road open at noon tomorrow. Get back as quickly as you can because the snow is drifting the 5- and 6-foot cuts full in a very short period of time."

What she didn't know was that the road had already been scheduled to be plowed at that time. The next week I received a call from the same woman with the same story—her mother wanted to go back again.

The Hunt Project became a one-road entry and the irregular winding roads from farm to farm were snowed in for almost a month. A hay and feed drop by plane was carried on by the U.S. Air Force. Settlers would call in their needs. The Air Force had a map with the names and locations of these homes. They didn't consult me. No settlers really suffered for food or fuel, but they did make some booboos. For instance, Forest Boerner was running out of feed for their milk cow. They had three children who needed milk. He said he needed about 10 bales of hay. My secretary notified the Air Force in Mountain Home. The next day Forest called and said, "Call them off!" They had delivered 40 bales of hay and 10 sacks of grain for his one cow—enough feed for several months.

One of the settlers asked me to witness and stand up for him on his marriage to his financee from Georgia. I told him he had better load up with supplies, as a very big blizzard was due the next day. They really must have loaded up. It was 20-some days before they could get into town. They had been snowed in most of a month. When I saw them, I asked, "What was it like being snowed in?"

They laughed and replied, almost in unison, "It was wonderful!"

Milk trucks were at a standstill. Dairymen had only enough milk cans for one day. I advised putting it into washtubs. When it was frozen, dump it out onto a clean sheet and keep it covered from dirt. It could not be used for fresh milk, but it was all right to make butter from. It was a common sight to see a sled loaded with tub-shaped milk cubes.

In the late 40s and early 50s Russia was recruiting communists in the United States. They were having considerable success. The phone call from the F.B.I. was a surprise. When each of us had established our identity, the agent asked, "Is your line private?"

"It is."

He told me they thought there was a large cell of communists being formed or recruited in the area. He asked that I check on an ex-naval officer who had settled in the Hunt Project. It was a surprise because the officer had been using me for agricultural advice. I was asked to report the license numbers of the cars that were stopped at his place and report who was visiting him. His mailbox was a quarter of a mile from the house and out of sight, along with several other boxes. I would check addresses and points of departure for the letters. The F.B.I. uncovered the communist cell in Twin Falls. When the ex-naval officer was accused of being a communist, which meant he was distributing material to overthrow the government, he denied it, saying that he had been a communist but had turned in his card. He had been enlisted when he was stationed at Murmansk, Russia. Somehow his communist connection became public knowledge and he sold his farm and left the area. The incident was one of the many duties that a county agent had to take part in.

During the winter Ethel's father, Guy Tobey, had a heart attack. He had a lucrative job as manager of Sea Side Flooring and Roofing in Los Angeles. The three telephones, many crews working on such projects as hospitals, battleships, large office buildings, supervising and making estimates finally took their toll. He was a gifted man. A salesman would call in the dimension of a job. He would doodle awhile with a pencil and piece of paper and give the figure for the bid. I asked him, "Dad Tobey, are you ever off in your figures?"

"Sure, I make a mistake now and then, but never over $100."

He was also a gifted musician and had tuned pianos for awhile in his early life. According to letters from Ethel's mother, he was getting along all right after the heart attack, as he usually tuned one piano and not more than two a day. He was very much in demand. When Jose Iturbe had concerts in Los Angeles, he insisted that Dad Tobey tune his piano. Iturbe played for him after he had finished tuning the piano, and

asked, "Do you play?" Dad Tobey played for him, and Mr. Iturbe sa
"You could have been a concert pianist."

When we visited the Tobeys during the summer, he seemed to be
his usual, cheerful self. His doctors checked him every month and the
damaged heart was holding its own without any symptoms of strain.

I was in the act of sitting down after returning from the speakers
platform during a Chamber of Commerce dinner when someone
slipped me a telegram envelope. I sensed that it was bad news; Ethel
was busy talking to someone and had not seen it. I turned away from
her to read that Dad Tobey was dead from a massive coronary attack.
Our family doctor was sitting next to me and I told him what had
happened.

"You take Ethel home and I will follow and give her a shot so she
will sleep."

On the way home I broke the news to her. She and her father had
been very close. Dr. Neher's shot really knocked her out. Dallas and
Lary were sound asleep in their rooms. Susan woke up in her crib as I
was getting ready to go to bed.

"Drink of water, Daddy." She drank half a glass and lay down.

"Do you need to go to the bathroom?"

"No."

"You'd better go now, so you will sleep longer." I picked her up
and started to carry her. She struggled to get down.

"I can do it myself!" She came paddling back, pulling up her
pajamas, and climbed into bed. I tucked her in after our goodnight kiss
and hug. By that time it was nearly 11 o'clock. What happened at one
o'clock that morning is going to cause skepticism and wonder, but not
as much as it caused me. This happened over 35 years ago and I still
wonder and try to explain it. It left me certain there is a hereafter.

The beautiful English setter, my pride and joy as a hunting
companion, always slept by my side of the bed. At one o'clock she
started barking. I sat up, turned on the light to see what she was
barking at. She was sitting at the foot of the bed, looking up and
wagging her tail and whining softly. I had a strange, uneasy feeling.
Susan awoke, stood up and reached her arms toward the foot of her
bed, and said, "Grandpapa." She laughed, turned around and snuggled
back into bed. The following came to me clearly like a voice, but
without sound.

"This is Dad Tobey. Tell Babe I am all right."

I asked, "Why don't you tell her?"

"We can't, because of all the trouble and chaos it would cause. The
world would be in turmoil with a whole babble of voices. Babe is
going to have a terrible time soon. Protect her if you can." Then there
was nothing.

I slept only fitfully the rest of the night, thinking of this strange
experience. It reminded me of the time in Wyoming when Claude

asked me what was around the bend of the Gros Ventre River. That incident I passed off as a good guess, plus some thought transference. To me it was hard to refute the following evidence. The dog had hunted with Dad Tobey many times and they were good friends. Susan was the apple of his eye. When she was visiting him in California, they were both early risers. He would take her to the bathroom and then they had breakfast together. He would put her back into her crib and go to work. In the afternoon she was impatient for him to come home from work.

I was wide awake and I had not been dreaming. It really happened.

I was not really a religious fanatic. I believed in Christ because He was real. To me God was the goodness, compassion, and sympathy of the world. In the hereafter you left your children to carry on on earth. You also passed on the help and kindness you had received to others. The helping of another human by word or action is like a wave—it ripples on into eternity. James Russell Lowell's "He who gives himself with his alms feeds three, himself, his hungering neighbor, and me" had a lasting effect on my life.

Ethel was taking the loss bravely the next morning. We had finished breakfast and were lingering over a cup of coffee, talking about plans to attend the funeral. It was then I told her of the visitation of the night before, but didn't tell her about the warning. We left that afternoon for Hollywood, taking Susan with us and leaving the boys to stay with their grandparents and go to school.

The funeral was at Forest Lawn two days after we arrived. It was Dad Tobey's wish to be cremated. Before the ceremony, the casket was in the Tobey home for viewing by friends. I told Susan she was going to see Grandpa, but she had to be quiet because he was asleep. Putting my finger to mouth, I said "Shh." Susan tiptoed in, looked at him in the casket, put her finger to her mouth and softly said "Shh." She reached out and touched his face and whispered, "He is cold." She also saw them close the casket and take him away in the black hearse. This made a lasting impression that would show itself later.

We suggested to Ethel's mother that she come to Idaho to live. She had enough to buy a house and live comfortably on their savings if she was careful.

"Idaho is too high for my heart. I am going to stay in California." She was always complaining about her weak heart but never took any medication.

POLIO

Early in the fall of 1947, the polio epidemic hit south central Idaho, centering in Gooding and Jerome Counties. By the time it ended late in 1948, nearly 300 had been infected, with nearly 50 deaths and a large number crippled or handicapped to varying degrees.

There were many reasons why they made me county chairman of the Polio Foundation. My office put out information and publicity furnished by the National Foundation, supervised fund drives, and distributed pamphlets on how to protect yourself and your family. We sponsored a trip to Boise to attend a two-day meeting on polio control which included a trip to the Elks Convalescant Home where there were people of all ages in various degrees of muscular impairment. At St. Luke's Hospital, the line of barrel-like respirators with the patients' heads sticking out while they worked with a whoosh and a whump, rhythmically going on and on, left me feeling very depressed. Some would never get out of the iron lung. I wondered how they could take it.

There was a lot of controversy among doctors about polio. Some thought it was contagious, some didn't. They had not yet discovered it was a virus. Sister Kenny of Australia had developed a method of treatment involving hot packs and stretching to keep muscles flexible. Some doctors were adopting this reasonable concept; others said it had not been proven and refused to recognize that a mere nurse could come up with a simple treatment that would be effective. The disease was puzzling, as quite often only one member of a family would be affected and rarely two.

Later it was decided that some people had very light cases, often undetected, that made them immune. The doctors thought that both Lary and I had had polio. I have one leg slightly shorter and foot smaller than the other and a permanent stiff neck, probably the result of polio in childhood.

About two days before Christmas vacation, Lary stopped in at my office for a ride home from school. My secretary was a large woman. To tease Lary she grabbed him and sat him on her lap. She had been nursing a bad cold for several days and I hoped he wouldn't catch it. The next day she was taken to a Boise hospital with polio.

Lary came down with a cold and fever the day after Christmas vacation. Dr. Neher said it was flu and recommended a week in bed and hot baths. When Lary complained about leg pains, I stretched and rubbed his legs. He was ready to go back to school when the vacation ended.

The women's club decided to hold a fashion show. They asked my tall, slim, beautiful wife to be one of the models. She decided that it would be necessary to get rid of a slight bulge in her tummy and get her weight down from 128 to 122 pounds. For nearly two weeks she practically starved herself and exercised. It was a cold and windy day when she hung out the washing and caught a cold. The next day she felt terrible and I made her stay in bed. When her temperature rose to 103, I called Dr. Neher.

"Doctor, she has all the symptoms of polio. I want her taken to Boise for a spinal test."

"You are over-concerned. It is just the flu and she will be o.k. in a few days. Besides, spinals are very expensive."

"I don't give a darn about expensive." Again he refused to send her.

There was no improvement the next day. Sometime during the early morning she woke me and said, "My arms are numb."

"Honey, we will take you to Boise and you will be all right." I tried to reassure her, but I was apprehensive and fearful for our future. I had difficulty in calling Dr. Neher at 3 o'clock in the morning. When I told him her condition and symptoms, I was furious at his casual reply.

"She will have to make a trip in the morning."

"Dr. Neher, you made one hell of a mistake. You get over here in 15 minutes and order the ambulance!"

The children had to be told. Everybody was dressed and wide awake when the ambulance arrived. Susan saw the black limosine and said, "Don't go, Mommy!"

"Don't cry, baby. I'll be back soon."

My last instructions were to Dallas. "You are the man of the house. Look after Lary and Susan, and tell Grandmother."

About halfway of the 100 miles to Boise, Ethel gasped, "I need air. I'm about to pass out!"

The ambulance driver turned on the oxygen and I put the mask over her face. She was gasping for breath and no oxygen came out.

"I told one of my employees to change tanks last night and he has not done it."

It was necessary to open a window to get fresh air in. It was very cold. I tucked extra blankets around her and prayed that she would not get pneumonia. Mel had the ambulance floor-boarded at 90 miles an hour. Dr. Neher had phoned ahead to St. Luke's Hospital and they were waiting for us. They immediately applied an oxygen mask over her face. A doctor came in and checked her vital signs with a stethoscope. He gave instructions to the nurses for medication and turned to leave.

"Doctor, can I talk to you?"

"What do you want to know?"

"She definitely has polio. Why aren't you prescribing the hot packs and stretching of the Kenny treatment?"

His reply was pompous, as if I were an ignorant layman.

"The treatment that the Australian nurse advocates hasn't been really proven, and in my opinion it is a waste of time." He turned and walked out. To me this meant disaster. I had been clinging to the hope that the treatment would be a solution. At that point I didn't have enough experience to demand a change of doctors.

We said goodbye. I promised to return on Saturday. The ambulance took me back to Jerome. There were many arrangements to be made at home. My mother, in her late seventies, could cope for a few days until I arranged for a housekeeper.

At first it seemed overwhelming. The uncertainty about Ethel's health and future added to my depression. It was necessary to keep a cheerful and optimistic front for the children. They had to have hope that their mother would get well enough to come back home.

I was able to find a warm, friendly lady, Mrs. Landreth, as a cook and housekeeper. She was taking good care of 4-year-old Susan during the day. A phone call came from Boise. Ethel's condition had taken a turn for the worse, and she was in an iron lung. My secretary said she would tell my folks and Mrs. Landreth, and I hurried out the door to my car. There was no way to describe my despair.

The nurse at the desk gave me the room number and directions. The closed door added to my apprehension. I knocked and a nurse named Ellie let me in. There was a head of light auburn hair sticking out of the barrel-shaped black contraption, which was rhythmically giving out a loud whoosh and whump.

She was lying on her back, with only the head resting on a pillow. There was a mirror above her head. She could look in it and see a person standing behind her head. The nurse who was sitting within her range of vision moved away so I could take her place.

"I'm still here, darling."

"Hang in there, honey." My throat became paralyzed.

"See the button on my throat?"

Then I noticed a silver-colored button with a hole about the size of a pencil. A plastic tube with an end like a nozzle was suspended just above the button. She had difficulty in getting enough breath to talk. She spoke slowly, resting after each few words.

It was touch and go. One nurse sat by her head, watching constantly to determine how much oxygen she needed by the color of her face. Another nurse spelled the first one off, washed, changed bedding, and fed Ethel with liquids through a rubber tube inserted in her nose. A third nurse relieved the first two at intervals in the 8-hour shift. This meant she had nine nurses in a 24-hour period.

The third nurse ran the small tube down through the button and it made a snorting sound as it sucked the mucous from her lungs. In the hall the nurse talked to me.

"She will live if we can keep the lungs clear. There is a good chance of her getting out of the iron lung."

"How long?"

"Probably five or six months. Your visits seem to give her new hope. When you miss an evening, she almost sinks into a coma."

About two weeks after Ethel entered St. Lukes, a nurse called me and said, "I have a phone call for you from a Tiny." The only "Tiny" I knew was Tiny Breckenridge. He might be calling me about seed potatoes. I picked up the phone.

"Hello, Tiny. It has been a year since I've heard from you. What gives?"

"Virg, the boys and I have just heard about Ethel. Just wanted to let you know we care, as you folks have been very special people in our lives. We have told Steve Meikle [the banker] that you can write a check on us for a thousand. If you need more, let us know."

I really choked up. It was wonderful to have friends that cared. I thanked him and told him that at present I was in good financial shape.

During the winter and early spring when she was clinging to life by sheer will power, I made the round trip of 200 miles each day, starting at 6 o'clock after dinner with the children, and returning home at 11 o'clock. The nurses said my visits gave her a lift and courage to continue another day. The few times I missed she would sink to very low and they were concerned whether she would make it through the night. Unless you have experienced what she was going through, there is no way to imagine lying there unable to do anything but turn your head and talk with difficulty. Later she told me, "I just couldn't believe this was happening to me. It must be a bad dream. I've got to get out of this prison. With practice I was finally able to turn my mind blank for hours at a time. I believed that every day I lived increased my chances of getting home to you and our children.

"It was a terribly difficult task for you to look after them, do your job, and visit me every night. You were getting thinner and thinner. I was living from one visit to the next. When you couldn't come, you called and that helped. Fear was always in my thoughts. Would I live, how badly would I be handicapped, would I be able to be a complete wife? How much of a burden would I be?

"Most of the time I just tried to live from day to day. There is no way I could have made it without your love and devotion. The nurses all love you for the way you stood by me. I also worried about what the family would do if something happened to you.

"Enough cannot be said about the care of my nurses, especially Ellie, Penny, and Polly. Their encouragement and expert care made me love them. You really fooled me about your bout with pneumonia."

Somehow I had caught a bad cold. Dr. Swindell, the heart specialist, had just finished checking Ethel's heart and assured me it was still strong. He told me to sit down. After listening to my heart a short time, he turned to leave and beckoned with his finger for me to follow him to the hall.

"You are going to bed for a week. You have pneumonia."

The long hours, strain, and extra work had finally taken their toll. I weighed 150 pounds, down from 175. Using the bedside phone, I called home and Dallas answered. He was very mature and reliable for his age. He was to tell Mrs. Landreth and my parents, and be responsible for looking after Susan and Lary. There was no need to tell them, as they would worry.

The nurse brought my medications. I gulped them down. It was one o'clock the next day when I woke up. My nurse was standing by the bed.

"Well, sleepy-head, we thought you would never wake up. Are you hungry?"

"I'm starved." I ate a big lunch, went back to sleep, and woke up at 5 o'clock when the doctor came to check my condition.

"Your lungs have cleared up a lot. I think what you needed most was rest and sleep."

This presented the problem of not letting Ethel know and worry, and daily visits to keep her alive. Dr. Swindell was aware of this. We worked out a solution. Every evening I got dressed. They wheeled me to her door in a wheelchair, then I got up and walked in to see her.

For the first three days it was just eating and sleeping at least 14 hours a day. They weighed me the fourth day and I had gained 8 pounds. I wanted to go home but the doctor insisted on one more night in the hospital. On the morning of the fifth day he discharged me, saying, "You're well."

I felt well rested and my usual energetic self. When I visited Ethel, she remarked with difficulty in her croaking voice due to the hole in her neck, "You have been looking better each day for the last several times." Then I told her what had happened.

"It is just like you to keep me from worrying. You think of everything!"

During the latter part of this period a new nurse was named head of the polio ward. She was from Germany and had a strong German accent. I was very impressed with her knowledgeable, professional manner. I noticed they were applying hot packs and stretching Ethel's arms and fingers. She could now move her legs. When I asked about the fingers on Ethel's hands yielding only a little to bending, the nurse shook her head.

"The Kenny treatment should have been started on the first day. It is questionable whether she will have much use of her hands."

"I insisted that the doctor start her on the Kenny treatment when she arrived, but he would not do it."

She shrugged and muttered what I thought was "Dumbkoff."

231

hen I asked the doctor about her chances for recovery, he was ...ommital. Freida was very precise in answering my questions.

"If we can keep her lungs from filling up and preventing her from getting oxygen, she will live. On account of pneumonia the X-rays show the amount of fluid is gaining. I am sure she will be able to walk. Her hands are stiff as boards and it is very doubtful if she can get very much or any use of her hands and arms."

A few days later I received a call from Penny, one of her nurses at St. Luke's Hospital.

"You had better come to Boise as quickly as you can. Her lungs are filling up and she can last only a few hours." I took off for Boise at 90 miles an hour. Fortunately, my service station operator, Mel Grindstaff, had installed new tires on my car without asking me. He said I was a poor credit risk with those old worn tires. Near Mountain Home I heard a siren and saw blinking lights of a patrol car behind me. I pulled over and rolled down the window. The patrolman turned out to be Homer Kunz, an old friend. When I explained the situation to him, he said, "Follow me," and led me at 90 into Boise with his lights flashing and siren going.

There was a small cubbyhole anteroom leading into the respirator room. I always stopped to pray there before entering the main room. As I was praying for her welfare, for the family, and for the strength and wisdom to take care of what might happen, I felt a strange calm. There was no sound, but my mind registered the following words:

"This is Dad Tobey. Babe is going to live, but she will be terribly handicapped. After your wedding ceremony, you told me that you would take care of your bride. You will have many years of trying times, but you will rise to it."

When I entered the room, the doctors were standing at her head. One was inserting the suction tube into the opening in her trachea, trying to suck out the mucus on her lungs. The tube could be in position only a few seconds, then had to be withdrawn to allow her to get oxygen from a tube a few inches above her. Her eyes were closed and her face was grey with a tinge of blue from the lack of oxygen. The doctor stopped trying.

"It's no use."

Freida grabbed the suction tube from his hand and said, "Get out of the way." What happened made me believe in miracles. She inserted the tube and twisted it slightly. The empty sucking sound changed. There was yellow fluid moving through the tube. She counted 10 seconds between each insertion. The doctors stood almost spellbound. Her doctor checked her heart.

"Her heart is going out."

Dr. Swindell disagreed. "Her heart is missing a beat now and then, but it is strong as a horse. That is one reason she is still alive."

Ethel's color was returning to normal. It must have been 15

minutes, but seemed like hours, when Freida stopped and handed the suction to the incompetent doctor.

"I will aspirate her every day for a few days and her lungs should clear up. She is going to live because no one who has fought as hard as she has is going to die. Virgil, go get a cup of coffee, and when you come back in fifteen minutes, she will be able to talk to you."

I broke in on the doctor's conversation with the statement, "I think I know how she contracted polio." I told them about my secretary holding Lary, and his subsequent illness which I felt was a mild case of polio (which examinations and tests verified), and his mother getting polio two weeks later. Her doctor really blasted me as if I were completely ignorant. When he said, "That isn't any proof whatever," I saw red.

"You haven't any proof that it isn't right. I have had more bacteriology than you have and I am more intelligent than you. You are incompetent. You didn't recommend the Kenny treatment at first, which could have prevented the stiffness in her hands, and possibly saved the movement. Today you couldn't do a simple job of work with the suction tube and you made an untrue statement about her heart condition. I want you off the case right now!"

Red-faced, he left the room with Dr. Swindell. Dr. Tremaine, a very kindly and knowledgeable man, remained behind. He patted me on the shoulder.

"You really gave him his comeuppance and he deserved it. From now on I will be Ethel's doctor."

Watching the clock and drinking coffee for 15 minutes, I wondered if Freida's prediction would be true. I hoped that the crisis was over. Our blurred and uncertain future was churning in my thoughts. When I walked back into the room, Ethel's eyes were open and she was smiling into the tilted mirror above her head.

"Hello, darling. I'm back. I feel better than I have for a month. I am going to get out of this damned respirator someday."

There was no stopping my tears as I put my head against hers and we each whispered, "I love you."

"Honey, I need some sleep. Will you come back at 6 o'clock? I had the biggest vanilla eggnog."

"How did it taste?"

"I can't taste it, as they put a tube down my throat and pour it directly into my stomach. It does feel good in my stomach, as I am hungry for the first time."

She told me that Polly, Ellie, and Penny, her three day-nurses, were so elated about her recovery after they had worked so hard to save her for a month that they decided to have a party. I was to meet them at the Valencia Club, a Basque restaurant.

After a couple of drinks, we all ordered the lamb dish for which the club was famous. Because of our exuberance the Basque waiter asked

233

us to be less noisy. The nurses insisted that I follow them to their apartment, as the party had just started. I remember only vaguely what happened, as I got stoned for only the second and last time in my life. When I awoke, my mouth tasted like what I thought the bottom of a bird cage would taste like. They served me breakfast starting with a glass of tomato juice with vile-tasting hot stuff in it. It stopped my woozy feeling. After a shower and change of clothes in my hotel room, I checked out and went to St. Luke's. With misgiving I entered the respirator room. I had considerable doubt as to how Ethel would react to the party.

She was smiling, and so were Polly, Ellie, and Penny.

"Hello, darling. How was the party?"

"Honey, I am not sure, as I really got a snoot full. There was a lot of laughter and I woke up in bed with no clothes on."

"Who was in bed with you?"

"There wasn't anyone. They were all dressed."

"Ellie said you were terrific and I told her you would be."

A week or so after her lungs finally cleared up and she was over the pneumonia, they closed the hole in her neck and she could talk without difficulty, except that she still had to pause while the iron lung inhaled for her.

"It is wonderful to be able to talk easily. There was so much I wanted to tell you and couldn't because it took too much effort. Honey, I am going to make it, so just visit me once a week and I'll still be here. I will miss you like the dickens. I had a chocolate milk shake and I drank it with a straw. It tasted wonderful. It was the first food I've tasted for nearly four months!"

Susan at first believed that her mother was dead. When I left to visit Ethel, she just looked and never said anything. Lary was almost stoic. You could never tell what he was thinking unless he expressed himself. It turned out in later years as he developed that he was keenly aware of my situation and had everything sorted out logically in his mind. There was no doubt that he missed his mother very much because he had been very affectionate and close to her. He was very protective and concerned with Susan's welfare. His grades remained about the same—about half B's and A's, in contrast to Dallas' all A's. Dallas was another problem. His grades went down to B's and C's. He had to be disciplined about coming home from school and getting to meals on time. He was more openly concerned about his mother's condition because he had lost classmates and some of them had come home confined to wheelchairs for the rest of their lives. Some were so badly handicapped that they never came home. I knew that he must have been in a turmoil, but didn't know how bad it was until I attended a P.T.A. meeting. I asked a teacher how he was doing and her answer shocked me.

"I don't know what to do with him. He used to be such a nice boy.

Mischevious, yes, but he did his work and got along with everybo . Now he gets into fights on the playground. Punishing him by not letting him out for recess hasn't worked. He has whipped all of the big boys in his class and now is almost through the next grade up. I am sure his problem is missing his mother."

Apparently, he was using his training to punch short and straight and was more than a match for the long, swinging punches. I went to Boise on Saturday that weekend, and on Sunday the boys and I went rabbit hunting. Walking along with Dallas gave me an opportunity to ask him about the fighting problem.

"You told me not to pick fights when we moved from Driggs. They started to pick on me, and when I told you about it, you said that if I have to fight, do it, and there is no point in fighting unless I win—so get in the first punch, make it a good one, and follow up."

Then I told him what the teacher had said about the fifth grade.

"Dallas, I too feel like striking out about our situation, but it would do no good. We have to make the best of it. You must realize that nothing remains static. Things change. Are you still being pushed around?"

"I guess not."

"Then there is no reason for you to go on fighting. You have proved your point."

Then I praised him for his help at home and the way he had assumed extra duties. Lary had heard the whole conversation and didn't say a word.

"A family that stays together can accomplish most anything they set their minds on. Actually, your family are the only ones that really care about you. If you should die, no one outside of your family would miss you for very long."

Lary said, "That's right."

I received no more complaints about fighting from the school authorities.

When Ethel's recovery was almost certain, I became able to think more clearly about long-range plans and a family program to cope with the situation. I needed help and guidance and my father, with his philosophical mind, was the one I turned to.

We broke it down into three categories, Ethel, children, and me, and listed facts about the situation of each. Ethel would be severely crippled, and we used the word crippled. She might be able to walk with help. Probably she would have no use of her hands. This meant she would have to be dressed, bathed, taken to the bathroom, have teeth brushed, and be fed. She would feel that she was useless and a hindrance to the family. She would be reluctant to ask for anything.

How could the family make her feel loved and needed? This was really the most important problem. Discussions were held with the children taking part.

It was 12-year-old Dallas who suggested, "We can get her to help us with our schoolwork, whether we need it or not. Every night we each will have her help some."

"Good. That way she will know what is going on in school. If something is bothering you, regardless of what it is, consult with her, as she is a very wise person. When you are taking care of her, always ask her first if she wants something done. Try to anticipate her needs, because if she has to ask for something, it will make her feel more dependent. She is going to be afraid that you, her children, will be ashamed of her because she is so badly crippled. Many people shy away from handicapped persons because it disturbs them and they are uncomfortable around deformed or crippled people."

"We can be proud of her because of the terrific fight she has made to live and be with us. Most anyone else would have given up. She is kind, beautiful, intelligent, and we are lucky to have such a good mother."

I explained that the family could not stay together without their help. They listed the things their mother had been doing for them and would no longer be able to do.

I asked the question, "If you lay something on the floor, who will pick it up? What are you going to do with dirty clothes? Your mother has always kept the house neat and clean. It will disturb her to have a messed-up house." This caused considerable discussion. They said they would try.

"I will try not to be too bossy. If I am, please overlook it, as I have to take new and additional jobs and will be under a lot of strain." We discussed the need for supporting and looking after each other.

Granddad said, "After all, it won't bother anyone outside the family as to what happened to you. Your family are the only ones who really care, so you love, protect, and not pick on each other." This last part was simply reemphasizing what we had taught them from birth. Before a baby was born we had them feel the new brother or sister move and reassured them that we would still love them just as much as the new baby. There had been no fighting and very little quarreling that was quietly and forcefully squelched by their mother.

I told them that it would be necessary for them to come home on time and to continue to let me know where they were at all times. Then I asked if they had any suggestions as to how I should do things. To my surprise, I found out how my children felt about me. Apparently, sometimes I had a short temper and acted too quickly without giving them a chance to explain, or I refused to listen to their side. On the whole, they loved and respected me and were proud of me and their family.

The family problems were to be discussed with her and let her make as many decisions as possible. She was to be assured that she was loved. Any show of reluctance to do something for her would be noticed immediately and would cause a set-back in our relationship. It occurred to me that drinking of any kind would jeopardize the family.

I had kept Ethel informed of the children's progress during the months that she could not see them by taking up-to-date slides and projecting them on the ceiling. On one occasion I did not show any pictures of Lary. She said, "Where's Lary?" and was agitated and apprehensive. I had left some of the slides in the car, and when I showed them to her, she was reassured.

In May, Ethel was transferred to the Elks' Rehabilitation Center for physical therapy. She was still in the iron lung. On my first visit to the Elks' she was all smiles. She could talk normally now, as the hole in her trachea was closed, and she could take food by mouth.

"Guess what, darling! I stayed out of the iron lung 6 minutes the first try. Dr. Tremaine said there is no question that I will get out of the lung. He said it is evident that my chest muscles were not as severely affected as they first thought. And that isn't all. Since the danger of contagion is over, you can bring the children next weekend. I am so anxious to see them! I can kick my legs real good. I can move my thumb and middle finger of my right hand a little bit. The stiffness of them prevents any more motion."

Elated and hopeful, I drove home, thinking about breaking the news to the kids. They were asleep when I reached home. When I told them the good news at breakfast, there was a celebration by the boys. I didn't realize at the time that Susan was quiet. Later I found out why. It was Mrs. Landreth's day off, so I cooked a breakfast of hot cakes, bacon, and juice. The children ate heartily.

The Cross family prepared for the memorable visit. The boys were to go in first and greet their mother who still had only her head sticking out of the respirator. They were cautioned to stand back of her so she could see them in the mirror. Susan and I waited in the hall. I was holding her in my arms and she was shaking a little. I thought it was excitement. When she saw her mother, she screamed and hid her face. She had seen her Grandfather Tobey taken away in a black hearse, so all the time she thought her mother was also dead, because she had been taken away in the ambulance. I brought her close to her mother's head.

"Susan, I am your mother. Look at me. I am all right." Susan turned her head slightly and looked at her mother with one eye. Ethel kept reassuring her. Finally she rushed over and gave her mother a kiss, saying "Mommy! Mommy!"

She ran out the door and down the hall, yelling, "I've got a mommy! I've got a mommy!" Dallas ran after her and brought her back for a goodbye. During the first 50 miles on the way home, she sat next to me. Every once in a while she would pat me, clap her hands, and say, "I've got a mommy!" Then she went to sleep with her head on my lap and a smile on her face.

On my next visit a week later, Ethel was beaming when I entered the room.

"I have stayed out of the lung for 15 minutes three times today without too much trouble. I have to concentrate on breathing as deeply as I can. It was difficult at first to get my chest muscles to move, but it is getting easier each time."

A few weeks later she was able to sit in a wheelchair during the day and use the lung at night. She did not know that a nurse was always watching her color and breathing to detect any failure. Sometime later the iron lung was turned off while she was asleep. A nurse was observing her condition at all times. She slept through the night. The next morning the nurse asked her how she felt, and told her what happened.

"From now on you will sleep in the lung just in case it might be needed, but we will not turn it on."

This called for a graduation party. I brought roses and a graduation card. The nurses had a graduation diploma. At home we also had a celebration of the wonderful news after so many months of anxiety. From then on the family visited her every Sunday. To pass the time traveling to and from, the children played the alphabet game with the signs furnishing the letters to see who would get the entire alphabet first. Soon they knew every sign on the 100-mile route. They switched to white horses, mules, and goats. They soon learned the location of every white animal between Jerome and Boise.

This was also a time to discuss what additional things we each had to do to maintain our home and family life, and to make it more pleasant for Ethel at home.

Four-year-old Susan said, "I can look after Mommy while you are at work and Dallas and Lary are at school. I can bring her a drink and do a lot of things."

It turned out that these family discussions were very valuable through the years to come. It eventually made a close-knit and loyal family.

Ethel was getting physiotherapy. She could walk with support and her leg strength was gradually improving. They installed overhead bars on her wheelchair with slings to support her arms so she could move them with her shoulders. The muscles had atrophied to about half their normal size. She did this hours on end with very little, if any, improvement. There was no movement in her left hand, and slight movement of the thumb and second finger on the right hand. They were able to loosen the board-stiff joints somewhat.

She was worried about my welfare. She didn't say so, but she was always trying to set me up with her nurses. Her physical therapist said that she liked to fish, but never got to. Ethel arranged for me to take her fishing and camp overnight. I said, "I'll wait until you get home."

"Honey, it is doubtful if I can respond. I worry about taking care

238

of you."

I received a telephone call on Wednesday from a nurse who said Ethel wanted me to come on Saturday, instead of Sunday, as I was taking a nurse to their big annual dance, and for me to come dressed accordingly. The tall, extremely good-looking nurse was an excellent dancer and we had a good time dancing together. It had been many months since I had danced. She had been to the punch bowl many times and was acting eager and amorous when I took her home. I kissed her and thanked her for a lovely evening.

"I am going back to tell Ethel goodnight."

"Don't you want to come in for a while?"

"It is one of the most tempting offers I have had, but I am married to the most courageous and wonderful woman in the world. Thank you again." I woke Ethel with a kiss.

"I thought you would stay all night!"

I gave her the same answer. "I will wait until you get home."

The next Sunday she said, "Eleanor said you were a wonderful dancer and told me about saying goodnight. She was disappointed that you didn't stay, and she said, 'I wish I could find a man like that.' I wouldn't have minded at all, but I am glad that you did what you did."

Early in July she told me, "You have always taken the boys up to Williams Lake for a fishing and camping trip. Go ahead and do it. I will be all right while you are gone."

Having a housekeeper and being at home with the children every day made things a lot easier. The boys and Susan were being prepared for the possible return home of their mother. About the first of December, Dr. Tremaine said he thought going home for a month would help her morale and she would be able to spend Christmas with her family. This was wonderful news. The carpet and curtains were cleaned and we helped the housekeeper get everything spic and span. I brought her clothes from home and the nurse dressed her in a new outfit. The nurse wheeled her out to the car and she stood up to get into the car with help. The folding wheelchair and the exercise gadget went into the back seat. On the way home she put her head on my shoulder.

"You are aware that I'm not going to be good for anything. Someone will have to do everything for me. I'm going to be an awful burden."

"Honey, stop that. We all have missed your presence, guidance, and wisdom in keeping a family together. We have been counting the days until you could be home. The kids have been briefed on our family problems. We have had several discussions about what the family can do to keep together and have a good family life. You are a very important part of keeping the family together with our loving, caring, and sharing. I have missed your advice and counsel while you were away. I love you. Hang in there!"

It was a joyous homecoming and we both cried as we walked into the house.

Ethel had no trouble drinking liquids with a large glass straw in a tall glass. She had to be fed every bite, and had trouble swallowing solid food. Bites had to be small, well chewed, and washed down with a sip of water. Eating took a long time, and she said she always stopped while still hungry because she just got too tired.

My folks and sister and her husband came over to visit. They had not seen her for 10 months, and all told her how good she looked. At 8 o'clock she whispered to me, "I'm very tired." I told the company she was tired and they left.

"I want to go to bed."

"Do you want to take a bath first?"

"No, I had one this morning."

In the bathroom, I brushed her teeth, washed her face and hands, and helped her on and off the toilet.

"I'll never get used to having people wipe me. It is too embarrassing."

In the bedroom, I undressed her and put on a new sexy red nightgown. There she stood. Her face and hair were beautiful. Her neck showed the small trachea scar. If her shoulders and arms were covered, you saw two beautiful breasts still firm in spite of nursing three children, a flat stomach, molding nicely into graceful hips and long legs. The shrunken arms were hanging down. The hands were not curved, but straight like boards. From the waist down her backside was normal. Her shoulders and upper back muscles looked like something from a German refugee camp. I had never seen her without a nightgown since polio. It was then that I realized the extent of the damage to my beautiful wife. We went to bed.

"Honey, put your arms around me. It has been such a long time since you have held me. I used to dream about it and long for it when I was in the respirator." She snuggled up and was acting amorous.

"You are too tired tonight—we can wait until tomorrow."

"I only said that so we could go to bed earlier. I'm afraid that I won't be able to respond and that will not be good for you. Take lots of time getting me ready. It has been so long."

Our love-making in the past had been very special to both of us. After we were through, she started to cry.

"What is the matter, honey?"

"I could not respond one bit. It was as if I had almost no feeling. I know it was not very good for you."

"It was wonderful!" To me it was a relief. Her inability to respond completely bothered her for many years.

The month was a pleasant one for all of us. Ethel told Susan to get her ABC book and she would teach her how to read and count. Susan brought out a primer, climbed into her mother's lap, and started to read the short sentences, like "See the cat run." Her grandmother had taught her to read.

Ethel had terrible periods of depression in which she felt she was useless and just a detriment to me and the family. I could only assure her that her presence was an absolute necessity in helping to guide the rearing of our children. I pointed out that there were so many things she could do without doing them physically.

"It is going to be up to you to manage the household. I have an exacting job to do and you can help and supervise many things that I am not used to doing or am very inept in."

After many discussions in bed and letting her formulate what she could do to keep the family together, she came to the conclusion that she could be an asset. Her list included only a few things at first and as our talks continued she kept adding to it. She became more alive and cheerful.

Her list included supervising household duties, dishes, schoolwork, clothes, health habits, recreation, and keeping me rational. We had a live-in cook and housekeeper, Mrs. Landreth, who was a kindly soul, but a terrible cook.

On New Year's morning, Ethel had a slight cold. Her doctor had warned us that if she caught any kind of cold to rush her back to Boise. We drove down alone to Boise. She was really cheerful and talked about the future. She planned to try very hard to get some use of her hands. After two weeks in the respirator, she recovered from the cold. Weekly family visits continued. Her mother came up from California for two months, spending part of the time in Boise with Ethel and the rest with us in Jerome. She was really a detriment, as she made her own bed but did nothing to maintain the rest of the house. My mother was doing the mending for the family, and my mother-in-law actually sent her things to be mended. Her constant criticism of my management only added to the turmoil and confusion going on in my mind. She was disturbing the household relationship.

Early in May I received a call from the supervisor of the Elks' Rehabilitation Center that Ethel was not making any further progress and they were running out of funds. I was to take her home on the coming weekend. Ethel had asked Dr. Tremaine how long she could live with only 75 percent lung capacity .

"At least five years and possibly 10."

"I am going to see my children through school and also see grandchildren."

"You are one tough, determined woman and you will do it if anyone can."

I expected her to be in very low spirits and was trying to think what I could say or do to help her out of the deep depression that I thought she would feel. Her beautiful smile and "Hello, darling!" just lit up the room. My own depression evaporated. On the way home I found out why she was so cheerful. Her mother never communicated with me but

241

had been writing to Ethel regularly at least once a week. She had arranged for Ethel to go to the Cabot Kaiser Institute in Los Angeles for therapy. Kaiser had done wonders with polio patients' recovery and was rated even higher than Warm Springs in Georgia. Ethel was to start treatments on June 5th. She said, "You can read the particulars in her last letter. You know how thorough she is about anything she does."

After dinner that evening, I read her letter to the family and we discussed the plans. Her mother had prepared a very workable program for her rehabilitation. She was to live with her mother and would be driven by a woman to and from the Institute six days a week. The cost would be very high and was to be shared by me with Cabot Kaiser. I had only a few thousand dollars left of the $20,000 that I had planned to buy a farm with. It had gone to the Polio Foundation, the Elks' Rehabilitation Center, housekeepers, and trips.

"Do we have enough money to do it?" Ethel asked. We did not.

"We can make it, but it will be very close." I replied.

"Let's make the most of this month."

It was her courage and determination that helped me carry the additional loads. My physical condition and ability to do the extra work was no problem. It was my mental condition that she really bolstered up. I didn't realize until later how much her strength and bravery helped me. I felt that if she could do it, I could keep up my end of the problems.

The trip to Los Angeles was uneventful. The closeness of the relationship in the family was beginning to manifest itself. Everybody was concerned about the comfort of the others. The children were definitely concerned about someone besides themselves. It was a hurried trip and we stayed only four days.

During the rest of the summer, the boys mowed lawns and carried on a night crawler business. Large night crawler worms were in demand by fishermen. The 6- to 9-inch long worms were excellent trout bait. When lawns were sprinkled or flooded, they came out on top of the grass to escape the surplus moisture. It was quite a trick to pick up the worm before it darted back into its hole. They had a series of boxes of peat moss in the basement, covered by wet burlap sacks. At 25¢ a dozen, they were making at least $2 a day. This was big money in 1950 for the 10- and 14-year-old boys. Six-year-old Susan sometimes took part in their evening harvesting and they gave her a token amount. We had a big lawn and a high worm population. They saved this supply for emergencies.

After consulting me about the operation, Dallas and Lary attached two 1/4-inch, foot-long steel rods to an extension cord, taping the end for insulation against shocks. A safe procedure was followed all the time with the rods pushed into the ground before the extension cord was plugged into the electrical outlet. They were all for trying it that night. We waited until it was almost dark. A street lamp gave us enough light to see. I suggested that we should harvest the worms in a systematic order like harvesting a field. They decided to work in 5- by 10-foot blocks. The ground was quite moist because it had been flooded two days before. The rods were pushed into the ground about 16 inches and the cord plugged in. We watched and waited.

"Dad, it isn't going to work, or there aren't any worms here."

"It is going to take time, as the electric impulses are going to be very weak because they have to pass through so much dirt. What they will feel is a weak tickling that will make them uneasy and want to escape by coming to the surface." About that time a worm wriggled hurridly out of its burrow. Then another one appeared. Worms began popping out all over. We laughed and yelled at our success. In a matter of a half-hour and four moves of the prods, they had gathered over 10 dozen worms. They still watched who was watering lawns so they could gather at night.

Our cook was just not a good cook. She had no imagination and she didn't use a cookbook, and continuously cooked the same thing unless she was closely supervised. The children complained about the meals. Their mother had been a super cook and they were used to having an interesting, attractive, and appetizing menu. Mrs. Landreth had Sundays off. They looked forward to the meals I cooked. Susan said, "When Mummie comes home, we'll have some good food."

In August we took our annual five-day fishing trip to the Sawtooth Mountains in the Salmon River country. Quail, the Lewellen setter, naturally had to go along. When we arrived at the ranch house of the owner of the lake, Wes Claunoh, who owned the only fishing boats and charged for boat and fishing privileges, greeted me.

"Boy, am I glad to see you. There are four dudes from California that haven't caught a fish, and they are bitching. They are going to leave today and I'll pack them out after I take your stuff in. I told them I had some fishermen coming in today that would catch them and turn them loose by the dozen."

He gave us horses to ride up to the lake, saying he would have our duffel up in a couple of hours. The trail was a steep, winding climb up and down nearly 1,000 feet. In fact, in a few places the horse's hind feet would be above his front feet as he wound back and forth to gain altitude.

When we arrived at the lake, there were four men unloading their gear from the two wooden row boats. We could hear them bitching and complaining about how they had been "took." The fishing was a rip-off to get their money. While we were waiting for Wes to bring our gear, I put my rod together with the reel. The fly on a 9-foot, 3-pound test leader was one fly the boys tied to imitate a fresh-water shrimp that was abundant in the lake. While we were waiting, fish started dimpling occasionally. A big fish dimpled and started showing its tail about 100 feet out in the lake.

Lary said, loud enough for them to hear, "It would be like catching fish in a barrel to catch that fish."

"If you're so smart, why don't you catch him?"

Lary nodded to me, and we got into the boat. He rowed slowly and carefully toward the spot where the fish had dimpled. We watched for a few minutes and the fish dimpled about 40 feet away. The weighted fly settled on the water first without a splash, then began to sink. I counted to seven, gave the line a slight pull, and waited a couple of seconds. The line started to move and I set the hook on a 3- or 4-pound rainbow. The fish was an aerial acrobat, being out of the water nearly half the time. The boys whooped and hollered, giving advice to get even with me for giving them the same when they had caught fish in the past. We didn't have a net. After rowing slowly to shore to beach the fish, Lary picked it up and looked at it.

"We just as well throw him back."

One of the California men said, "No! No! Keep him."

"He's just a little gut," said Lary and threw him back in the lake. In a few seconds the fish righted its self and swam away. One of the men came over and said very humbly, "Would you help me catch a fish?"

"I would be glad to. Let me see your pole." Lary took the leader and fly off my pole and attached it to the man's line. They climbed into the boat and Lary rowed out about 100 feet into the lake. He told his companion to get ready to cast into the center of the dimple when a fish rose to the surface and wait until the line started to move, then set the hook. They didn't have to wait long for a rise about 30 feet away. The cast was perfect. The fish took the fly and the man yelled with joy and excitement. It was a nice fish of nearly 3 pounds. Fortunately, he had brought along a net. He held the fish up for his companions to see. They got into their boat and started beating the water with no success. When Lary's companion had caught five fish, Lary told him he had his limit in pounds and they stopped. As they were beaching their boats, Wes arrived with our gear. He looked at the fish and said, "I told you the fishing was good."

Lary removed my leader and fly from the Californian's pole and informed the four of them that they must use a small leader, not more than 3- or 4-pound test. The leaders they were using were so large that they spooked the fish.

"I took fly-fishing lessons until I learned to cast quite well. The others told me they knew all about fly-fishing and I followed their advice. I wish I could stay and fish with you, but I have to get home." He handed Lary a $20 bill, which Lary shared with Dallas.

"Will you be up here next year?"

I said, "We always come up on this date."

"I may be seeing you."

We called Ethel once a week and each of us talked briefly on account of the expense. She was cheerful and said she was going to have a surprise for us when we came down for Christmas. Expense was a very serious problem, as I had nearly exhausted our savings. Also, I felt we had to move out of the neighborhood. Dallas remarked that the Smail and Neher boys didn't have to mow their lawns — their fathers hired them done. We were in a small town and we lived on what was called "Snob Hill." An acreage would keep the boys busy and allow them to have stock for 4-H. There was a two-acre plot on the northwest corner of town. I bought it with my last $1,000. It would be a lift for Ethel to have a new house and different surroundings. The fenced acreage would allow us to have livestock. The family all loved animals of all kinds and this would give them something to do as well as make money for them.

Going to California for Christmas was a must for all of us. It would give her a boost in morale. It would help all of us to be together again and further cement family ties. I had almost 15 days of annual leave. The plan was to spend 10 days of it. It would take three days traveling and we would stay seven days. We planned to leave on December 20 and start back on December 28. We received a surprise in the mail. It was a card addressed to me by Ethel's mother. The message on the card was legible but like a child's first effort to write. It said, "Darlings: I can write. See you soon. I am tired. Love, Ethel." I read it aloud to the children. They took it and read it aloud. Susan said, "Mummy is getting better."

This gave us all a boost in morale. To me it was the most wonderful news I had in a long time. It meant she would not be entirely helpless and would possibly be able to do other things with her hands. At times I felt that our situation was hopeless. We were deeply in debt, as I had mortgaged the once-paid-for house.

Our spirits were high as we left at 6 o'clock in the morning. The Tudor Ford had been packed the night before. Mrs. Landreth had breakfast ready at 5 o'clock. The children were excited but still sleepy, and I told them to get some sleep, as they would need it later on. Dallas at 17 was an excellent driver, and I told him we would take turns. Soon they were all asleep. The road was smooth and the car seemed to travel without any effort at 60 miles an hour. Leaving the green farm land of the irrigated Twin Falls area, we were soon in Nevada with its endless miles of sagebrush, hills, and desert terrain. Some describe Nevada as having more miles of nothing than any state in the Union. Every 2 hours we stopped and walked around for a few minutes to stretch our legs and keep alert. Dallas and I traded driving every 2 hours. It was a long, monotonous trip, with few changes in scenery. There was an occasional ranch, or a stream and hills with a few scrubby juniper trees.

We ate a hurried lunch of soup and sandwiches at a service station cafe and continued on. It was 5 o'clock when we drove up to a casino restaurant. We ate hurriedly, as we wanted to drive a couple of more hours before dark. From our table we could see people playing at a roulette wheel. I decided to play $5 on the roulette wheel. They were all for it. The problem was to decide what number to play. Dallas said, "Let Lary do it. I actually think he is psychic."

"O.K., Lary, you are it."

"Give me a little time to think." He closed his eyes for a minute. "I see the number 21." I walked over and put a dollar on the 21 and a dollar on each corner. The wheel spun one way, the deal with numbers in another. The ball bounced around and stopped in 21. I cashed in the $68 which paid for our trip. Nothing but pure luck.

The last rays of the fiery red sun disappeared from the horizon 2 hours and a 100 miles later. It was my turn to drive and I felt rested. In fact, I was so hyper I knew I would be unable to sleep. The family conference was unanimously in favor of going on. At 12 o'clock we were nearing Los Angeles. They were all sleeping and I was feeling sleepy, so I pulled off the road and took a nap at a service station.

The traffic starting at 60 miles from Los Angeles slowed us and we arrived at 8 o'clock. Ethel had left with her driver for Cabot Kaiser half an hour earlier. Her mother, who was a marvelous cook, served us a sumptuous breakfast and we all went to bed for a nap. When Ethel arrived home, we had a tearful, but joyous reunion. Some of the sparkle had come back to her eyes, and I could see by her cheerful smile that her attitude toward life had changed to a definitely hopeful outlook. We were all in high spirits.

"Do I have a surprise for you!"

"Tell me, honey."

"Wait until tomorrow when you take me to physiotherapy."

"I guess I'll have to wait, as you have always amazed me with your surprises."

There were a number of patients in the physiotherapy room with many different appliances that they used to help their individual muscular involvement. They would exercise and rest. Ethel's first exercise was in the yard. She actually trotted with the therapist. It wasn't a good trot, but it was a trot. She could walk. I could not help having tears of joy.

While she massaged Ethel's hands, the therapist had much to say in praise of her determination to improve the use of her muscles.

"In all my experience I have never seen anyone try harder and make as much improvement as she has with what she has to work with. Most patients would give up completely and just be resigned to their condition. We all love her for her almost unbelievable effort and persistence."

With glass, wood, and epoxy, they had made a gadget that fitted over her thumb and second finger and enabled her to hold a pen. She practiced writing. It was a laborious process.

246

"I have to concentrate and try to command the fingers and muscles to make each move. Sometimes it takes a little time for them to respond. At first I could only make lines, but it is slowly becoming easier to form the letters. It took me an hour to write the card to you, and I was exhausted when it was finished."

"I have really had my surprise."

"You haven't had it yet. Wait until the therapist for my next treatment comes."

The nurse gave me instructions as to the daily stretching of her neck, arms, and hands, and had me practice it while she counted and instructed me.

After a 15-minute rest break during which we walked and talked about the children, a voice said, "Time for your fitting." This therapist had been a state and national 4-H winner in Home Economics. When the supervisor found that she was handy with tools, they gave her a workshop and tools. With an unusual mechanical ability bordering on genius and her knowledge of muscles, she designed gadgets to enable the patients to make the most use of their damaged muscles. She held up what looked like a cross between a fork and a spoon, with tines and a bowl-shaped base.

"This is a spork. There is an excellent chance that you will be able to feed yourself in six months."

She fitted the long, slim handle of the spork into a cast of Ethel's thumb and second finger. Then she clamped a board on the table with a short piece of pipe in it. A rod went into the pipe that was connected to an open sleeve-like contraption with a hinge on the back. She strapped Ethel's arm into it. The gadget allowed her to move back and forth, sideways as well as up and down, with shoulder action.

"This is going to be your surprise. Imagine, in six months I am going to get a bite when I want it! No one, even you, has timed my bites right."

The smile on her face showed her faith and desire to reach that goal. It was her courage and determination never to give up that helped me to have hope for the future.

The ride home was uneventful. We tried using Lary's psychic perception on the roulette wheel, but he missed on five straight numbers. His genie must have been taking a vacation.

COMING HOME

We moved into our new house in May. Our housekeeper had moved out of town. We were cooking and housekeeping for ourselves.

It would be impossible for a man to realize the extent of daily problems that confront a wife in the management of a home and children until the responsibility is his alone. There were so many things that I had taken for granted which now became additional work to do. The family discussions that we had held helped. The children were cooperative and assumed duties and carried out their responsibilities with very little supervision. Meal planning, ordering groceries, paying household bills, helping with homework, doctor and dental visits, and countless other chores all took time. An extension agent has a very demanding job which is very much full time, and many evenings have to be spent in giving lectures and attending meetings. It was hard to find 5 minutes. My hours of sleep suffered.

Ethel's mother wrote a letter saying that Cabot Kaiser would release Ethel on June 1. They felt that the only progress she would make from now on would be up to her. They wanted me to come down a week ahead to learn the daily therapy and stretching muscles and tendons. There was no doubt Ethel had made considerable improvement because her letters were a whole page long.

All of us went to Hollywood to bring her home. She had returned from her therapy session at Cabot Kaiser when we arrived. What a joyous occasion! There was laughter and tears. Dinner was a great boost to everyone's morale. Ethel could feed herself with the gadget that the therapist at Cabot Kaiser had invented for her. By pushing down, the arm would rise up and by swerving her body, the inert arm could be moved up and down from the plate to her mouth. It was still a difficult process for her, but the therapist told her that she would gradually improve for a long time. Her Swiss steak had to be cut in small pieces because her throat was still partially constricted. The spork worked remarkably well in scooping up bites. We all slowed our rate of eating so she could keep up with us.

About halfway through the meal, she said, "I am still hungry, but my arm and hand are too tired to continue eating." I finished feeding her with her spork.

She said, "Don't worry, darling. It won't always be like this. I will get stronger in time."

The spork, clamp, sleeve, straws, and the board with the pipe

248

fitting that held the sleeve upright fitted into a carrying case for traveling; otherwise it would be left clamped on the table.

There was a lot to learn about the daily stretching and flexing of the muscles in the arms, hands, and neck. The therapist had me do the therapy under her supervision. Little did we know that this would go on for the next 20 years.

One evening we visited J. M. Whiting, my old superintendent of schools from Heyburn. The boys were fascinated with their first look at television. J.M. lived a few blocks from the Tobeys and he invited us over to watch the wrestlers on TV. The boys were appalled at the barbaric mayhem. I took them to a gym the next day where they saw the same wrestlers rehearsing and realized that the performance was really a fake.

The boys never forgot and every once in a while remarked about how they saved Virg. They rarely called me Dad or Father. We were returning from a show on Hollywood and Vine, a few blocks from Tobeys' residence. They paused to watch the stream of cars from the walkway over the freeway. I walked on. I was by a 6-foot hedge two blocks away when five young men came out of a driveway and blocked my progress. I backed against the hedge to keep from being surrounded. From their black shiny zoot suits, I knew I was in trouble. Zoot-suiters had been terrorizing people in Los Angeles for months. I had my hands against my chest. I was going to use thumbs, knees, feet, head and do as much damage as I could before they got me down. I glanced back to the freeway. Lary and Dallas were talking and waving their arms and walking slowly toward me. They were still a block away.

"Lary, there are several people ahead. Do you suppose Virg is in trouble?"

"Let's take a look."

They didn't run, but started to walk briskly. This gave me hope. The punks noticed their approach and crowded in on me to let them pass. My sons and I had an agreement that if you were crowded or in trouble and another nodded, you nodded back and it was time to take action. Dallas nodded; I nodded. One hundred-eighty-pound Dallas, who had been bucking 100-pound hay bales, reached out and knocked two heads together. I floored one with blows to the head. Lary, only 140 pounds, jumped on one and rode him to the ground. The last one was clobbered by both Dallas and me. They were all down whimpering—five 16- to 19-year-old punks, none of whom could make a high school football team. They had to travel in gangs and pick on single victims.

Lary said, "It serves you right for monkeying with anyone from Idaho. Dallas, what shall we do with them?"

"Lary, the first thing is they have too many clothes on." With the help of two of their broad belts with big buckles, the punks were persuaded to strip completely. They stood complaining and shivering in the chilly night air.

"Start running. It will warm you up." They chased them down the street, encouraging them with whacks from the belts.

"What about their clothes?" I asked. Lary and Dallas gathered the clothes, took them to the overpass and threw them down to the freeway. The police picked up the naked boys. The article in the newspaper said they told the officers they were minding their own business when three huge men from Idaho came out of an alley, beat them up and took their clothes. I called the editor and he promised no names, and the correct version came out in the paper the next day. Two days later the fleet came in and sailors had a ball catching zoot-suiters and stripping them. This ended zoot-suiting in Los Angeles.

On the way back to Idaho, we stopped at a service station. I paid the attendant with silver dollars and a bill, which he placed on the hood while he cleaned the windows. We were at least 2 miles out of town when I noticed the money still lying on the hood. I turned around and took it back to the station attendant, which impressed the family.

"Crosses never steal. They don't have to," I told them.

Breakfast was our first meal at home. We discussed the cooking and housekeeping problems. Our new house had four bedrooms, two upstairs and two in the basement. If each child had a room of his own, which they wanted and we thought they should have, there would be no room for a housekeeper. Ethel listened to our conversation, then expressed her opinion.

"Virg is a better cook than any of the three housekeepers we have had. All of you can cook if you have to and I can help you. We can have a housekeeper come in for a half-day once a week to clean house, do the laundry, and change bedding."

"If I am going to do most of the cooking, you children will have to pitch in and help."

The children thought it was a great idea.

Ethel said, "Get a pencil and paper and we will make up a schedule for everyone on a daily and weekly basis." It turned out that she had been thinking for a long time about organizing the household. We all chipped in with suggestions. It was pointed out that by having a schedule, we would be able to get the work done more efficiently and have some time for recreation. We prepared an almost complete schedule for weekly duties, as well as weekly rotations. Since there were three children, the schedule was on a three-week rotation. It was a relief to know that Ethel could and would take over some of the managerial duties in the household. More importantly, it helped her to feel essential.

My schedule started at 6 a.m., getting dressed, washing up,

starting breakfast. Six-thirty was wake-up time for the rest of the family. Ethel had to be dressed, taken to the bathroom, washed, and made ready for breakfast. The children had to make their beds and get themselves ready for school. Breakfast was almost exactly at 7 o'clock and finished by 7:30. Bathroom and brushing teeth for Ethel, while the kitchen was cleaned up and dishes put in the dishwasher by the children. It was actually a three-ring circus. It was a relief to me to get to the office at 8 o'clock and breathe. I went home at noon to fix lunch for Ethel, unless I had to be out of town. We had a housekeeper twice a week and I tried to arrange out-of-town meetings on those days. Sometimes I took Ethel with me. The children had a good hot lunch program at school.

At 5 o'clock I hurried home to prepare dinner. There were many night meetings and I was rushed for time. The children had to be present at 6 o'clock for dinner, with absolutely no excuse. After dinner, each carried the dishes to the kitchen, cleaned the scraps off, and put them in the dishwasher. In the evening, the children did their homework. They were allowed one hour of television. Often they had time to play games.

There were many school activities that had to be planned for. There was chauffering, and I took over whatever chores they were unable to do. This schedule left no time for grocery shopping.

I was complaining to my home agent, Edna Weigen, about the time it took to plan meals and shop. She suggested that I should plan meals for several weeks ahead of time and make one order for each week's supplies. I could phone in my order from the office and the store would have it ready for me to pick up after work. I told Ethel about this.

"Let me think about this for a day or so."

After dinner a couple of days later, she informed us of "the plan." First she asked Lary to make a list of the favorite dishes that each member of the family would like. To this she added wholesome main dishes that would be easy to prepare. From the list 21 menus were chosen, each with four or five alternates. This would be a three-week rotation. She suggested that we have the home agent balance the main dish with vegetables and fruit for a healthy diet, and to recommend amounts. I showed the list to Edna.

"I can use this! I'll have Eleanor [the secretary] make copies of it for both of us. I'm conducting two-day afternoon classes in meal planning and I will use it for group participation."

The result of their work was very promising, as they even had the amounts of each food item for a family of five. Edna helped me make up the weekly grocery lists. It wasn't perfect at first, but after several months of revisions and changes, some in the selections and some in the amounts, the sequence of what should be used early in the week because of spoilage, we came up with a set of lists that could be left in the grocery store. All I had to do was call and say, "Please have list number 1, 2 or 3 ready for pickup at 5 o'clock."

The children soon learned the menu rotation and made remarks like, "Goody, it's chicken and dumpling week!" The meals were good. Ethel had been a superb cook and her suggestions and supervision, and *The Better Homes and Gardens Cookbook*, made me a competent cook.

Shortly before fair time, Edna, the home demonstration agent, suddenly became ill. She was to conduct an adult cooking class, and it fell upon me to conduct the class, which I did, using the women as resource people. This went back to the days when I had to take over an algebra class because they had run their teacher off. If I couldn't answer a problem, I would call on one of the bright students to explain it. The cooking class went o.k. except that I really put my foot in my mouth when one woman said she hated to cook. I guess it was my own predicament that caused me to make an incendiary statement.

"Cooking is relatively simple, or women couldn't do it."

They really booed me, but mostly in a good-humored manner. My face was really red when my remark was printed in the next issue of the weekly newspaper. In order to protect myself, I decided to enter an apple pie and a loaf of white bread in the county fair. The pie was perfect on the first try, with a flaky, light brown crust. The bread took three bakings to get a satisfactory loaf. The judging was going on while I was watching Dallas and Lary show their Holstein heifers. When that was over, I strolled over to the food section and, to my surprise, there was a blue ribbon on each of my entries. Editor Bill McKnight just happened to be passing and I called his attention to them. He had tried to give me, his fishing buddy, a bad time by printing my ill-advised remark. His next issue announced, "County Agent Proves That Cooking Is Easy" and listed my two blue ribbons. Actually, Ethel deserved the credit for them because of her meticulous supervision of the project. When Dallas saw the ribbons, he said, "Mummy, you were the bestest cook in the whole world!"

Everyone did some food preparation: even 7-year-old Susan, with her mother's supervision, could make a beef stew after returning home from school and have it ready for dinner. Lary was a Kraft Dinner specialist. He enhanced it with green peppers, onions, ham, and cheese, and that was his favorite meal to cook. Dallas could cook almost anything.

Ethel had a phone business that gave her something to do to pass the time and earn a few dollars a month. We modified the telephone, using springs and a foot lever to raise the bar and a fixed headrest. The operator would keep the line open for her. She was able to memorize over 150 phone numbers, and would call the Rotary and Chamber of

Commerce members to remind them of their weekly meetings. The brief conversations added interest to her day.

It was amazing how well Susan anticipated her mother's needs. Ethel rarely had to ask for anything. We tried to make her feel useful, needed, and as independent as possible. At first she seemed to be reluctant to discipline or correct the children. Possibly she was afraid of losing some of their love for her, because of her condition. My corrections and remarks were sometimes too hasty and abrupt. She never interfered, but discussed it with me when we were alone. My contention was that they expected to be corrected and would respect her for it. Children, when pressured by their peers to do something that they know is wrong, like to have an out by saying, "My parents wouldn't like that," or "My parents would just about kill me if I did that."

Actually, very little discipline was needed. Guidance when they were first able to comprehend really paid off. They were exuberant, fun-loving people, full of spontaneity and wit. If you want your child to drive safely and handle a car properly, the training should start when he is six years old or less. Get him to comment on good and poor driving. Your personal behavior in following ethics, rules of conduct and laws will carry over into the behavior of your children.

Ethel and I as parents tried to show them the value of honesty. Starting when they were quite small, I told the boys that because of their inheritance they would be larger than most of the boys in their class. They were not to pick on others because of it. In fact, they should help protect smaller boys from bullies. As the three children were growing up, we tried to see that there was no sibling rivalry or competition between them.

"The only people that really care about you are your folks. If you should die or get killed, it would make hardly any difference to other people," Ethel pointed out. "Support each other. Be proud of what your brothers or sister have accomplished because they are Crosses. All of you are different, even though you have the same parents. There are thousands of genes that you may have inherited from other ancestors, and your skills and talents may be in different fields. When any one of you accomplishes something, we are all proud of you. Whether it is good or bad, it reflects back on the family." Ethel's affliction with polio actually made the family a very close one with everybody looking out for everybody else. The children were proud of their beautiful mother and liked to show her off and be with her, which pleased her very much.

Ethel never complained about her condition other than to bemoan her inability to do something, which was rare. One day she said to them, "I cannot do things that other mothers can do, like taking care of your clothes and a lot of other things."

I felt like hugging Lary when he said, "Mummy, when I come home from school you are always there. If I need help or advice you are there—and that's more than most of the boys have, as their mothers are always running around. I've noticed they don't pay much attention to their children except to say, 'Don't do this or that.' You have always been ready to help us when we needed it."

When Lary was in the sixth grade, he went to bed with a bad cold and fever. The cold lasted only a few days, but he still had a low-grade fever. He complained of stiffness and soreness in his knee joints and we were afraid that he might have rheumatic fever. We took him to a pediatrician in Twin Falls. Tests showed his sed rate was up. Bed for six weeks, and going only to the bathroom very slowly and then back to bed. His schoolwork was sent home and Ethel was his teacher. At the end of six weeks he still had the slight fever and his sed rate was still high. Back to bed again with the continuation of the same medication. Tests showed the same results. The specialist's bill was very high and I still owed about $100. The pediatrician at Twin Falls also said Lary had a bad heart. He had been in bed for four months and no change. I called Ethel's doctor from the Elks and we made an appointment.

Dr. Tremaine first sent us to a heart specialist for a check of his heart condition. Then he also checked Lary's heart and tested for rheumatic fever. We met with the two doctors in the afternoon. The heart specialist said there was a slight noise due to scar tissue from measles, but his heart was strong and functioning perfectly. Dr. Tremaine agreed.

"I concur. Lary has a bad sinus infection in his right nostril that is causing the low fever and the sed rate. His local doctor can treat this. He isn't on the verge of having rheumatic fever and has never had it. Lary, do you play baseball?"

"Yes I do, Doctor."

"Well, take it easy for two weeks because you might hurt your arm."

"Do you mean I can get out of bed and go back to school?"

"You surely can."

When I got the bill from the pediatrician in Twin Falls, I telephoned him and said I wasn't going to pay the bill and why. Two weeks later, the arrogant and abusive owner of the local bill collecting agency called and tried to collect. I told him that if he didn't have my bill marked "Paid in Full" handed to me in person by Wednesday noon, I would file a suit for medical negligence, malpractice, and incompetence against the doctor. I would not accept mail delivery.

"You mean that?"

"Don't show up with the bill and you will find out." He came on Wednesday with the bill marked "Paid in Full."

Our new place had 2 acres of very level, fertile land. One half of it was fenced and put into pasture. A loafing shed or barn served as shelter. The other half was planted with strawberries with rows of sweet cherry trees. The pasture was for calves or stock for the boys' 4-H projects. They wanted to raise and fatten out whiteface steers. Champions really brought a lot of money at the fat livestock sale. Sometimes the figures ran into thousands of dollars, depending on the sponsors. My friend L. Wiseman, who ran the sale yard, said he would be on the lookout for steers that could possibly be good to fatten out. On a sale day in April, he gave me a call saying there were four whiteface calves to be sold and two of them might make good fat steers. They were about the right size and two of them had the right conformation. I noticed that they seemed to be wild. Possibly they were afraid of the strange surroundings. When we turned them loose in our pasture, they ran to the far end. Lary and Dallas looked them over.

"I wonder if we will be able to tame them?" Lary said.

"It will take a lot of time. Even Virg with his knack for handling animals will have his hands full." Truer words were never spoken. They started to come to the feed rack. Everyone talked to them to get their confidence, but when they were not eating at the rack, they stayed at the far end of the pasture, away from man as far as the fence would allow. One of the steers that had the best conformation seemed to be less afraid of us. We could walk up quietly, but when we patted him, he would jump and run. He didn't like to run very far. If we could get a halter on him and have him tied up for a few days while we curried and petted him, he would get tame enough to handle. When they saw the halter Dallas was carrying, three of them ran wildly with their tails in the air toward the other end of the pasture. One ran into the shed. In fact, he hit the back wall and fell down. He was groggy and we were able to get the halter on. It was then I noticed that his eyes were glazed with white. He was nearly blind with pinkeye.

One of the neighbors told us he thought the calves had been on a rodeo circuit as roping calves and we would never be able to tame them. He was right—we never did. Two of them bloated. We sold one and butchered the other. It was a very unprofitable venture.

This was the first of a succession of animals. The Silvers gave Lary a banty rooster and two hens. We had banty chicks that the cats were after. Dallas tossed coins in a saucer and won five baby ducks that grew up to be bottomless pits for feed. They thought Dallas was their mother and followed him around quacking as loud and frequently as they could. When I suggested that we eat them, I met with a wall of indignation. We sold the lot for $5. It was a relief to get rid of them. Susan visited a friend in the country and came home with Nanny, a cute baby goat. It followed her everywhere. She and her friends taught it to play hide-and-seek. It became a pest, as it liked to climb up and stand on top of cars. It loved to eat clothes right off the line. Flowers of all kinds were favorites for dessert. Harold Campbell needed goat's milk for a weak stomach and we were magnanimous in letting him have Nanny. For years she followed him around his ranch. She would jump into the back of his pickup when he went to the field to irrigate. She liked to hunt pheasants with him and helped find the birds.

Next was Lambie, a small lamb that strayed from a driven herd and was wandering around bleating on the highway. Susan raised it on a bottle. She won a prize as an 8-year-old Little Bo Peep with Lambie in the Fourth of July parade. I liked mutton, but the rest of the family said they would never eat a bite of it. Susan was at school when I sold Lambie to the sale yard. She didn't speak to me for over a week. Finally, she broke the silence.

"If I can't have Lambie, where is my money?"

I handed over the $29.75. All of the Cross offspring were in 4-H Clubs from the time they were 10 or 12 years old. Susan was in food and clothing. Dallas was champion in fitting and showing at the county fair and reserve champion at the district fair with a Holstein named Ballerina. That was an appropriate name for her, as she really showed off when she was being led before the judges' stand. She loved Dallas and would bawl a greeting as she ran toward him. Lary and his heifer were evenly matched. Neither was capable of winning.

ARROWHEADS

The Hulls, Everett, and his father, had been friends of the Tobeys for many years. They had driven from Kansas with two wagons pulled by large draft horses carrying their household goods. An extra team was led behind a wagon. They had stopped at Twin Falls after the turn of the century when the Twin Falls tract was first being settled. There they heard of the gold strike in Jarbridge, Nevada. They decided to delay their planned trip to California.

There were various stories as to how the gold was discovered. The most plausible was that a cowboy who was helping drive cattle from Nevada to the railroad at Minidoka, a distance of 200 miles, was chasing a stray steer when he ran onto an unusual outcropping of rock. He put a piece of the greenish quartz into his saddlebag and forgot about it until he emptied his saddlebag almost two years later. A prospector saw it and started looking for and found the initial discovery.

The Hulls drove to Jarbridge. It was a typical lawless boom town. A shack next door to a saloon had collapsed due to deep snow. They traded a team of horses for the property. A tent by the river was their home until they got the shed fixed up.

The claims and mines were mostly east to west on the high hills and mountains. When Everett and his father went up into the hills, almost all of the good claims had been filed upon. The ore was in green quartz in the rocky granite outctrops. They did find a 20-acre plot of flat land covered with soil and shale with no outcrop. They filed on it and had it recorded in the office at Jarbridge.The next day they took picks and shovels to do their 4x4x6-foot assessment work needed to hold it for a year. A miner riding a horse stopped by.

"You have filed on the least likely place in the vicinity," he told them. "The only way you can properly explore this claim is to have a big team of horses and a fresno."

"We have the horses."

"The gold-bearing quartz runs north and south, so you dig east and west across your claim."

They thanked him and bought a rusted fresno scraper. Everett drove the four horses and his father, a strong man, handled the heavy bar. It was slow, hard work. They would hit rocky spots. Actually, the soil was only about 2 feet deep. When they hit an outcrop, they would use the pick and look. Twelve-year-old Robby followed the fresno and looked at the rock they exposed. They had been working a week and the father was about to tell his wife thay would move on to California as planned.

The next day they were making the third cross-cut about halfway up on the claim when Robby came running, yelling, "Daddy, Daddy, look what I found!" He was waving a small piece of rock that was almost black on one side and green on the other, with fine yellow threads scattered through it.

"Where did you find it, Robby?"

"Back there a little ways."

They were able to follow Robby's tracks back to the spot where he had found the rock, but there was no outcrop there. It had to be from the area they had previously worked. It was nearly noon the next day when they finally found it, after going over the 200-foot area three times with picks and shovels. It was the tip of an outcrop. In a few days they were using the horses to pack ore to the processing mill.

Mrs. Hull hated Jarbridge and wanted to leave. She kept complaining that it was not a place for a God-fearing family. The winters were very severe, and even though they had built a log house, she feared for the health of Robby, as he was quite frail. The only doctor was a questionable drunkard.

The Hulls didn't drink or gamble and they were getting rich. Near the end of the second year, Robby caught pneumonia and died, probably due to lack of adequate medical attention. They fresnoed rock and soil into their mine shaft. Taking only their clothes, they rode the stage coach to Twin Falls and took the train for California. There they bought a large acreage of land close to fast-growing Los Angeles. They lived in a mansion in the fashionable part of town. Undoubtedly, at one time they were millionaires.

They became involved in huge land and building developments and were heavily investing in stock market futures. Mrs. Hull died of shock when the Depression wiped them out.

In 1935, Everett and his father were back in Idaho, tuning and repairing pianos. There was no competition and their work took them to many remote areas where pianos had not been tuned for years. Everett began to hunt arrowheads and gem stones and in a short time knew most of the areas of old Indian encampments. His collection finally reached over 1,000 arrowheads, spear points, and flint knives.

When his father died at 90, he was lonesome, as he had no living relatives. Our family adopted him and had him to dinner when he was in Jerome. He started to take Dallas and Lary on rock and arrowhead hunting trips. Wind uncovered arrowheads and Indian artifacts in many of the ancient campgrounds in Hagerman Valley and Owyhee County. Their collection began to be impressive.

The following incident makes you wonder as to what controls our destiny. Is it planned or is it chance that determines when we are saved from sure death or we die because of a few minutes or a few brief seconds? Why was someone out there to save us? Why did the tree blow down when a truck was passing? Life is really a fragile thing that can be snuffed out easily by unexpected happenings. We always think this can happen, but to someone else.

Sunday was a fine day. Dallas and Lary packed a lunch, planning to ride their bikes 3 miles to the top of Snake River Canyon. They promised to be home for an early Sunday dinner at 5 o'clock.

Leaving their bikes at the top, they climbed down the almost vertical canyon wall to the river 400 feet below. There was a steep trail with many places where you had to use both hands and feet. They were in the Blue Lakes area in sight of the famous Perrine Ranch. The first of the large springs entered Snake River there. Because of protection from wind, reflection from lava rock walls, and the abundance of fish and clams, Indians had camped there for hundreds of years and it was an excellent place to find Indian artifacts. It was fall and the Perrine Ranch had turned the water out of their irrigation ditches. Water washing the banks and bottom of the stream often uncovered arrowheads that had been buried by a foot or more, due to the increasing soil depth. The area was literally sprinkled with pieces of black and colored obsidian that had been chipped off by arrowhead makers.

It was nearly 5 o'clock; dinner was almost ready and there were no boys. In our close-knit family it was necessary for everyone to be punctual for the household to run smoothly. In the past there had been few misses on agreed schedules. Ethel began to worry that something had happened to them. The climb into and out of the canyon was dangerous. I tried to reassure her.

"They have been well trained not to take any chances and they will be here on time."

At 5 o'clock there was still no sign of them. I decided to hold up putting food on the table, expecting them to arrive any minute. At 5:30 I started to put food on the table, deciding to eat hurriedly and drive to the canyon to see if their bikes were still there. We heard a car drive up into our circular driveway. It was a white ambulance with a big red cross on it and the sign Twin Falls Municipal Hospital. Ethel was staring at it with her mouth open and her face grey. The ambulance stopped. Lary stepped out of one side and Dallas the other. The driver opened the rear door and took out their bikes.

They had climbed down the canyon wall and were hunting arrowheads in the canal's ditches. They had found three perfect points and several slightly damaged ones. They said it was about 2:30 when they decided to walk back up the main canal toward the trail. Somewhere along the bottom of the trail they came to small footprints.

259

A little farther on, someone had pulled two tall plants with a flat cluster of white blossoms on top and a long white carrot-like fleshy root. Lary picked up one and said, "Someone took a bite out of this one." Dallas was holding the other and said, "There is a bite out of this one. I hope they didn't swallow any."

"Why?"

"That is water hemlock. It contains cyanide. Socrates ate it and died." He took out his knife and sliced into the root. It was full of clear white bubbles like cells. "Virg told me these cells contain the poison." Further up the canal they saw where the two bites had been spit out.

They started to climb the canyon wall, resting after the first 100 feet. It was then they heard crying and sounds of someone in pain. Hurriedly, they climbed up another 100 feet and saw the two boys. They were huddled up moaning and holding their stomachs. There was no way they could carry the boys up, so they decided to carry them down and get help. They had noticed a man with a pickup truck cleaning ditches about a quarter of a mile from the foot of the trail. How Dallas, 16, carrying the 12-year-old boy, and Lary, 12, carrying the 8-year-old, made it down that canyon was a miraculous feat of courage. The sick boys could not hold on. One hand had to hold them by an arm. Sometimes they had to put one boy down and help get the other over a dangerous steep place. Dallas said the smaller boy's eyes were rolling back in his head and his breathing was getting shallow. When they reached the bottom, Lary ran ahead to get the man in the pickup. The younger boy passed out and Dallas gave him artificial respiration to revive him partially. They put the boys in the back of the pickup and gave them artificial respiration on the way to the hospital. They had learned the procedure in Scout work. In a few days the story of their heroism was in the daily papers and had spread all over the area. The doctor said both boys would have died in a half-hour or less if they had not reached the hospital in time.

STRAWBERRIES

We planted an acre of strawberries which would bear fruit the next year. The second year after planting the strawberries and young sweet cherry trees, the berries started to ripen in June. Thirteen-year-old Lary, whose right hand was in a cast due to a wrist injury, took over the harvesting. The picking crew was entirely girls of different ages and paid by the box or 60¢ a crate. He kept the books, checked to see they were not damaging the vines, or picked fruit and assigned rows to the pickers. Ethel took and solicited orders over the phone. One half of the patch was picked every other day. For nearly a month, the average daily harvest was 40 crates or more. After the cost of picking, crates, boxes, delivery cost, and paying Lary, the net for the two years of production was nearly $4,000. This whittled down the original $10,000 polio debt.

Dallas was bucking hay for the Capps brothers seven days a week, making at least $5 a day.

In the fall at the end of the second season, grass had grown up and died in the rows of the 3-year-old planting of 4-year-old cherry trees. The city decided to put in a through street, as our acreage had been zoned into the city. This meant taking down the stock shed. It was shortly after the city work crew had quit work for the day that a fire broke out and destroyed all of the cherry trees. The city officials flatly refused to accept any blame for it. My only hope of getting anything for the cost of the shed, trees, and labor was to take it as a loss from my income tax. My income tax was about $750. The tax return listed the total amount of the loss as $1,500, on which I could get a refund for taxes the year before. They paid a refund of $750, not $1,500. The next year I put in for the $750 they had not paid. To my surprise, they accepted the return and sent a check for $750, which I deposited immediately. Two weeks later I received a phone call.

"This is the Internal Revenue Service in Twin Falls. You received a refund check for $750."

"I did."

Then I was told to pay it back immediately, as it had been disallowed the year before. The agent first tried to bully me. I had a bulletin prepared by Tony Horne, extension horticulturist, showing the value of fruit trees at different ages, which substantiated my claim. He was insistent until I told him I would file suit if he took action against me and would insist on a jury trial. He was against that, but said they had to collect something. I opened my checkbook and showed him my balance of $40. (It was near the end of the month.) I wrote him a check for $30.

"I don't like it."

"You mean you won't take it?"

"I didn't say that."

I gave him the check. We shook hands, and I thanked him and left. That ended my fear of the IRS. They are mortal and susceptible.

When Lary was in the eighth grade, he insisted on taking his mother to school on a Friday. He did not tell her that he was in the championship spelling bee. Ethel said, "He must have been sure that he was going to win it." He did.

The grade school teachers had Ethel give a talk on polio and Salk vaccine when Susan was in the third grade. One of her classmates must have been very jealous of Susan's popularity. At recess she spitefully said to Susan, "At least my mother isn't crippled."

Susan looked at her. "My mother is not crippled; she is handicapped and it isn't her fault. She is prettier than your mother and her children are a lot better mannered and smarter than your mother's."

The children were proud of their mother and liked to show her off. One of these incidents was when Dallas said, "Get Mummy dressed up, as I am taking her to school with me on Thursday." Needless to say, Ethel was also proud of her big, handsome, and very popular son.

The Cross family attended all football games starting with Dallas'. My father, in his 80s, was an ardent fan and often traveled 100 miles each way with us to see a football game. When Dallas was a sophomore, he hit upon the idea of getting his mother involved and interested in the game. Every year they learned and reviewed the rules. Then they learned the plays and signals. During a game she would hear the signal calling of the quarterback, and say what the play was going to be. She was a good armchair quarterback, as she could call what play would work in a given situation.

ROCKETS

High School Principal Pete Taylor called me and said that it was very important that I come over to his office right away. I could not imagine Lary's getting into trouble. It ran through my mind that he might be hurt or dead. You can imagine my relief when I saw him and his close friend, Bob Boren, sitting with sheepish grins on their faces. I wondered what these two brains had been up to.

Periodically a rocket was seen over the Butte 3 miles east of Jerome. It was estimated that it was going 6,500 to 8,500 feet high. This was a violation of the air space and endangered airplanes. Because of this violation, the F.B.I. was called in. The two agents were very nice and assured Bob's father, Gib Boren, and me that the boys were in no danger of prosecution. They emphasized that there must be absolute secrecy about the incident. This also included Pete Taylor, the principal. We, the parents, were not to ask any questions, nor were the boys to volunteer or discuss anything about the rocket. That evening at home no mention was made of the matter, though I was burning with curiosity, and felt awkward and left out.

The next afternoon we were again summoned to the high school. The F.B.I. agents were replaced by two men from White Sands Missile Base in New Mexico. Again the parents were warned to keep absolute secrecy about the entire incident for the boys' possible safety. They could not believe that the two boys could concoct a propellant from a high school chem lab and propel a three-stage rocket that high. The boys had another rocket in Boren's garage, completed except for the propellant. The men from the missile base had them go through their procedure and watched the successful launch. It must have gone off well. They said it was almost unbelievable what the boys had accomplished. Again they cautioned us about secrecy for their safety and said that this must never be made public; terrorists and other countries would use any means to get this information. The only reference that Lary ever made about the incident was that they told him when he finished college, a job would be waiting for him at White Sands. Gib Boren and I mutually agreed that we were lucky they didn't blow each other to pieces.

263

OUR SONS

Whether it was the good diet of my mother's or the inheritance from our Indian ancestors, or a combination, our family was very healthy. We rarely had colds and almost never missed school on account of any illness. It was nearing graduation time for Dallas and he had never been absent or tardy for the 12 years. The school officials were going to feature this at commencement. Dallas told his classmates that he was going to play hookey and miss a class just so he would not have to face a crowd and be embarrassed by the fuss they would make over him.

Pete Taylor, the high school principal, was really a super human being. He was liked and respected by students as well as parents. His office overlooked the walk into the building. When he saw Dallas leave the building during a study hall period, he put on his hat and followed him about two blocks behind. Dallas had just sat down on a stool by the counter in McCleary's drugstore when Pete walked up.

"Dal, have a Coke on me."

"All right. I'll have a cherry Coke. Thank you."

"Make it two. Dallas, it is quite an honor to never have missed a day of school and you should be proud of it. In my 20 years of teaching, you are the first student in my school to achieve this honor. You are going to receive the plaque and there is nothing you can do about it because we will give it to you regardless. As long as you are with me, you are in school."

Dallas finished his Coke and sheepishly went back to the next class.

Undoubtedly, the polio disaster and the resultant close cooperation of the family members made a cohesive, loving family. In the years that followed, we felt blessed with our almost trouble-free offspring when so many parents were having one problem after another as their children were growing up. The following incident graphically illustrates the value of early parental training and guidance.

On Monday morning after I returned from a week of conferences and teaching at the University of Idaho, my secretary, Eleanor, greeted me with a question.

"Have you heard about those boys stealing?"

"What boys?"

She then named a list of 20, which included a doctor's son and an attorney's son. Many of them were Lary's close friends. I was

264

apprehensive.

"Was Lary included in this list?"

"I'm sure he is," Eleanor said maliciously. She had been trying to undercut my job because her county commissioner "boy friend" would give it to her husband, John. I asked the sheriff if Lary was mixed up in the mess. He said Lary was not on any of the warrants he served. Most of the warrants were served by his deputy, who was out. The probate judge was out of town. My next contact was Fred Abrams, Chief of Police. Fred was a friend of the young people of the town and they liked and respected him. He held out his hand to greet me.

"Congratulations." Hope flooded my mind.

"Congratulations for what?"

"For having such a fine son as Lary. He and Larry Silvers knew about the widespread gang-like stealing from stores that has been going on for several weeks. They walked away and did not say anything so they couldn't be called squealers."

Now, many years later, I still get an overwhelming feeling of pride in my son. Back in my office, I read the article in the *North Side News*. Because of the magnitude of thefts, the guilty boys were sentenced to a year at St. Anthony Reform School. Being juveniles, their names were not published. They were given one year probation provided the following stipulations were met: sell their cars, be off the street and at home by 10 o'clock, no riding in a car driven by a juvenile, which included themselves. They were to keep what they had stolen for one year and pay for it from what they earned by physical labor. When I told Ethel about it, she was misty and ecstatic.

"That is just like what Dallas did a few years back!"

When Lary came home from school, I asked him, "Were you mixed up in this mess?"

"No, Virg. Crosses don't steal is what you and Mother have always told us. Besides, Dallas walked away from another mess like this three years ago, and he isn't any better than I am."

Ethel said, through tears, "I wish I could hug you!" Lary walked over and gave her a hug. Incidentally, Larry Silver and Lary Cross were inseparable buddies, one an all-state halfback, the other an all-state guard and linebacker.

That night we talked over how he could be rewarded without making a big to-do about it. The next Friday I told Lary that we probably had enough money to buy him a car. He wanted one to pull a spray rig. If he wasn't too busy tomorrow, we could go to Twin Falls and look for one. His grin lit up his whole face. His eyes sparkled.

"I am very, very busy, but I can tear myself away for all day tomorrow!"

He picked out an Austin with a trailer hitch. The last thing I asked him when he got into the car was, "What will I do when you get a traffic ticket?"

"That's easy. You will sell the car. Right?"

So Lary got his car. Most of his friends couldn't ride with him because of the judge's order. There must have been considerable jealousy and envy, because when Lary drove up to park in front of the school during noon hour, Fred Abrams, Chief of Police, drove up with his lights flashing and parked behind Lary, who was trying to figure out what he had done wrong. A group of boys gathered saying, "Cross, you are going to get yours!"

Fred Abrams got out of the police car, walked up to Lary, and held out his hand.

"Lary, I just want to compliment you, as I like the way you drive." This was typical of Fred's association with young people.

I will never know how much planning and preparation Lary made to win a trip to the National 4-H Club Conference in Chicago by being a state winner in one of the many fields. He had tried dairy but definitely was not an animal person. His work in the rural electrification club was outstanding, but sons of electricians were almost sure winners. When Lary was a junior, he got four of his friends to join him in a 4-H Entomology Club with his mother for a leader. His collection of insects got a blue ribbon at the county fair, but he wasn't even close at the district fair. He knew I was advising growers on insect control practices. Our neighbor had been running a commercial spray outfit for controlling lawn weeds and insects. He moved away during the winter. In the very early spring Lary contacted Roland Portman, the extension entomologist. Roland knew of Lary's capabilities and thought it was an excellent idea for him to start a very profitable summer business operating a spray rig. The materials to use were outlined in a complete and specific *Idaho Bulletin* that Portman had just published. Lary could identify insects. Mr. Portman showed him how to set up his record keeping, and furnished him with professional mounting material and boxes. The problem was to get a trailer with a sprayer on it. To get a 200-gallon tank, pump, hoses, nozzles, and trailer would cost about $1,000. Lary said he had $200 saved from hay bucking. Dallas could ante up only $100. I was still so deeply in polio debt that $200 was the most I could scrape up. Lary, Ethel, and I discussed the problem. We told him, "You might as well plan on bucking hay again this summer."

A few days later I was depositing my paycheck in the bank when the bank president called me to his desk. He was laughing.

"I just loaned a 16-year-old boy $500. You will have to sign his note because the bank auditors will really frown on an unsecured loan to a 16-year-old!"

The next thing Lary did was to trade his Austin for an old, but reliable pickup to pull the trailer. The pump power in the Briggs and

266

Stratton motor would send a stream at 300 pounds pressure to the tallest tree. For a trial run, he sprayed our lawn and trees. Everything worked with very little adjustment. He put a small ad in the newspaper guaranteeing complete satisfaction. By the first of May he was busy after school and all day Saturday and Sunday. He really put in long hours, as news of the quality of his work spread throughout the county. At the end of the season he had boxes and boxes of mounted and classified insects with common and Latin names, as well as a neat, complete record of amounts, costs, hours, and profit on all spray jobs. At the end of the season he was able to pay Dallas $250 for his $100 investment, repay the bank and begrudgingly paid back my $200. He still had $800 left, which would see him through school when he entered the university that fall.

The 4-H Club, with Lary as president, met regularly in the evening every two weeks. He kept kill bottles and with a net gathered specimens to mount every day. His bug collection and spray business records comprised his 4-H entomology project which was a state winner. Jerome County had an unprecedented number of state winners and was named as having the most outstanding 4-H Club program in the state, which gave me a trip to Chicago as a chaperon for the delegation from Idaho. They were a superior, well-dressed, and well-groomed group of 20 teenagers who boarded the Portland Rose at Shoshone. When the last delegate boarded the train at Pocatello and all were assigned their seats and berths in our separate Pullman, Lucia Wilson and I called them to a meeting for instruction on conduct and proceedings. Lucia was chaperon for the girls and I for the boys. We discussed conduct on the train, in the hotel, and meetings.

I asked, "Are there any other questions?"

"Mr. Cross, how shall we treat these girls?"

"They are something very special. They are the cream of many thousands of Idaho girls, so we treat them as if they were royalty, which they are. Hold their chairs and wait until they are seated. Be so polite that they become aware that you are the most polite and special boys that they have ever met." Previously I had gone over the programs of 4-H Congresses and had talked to other agents, so I had a good idea of the activities.

"There will be a lot of dancing, and you will have a chance to dance with many new and very pretty girls."

This comment brought on very vocal approval.

"There is one thing we are not going to overlook, and that is the Idaho girls. Most dances are tag, so you are to see that every Idaho girl gets on the floor. After you are tagged, she will get to dance the whole dance."

The conductor arranged that we would eat in the diner at the same time. I would sign for the meals. The menu and prices were mind-boggling for them. The three girls who were seated at my table all ordered rib steak, like I did. One of the girls from another table came over and said, "Mr. Cross, what shall I order?"

"Whatever you would like from the menu."

"But it is so expensive—$7.50!"

"So what? You have earned it. Enjoy!"

Five more people moved into the partially-filled Pullman car in Salt Lake. They were Pat Boone and his family. He sang for them and led them in a song or two.

One girl remarked, "Imagine seeing Pat Boone in person!"

At the Stevens Hotel in Chicago we were shown to our rooms which were grouped together in the same corridor. Meal seating was in tables of 12, first come, first served, in order to encourage mixing. There were programs of all kinds, but they were short with many choices for the delegates to attend. In the evening there was a dance in the ballroom with Guy Lombardo's orchestra. There were free periods and time to shop. We of the country were fascinated by the Christmas decorations in the stores. The Lionel train exhibition was simply overwhelming.

Lary was very busy. He would say "hello" and "goodbye." Lucia Wilson said she entered the elevator with him and he greeted most of the occupants by their first names. When she asked how many names he knew, he answered, "Oh, two hundred or so." He came to the room one evening with some packages to put into my suitcase. He had been Christmas shopping for the family at Marshall Fields. It was apparent that he had spent more money than he usually carried.

"How did you pay for them?"

"By check. The saleslady said she couldn't take an out-of-state check, so I insisted on seeing the manager. He asked a lot of questions and I showed him my bankbook. He told her to cash Mr. Cross' check for whatever he writes."

We were going as a group to the dining hall for dinner. Barbara, one of the Idaho girls, stopped in front of me.

"Mr. Cross, there is the cutest boy from Gawja."

"What you are saying is there's a dance after dinner and you want him to take you to it?"

She blushed. "That is right."

"Point him out and follow me and I'll do the rest." He was really handsome and when he sat down I stood behind the vacant chair next to him and asked, "Is this seat taken?"

"No, sir, it isn't."

"Thank you." I held the chair for Barbara and seated her next to him. I sat at another table and later she brought him around to meet me, giving a slight wink. After that, I was kept busy playing Cupid.

One evening I sat with Lary. On his other side was the president of

Hercules Powder. He was interested in Lary and his business venture. He congratulated me on having such an outstanding son. Lary had won national honors for his project in entomology.

"Lary, when you finish college, look me up and you have a job."

"Thank you, sir. I am going to be an electrical engineer and I am afraid of explosives."

"We have an insecticide department, so keep us in mind."

The next summer the boys and I were hunting arrowheads and other Indian artifacts along the Snake River near King Hill. Heavy rains had washed the banks, leaving an occasional point exposed. I found a beautiful point and held it up for them to see. They wanted a closer look at it, and being ornery, I started to run. I hit a slick, muddy spot and fell, sliding on my face. I was a mess of sticky mud from head to foot. They helped me to my feet and led me to a pool where they doused me in to wash off the mud from my clothes, face, and hair. It was a warm day, so it wasn't too uncomfortable.

After dinner that night I made a big bowl of popcorn and ate plenty. About bedtime I had an abdominal pain that kept getting worse. Ethel called Dr. Neher and he gave me a shot, saying it was a gas attack due to something I ate. The shot didn't help and the boys drove me to the hospital. There I was given a sedative. The next day I had X-rays and visits from Dr. Neher and his cousin, a doctor from Shoshone. That evening they called in Dr. Smail. They ruled out gall stones. They were perplexed by the symptoms.

All this time I was under sedation. I could hear and comprehend everything they said, but didn't say anything and kept my eyes closed. I thought it was definitely gall stones and if the damned fools didn't figure it out, I was going to die just to prove how incompetent they were. The next morning I was worse, but again heavily sedated. Ethel and Dallas came to visit me. Dr. Neher told her in my presence that something had to be done soon, as my vital signs were getting lower and lower. I could hear him but didn't open my eyes. When he left, Ethel came to the side of the bed.

"Darling, can you hear me?" I opened my eyes, tried to smile.

"I can hear you."

"Virg, you can't quit. Everything depends on you." She said later that I acted wide awake.

"Get Dr. Smail and the doctor from Shoshone off the case. Get Dr. Soli. He is in the building. It is gall stones."

Ethel and Dallas went to the chart desk, where they found Drs. Neher and Soli. Ethel told Dr. Neher in no uncertain terms what she wanted. He nodded and they came to my room. Dr. Soli examined me and said, "Gall stones." I opened my eyes, and he said later that I winked at him.

Neher and Smail were arguing with him in the hall and I could hear them.

"If we are going to save him, we have to operate immediately," Dr. Soli said. He ordered the nurse to prepare the operating room and give me a shot in the vein.

When I woke up with very little pain, Dr. Neher came and showed me a bottle of gall stones, saying, "Look what I found!"

"Doctor, you didn't find them. Dr. Soli did."

My recovery was very slow. In February I had a hemorrhoid operation. In March we were moving a piano to the basement of the court house and as we were going down the steps the fellow on the bottom slipped and I got the whole weight of the piano and had to have a hernia operation. Three major surgeries were just too much for even a healthy man to recover from readily. I was having daily shots for pain for 19 days and began to look forward to them. The nurse gave me my evening shot, and the syringe broke with very little of the contents going into my arm. She was a heavy-set, lazy person and said, "You got most of it." At 11 o'clock I still couldn't sleep and asked the new night nurse for a shot. She looked at my chart and said I couldn't have another so soon.

"The needle broke and I got very little of the last one."

"You still won't get a shot."

"My bowels are uneasy. I want an enema." She gave me a shot and I went to sleep.

I went to the office after a few days at home, working only half a day. I was not to be jarred or exercise, and move slowly for two weeks due to complications from infection. Milford Jones came into the office. He was in trouble, as he had planted nearly 300 acres of newly purchased land to seed peas. A heavy frost had damaged them. The fieldman for the seed company had advised him to plow them under and plant barley. Milford said this would break him, and pleaded with me to take a look and see if they could be saved. I got into his pickup and we drove to my house to get some pillows, as I couldn't stand the jarring and jolts of the long ride to the pea field. I sat in the car and he brought me samples of the damaged vines.

"Milford, see that little tip? That is the terminal bud. It is not damaged. In fact, none of the plants I have looked at are damaged."

"What does that mean?"

"It means that the peas will bloom and mature. In fact, this is a rare phenomenon, as there will probably be at least 25 to 30 percent increase in bloom and you will have one hell of a crop."

He wiped his eyes. It must have been hard for him to realize that his crop was not permanently damaged.

"Are you sure?"

"Milford, I was never more sure about anything." He shook my hand and gave me a hug and took me home. I was completely exhausted. Milford had the super crop as I had predicted. Just before Christmas, he gave me an envelope that contained a bill with three zeros on it.

QUAIL AND PHEASANTS

Jerome and Gooding Counties were nationally famous for pheasant hunting during the 40s and 50s. Sun Valley, 60 miles away, was a favorite stop for screen celebrities. Silver Creek and Wood River provided super trout fishing. Lary and I were eating a late snack at the Y Inn at Bliss. The pheasant season would open at 12 noon. Seated at a table across from us was a large, heavy-set, bearded man, a medium-sized, good-looking man, and a large, middle-aged, blond man. The blond man was evidently the owner of the new wonder dog, a Weimaraner. This newly imported breed was listed as super intelligent hunters. The owner was putting him through his repertoire of commands. Baron von Steuben could obey almost any command. He could even use the stool in the bathroom. When the owner bragged how easily they would get their birds with Baron von Steuben, Lary whispered, "I wish we could have a dog like that."

"Lary, don't sell Quail short. She is a superb hunting dog. Talk is cheap."

We were sitting on a ditchbank waiting for 12 o'clock. Lary was impatient and kept asking the time. At 11:40, a car drove up on the opposite side of the field. Four men got out, loaded their guns, and started walking toward us. Birds started to get up and they shot toward us. We decided to leave. As we were opening the car door, about 20 birds got up at once and flew over the car, landing in a beet field about half a mile away.

"Quail can find them in the beets and we will get our limit of four right away."

We had to drive around a mile and a half to get to the field. Baron von Steuben and the three men were hunting the field. Lary suggested that we find another field.

"Lary, I want to watch the wonder dog work."

The Weimaraner was working beautifully, crossing back and forth about 30 yards in front of the men. Lary was urging me to go to another field. The dog should be setting birds. Finally, he went on point. The bird fell and he retrieved it perfectly. When they neared the end of the field, he set another bird. It was a calm, clear day and voices carried a long way. The dog's owner said in a loud voice for our benefit, "There is no use of them hunting this field with that mutt. Baron von Steuben has been through it."

"Lary, at least 20 birds lit in that field and that dog only found two.

The rest are still there."

We had not gone over 50 yards when Quail made her first point. She continued to find birds one after another in a hurry. By the time we reached the end of the field, we had six birds. The three men were still standing by their car when we left the field. The large, heavy-set man winked at me.

"Where did you get that mutt?" I winked back.

"At the dog pound for $2.50."

He said, "I am Andy," and he introduced Bing Crosby and the other man whose name I do not remember, as it sounded like an Eastern European origin. Winking again, Andy said, "Will you take $500 for that dog?"

"No way."

Bing said, "Do you mind if I go over and shoot that bird?" He pointed across the road. There was Quail on point.

"Be my guest."

He shot the bird and Quail retrieved it for him.

"You have a great dog." I really felt sorry for the owner of the dog and his companions. They were happy to accept my invitation to hunt another field with us. Birds were plentiful in the next field and Quail set birds in front and in back of the Weimaraner even after he had covered the ground. We took turns shooting. They were betting a silver dollar a shot. An hour later, Lary and I had our limits.

"Are you going hunting tomorrow?" Bing asked. He winked. "Baron von Steuben must have a cold. He can't smell. Could we hire you and your dog to hunt with us?"

I told him we would hunt with them, but paying me was out of the question. We had breakfast together at 6 o'clock the next morning at the Y Inn. They had a betting game going. When it was your turn to shoot and you killed the bird, the other hunters each gave you a dollar. If you missed, you had to pay each of them. They asked if I wanted to join them and said Lary wouldn't need to. Lary said he had money and wanted to bet. They agreed that would be o.k.

Lary whispered, "Did I sucker them!"

I didn't miss a bird. Lary didn't miss a bird. Bing was a good marksman, and he only missed two. Andy missed a few more. The owner of the dog could not hit a barn door even if he was inside it. We finally allowed him two shots. When we quit, he had killed only one bird. As we drove home, Lary counted his dollars, all seven of them.

"I feel sorry for the owner of that dog. He paid $2,000 for this new wonder breed of dog and over $1,000 to have him trained. When Andy offered you all that money for Quail, I was afraid you would sell her."

"Lary, he was only fooling, because he winked at me as he said it."

They still tried to give me money, which I refused. Two weeks later I received a hunting coat with all the trimmings, which I used for

273

many years.

TAYLOR WILLIAMS AND HEMINGWAY

Taylor Williams was the specialist in sporting goods for Myers Hardware in Gooding. To me as a child he was tall, slim, dark-haired and had a smile while he patiently helped me select fishing tackle when my purchases were never over 50¢. I must have been 14 or 15 when I met him fishing below the upper Salmon Falls. I was bait fishing with either worms or soft shell crawfish. He was casting a fly 50 to 75 feet. Every so often he would hook, play, and land a big rainbow trout. I stopped fishing and followed him a distance, out of his way. I was thinking that someday I would own one of those expensive fly rods and reels and learn to fly-fish. Taylor finally noticed me and asked if I would like to try casting the fly.

"Mr. Williams, I don't know how."

"It is easy. I will give you a lesson."

In a short time he had me casting easily 25 to 30 feet. I got a strike and brought in an 8-inch jumping, struggling rainbow which he turned loose. I never really started to fly-fish until after I finished college.

When Sun Valley opened up, Taylor became the fishing and hunting guide for the lodge. His gentlemanly ways and his excellent teaching ability made him a favorite with the many stars and celebrities who patronized Sun Valley. When Ernest Hemingway moved to Sun Valley, Taylor became one of Hemingway's close friends. Hemingway took him fishing to many parts of the world. Wood River and world-famous Silver Creek were among the best trout streams in the west. Taylor was busy giving lessons to beginners.

I had gone to Hailey to check the 4-H camp grounds with the Blaine county agent. On the way back I turned off at a side road and drove to a stile over a fence near Silver Creek. After putting my rod together and tying on a leader and a renegade fly, I climbed over the stile and put my waders on. When I came to the shallow crossing on the wide, crystal-clear stream, there were two men fly-fishing at least 100 feet upstream. I would be all right to cross, as trout swim downstream when disturbed and they had fished the water in front of me. When I was halfway across, the heavy-set man turned and said, "You are an ill-mannered bastard!" When I reached the bank, I stood up.

"Just because you write books that I and other people like to read gives you no license to be rude. If you will come out of the stream and take off your waders, we will see who is the biggest ill-mannered bastard. You have all the advantage, even though we are about the same age and size. You have fought professionally and I am just a clumsy farm boy."

Taylor Williams said, "Hi, Virg." He turned to his partner.

"Ernie, I have known him since he was in grade school. He is trying to sucker you. You wouldn't have a chance. You are in terrible condition and he is always in shape."

"So he's that kind of a guy." He laughed and waved his hand. "Come join us."

I fished for several minutes just so I could say I fished with Hemingway, then excused myself because I had to get home. Hemingway was really pleasant and charming in the half-hour I was with him.

The celebrity that I enjoyed the most was "Old Mister Boston," as he was called. Berkilwitz was part-owner of the Boston distillery that made Old Mr. Boston gin. He had bought the Sand Springs Ranch northwest of Wendell. Sand Springs was a river-sized stream that gushed up from the underground lava channel. It was cold, pure, and ideal for trout. There were marshy areas along its banks as it flowed to the canyon wall to reach Snake River 400 feet below. When the wind blew a gale, the ducks would go there by the thousands, as it was sheltered by trees from the wind. I had fished and hunted it for many years. When Berkilwitz bought it, he put up a high fence, posted it, and even had a watchman and dog to keep out poachers at night.

It was nearly 4 o'clock and windy when I finished my farm visits near the Sand Springs ranch. It was in the late fall and ducks ordinarily would be feeding in the corn fields. I could see ducks flying into Sand Springs ranch and alighting. I drove up to a "No Trespassing" sign and parked. Placing my gun on the ground, I climbed over the fence. It was about a 100 yards to the willows bordering the stream. I just walked into the edge of the willows and dropped a mallard hen. I thought I heard someone shout, but I wasn't sure, as I was busy dropping another mallard. An angry, red-faced man broke through the willows.

"You are trespassing."

"I know it."

"Do you know who I am?"

"I think you are Mr. Berkilwitz or Old Mister Boston, as you are called."

"I am going to call the sheriff and have you arrested."

"Go ahead and turn me in. I have hunted here since I was a small boy and the fine will be worth it."

"You S.O.B. At least you can take turns. It is going to cost you a dollar if you miss and I'll pay you a dollar when you hit. Do you have any money?"

"Seven silver dollars." We matched for first shot and he won. He was really an excellent shot and he finished $2 ahead. He acted as if he had won 10,000 because it pleased him so much to beat me. When I started to leave, I heard, "You smart-ass, don't you come back. But if you do, give me a call first. I like your money!"

I called him Friday evening and said, "I am going to climb over your fence tomorrow."

"Virg, don't do that. Drive up and park in the yard."

When I drove up into his yard, he came out to meet me and insisted I go into the mansion with him. He could have been rebelling against his numerous guests. I was dressed in not-too-clean hunting clothes with an old battered hunting cap. He proudly introduced me as his hunting partner. Their response was as disinterested as mine. I could shake a limper hand than they could.

On our way to the field, he said, "Those are my wife's guests. All they want to do is drink, play cards, and screw. When they get bored with Sun Valley, they come down here to get bored."

During our several meetings, I learned a lot about the 50-year-old man. There was no way that I would have traded places with him, in spite of his wealth. His family was a mess. The children were over-indulged and in all kinds of trouble. Everyone kowtowed to him, trying to get at his millions. In contrast, I had a healthy, law-abiding, and almost trouble-free family.

He would call at least once a week to get me to come out during the week. I also tried to hunt on Saturday or Sunday. We continued our dollar betting on each bird. He almost never missed. I was good, but he was a little better. Only once did I take home an extra dollar. His highest day was $2. As we walked back to the house, he would clink them to bug me. We were never polite to each other. He postponed his leaving for nearly a month until early December. We shook hands and told each other how much we had enjoyed each other's company.

"I'll be back in June and I will teach you how to fly-fish, which I hope you'll be able to do better than you shoot."

I received a Christmas card from him, but that was the last I heard. He died of cancer in the spring.

THE PARROT

Shortly after I started to work as Vocational Ag instructor at Aberdeen in 1930, the annual conference was held at Pond's Lodge on the North Fork of Snake River close to Yellowstone Park. The week in the pristine setting of pines, clear streams, mountains in the background, the smell of pine needles and glorious, bright, cool days was a new experience for me. The Ponds were an elderly couple and their newly-married son, Homer, helped manage the combination lodge, cabins, store, and recreational center. After accompanying him on an evening of fishing, we became close and lasting friends over the years.

The meeting room was large enough to accommodate several hundred people. In the back near one of the doors was a large, young, green parrot in a cage. Someone said friends had given it to the newlyweds as a wedding gift. Another said the Ponds had brought it back from Mexico when they returned from an L.D.S. mission. Al Funke sat by the parrot, back a long way from the speaker's table. Al was planning to quit in a month for another job, as he didn't like kids or teaching. Al was a devout Catholic and was very definitely anti-L.D.S. Every day he sat by the parrot, saying he was by the door in order to smoke his pipe, much to the horror of Mrs. Pond. Al pretended to be taking notes, but all the time he was talking to the parrot in a low voice. He appeared to be repeating the same things over and over. I could not tell what he was saying to the bird, but having known Al for three years, I was sure it wasn't good. I found out what it was many years later.

Nearly 10 years later we were having a three-day conference of extension agents at the Pond's Lodge. Homer greeted me warmly and we talked about getting together for some fishing after dinner that evening. His parents had retired three years before and he was now manager. Periodically during the past 10 or 11 years I had dropped in to see him. The parrot had never done anything but sqawk and screech. This time I looked and there was no parrot.

"What happened to the parrot? Did it ever talk?"

Homer broke out in a fit of laughing until he was red in the face. "The parrot talked all right—and how! In fact, it probably caused my mother to retire. As you know, she was a very devout Mormon and was head of the state relief society for the church. This was a good place to hold the yearly conference. The ladies were standing around near the door talking and waiting for the meeting to assemble. A woman walked up to the parrot's cage, tapped on it with her finger and said, 'Polly wants a cracker.'

"My mother was standing close to the cage. She fainted when she heard the parrot shriek in a loud, rasping voice, 'Go fuck yourself!' and repeat it twice. That is when my mother really went into retirement. We gave the parrot to a saloon-keeper in Rock Springs, Wyoming, but he had to get rid of it because it was just too foul a fowl."

MY MOTHER-IN-LAW

When someone asked about my mother-in-law, also named Ethel, I said, "She was a dragon." Actually, she was not that bad. She was born Ethel Jondreau. Her mother was a sister to Admiral William Leahy, her father a French entrepreneur in Wisconsin. Her father moved out on the family, taking a younger woman with him to Canada, where he became a millionaire. He did support the family on a rather generous level. Ethel graduated from the University of Wisconsin and her brother, Rome Jondreau, became a Commander in the Navy after graduating with high rank in his class at Anapolis.

She was quite a domineering person because of her superior intellect. She resented the fact that she had not reached the proper status in society. She and Guy Tobey lived together without very much affection or closeness. This probably accounted for her "short visits" to us in Idaho that lasted for at least a month to six weeks. She dominated her daughter from childhood on, and seemed to think that she had a right to take over control of our house and rearing of the children.

Ethel and I had always discussed family problems with each other. Her mother's intervention in the household affairs led to friction between us. On account of your wife you do try to go all out in getting along with Mother-in-law. When Dad Tobey was with her, the visit lasted no more than 10 days, and he kept her in line. I enjoyed him very much and we were very good friends. At the end of her prolonged visits, Ethel and I were sleeping in different beds. When we put her on the plane in Idaho Falls, Ethel said, "Buy a bottle. We are going to celebrate!" And we did. Fortunately, the long, unpleasant visits didn't happen until we moved to Driggs.

It was late in August and Ethel was expecting Lary in two months. Her mother and Aunt Rose Blomgren came up to visit us. They wanted to go through Yellowstone Park. They would take our car, as I had some work and meetings to take care of. At dinner the evening before they were to depart for the park I gave Ethel instructions about safety, saying to stop at the top of the Teton Pass, put the car in low gear and never take it out. None of them had been to the park and were not aware of the danger of bears. I had been there many times and there were always several people in the hospital recovering from bear attacks. I warned them to keep the car windows closed at all times because they were taking 4-year-old Dallas. Someone should be in the car at all times with Dallas. Ethel's mother resented my briefing. Possibly I was too dictatorial, and it annoyed her to have someone tell her how to do anything. They were planning on staying four more days after their return from the park.

When I returned home from the office two days later, they were home and supper was nearly ready. Dallas was playing with a friend next door and came home just in time to get to the dinner table for grace. I sensed that the conversation at the table was somewhat strained. I noticed that Dallas had Mercurochrome painted on the back of his left hand.

"What happened, Dal? Did a bear scratch you?"

"A big black bear, Daddy."

Ethel put her finger to her lips and said, "I'll tell you about it after dinner."

Ethel's mother acted very quiet and even subdued all through dinner. Right after dinner she told her sister, "Rose, let's go to the drugstore. I need some lotion for the mosquito bites I got in the park."

I asked Dallas how he got that scratch.

"I told you, Daddy. It was a big black bear. He crawled all over me on the back seat and I was scared, but I didn't cry or anything. I curled up in the corner and was quiet, just like you told me to do if a bear caught me."

"Ethel, is he telling the truth?"

"He is. There was a bear begging beside the road and Aunt Rose wanted to get a picture. She got out of the car and couldn't work the camera. I got out of the driver's seat and closed the door, leaving the window open about 2 inches. I told Dallas and Mother to keep the windows closed, like Virg said. Mother was sitting beside the driver's seat. I heard her scream and saw a bear climbing through the window she had opened. She climbed out the other door. The bear climbed into the back seat where Dallas was. I was petrified. Dallas wasn't moving or making a noise. He was rolled up into a ball. Mother opened the car door, put a hand on the bear's head and pulled Dallas out with the other hand. The bear bit through her coat but didn't touch her flesh. Her heart didn't act up as she is always complaining it will. What are you going to do?"

"I'm going to send her home on the bus. Do you want me to tell her or should you do it?"

"I'll do it. She is overdue to go home."

Her mother was quiet when she boarded the bus. My later version of the story was that when the bear got a look at her, he jumped out of the window, swam across the Yellowstone River, and galloped off into the sunset with his hind feet crossing ahead of his front feet.

She came up again in October for Lary's birth. The rest of the time she came with Dad Tobey. As far as she was concerned, I could never do anything right. Ethel wasn't her usual cheerful, energetic self when her mother was around. Her mother had dominated her too long.

She and Dad Tobey came up again when Susan was born. I did

appreciate her help. Dad Tobey and I had a mutual respect and fondness for each other. He was in seventh heaven at Driggs, enjoying the fishing and hunting. As they were leaving, she said, "If you have any more children, I'm never coming back!"

Dad Tobey said, "If Babe wants another baby, have one. She kept me from having more than one."

Ethel said, "I won't promise. Our children are so healthy and such fun, we just might have another."

When Dad Tobey died, he left his wife with Social Security and nearly a $100,000 in cash and life insurance. This should have been enough to last at least 15 years according to the times and her present life-style. What happened to it in three years, we will never know.

I happened to answer the phone when the voice said, "This is Mother Tobey. I am sick and out of money. Will you come and get me?"

"I'll drive down and pick you up. I can be there day after tomorrow."

"I can't stand the ride in the car."

"O.K. I will be there day after tomorrow and we will take the plane back."

Ethel had been listening to the one-sided conversation.

"That was Mother."

"Yes, she said she is sick and broke. She wants me to come and get her. I will take the bus down because it is cheaper. I hate that 20-hour bus ride."

"Virg, I can't even guess what she did with all that money. She must have tried to invest it and got swindled. We will never know, as she has always been very secretive about money, even with my dad."

My dentist gave me a sleeping pill that I took in Nevada and woke up at 8 o'clock the next morning with my head in the lap of a kindly black lady. Mother Tobey had arranged plane reservations for that afternoon. She had to be helped by holding her arm when she walked, complaining that her back hurt.

She had to be waited on and barely made it to meals. Her back condition deteriorated rapidly. After I had to help her on and off the toilet for a month, Ethel said, "You have enough burden with me. She has to go to a nursing home."

The county commissioners were very helpful and we placed her in a rest home only a few blocks from our house in Jerome. This made a daily visit easy. She died a year later.

URANIUM

In 1957, the great uranium rush was on. Pick had sold out for millions. Scintilator and Geiger counter manufacturers and dealers had trouble filling orders. The four corners of Nevada, Utah, Wyoming, and Arizona were the hot spots. Uranium was being found in most of the western states. It seemed like everyone was trying to strike it rich. The number of 20-acre claims had been estimated at 20,000 by the U.S. Bureau of Mines. After filing and registering it with the county recorder, you had 30 days to do your exploratory work. If you did not complete your exploratory work within the 30 days, your claim could be jumped. This amount of work had to be done every year to hold your filing. The western states had millions of acres of federal and state lands that were open for filing mineral claims.

I wasn't any different from the rest of the treasure seekers. Everyone had dreams of becoming an instant millionaire. My financial situation must have been worse than most. I still was paying on the more than $10,000 indebtedness for post-polio treatments.

During our annual extension conference at the University of Idaho in Moscow, I went to the library of the School of Mines and found the bibliography of all the uranium publications in the U.S. The U.S. Bureau of Mines sent me the publications. One publication was very interesting with just a few lines, such as, "Uranium found on Cherry Creek near Stanley, Idaho, in 1912 by Sturkey while mining for gold." There were another few lines in a publication to the effect that a German named Oppenheimer in 1920 was inspecting the uranium provinces of the world. He had written a report on it. It also listed where it could be found in German. In another publication there was a notation that the Massachusetts Institute of Technology had identified the sample sent in by Sturkey as uranium.

In regard to Oppenheimer, it turned out that after World War I, Germany was working on producing the atomic bomb so that they could conquer the world.

Using official University of Idaho stationery (which is a no-no) to give my request authority and a $10 money order brought me Oppenheimer's report, but it was in German. My German was limited to "Yah" and "Nein." With a German-English dictionary and my wife, Ethel, we were able to get a rough idea where Oppenheimer had seen the uranium ore.

A phone call to a super secretary at M.I.T. was lucky. She just happened to know the secretary that worked in the office that kept record files. A home phone call to this secretary brought a copy of M.I.T.'s report to Sturkey. As I remember, it read something like this:

August 18, 1912

Dear Mr. Sturkey:

Your sample of ore is not radium. Our electronic analysis shows it to be 1.045 percent U308 (uranium) which is greyish-white trash metal, but may have some value in the future.

Translating Oppenheimer's report, the vein was uncovered by Sturkey while placer mining. It was about halfway down the hill that went into Kelley Creek. Our sheriff was reared in the Ketchum area, so I asked him and he said it was close to Stanley.

There was nothing we could do about it all during the winter because of the very deep snow that would not melt until April. Being worse than broke, having no Geiger counter or scintilator, which would cost over a $1,000, had me completely stymied.

In April I overheard a conversation between Bob Bellini and another Elk at the Elks' Club. Bob was a short, stout, jovial Italian who ran a machine shop. Apparently, he had a Geiger counter and scintilator. So far he had only found traces of radiation activity—none over the .25 scale, which would be worth investigating. I asked Bob to come over to a vacant table and told him about the research that had been made of uranium findings in Idaho. We agreed to form a partnership. He was to furnish the Geiger counter and scintilator, gas and meals. I was to furnish the car. He agreed to follow any decision on selling out.

Our first trip was to a uranium find of the early 20s southwest of Buhl. We located the find easily. The mining record filing in the courthouse gave us the section and part section it was in. It was in a lava flow. All of the carnotite had been dug out, leaving a perfectly smooth, round hole 10 or 12 feet across and 25 feet deep. It widened to 15 feet in the middle and tapered off smoothly like a ball at the bottom. Radiation was high but there was no uranium ore left. It was like a huge bubble had formed at the lava flow. Mining geologists were at a loss to explain it.

We made several futile trips after that. The locating was fairly easy and there was radiation but none high enough to warrant any further exploration. Our trips were on Sundays. Early in September I picked Bob up at 5 o'clock in the morning and we headed for Stanley. We had breakfast there, and someone told us how to get to Kelley Creek.

When he saw our fishing poles he said, "You won't get a trout over 10 inches in Kelley Creek."

"We like them small," Bob said. We finally drove up a hill and started down the other side. There were all placer diggings in a rather deep, dry gully that had been placer mined. There was no stream flowing as in Oppenheimer's description of the location. Years later I found out from John Weednan, who stayed in the cabin and worked with Sturkey, that they had brought a stream of water from Kelley Creek, and when the operation ceased, they had turned it back into the main stream.

We used the scintilator and Geiger counter and found high radiation. In panning some of the hot spots, we found very small, short rods, 1/32-inch long and about the diameter of a fine pencil mark. Through formal and informal study, I had almost a working knowledge of geology. These rods were bannerite, very high in uranium. We found hot spots in the old tailings from the sluice boxes that ran the instruments way up on the scale. We dug holes several feet deep in these tailings and the radiation level never changed. The bannerite was heavily concentrated in the sluice box tailings. We left tired but not discouraged. Bob said, "It is here someplace. It may take us all summer to find it, but we will find it! Can you go next Sunday?"

"I don't know why not."

The next Sunday we drove down the road. It went only one way—downstream. About a half-mile down, there was a small stream crossing the road from the left from a draw that went steeply up a long hill. We decided this might be the stream Oppenheimer referred to. We went up the small, clear stream whose banks showed very little radiation readings. About a half-mile up the hill, the stream gave out. Bob said, "There's a lot of granite outcrops on the right side. Ore is found in granite batholiths. Let's check them."

We worked back and forth a 100 yards apart. The scintilator was on the .25 mark. If radioactivity was higher than that, it would turn off. We stopped for lunch at an outcrop that was much larger than the rest. To mark it for reference, we piled up several rocks. Bob put an empty pop can filled with dirt on top.

Late in September, at 7,000 feet, frost had made the lower valley a kaleidoscope of yellows, browns, and reds of maples, alders, sumac, willows, and quaking aspen, whose leaves are never still, intermingled with green of the pines. There wasn't a cloud in the sky. The air was clean, scented with the smell of pine. We took a short nap in the bright warm sun, then continued our search, walking parallel from outcrop to outcrop across the long slope. We thought it was about a half-mile from where we had eaten lunch. I walked over to a small outcrop and put the scintilator on it, and noticed that it was off. The outcrop read negative. So I set it back on the .25 scale and retraced my steps, as I was following a faint game trail. It was only a short distance when it went off again. I took it off the prospecting setting to full reading. It almost went off the scale, which meant that if it was uranium and not thorium, it was of commercial value. The outcrop was only 9 or 10 inches high and about 18 inches across.

Thoughts ran through my mind so fast that I was completely paralyzed. Money, out of debt, college for the kids, a better way of life, a farm; what do we do now?

"Bob, come here. I think the scintilator is haywire."

"You're crazy, Virg."

"No, I'm not. Come here and check this rock." He came puffing up the hill from a block away. The Geiger counter didn't flash as it would on a lower reading, but kept a steady, bright light.

"Take it off—it will burn up," I said. But he continued to run it all over the rock. Suddenly, it quit. It had had it. We didn't have any tools to stake it with. It was so remote we figured no one would find it anyway and we would stake it next week. We were so excited that, stupidly, we didn't mark it because we could locate it again from the markings we had left at the lunch area. The rock was hard. With a miner's pick we chipped off a piece a few inches long. The top side was brownish, but the other side was a granular grey, metallic surface with a small tinge of yellow. Away from the original rock, it still showed high radiation. We were so high and excited that we didn't pay any attention to our way back to the car. Every so often we stopped and checked the rock to see if it was still radioactive.

The next step was to file several claims of 20 acres each, pay $2 for each claim, and file it in the county courthouse. Within 30 days we had to make an excavation of 256 square feet (or 4x4x6), in order to hold the claim for a year. We could hold the claim indefinitely if we did this much work each year. All of these things we talked about going back. In Hailey we stopped for a sandwich and a cup of coffee. The waitress said, "Hello, Mr. Cross," and gave me a hug. She was captain of the girls' high school basketball team that I had coached 15 years before.

"What are you doing here?"

"Nellie, we are looking for uranium."

"Have you found anything?"

"Maybe."

"Why don't you ask him. He's a government geologist." She indicated a man sitting a few stools away. I walked over to him, introduced myself, and asked, "Are you a government geologist?"

"I am. My name is Ralph Graves." I showed him the rock.

"Put it in your pocket. I will talk to you outside."

His first words were, "It is a piece of high-grade uranium ore. Have you filed on it? Do not show this to anyone, or say anything about it to anyone, until you have filed on it."

During the week we talked and made plans to go back the next Sunday with stakes and filing papers for five claims. On Sunday we started early on our trip to the find. The assay report from Salt Lake City verified that it was high-grade uranium ore and of good commercial value.

The outcrop was probably the top of a vein. The scintilator would tell us its direction by radiation readings, and this would determine the direction of the four stakes for the claim's boundary. If there was a series of claims, the staking had to be exact. If your claim exceeded the prescribed width or length, that portion was open to be filed upon. One of the famous examples of a colossal error was at Tonopah, Nevada. A young mining engineer filed on the ground that had the hoist and a shaft of over 1,000 feet deep. Someone had missed filing a claim on a 100-foot strip. The mine owners settled for over a $1 million.

We stopped for breakfast at the restaurant and lodge at the foot of Galena Summit, where the film "Bus Stop" with Marilyn Monroe was made. The spry, 75-year-old woman was an old friend. She had a bit part in the film and it was all she could talk about.

The drive over the 8,000-foot summit was slow on account of the many curves and switchbacks. You could look down and see several sections of the road lying parallel below you.We drove up Cherry Creek to the small storage reservoir where we had left the car on the first trip. Bob was bothered by the high altitude. We followed some blazes on trees that we had made belatedly on our trip down from the find. We easily found the outcrop where we had eaten lunch. The outcrop containing the ore was uphill in a southwest angle, about one-half mile, I thought. I remembered that it was on a small trail made by deer and small animals. The hillside was one small trail after another, most of them angling. The hill was covered with grass, scattered scrub pine, numerous outcrops of rock varied from level to a foot above ground. It had rained and washed out all of the tracks from our first trip.

"Bob, this looks like about the place. It has to be around here close. Let's put a shirt on a shovel and work in a circle away from it."

Six hours later, two tired and discouraged prospectors walked down to their car. The next Sunday was a repeat of the previous one. The route we followed down the hill was different. The outcrop was nearly 6 feet high and several feet long.The scintilator went all the way on the highest scale. This time we blazed trees all the way down to the car.

The problem of staking and assignment work was easily solved. We traded a third interest to the Halverson Construction Company. They in turn put in a road, surveyed and staked the claims, and bulldozed out the necessary assessment work. Vitro Chemical Company of Utah sent in their mining engineer. At his request, Vitro

287

sent in two more engineers, who landed at the Stanley air strip. They made an offer of $175,000 down with a graduated 10 to 20 royalty. If they didn't start to mine it within two years they would pay $50,000 a year for each year that they did not mine, up to $1 million.

I envisioned my third getting me out of the polio treatment debt, a new life, and security for my family. Pick had just received his millions for his uranium find. Bellini and the Halversons said no to the offer. They wanted a million down. An early unexpected October snow stopped all operations. I had borrowed over $10,000 from banks, friends, and loan sharks for physical therapy treatments at Cabot Kaiser and other hospitals. I was paying interest on interest. Each of the three partners had 30,000 shares of stock. I was so put out with the stupid greed of my partners that I resigned the secretary and treasurer positions and offered 25,000 shares to my partners for $5,000. They jumped at the chance, mortgaging the machine shop and the caterpillar. With this windfall, I paid off some of my debts.

Vitro made another lesser offer in the spring, based on diamond drilling. The diamond drills failed to show enough ore to warrant development. Sturkey's location of the uranium is listed in U.S. Bulletin 9.

Dallas had a very successful year at Boise State. He transferred to the University of Idaho and had an outstanding spring football year. He was taking pre-med and his grades were very good. At the close of school early in June, the family drove up to bring him home. We arrived back in Jerome on Friday. It was necessary that I go to the uranium claim on Saturday to supervise some development work. Dallas wanted to go with me. We took sleeping bags, planning to stay overnight because we were leaving so late. We stopped for dinner in Stanley which is an outpost deep in the Sawtooth Mountains, really a primitive area. It had a couple of cafes, a bar (Wirtz), a post office, and service station. There was a dance in progress in a room adjoining the bar. The dancers were mostly college kids and Dallas knew some of them. He said that he would like to dance a couple of times.

"O.k., I'll have a drink at the bar. There is no hurry because we are only 5 miles from the diggins."

I was sitting at the bar listening to the music and sipping my drink when someone sat down on the stool next to me. I didn't pay any attention to him until he made some remark to me. I answered politely but casually. He took affront at what I said. When I tried to placate him, he took umbrage at everything I said. He was probably 10 pounds heavier and 10 years younger than I. It was apparent that he was a bully spoiling for a fight. I looked for Dallas, but he was nowhere in sight.

"I don't want any trouble. If I have offended you, you have my apology."

This didn't appease him and he became more abusive. Finally, I decided I would stand up, flick out my left hand to the left and try to Judo cut him with my right. If this worked, I would grab his hair with my left and my right fist would settle the matter. If that didn't work, I would probably get the hell beat out of me. As I slid off the stool facing him, he was jerked up from his stool by a 6-foot, 3-inch, 220-pound angry man.

"This is my dad you are trying to pick a fight with. I'll give you your choice. You can walk out or be carried out, or be thrown out through that window." The man was teetering on his toes, looking at Dallas' big right fist.

"I'll be looking for you in the morning and if you are still here you will go out flat on your back," Dallas promised.

The man gasped, "I'll walk out."

Dallas wheeled the man around and booted him. Wirtz declared drinks on the house. It turned out the man had been bullying the town for two days.

Dallas said, "Daddy, I've seen you in action and I think you could take him. I just didn't want to see you cut up." They were still celebrating the next morning.

HONOR GUARD

After his second year of college, Dallas enlisted in the Army during the summer. After finishing boot training, he was in the Honor Guard at Arlington. He and one of his buddies had been picked from 3,000 recruits at Colorado Springs training camp. Candidates for the Honor Guard had to be at least 6 feet tall, excellent physical specimens, handsome and intelligent with an impeccable background in regard to loyalty and conduct. Ethel and I were very proud of him.

Ed Sullivan announced on his 7 o'clock television program that the drill team from the National Honor Guard would do their rifle drill. This awakened me from a drowsy state of mind. Suddenly, there was the drill team and Dallas was first in the row. I jumped up and went to bring Ethel from the kitchen, telling her to hurry and look at the T.V.

She gasped, "That is Dallas!"

We watched with pride and amazement at the complicated dexterity of the drill. All the family was now watching and the phone started to ring. We decided to let it ring until the show was over. It turned out later that my sister was trying to call to tell us to watch the show. After it was over, the phone was ringing constantly with friends calling to tell us about it.

About 2 o'clock on a Friday afternoon, I returned from my weekly broadcast at Twin Falls. Eleanor, my secretary, said a man from the F.B.I. was waiting to see me in the sheriff's office. There is no way you can help wondering—Does it concern my family? What do they want me to do now?

I called the sheriff's office. The F.B.I. man said he had some questions he wanted to ask me and for me to come up to the sheriff's office. I asked him to come down to my office for more privacy. He agreed, came in and shook hands.

"Don't be alarmed, but the questions are about your son, Dallas."

"What has he done?"

"Don't worry. He is a great boy and you should be as proud of him as the Army is. What we want to know is where he was between June 14th and July 8th last year. We have a complete record of his whereabouts except for those dates."

"He wasn't home during that time. He bucked hay all summer for Johnny Capps. I believe he was in the Hailey-Bellvue area during that time. They worked seven days a week."

"Where is Johnny Capps?"

290

"He lives about 10 blocks from here. His name is in the telephone book."

The agent called Capps and asked him about Dallas. Capps verified my statement, and invited the agent to come and see his written records.

A month later we received a letter and newspaper clippings from Dallas, showing the Queen of England walking with a tall, handsome soldier. He was one of her guards. He told us that his orders were to keep watch at all times and at the sign of any violence or shots, to put the Queen on the ground as quickly and gently as possible and cover her body with his until ordered to get up by an officer.

He said the Queen was nice and talked to him a lot, asking questions about his family, where he was reared and what he had been studying in college. She was a very gracious and considerate person. He informed us that he considered his mother to be prettier and smarter than the Queen of England, however. He criticized the Duke for paying too much attention to pretty women and thought it must be embarrassing to the nice lady, the Queen.

A short time later we received a package that contained a pair of white gloves wrapped in cellophane, with instructions to keep them, as they had shaken hands with President Eisenhower. Dallas was delegated to the eight-man squad that met the Presidential helicopter. It was their duty to check the F.B.I. men who ushered the President into the waiting car or to the White House. The security men were issued brass buttons, and just before the helicopter landed, the squad was told where the F.B.I. men would be wearing their buttons. The squad was to face outward, have bayonets at ready, and order "Halt" when the F.B.I. agents were 10 paces away. They were to show the position of their buttons. If they continued to come forward, second and third "Halt" commands were to be used. If they still did not halt, run them through with the bayonet at the third rib and out the back.

Dallas said, "We thought it was fun to be grim and ready to use our bayonets. The F.B.I. agents showed their buttons in a hurry. President Eisenhower shook hands with each of us, and asked where we were from. I told him that Idaho has better fishing than Colorado."

He said, "That's what you think, soldier!"

What really made the squad love Ike was the day he went to their front, gave the command and marched them to the White House, putting them through drill with them singing out their cadence.

Dallas and Geraldine Smith, high school sweethearts, were married during the Christmas holidays in the second and last year of his Army service. The tall and very good-looking young couple honeymooned in a cabin at Sun Valley which was loaned by a friend. They reported that they had to shovel their way in through the snow to the cabin door.

When they returned to Washington, D.C., Ethel told them to call on Admiral Leahy, who was Dallas' great uncle. He was glad to see them, but asked Dallas, "Why aren't you in the Navy?"

"Sir, I didn't want to spend four years in the service."

"Do you like to dance?" He gave them two invitations to the French Embassy ball.

"What shall we wear?"

"Your uniform will be perfect. Gerry, wear your wedding dress."

They were by far the youngest couple at the ball. They danced beautifully and never were allowed to sit out a dance.

I answered the telephone in my office. Dallas' voice on the line said, "Don't say my name. I will call you collect at home." There was the click of the phone hanging up. At 7 o'clock the collect call came from a pay phone. There was a 15-year major who was sour because he had been passed over for promotions. He was taking it out on the Honor Guard personnel with unjust and ridiculous criticisms and punishments. He was causing some to go A.W.O.L. He had the Honor Guard squad at parade rest a half-hour before Ike's arrival at the airport. Then they received word the plane had gone back to Florida. As a result, the major had kept the Guard at parade rest for two and one-half hours in the hot sun and two of them had fainted. Dallas gave me the major's full name, and wanted to know if I could do anything about it without involving him.

I called Senator Dworshak and told him the situation.

Henry said, "If I raise hell, Dallas will get the blame. Let me do some checking and I will call you back."

Later he returned my call and said, "There is a senator from New Jersey who owes me and has no one in the Honor Guard." Two weeks later the major was in the ROTC of a woman's college in the Dakotas.

Dallas started to work at the Maryland Biological Institute when his enlistment was over, and enrolled in evening classes at Washington and Jefferson University. In a short time he was moved from checking appliances and equipment to actually doing cancer research. During this time they had a baby girl and named her Karen. He had been working a year and going to school when he called me collect.

"This is Dallas."

"Yes, you can come home and stay with us this summer. That is, if Gerry will cook. I know you are anxious to get your degree. I will tell Capps you are going to buck hay." We always had a lot of ESP between us.

"Dad, will you tell Lary that I would like to run the spray rig?"

"That spray rig is Lary's. He paid you back twice over and I will not ask him."

"You don't need to ask him. Just tell him I'm going to be home in two weeks. I know you are going to call him about spring football tomorrow. Call me and tell me how he is doing. They really had a great

292

freshman year."

"I will be glad to do that and I know he will be glad to see you when he comes home."

When I called Lary at the university and asked him how he was doing, his reply was, "I am tougher and stronger than they are."

"Guess what? Dallas is coming home in two weeks."

"Gee, that is wonderful. Tell him to take over the spray rig and get me a job bucking hay."

When I called Dallas and told him of the conversation, he said, "That is my brother and I love him. You and mother taught us what a family love really is."

I contacted Keith Evans, a college classmate of mine, who was in charge of the federal grasshopper control program. He hired Lary to make surveys of grasshopper egg beds all over southern Idaho. The job paid well.

POTATO RESEARCH

Many of the older farmers were very slow to accept the findings and research for improving their farming practices. Many were contemptuous of the university graduates. They felt we had no practical experience and they, because of their experience, knew more. They did not realize that they would be out of farming unless they improved their production. When Roosevelt made farm subsidies it opened the door for investors with money to buy large tracts of land, for which the subsidies, from the government helped pay. To Roosevelt should be given the dubious credit for putting an end to the family farm which had been the backbone of American agriculture. This infamous act led to a confusion of surpluses and more subsidies. I hope the misguided economists who thought up the program are messing up the place where, I think, they have gone.

The most effective way to get a new, improved method into operation was to persuade a young farmer to try it. Tours of these demonstrations were effective. In the 50s we had a whole new breed of young, better educated farm operators. In the past, fertilizer was a matter of plowing under crop residue. Now it could be bought in sacks.

I was an Animal Husbandry major. For Idaho potato farming to play the major part in my life would appear to be ridiculous. I became interested in potatoes at Aberdeen. My agriculture students had potato projects that I had to supervise. Actually, I had very little knowledge of the overall culture and problems. One of the first things I did was to request the extension potato specialist to spend a day training me to identify diseases. The request was also to make the extension personnel become aware of my existence. The Aberdeen Experiment Station personnel were very cooperative and seemed pleased that I showed interest in their work.

By the time we moved to Shelley, which was then the center of the potato growing industry where potato was king, I was well informed and qualified to supervise the boys' projects. Extension Research Bulletins were an excellent source of information. Teton County raised only certified seed. In addition to raising certified potatoes with Claude Dalley, I held roguing schools to teach growers to recognize diseased plants which needed to be "rogued" out of the field because they would lower the yield if they were used for seed.

E. R. Bennet had been the potato production specialist for many years. He was only seven or eight years from retirement, and I asked myself why not prepare to take his place. Being slightly color blind was an asset to me. When I looked over a potato field that appeared to be the same shade of green to other people, diseased plants would stick out like a sore thumb to me. Usually they were in various shades of yellow. During the roguing training schools I became famous and they attributed it to my keen eyesight. At the experiment station I could point out barely discernably diseased plants and they would verify it by microscopic examination or other tests. The training my father had instilled in me on observing everything around me helped.

Idaho's average yield was a standstill at about 215 sacks per acre. When land was first cleared of sagebrush, yields were 300 to 400 sacks per acre. After a few crops of potatoes were raised, the yields dropped down to the average. I had success in getting young farmers to use the findings of the Experiment Station. As a result, Jerome County changed from the lowest average yield to the highest in the state. As has been mentioned, new land would yield 50 percent above the average and gradually go down until the farmer would say, "It is spudded out."

Two diseases, rhizoctonia, a soil-inhabiting fungus which causes damping off of seedlings, blight of foliage, root and stem rot and rotting of potatoes, and verticillium wilt, which causes yellowing and wilting of the plant, were causes of the decline in production as the number of organisms built up in the soil with each crop. It was no surprise when C. O. Youngstrom, Director of Extension, offered me the job as potato production specialist with a 30 percent increase in salary, as well as a challenge that I thought I could meet. It was a tempting offer, but it would mean traveling all over the state. My family could not function with me being away from home several days at a time. Constant care of their mother would be too great a burden for the children. They would have to cook or we would have to hire one. Two teenage sons needed the guidance of their father during that critical period. With great reluctance, I had to turn down the job for which I had prepared myself.

Richard Ohms was appointed to the position. On his first scheduled tour to meet and get acquainted with the agents and the problems of the industry, we started a very close friendship that has lasted 30 years. It did not take me long to realize that he is a very special person. I was prepared for a researcher with tunnel vision. His comprehension and intelligence was awesome. In a few short years our cooperative work increased Idaho yields over a hundred sacks per acre.

Discoveries are often made by accident or by chance. The Soil Conservation Service was getting farmers to arrange their fields for more efficient use of machinery and water. There were at least three instances where ditches with grassy banks were eliminated and were just part of the soil. Late in August or early September, the vines would be dying from verticillium wilt. You could see where the ditches had been, as the vines were green and healthy. When you sliced into the trunk and roots of a plant the zylum and phloem tubes that carried nutrition to and from the manufacturing leaves were clean. The fusarium fungus clogs these tubes, leaving a yellow discoloration. The answer didn't come very soon. I kept putting it back into my think tank. Finally I wrote on paper:

Ditch—water. Ditch bank saturated with water. Soil organism— different water tolerance. High water content—different organism. Conclusion—Verticillium wilt cannot live in saturated soil. Solution— Saturate soil by heavy application of water. For how long? The roots were clean and white and free from rhizoctonia and there was a heavy set, as the stolens that connected the tubers to the roots had not been cut off. They are following grass and alfalfa as was the common practice. Grass must inhibit the development of rhizoctonia. Grass also has abundant root growth . Root growth is organic matter which makes loose mellow soil. Loose soil is aerated and has high oxygen content. One or both—combination?

During a farm visit to Roger Fiola, I found what I was looking for. Roger was cussing a neighbor who had failed to turn off his irrigation water and had flooded Roger's 5-acre field that was between two fields of alfalfa. Now he would have to wait until it was dry enough to plow. He said he wouldn't get a good yield on the grain field.

"Roger, it will out yield the other field."

"Why will it?"

I told him the amount of commercial fertilizer to apply in the fall and spring. On Dick's first visit I insisted that he see the Fiola farm. He was amazed at the results. The potatoes in the alfalfa were turning yellow and beginning to die. Potatoes in the grain field were green and waist high. When we dug to see the tuber growth, it was really astonishing. Dick said, "The yield will be 400 sacks. You may have solved the problem that the experiment station has been spending several hundred thousand dollars a year on for almost 20 years. I will look up and go over the research that has been done by other states and maybe we can fill in some gaps."

"Dick, I have a fellow from Iowa that has never irrigated or raised a potato. He has 160 acres that I am supervising. It is under sprinkler irrigation and he is going to get at least 400 sacks. I believe I have stumbled onto something." The next day we visited the new grower. Dick remarked that the soil was light and loose and asked what I did.

"I had him install smaller sprinkler heads and adjusted the pressure for a gentle application rather than heavy pounding that filled the soil to a depth of 18 inches where the potato roots are." Potato growers were having a difficult time raising a good crop of potatoes with sprinkler irrigation, as they were applying water too fast and rhizoctonia thrived in packed soil.

Two weeks later I received several pages of research findings from other states with a footnote from Papavisas Cornell-Davis Illinois. Like all researchers, they were trying to solve a particular problem. Each had a few byline notes that they could take rhizoctonia fungus in a petri dish with a culture medium, place fungus from grain in the dish and the rhizoctonia would disappear. He also gave me a list of plants that were host for rhizoctonia: beets, mustard, beans and radishes were among the worst.

For 50 years the standard rotation used was three years alfalfa, one year of potatoes, one year of beets, then back to grain to alfalfa—and a potato crop. Now farmers could raise one or two years of grain, then a crop of potatoes. Idaho was able to increase the production at a time when potato products were coming into their own.

Potato dealers were either just plain thieves or honest. The honest dealers were in the minority. Processors tried to buy cheaply and they influenced the forecasts of yields. Often the forecast would be wrong, as they would predict a big crop. In the spring when supplies ran short, prices would often double. For years I had been checking a large number of fields in all of south central and southeastern Idaho. I checked them for stand count in a 100 feet of row. Stands varied according to rot due to inclement cold weather. In the fall I checked them for tuber weight in 10 feet of row. I did this so I could advise farmers whether to sell or to hold.

BURLEY

On the 1st of March, 1960, Lew Williams, district agent, came into my office. After an exchange of greetings and handshakes, he asked, "How would you like to change jobs?"

A lot of things went through my mind. Was I being eased out by a county commissioner because I had fired my secretary (his girl friend) for harmful disloyalty? Or what?

My hesitation caused Lew to say, "I am sure you will like the change. It is just suited for you and means a good boost in pay."

"Lew, what do you want me to do?"

"The Potato Commission and the university want you to be the district potato specialist with headquarters in Burley."

"When do I move?"

"You are to be on the job by April the first."

"Well, it's time that I moved, as 15 years on one job is long enough."

When I had been offered the position of state potato specialist and had to turn it down because of being unable to travel, it was a definite disappointment. When the Idaho State Potato Commissioner decided to put in an area specialist with headquarters at Burley to serve six counties in South Central Idaho as a trial to see if it warranted putting in two other similar agents, it never occurred to me that if the program did not succeed in two years I would have to get another job.

When I talked to my family about the move, Ethel said, "A change will do you good. This is a challenge and you like challenges."

Lary said, "Now they will find out how good you really are."

"I hope so."

Susan deeply resented the move. She was very popular in school and feared moving to a strange town with no friends. In fact, for weeks she would not speak to me.

Our ad in the newspaper sold our house in two days to a young optometrist. Susan would not go to Burley with us to look for a new house. At the time, Burley was in a temporary depression and houses were not selling. We looked at several desirable homes. I asked Ethel which one she liked.

"I like the yellow house on Miller Street. It is only two years old. The children's bedroom has to be repainted because of the crayon marks on the walls. There is a nice lawn. Just think of the fun you will have using your expertise to make improvements."

"That sounds like a lot of work."

"You will not have the night meetings, 4-H camps, and will have more time to do things at home."

The owner of the house had to move to a new job in Elko and needed $5,000 to pay down on a house he had purchased there. He did not like my offer, but accepted it.

Ethel was right about my having less overtime work, as I was pretty much my own boss. I submitted my program to Dick Ohms, the state potato specialist. He said it was excellent. The powers that be okayed it.

Ethel and Susan would stay in Jerome until school was out. I moved a bed into the new house and stayed there during the week, returning to Jerome for weekends. During the two months, I repainted every room inside the house. I was able to get spruce trees from overcrowded plantings that had been made by government subsidies on the new settlers' farms, and planted a border of spruce trees around the backyard, with a maple and birch tree to complement. I did not have to buy any shrubs because of the cuttings furnished by friends.

It was a case of Mohammed going to the mountain. After sitting at my desk for a week preparing a plan of work, publicity articles and arranging for a radio program, I had received no request for help. I had to go to the mountain. I asked one of the county commissioners, "Who is the most successful potato grower in Cassia County?" He didn't even hesitate.

"Blaine Curtis is a big wheel in the church and probably the most successful potato grower in the area."

I drove up just as Mr. Curtis had turned to go back up the half-mile row on his tractor. He didn't see me. I followed the planter at a slow walk. After a while, I startled him when I tapped him on the shoulder.

"Who the hell are you?"

"Blaine, I am your new potato specialist. Your number three planter is missing. You either have a bent pick or a rock is dulling them."

He laughed and shook hands. When we dug up the site behind the third planter row, sure enough a rock had dulled one of the picks on the revolving wheel, and it could not pick up the potato piece. There was a slight jog in the long rows.

"You need a cup of coffee," I said. "Come back in an hour and I'll have your rows straightened out."

"You can do that?"

"Easily."

"Virg, I will get the coffee at the store. My wife is a strict Mormon and I have to get my coffee away from home."

He spread the word around that the new agent is one of us and knows his stuff. This was the start of a long-lasting friendship. Blaine, following my recommendations, had a 325-sack yield instead of his usual 225.

My first office call was from Warren Heins. He was a well-educated, ambitious young man. I had said to myself, "If the first customer is the right kind of person, I'm going to make him a millionaire." Warren was trying to farm 240 acres of land that had a previous history of many potato crops grown by an entrepreneur named Camp who moved on to new land when the old played out. There were thousands of acres of land in the same condition. Warren was applying too much water and the soil was packing and stiffling plant growth. After changing his irrigation methods, he had a crop of 275 sacks, which was a good yield at that time. An unsuccessful neighbor offered him an additional 160 acres and I persuaded the bank to go along with him. Following my rotation, fertilizing, and irrigation practices under my supervision, he became the most successful potato grower in Idaho. At the end of eight years, he had 1,800 acres free of debt and the banker listed his net worth as over $2 million, which was a long way from the original appraisal by the bank of $10,000. His farm was used as a demonstration place for tours and was instrumental in getting Idaho potato growers to improve their methods, resulting in a production increase of over 100 sacks per acre in 10 years. Warren and I were featured in a long article in the *Idaho Farmer*.

There was no way that I could have improved on the first spring and summer in Burley. My calendar was full of requests for assistance and the results of the farmers following my advice were very outstanding. It was gratifying to be accepted, busy, and getting results far beyond my expectations for the first year. Two young growers on new land in the Malta area, which was notorious for not raising high yields of potatoes, agreed to let me completely supervise their operation. On the farm tour their crop looked as if it would be close to the unheard of yield of 400 cwt. per acre. This really impressed the 150 growers that were on the tour.

The Idaho Potato Commissioners, comprising growers, shippers and processors, decided to try to move more potatoes of the unusually large 1960 crop. They decided to put three men in the field to promote the sale of Idaho potatoes. They decided to hold a contest in which the managers of different stores were to compete for up to $5,000 prize money. Approximately $50,000 was appropriated for prizes.

The Commission would furnish advertising flyers and pay influential judges for the contests. We were to contact the produce managers of grocery chains such as Kroger's, A & P, Safeway, Albertson's, etc. We were briefed for two days in Boise. Our pitch was that we had an unusually high-quality crop and we wanted to move more of them. The contest would increase their sales with no cost to them. My area was two weeks in Detroit and two weeks in

Chicago.

It was about the middle of October when I boarded the two-motored puddle jumper in Burley, wearing casual clothes. My good dark suit, white shirts, and ties were in my suitcase. The runway was rather bumpy, the load heavy. I was beginning to wonder if the plane could get aloft before it ran into the river at the end of the runway. It was then I formed my permanent opinion about flying. Everything was all right except the takeoff, the flight, and the landing.

In Salt Lake City the stewardesses were very pretty, polite, and concerned. No smoking, seat belts. My seatmate next to the window was amused at my obvious nervousness.

"First flight?"

"Yes."

Over the intercom came, "This is your captain speaking." He introduced himself and proceeded to tell how safe the big four-motored Douglas was and that it actually "just about flies itself." I felt better about the impending flight. Apparently, he had forgotten to turn off his mike. We heard him say, "I hope we can get this clumsy bastard off the ground." Then he came out and grinned. We took off but had to circle round and round to gain enough altitude to cross the mountains.

It was then I noticed my seatmate. He was clean-cut, dark-suited, very athletic, and intelligent looking. I was trying to catalog him but could not. His hair was about as receded as my own. I said, "I like your barber."

"If you didn't have the same kind of haircut, I'd pop you one!"

"I'd pop you back."

"I'll bet you would, with those wrists. Where are you from?"

"Around Burley, Idaho."

"Do you know Bannister?" This surprised me.

"I know him quite well. I cooperated with him before, during, and some after the war."

"Do you play gin rummy?" This was my road game.

"I play it occasionally, but I'm not really too sharp."

We played for 5 hours, taking time off for lunch. He was good. Almost no money changed hands. When I asked what he did, he said that he was in government service. It was then I realized that he had all the markings of a federal agent. We were both staying at the Fort Shelby Hotel. He said that he would give me a call.

It was a relief when that plane landed safely in Detroit. I went to the baggage turntable. No suitcase. After waiting an hour, I went to the baggage desk. An inquiry revealed that my suitcase was on the way to Shannon, Ireland. The Commissioner had made my appointments with the produce managers ahead of time. I had appointments for the next day and no suitable clothes. I complained to the passenger seated by me on the bus and he said, "No problem. You are staying at the Fort

Shelby. Three blocks from there is a secondhand suit store. You can get any grade of suit you want that fits at half price."

I registered at the hotel and left my small bag in the room. The suit store was large. The proprietor listened to my story and showed me a charcoal dark suit. It was from Saks Fifth Avenue.

"This suit has been dry cleaned as prescribed by law and never worn. It will fit and we will shorten the cuffs."

"Was it stolen?"

"Probably someone made a killing at the races and bought a suit. Then he lost, so he pawned it." Three days later my well-traveled baggage was delivered to my room.

The next morning I hired an independent taxi. The driver was so cooperative and likeable that I used him for the entire two weeks. I was to be allowed 12 minutes to make my pitch with the produce manager, as he had a tight schedule of interviews.

I introduced myself and said, "I am a farm boy. My forte is potato production. As a salesman, the only thing I ever tried to sell was bluing in order to get an air gun—and my mother bought most of it." This really set a pleasant tone. Then I told about the excellent quality crop of potatoes and the contest with money for their managers, and last but not least, how it would increase their sales at no cost to them. Then I would say, "That is 8 minutes." Generally the reception was good and after a few pleasantries the manager would call in an assistant and tell him how many cars to order. The assistant and I would then complete the transaction. In the evening I would cut a tape of the results and mail it to Boise.

On Saturday I made appointments with chefs of top hotels and restaurants to show them how to bake an Idaho potato. The usual practice was to bake it in foil, which broke down the starch cells and resulted in a mushy, glaciated potato. I also showed them how to make French fries. They enjoyed giving me a high white chef's cap to wear while they baked potatoes and made French fries their way and I did it my way so we could compare the results. The dice were loaded and I won every time.

Fred, my seatmate on the plane from Salt Lake, called on the third evening and said, "I am in the bar off the lobby. Come down and see me." We greeted each other as friends.

"You have FBI clearance and your name is Virgil Cross?"

"Right." He went over to a phone and dialed. I could not hear what he said. When he returned he told me, "Virg, you really do have FBI clearance. I am surprised at your rating." He showed me his card stating that he was FBN—Federal Bureau of Narcotics.

"Virg, would you like to go with me on a bust?"

"I surely would!"

"We have followed a shipment from the Orient to Vancouver and tracked it all the way across Canada. We have observed its few stops and checked the participants. I am sure it is bound for the United States and will cross at Windsor. We want to catch the principals. It will be waved through customs."

We got into a beat-up-looking car. His reply to my rather querulous look at it was, "This is a car seized in a raid. It has over 400 horses and can go at least 125 miles an hour." We stopped on a hill overlooking a street down below. Fred was getting a report of the progress of the truck that was supposedly hauling furniture. He checked three other parties and they were in place. He picked up a short machine gun and said, "If there is any shooting, get down and stay flat until I tell you to get up. Here comes the truck."

The truck stopped a couple of blocks away and two men from another car got into it. Fred said, "Good, we've got the big ones." When the truck moved past an intersection, he gave orders to block it and big semis blocked it front and back. Men swarmed out and surrounded the truck. It turned out to be one of the largest drug busts. Fred took me back to headquarters, introducing me and saying I was from D.C.

One morning I entered the elevator and said "Good morning" to the other passengers. There was a silence, then a few belated good mornings and some laughter. A salesman said, "When I boarded the elevator on the fiftieth floor of my hotel in New York and said 'Good morning,' all of the people got off and left me."

I had just finished breakfast and was walking through the lobby on the first Sunday morning. I noticed the large number of huge men in the lobby.

"Hello, Virg." I looked around to see the familiar face of Wayne Walker, defensive end for Detroit. He had been a fraternity brother of Dallas'. We exchanged pleasantries. He asked what Dallas was doing, and whether I would be going to the game.

"Wayne, I don't have a ticket and I understand they are sold out."

"I'll see about that. Wait here." In a few minutes he handed me an envelope and we shook hands and said goodbye. When I presented my ticket at the gate, I was directed to the Press Box and watched Detroit beat San Francisco. When someone asked me who I was with, I said, "Detroit."

The two weeks in Chicago really kept me busy. By Friday I was ready for a day of rest. On Saturday evening after an early dinner I got off the elevator on the seventeenth floor of the Stevens Hotel to go to my room. There was a lobby on each floor. A well-groomed, very pretty, middle-aged lady asked if I had seen the desk clerk. She had rung for service and received no answer. She was going to the theater and needed a maid to button her dress. I volunteered. After checking my business and asking some questions, she rather reluctantly agreed to accept my help. She had two tickets to "My Fair Lady" and invited me to see the play with her. Afterward, I boarded the train for Idaho.

Dallas and Lary were about as close as two brothers can be. They had mutual respect for the other's talents. It seemed as if they stayed awake nights thinking up mischief.

I had ordered a half chicken from a restaurant in Burley that really served super chicken. The menu said half a chicken, but when my order came there was a wing, half breast, half back, drumstick, but no thigh. I called the manager-owner over and said, " I didn't get half a chicken as the menu advertised. There is no thigh."

"That is the way we serve half a chicken."

"It comes under the heading of unlawful or false advertising. You are liable for state and federal prosecution."

"You don't have to pay for the meal."

"I will pay for it, but don't let it happen again."

The following Sunday was one of the few days that Lary and Dallas could spend together in the summertime. I told them of the chicken incident. Lary had a car with U.S. license plates because he was doing a federal survey on grasshoppers. They were dressed up and getting into the official car. Dallas was carrying our camera. I didn't have time to tell him it was out of film as they drove away. After an hour and a half they returned to the house, laughing. They had driven the government car close to a window opposite the cashier's desk in the restaurant. Each ordered the half-chicken dinner. When it was served, a piece was missing in each. They spread the chicken pieces out on two napkins. Then Dallas went to the car and brought in the camera. While they were snapping pictures, the proprietor came over.

"What is going on here?"

"You are in violation of Act 37, Chapter 423, Section 5, Paragraph 6 of Idaho Code Annotated [citation purely fictitious] regarding false advertising and it could carry a heavy fine."

This really shook the man up, and he pleaded for leniency.

Lary said, "Since this is his first offense, do you suppose we could get by with giving him a warning? I'm sure he will not repeat the infraction." The owner hastily assured them he would conform to the law.

"The chicken is good and we will just forget the whole thing." They ate the chicken and ordered pie a la mode. The waitress informed them that their check had been paid. They thanked her and left a tip.

Ethel and I were watching the Johnny Carson show on television. Dick Gregory, actor and black agitator, was a guest. This was about the time of the Kent State incident. Gregory had tried to hold a march at the University of Idaho.

"What happened at Idaho?" Carson asked.

"Those cowboys don't know anything and they aren't even civilized. I don't want to talk about it."

"You didn't hold any marches after that?"

"That was the end of it in the West."

Ethel said, "I wonder what happened at Idaho to stop the march? I wouldn't be surprised if one of your sons was involved in it."

"Honey, I will not take all the blame. After all, the girls who played basketball with you said playing against you was like fighting a bear."

About a month later, I was attending a refresher course at the university and President Theophilus called me to his office. He told me what had happened. After the march had been dispersed, he called Lary in. It turned out that he was one of the organizers. The athletes and fraternity hall students had organized to prevent damage to the campus. They had contacted the police and got them to promise to stay away, also radio and television media promised no publicity. They alerted the infirmary. The group formed a line preventing entrance to the campus buildings. Lary was the spokesman.

"We are here for an education and do not want to have a building ruined or education disrupted. You can march around the campus and hold your meeting in the old football stands."

Don R. said he was in the I Tower with other faculty members, watching the confrontation with field glasses. He kept his focus on Lary. Two big, black Idaho tackles were on either side of him. The marchers, mostly out of state, defied the order and charged. In a few minutes the punching of the men and slapping of the girls left the marchers sprawling on the grounds. In minutes the mob was running and leaving a lot of their number on the ground. Theophilus said, "Lary was really something in action!"

One of the girls asked a fellow house member who had a black eye, "Are you going to march again tomorrow?"

"And get my head knocked off? No way! From now on I'm going to keep my mouth shut."

POTATO FUTURES

When I moved to Burley to take the area specialist job, I had compiled 10 years of crop data and could be very accurate in my estimates of the potential crop. The new processors did not have this yield data. Somehow K. C. Barlow, a large potato grower from Burley who was Speaker of the House, heard about my estimates and contacted me. It was good for the university to have a useful and friendly contact with the legislature. He called me from time to time as the season progressed to check on the condition of the crop. Apparently, he kept close track of me, as I received a call while visiting in California.

I was attending an early fall conference at the University of Idaho. A secretary came into the hall and handed me a note that read, "Go to the Dean's office. Important." I wondered what in hell I had done now to get my foot into my mouth. The Dean was talking over the phone and said, "Here he is now," and to me, "It is K. C. Barlow." He handed me the phone.

"How did you find me?" I asked.

"I even have the phone number of your home and your secretary. What are you telling your farmers?"

"My findings show the stand is down about 5 percent from normal and the tuber weight down close to 15 percent due to the lower number of thermal units because of an unusually cool summer. Based on previous records, the potatoes will be scarce and in demand by late March. There are a lot of fields I didn't see."

"Where did you take your samples?"

"K. C., I took them in the same area and farms that I have been using for the past 10 years."

"The reports I have been getting say the crop is beautiful and most of the industry is predicting a bumper crop."

"The plants look beautiful, but you don't put them in the cellar."

"Virg, I am having a hard time believing you, but you have always been right in the past. If you aren't, I'm going to lose a bundle." He said thank you and hung up. The Dean wanted to know what that was all about.

"The information is available to any of my growers upon request."

"That is all right. Do you publish this information?"

"And get my hide hung out to dry? The answer is definitely no."

He said, "Keep it that way." I found out later that K.C. was a big player of potato futures and had become a rich man doing it.

When I moved to Burley, one of my first visitors was Ray Barlow. His visit resulted in my being able to retire early and comfortably. Ray had resigned his position as a Professor of Economics at Arizona University. His specialty was stocks, stock markets, and futures. His father was K. C. Barlow. K. C. was rapidly failing with cancer and Ray took over the management of the 1,500-acre farm. He knew that I had been furnishing K. C. with potato crop information for 10 years. He wanted to know about the condition of the present potato crop.

"The stand count is average. The crop looks beautiful, but it may be short. This year is very similar to a crop six years ago. Your father should have made a killing."

"He really made a killing. He made several hundred thousand dollars. Did he give you anything?"

"No."

"He was a tight-fisted old bastard." Later I found out Ray hated him for the way he had treated Ray's mother, as if she were chattel.

"He got that way honestly, as his father was a Mormon patriarch with seven wives. He has a big statue in the family plot in Salt Lake, with small slabs for the seven wives in front of the statue. You know Mormon wives are trained to serve their husbands, have children, and be faithful to the doctrine of the church."

Ray was preparing to leave the office. As an afterthought, I said, "I am going to check tuber weight in Eastern Idaho this Saturday. Would you like to go with me?"

"Do you have a scale?"

"I don't need one."

"I'll pick you up in my car at six in the morning." By 8 o'clock we were digging up 10 feet of potato rows.

"Get your notebook out. This first hill weighs 3 pounds and about 4 ounces."

He set up a small box and his scale and said, "I'll be darned. Three pounds, 4 ounces!" He checked the weights of the next three hills.

"I shouldn't have brought this scale. You are a human calculator."

On the way back we talked about the small size of the tubers and lack of weight. I told him, "I can't really give an accurate estimate until I check on data from other years. I am going to the National Potato Growers' Convention at Fort Collins on Monday to give a paper on control of rhizoctonia."

"Maybe between us we can get something really big going. Potato futures are based on the price of Maine potatoes. The Idaho crop has some influence on it. Colorado, Wisconsin, and North Dakota also influence the market. Maybe you could establish contacts with growers and specialists in those areas."

I arrived at the meeting early. A tall, pleasant-looking man wore a

Maine name tag. We hit it off immediately. I said, "Since we grow more potatoes than you do, I'll buy you lunch." Treston Bubar was a big Maine potato grower and he played the futures market. It was a mutual advantage to exchange information. It just happened he had a state concession on materials to prevent sprouting in storage and he treated almost all cellars in Aroostock County. Contacts were established with specialists for exchange of crop information for the mutual benefit of our growers. When I told Ray of the contacts, he clapped his hands and said, "We can really get something going now."

The report that all states would have nearly a 5 percent increase in production from the slightly below-average crop of the year before really made him beam. Ray said Danny Reitman had been putting out the prediction that "Idaho is going to have a bumper crop."

"Who is this Reitman?"

"He is an Italian Jew that buys and ships potatoes. He is a licensed broker with a seat on the stock exchange. He is advising his clients to go short. Danny drives along and eyeballs potato fields, then he puts out his estimates to the brokers. My father quit using him when he found you and he said Danny was really lucky in his estimates, but really flubbed sometimes.

"Ray, Idaho will be down 10 percent or more. That is hard to believe, but my samplings show that to be true. Now is the time to go long, as it will be a month before they find out at digging time."

Ray said, "Let's not get in a hurry. We won't play the market this year. We would be making peanuts. Let's bait the trap and catch a silver fox next year. This year we would only catch muskrats. Who is your broker?"

"I have some dealing with Goodbody."

He said, "My dad dealt with Merrill Lynch. This year you will furnish for free timely information on the Idaho potato crop to their commodities broker. I will do the same. We will furnish slightly different figures and different terms, as we will compare our reports before we give them out."

No attention was paid to our first report on the Idaho crop. After harvest it was apparent that we were right. Treston called me one evening and said the harvest was going to be down nearly 5 percent due to flooding and ponding of wet places in the fields. We passed it on to our broker the next day. We also gave the estimates of specialists from other areas. By this time our accurate reports were being put out on the big board.

Ray said, "Now we have them where we want them. We will continue to put out nothing but accurate information, after we have established our own position, as the market has been going up and down based on our reports."

The next year the early U.S. Department of Agriculture report said the potato crop would be a large one based on the increased acreage due to the previous year's high potato prices. Idaho acreage was up by nearly 10,000 acres. It was a large acreage, but due to the late spring planting, was late. My report to Treston was that the Idaho crop would be about the same as the previous year, in spite of the increased acreage. He reported similar conditions. The Idaho crop looked good all summer and this information we reported to the brokerage firms and commodity specialists. Reports from the Dakotas and Minnesota were similar.

Ray got together with four other potato futures players. Two were from out of state. They agreed to give me 10 percent of the profit and no responsibility for losses.

Processors and potato dealers were contracting smaller amounts than usual. They were paying $1.50 field run which was a ridiculously low price, below the cost of production. The result of our field sampling on August 15 was surprisingly lower tuber weight per hill than normal. On the way back we stopped at the Aberdeen Experiment Station where researcher Wille Irritani kept a record of total thermal units. His records showed they were considerably below normal. Because of this and his sampling of experimental plots, he estimated a yield of at least 20 percent below normal.

Our last sampling of the tuber weight was startling. They were down even more. With only one month of growing time left, there was no way they could come close to catching up. Just to make sure, we stayed overnight and sampled fields the next day. Treston's report, which we passed on to the brokers, was that heavy rains had caused some flooding in low spots, but Maine would still have an average yield. We also added that due to the lateness of the crop, frost could definitely lower the yield in most areas.

The weather Bureau forecast a possible freezing temperature for the northeastern U.S. The price of Maine future potatoes jumped 25¢ or $125 a carload on the futures market. The report of damaging frost in Maine caused the market to jump $250 a car.

I saw Danny Reitman at the Elks' meeting that night and told him about the frost. He said, "I know about the frost and my reports from Maine say that it only singed the top leaves in a few places. They are still going to have a big crop. Why don't you come down to my office and short them. This is a sure thing and you could make a bundle." I had already received the information about the severe damage from Treston.

For a while it looked as if Danny was a genius with his Maine May delivery shorts. His contract to sell Maine May potatoes at $2 per 100 appeared to be money in the bank. After the scare the market went back to $2.25 and if the U.S.D.A. crop forecast should be changed, it would go much higher. For 10 years I had been making a forecast as to what the government's forecast would be, and I was never less than 94 percent correct. The processors and shippers must have sensed a possible crop shortage and were now contracting as fast as they could at $2 per cwt. I gave my report of the pending short crop to the five partners and they took their positions on the long side. University policy prevented me from publishing news articles of my estimate of the total yield. My growers were being robbed by the processors and shippers.

A call to the editor of *The Idaho Farmer* brought results. He agreed to meet me at 6 o'clock Sunday morning and take a tour to sample potato fields in Eastern Idaho. I knew what was happening in my area in South Central Idaho. We spent all day digging and weighing the potatoes in a 10-foot row in field after field. When he compared these figures with my records of the past 10 years, he was amazed. Two days later *The Idaho Farmer* published the information that Idaho's potato crop would be down 10 to 20 percent due to the unusually light weight of the tubers. He printed pictures and I was in some of them. The article mentioned that he had made the trip with me.

Then all hell broke loose.

First I received a call from the Director of Extension. He really lit into me, saying it was not the function of university personnel to engage in determining the yield of a crop. That was the responsibility of the U.S.D.A. He said he had received complaints from some of the most important people in the state requesting that I be fired. One of them was Jack Simplot.

I said, "We took his car. I was not on duty, as it was Sunday. The reason for the trip was to protect my potato growers. Their organization is matching federal funds for my salary."

This didn't appease him. He said, "I may have to fire you."

By this time I was furious because I thought he should back me up, and not bow to special interests. I said, "The Idaho Potato Growers are the most powerful farm organization in the state; several big growers are in the legislature. I have already received calls from two of them thanking me for the good work. If you fire me, you could follow within 30 days." He sputtered something and hung up. I was sitting at my desk confused and wondering what trouble my big mouth had caused, when the phone rang again.

"This is Don R. Theophilus, Virg." Now I knew that there was big trouble because when the President of the university calls you, it is serious.

"I read the article. Do you know what you are doing?"

"Don R., you have known about my forecasts in the past and they are available to any farmer who asks for them. After checking and double checking, I'll bet my job that it is right."

He laughed and said, "That is what I did when Jack Simplot called and said you should be fired. I told him I have known Virg since he was a freshman in college. He doesn't lie and I have known for years the forecasts of the potato yield available to farmers, and they have been accurate. Then I told him if you are wrong, I'll fire you as he suggested. If you are right, I'll give you a limit raise. I also received calls from two legislators praising you. Good luck!"

I didn't blame Jack. He was a good and kindly man.

The article started everybody sampling potato fields. The result was on Friday, five days after the article in the paper, contracts were up to $2.75 a hundred and they kept climbing all year to $4.50 a hundred. The article had made the growers many millions of dollars. Later in the year, Don R. told me that he talked to Jack Simplot when the legislature was meeting in Boise and asked him, "What about Virg Cross?"

Jack said, "He was right and he cost me several million dollars."

The futures kept going higher and higher. When the five associates closed their contracts, they had made $750 a car and they had really plunged.

Danny Reitman, the potato dealer and futures broker, was short, dark, about 5-feet, 9-inches tall. His compact build gave him a look of strength and power. He was always immaculately dressed. He was smooth, in fact too smooth, not only in his outward manner, but in his conversation. He was a generous spender at the bar and tried to be a big wheel. I felt uneasy around him.

My next-door neighbor and bowling partner was a trouble-shooter for the A & P grocery chain. He had been a neighbor of Danny Reitman in Chicago. He said Danny was in the produce business there. He was also a close companion of well-known Chicago gangsters. Danny had a gun in holster strapped to his steering wheel. He added that when things got too hot in Chicago, Danny moved to Burley to turn legitimate. His associate, the infamous Bugsy Siegal, moved to Las Vegas where he was later killed. It was rumored that they had a mutual insurance policy for $500,000 which Danny received.

After the report of the short crop, Danny called me. He was short on the futures and had to put up more and more money to cover the margin. He had really plunged. He said, "You are wrong on your forecast. You will have to retract in the newspapers."

"Danny, the report is correct. You have made one hell of a mistake."

"You are going to change it. There are ways of taking care of people like you."

This conversation took place about nine in the evening. I asked him to meet me in the Elks lodge room at 2 o'clock tomorrow and we would settle the matter. His statement about taking care of people like me scared me. I called my son, Dallas, and we discussed what to do. I prepared certified letters to the police department and to the F.B.I. in Pocatello telling of the conversation and threat. Martha Briscoe had the address of Danny's son and family in Chicago, also the address of his daughter. I was going to fight fire with fire and maybe he would back away after I told him what I had done.

I stood up when Danny walked into the room. It was warm and he removed his coat and hat. I didn't know what to expect. He was smiling as he walked up to me. When he started to step forward with his left foot, I ducked to the right and was just in time, as his right fist grazed the corner of my left eye and made a slight cut. Knowing my own strength, I grabbed him and we struggled for a few seconds. When my right leg kicked his left heel, he fell with me on top. His head hit the floor hard, partially stunning him. Choking and pounding his head on the floor took all the fight out of him. I stood by waiting for him to recover enough for me to talk to him. He finally sat up and said, "You are a dead man."

I kicked him, like I would punt a football, in the ribs. He rolled over and a kick on the other side finished him off. He was doubled over and really hurting. Finally, he got up and sat in a chair. Then I informed him about the letters and read off the addresses of his relatives.

"If the police and the F.B.I. don't get you, this is what is going to happen. We are not mafia and families don't mean anything to us. In my family there is a frogman, a commando, and a marine. They have been notified. If anything happens to me, neither you nor any of your relatives will be left alive." It must have worked, as I had no more contacts with him. A short time later he moved to California.

My association with the five partners in potato futures made eight very profitable years. We disbanded when Jack Simplot and his partner illegally tried to corner and influence the potato futures.

SUSAN

Susan resented the move from Jerome to Burley with words and tears. She was a very popular, beautiful girl with many friends from the first grade to her junior year, and a straight-A student. She was also in line to be Queen of Job's Daughters. Burley High School was predominately L.D.S. We told Susan to go to the L.D.S. Church and see how she liked it. After all, we were in an L.D.S. community and it would be easier to live there if we got along harmoniously with the natives. She attended church several times. Trying to get another convert, they promised she would be elected student body secretary if she would join the church. The church did not appeal to her and she told us, "No more L.D.S. Church. I am going to the Presbyterian Church."

She had decided not to date for a while in order to look the field over. Burley had a big all-state football player who kept asking her for dates and she told him she was not ready to date yet. After a month or so a very nice, nonathletic student asked her for a date. They dated for school affairs. We were pleased, as he was a top student from one of the best families.

Susan was still angry about moving. She had stopped confiding in me and this bothered me greatly. She was as close to her mother as a daughter can be. On a Sunday morning early in December, Ethel and I lingered over the last cups of coffee after Susan had left for church.

"Virg, Susan is having a terrible time at school. It is affecting her grades and she has been crying in her room at times."

"What is going on?"

"She refused to date that big Higgins boy several times. Now he and two of his buddies are making life miserable for her. They harass her at dances, in class, and after school. This has been going on for a long time."

"Ethel, why didn't you tell me sooner?"

"Susan said, 'Don't tell Daddy. He is too rough and can be downright violent when he is mad.'"

That afternoon I told Susan that I would go to the authorities at school and put an end to the harrassment. She said, "There is no need for you to go to the principal. Everything has been taken care of and is going to be o.k."

Lary came home from the university for Christmas vacation a few days early. He had been home a few days when I received a phone call from Mrs. Higgins saying she wanted to see me. I answered her knock at the door. We sat down. She said, "You should see my son."

I never gave her a chance to say more. I proceeded to tell her what her bullying son had been doing to Susan.

"That monster son of yours wanted to know where my son's father worked. He also asked if he had any brothers."

"Your son was lucky. Lary's older brother Dallas, the big mean one, will be coming home tomorrow. He is very fond of his sister."

When I asked Lary what had happened, he laughed and said, "Susan fingered him for me. When he got into his car, I got into the front seat with him. I told him, 'I want to talk to you about my sister Susan.'

"He said, 'That is all right with me.' Apparently, he had a lot of confidence because he was 2 inches taller and probably 20 pounds heavier than me. He drove to a field on the edge of town, got out of the car and took off his coat. It ran through my mind that I might take a lot of punishment, but having just finished football, my conditioning would wear him out. He fell for the old slicker Cross trick. I flipped out my left hand, looking at it and simultaneously swinging a right just above his belt buckle. He grunted, lowering his guard, and I decked him with a left square on his chin. My right hand and arm tingled and my left hand was slightly numb. When he got to his knees, he refused to stand up and blubbered, 'You can't hit me—I'm a juvenile.'

"How old are you?

"'I won't be 19 until January.'

"Well, I'm just 18.

"He had a lot of long hair which I grabbed and I proceeded to slap him with a gloved right. The idea was to mark up his face without serious injury. When I was through, his face was a bloody mess. I helped him into the passenger seat. It was then I asked him if he had any brothers and where his father worked. I also told him that if he or his buddies bothered my sister again in any way, she would be wearing his two front teeth for earrings. I drove the car to our house and he drove home."

The next day, Dallas, 6-foot, 3-inches, 220 pounds, arrived home. The two brothers greeted Susan at the school steps. She pointed out the ex-bully and they nodded, no doubt giving him cause for considerable apprehension.

When I asked Susan how she was being treated at school, she said, "Daddy, I told you it would be taken care of. All the boys are so polite to me. That creep and his two buddies move clear away from me when I walk down the hall or into a room. My big brothers have put the fear of God into them."

At Burley High Susan had dropped from a straight-A student to a C student. She said she just didn't belong in that school, and felt that because she had refused to join the church, she was not getting the grades she should have. I looked at a biology paper on which she had received a C+. I taught biology in Heyburn High School. I thought it was an excellent paper. She said that Susie Curtis had copied it almost word for word and received an A on it in the other class.

Jim Andersen, Susan's steady boyfriend, was attending Idaho State at Pocatello. During spring vacation he was arrested and put in jail for the weekend. He was a car buff and almost a genius mechanically. He had been picked up several times for speeding. Apparently, this time he either resisted or hit an officer. We had felt that Susan and Jim were getting too intimate and this was a good excuse for breaking up the relationship.

Ethel said, "Lary wants Susan to go to Moscow this spring to take the pre-exams and get acquainted so she can get interested in going to the university."

Lary, having hashed for four years at the Alpha Phi House, was an honorary member. He said the girls at the house were looking forward to meeting Susan and she could stay at their house during her visit to Moscow. Susan was rather reluctant about going. Ethel said she had been beaten down so much that she expected the worst.

Susan flew to Lewiston and took the bus for the 40-mile ride to Moscow. Lary met the bus and took her to the Alpha Phi House.

The girl that stepped off the plane at Burley was altogether different from the one that had left a week before. She yelled, "Daddy!" and gave me a kiss. I could see that she had a wonderful time and was walking on air.

Her mother said, "Susan, tell us about your visit."

"Mummy, it was wonderful. The first evening President and Mrs. Theophilus were the dinner guests at the house. Everybody stood when they entered. He saw me and said, 'Susan!' and they both gave me a hug, and I was seated between them at dinner. They wanted to know about our family. It really impressed the sorority house members.

"When the members asked if I was Dallas and Lary's sister, they said 'You are a brain.' I told them that I was only a B student and they laughed like they didn't believe me. When I took the exam I rated as a sophomore, second semester. I feel like I am really somebody, being a Cross. They can no longer get me down because I feel so good about myself and my family."

That fall we took Susan up to Moscow a week early for rush. My advice was to try for one of the lesser sororities like Alpha Phi's rather than the elite Kappas and Pi Phi's. I knew how cruel and disappointing rush could be and didn't want her to be hurt. The selections of the pledges and the sororities had to match. If your final two selections did not nominate you, you were out. Each day was an elimination.

315

When we returned from our Canadian trip, she had a Pi Phi ribbon. Her two choices had been Pi Phi's and Kappa's and they matched her.

Susan made her grades with a three-point average. During her sophomore year she began to have headaches. She said everyone expected her to get straight A's and the pressure was getting to her.

When I came home from work, Susan had arrived for Christmas vacation. There was a tall, rather good-looking boy with her. She introduced him and I recognized the family name. He was a member of a very influential family in Pocatello. Undoubtedly, Doug was a prize package. He asked me if it would be alright for him to be pinned to Susan. I said it would, if it was alright with Susan, but I felt a bit doubtful about him.

Dallas and Lary arrived a few hours later. After dinner they invited Doug to go downtown and have a beer with them. When they returned at 10 o'clock, the brothers said they wanted a word with Susan. Several minutes later, Susan came out and spoke to Doug.

"You will have to leave. You can't stay here."

"Why?"

"Because you don't belong here."

"Susan, who do you think you are?"

"I know who I am, but I don't know about you." Later I questioned Dallas and Lary. They said that after a few beers Doug began to brag about all of the girls he had sex with, and even named names. They said he was a creep.

Susan's headaches got worse, especially at exam time. She could tutor a class at the house and they would get A's and B's, but she would be lucky to get a C due to the terrible headaches. Shots given by the doctor would give relief. She hated the shots, as they knocked her out completely and she had to go to bed. We sent her to Mayo's, and they said the headaches were not physical or migraine. Dallas, who was administrator of the Veterans' Research Program in Kansas City, came to the rescue. There was a research program in its infancy at the University at Topeka, Kansas, that was using thought transference to cure a condition such as hers. Due to wide publicity of his research, they accepted her as a guinea pig. The researchers were so delighted with her and the progress she made in three weeks that her records were sent all over the United States and even to Europe. By concentrating, she could send blood to her hands and feet, raising their temperature two degrees, thus taking blood from her head and stopping the headache. For years, if she felt a headache coming on, she would excuse herself and go to the bedroom for 10 or 15 minutes and come out headache-free.

Susan did not want to back to the University of Idaho. It was hard to live up to the reputation of her brothers and cousin Lynn Hintze.

Ethel asked her if she would like to go to Idaho State at Pocatello.

"I would. They never heard of the Crosses and I can just be myself and chug along getting my C's and B's and be happy."

Jim Andersen was taking Civil Engineering at Idaho State. During the summer he was welding in a steel fabrication plant in Pocatello. His record was excellent. I was mowing the lawn when he walked up to me and said, "Mr. Cross, I would like to start seeing Susan again."

I held out my hand and said, "Welcome back, Jim." A few days later Lary and Dallas invited Jim out for a beer. As they went out the door, I looked at Susan.

"I am not worried. They will like him. He is not another Doug."

In an hour the three came in the door laughing and there was no conference with Susan. When Jim left, Lary remarked, "Susan, hang onto him. He is o.k. and is really going to go places." He was right— in spades.

At the start of his senior year, Jim was financially unable to enroll in school. He was informed that he would be drafted, so he enlisted in the Marines and was sent to Camp Pendleton. Susan was in school. When Jim came home on leave in October, they were married at the Presbyterian Church in Burley. Susan insisted that the church bells be rung, as it was a joyous occasion. Jim's father, Tola, had just attended his first gentile wedding. All previous ceremonies had been conducted by bishops of the L.D.S. church. He remarked to his wife, "That is really the way a marriage ceremony should be!"

Susan finished her school year and joined Jim at Camp Pendleton. We visited them there, and Susan went to play golf with us. She slipped her purse under the seat of the car.

"Daddy, be sure to lock the car." I did. When we returned, there was a golf-ball-sized hole in the ventilator side window. Susan checked her purse and began to cry. She had just cashed her paycheck and the money was gone. I was flush from potato futures and handed her two $100 bills which covered the loss. Her reaction was a long hug and kiss.

"Daddy, you are the best daddy in the world."

Ethel remarked, "That is what I've been telling you for years."

Jim had only six months left to serve on his two-year enlistment when he was ordered to Vietnam. The big push was on and they needed welders and expert repairmen. His first stop was DaNang which went under the long siege the day after he arrived. He was given a repair truck with a driver and another helper. In the brief six months, his driver was killed and the rear was blown off the truck two times, but to our great joy he finally made it home. After finishing school, Jim went to work for Chicago Bridge and Iron. They had a training program for new employees in which they did every job for the company over a period of four years. Jim finished the training in two years.

PANDY

Pandy, short for Pandemonium, a Siamese cat, deserves some space. We got her as a kitten in Burley. With the advent of potato money and getting rid of the polio debt, we bought expensive new furniture. Pandy started to tear the new davenport and Ethel said, "Take her to the vet and have her put to sleep."

Reluctantly, I left Pandy with the vet's assistant, saying "Put her to sleep and send me the bill."

The phone rang very shortly after I reached home.

"You have to sign a paper if you want the cat put to sleep," she said. So I had to go back. I could hear Pandy's awful squalling. She was very unhappy. The assistant said, "She is a beautiful cat—why don't you have her declawed instead of putting her to sleep?"

"Fine. Call me when she is ready to go home." I did not tell Ethel. About a week later Jody Lewis was visiting and answered the phone. She said, "Your cat is ready to come home." This was a great surprise to Ethel. When I explained what happened, she said, "I'm glad you did."

So we brought Pandy home. Eventually, she had kittens. We had fixed up a maternity box in the basement. The seven kittens were born downstaris and Duchess, the Dachshund, helped her clean them up. In a few days Pandy was bringing the kittens upstairs and putting them behind the davenport, and I was carrying them back downstairs. There was a temporary truce and for the 10 days they were in the kitchen. When she moved them into the corner of the living room, we gave up and moved their box, but not their litter box. It was comic to see the kittens run the length of the living room into the kitchen litter box and squat just in time.

Actually, Pandy was Susan's cat and went with them to Salt Lake, to San Francisco, to Pendleton, back to Salt Lake, to Memphis. When Jim was promoted to number two man on the huge dam being built on the Orinoco, Venezuela, Susan tried to take her in a cage on the plane. The ticket counter said, "No cat on the plane regardless of cage." Susan marched into the office of Frank Bouman, President of Eastern Air in the Miami airport, and came out with a lifetime pass for Pandy. Jim said, "Pandy liked to kill Venezuelan snakes and rats, but was afraid of the 7-inch long cockroaches."

Pandy died at the age of 17.

LARY QUITS COLLEGE

At the end of the nine-week period of his senior year in college, there was a phone call from Lary. Ethel and I got on separate phones. His reply to our question, "How are you doing?" was, "I am coming home."

"I know you aren't broke because I just checked your bank balance. Have you gotten a girl in trouble?"

"Virg, you trained me better than that. I talked to Guy Weeks and Roland Portman. I am coming home tomorrow. See you then." He hung up.

Ethel said, "Do you realize he has never had over four days off a job or school since he was 14?"

"I guess he is just burned out. He said his grades were 3.4. He needs a rest."

He just sat around and read, getting up in the morning when he felt like it. When I asked him if he wanted to go pheasant hunting in the Wendell area on Saturday, he said, "I'll tell you Saturday morning." I really got disgusted with his desire to do nothing. It was after Christmas when he applied for a job at a service station. When the owner chose a fellow who Lary said "was a wimp" over him, it made him mad. Thiocol of Brigham City was hiring. Somehow Lary convinced the head of personnel that they could use him. The personnel officer told Lary that since he would be working on a top-secret project, he would have to be cleared by the F.B.I. and it would take at least two weeks. He started to fill out a questionnaire to send to the F.B.I. When it came to father, Lary said, "My father has clearance with the F.B.I."

The personnel officer didn't pay much attention and continued to ask questions and fill in blanks. When asked about what his brother did, Lary said, "He is in the National Honor Guard at Arlington and has top clearance." The man dialed a number, asked some questions and said, "Thank you." To Lary he said, "You can come to work Monday."

Lary was visiting us when the first man landed on the moon. He watched television most of the time for 24 hours. He got credit for important work on the development and testing of the retroactive rockets that controlled yaw in flight.

In the spring Lary brought home Caroline and her young son. She was very personable, pretty and undoubtedly intelligent, as she was utive secretary to the president and manager. The next time he brought her, he asked to be married at home, our blessing and the old Buick car that was in good shape. He said, "I know you object to a woman with a child but that is what I want." Our friend Martha Briscoe took over all of the wedding arrangements and they were married in June. The reception was held in our beautiful backyard.

Caroline's maid of honor at the wedding told me that Caroline had married a returned Mormon missionary. When they went back to Utah, she discovered that he was a fundamentalist who believed in polygamy and wanted her to live in a polygamist colony near the Arizona border. She divorced him. Her son Gary was born after the divorce.

Caroline wanted a father for her child. She checked over the list of single employees of professional status at Thiokol. Lary was last on the list. Caroline was well liked by the wife of the manager and enlisted her help. The boss invited the candidates to dinner, one at a time, and the women checked them over. It was arranged that the prospect would see Caroline home after the dinner. Lary was the last one. Caroline said she thought during the dinner, "Oh no, not him," but later decided that he would be the one.

When I told Ethel about this, she said, "Caroline deserves to have him after all that effort. She will be a good wife and a match for him."

That fall Lary went back to school and Caroline worked as a secretary. A Douglas representative interviewed him at school and invited him and Caroline to dinner that evening. During the interview they had never asked him about grades. Lary said, "You don't seem to be interested in my grades."

"We can find that out at the registrar's office." They asked him about his family and the work that he had done. When they found out about the spray business, they asked detailed questions. He was hired and after arriving in San Francisco he was told that they had been searching for the 10 top electrical engineering graduates in the country, and he was one of them.

When he told me the others were from M.I.T., Stanford, California Poly, Indiana, etc., I said, "You are in fast company."

"They are in fast company. They probably have had better equipment than I had at the University of Idaho, but we were trained to think. If you couldn't reason, you flunked. They can't out-think me and I can outwork them."

During the six months training period, the M.I.T. graduate said to him, "Cross, you are trying to climb over everybody."

"I am doing the best I can. I want to succeed. Good luck." He was to be stationed at Lanpoc and be in charge of the intercontinental missiles in cooperation with an Army General. They hit within a half-mile of the target in Kwajalein, over 3,000 miles away.

Ethel, Susan and I were visiting Caroline and Lary. Lary said, "At

320

9 o'clock tonight we are launching a missile, so be ready to watch it."
We watched but nothing happened. Lary called and said that he would
not be home until sometime tomorrow because there was trouble. A red
light had gone on 15 seconds before launching. At 8 seconds before
takeoff, Lary scrubbed the mission. This caused quite a furor with the
management, as it cost $200,000 to abort the takeoff.

Lary said, "If I have done what you think I have done, I should be
fired. I thought it was better to lose $200,000 and be safe than to lose
$2,500,000. Put a full-time guard on the rocket and give me until noon
tomorrow and I'll tell you what went wrong. I'll have to question the
men that serviced it."

He spent the rest of the night going over the schematics. He
thought it was a faulty solenoid. When he questioned the engineers and
technicians that had serviced it, he asked them about the solenoid that
was found to be faulty. They said, "It was alright. We had to replace
the old one that was faulty so we put a new one in."

"Did you test it?" They looked at him with a scared, blank look,
and said, "No because it was new." Douglas fired one engineer, gave
the other one 60 days without pay, and a week without pay to the
technician. Lary got letters of apology from all of the brass. They did
not have the least idea what had happened until he found the trouble.

After one year Lary went back to school, got his master's degree in
electrical engineering, and went to work for General Electric in Boston.
They had promised him that he would work on design, but the
manager said, "We are crowded for time on a government missile
project and when we get it completed, we'll put you on design. It
should not be over six months." Lary did not like missiles. To him
they meant death and destruction. A year later he was still working on
missile research. He told his supervisor that he wanted an immediate
change.

"Cross, if you don't want to do this work we can get somebody
else."

"I am giving you 30 days, and you can explain it to the vice-
president."

He applied in person to Sanders Associates in New Hampshire,
and insisted on seeing the vice-president. The officer was sceptical of
his resume and needled him about being so good. Lary gave him the
phone number of the vice-president of Douglas Aircraft and said, "Call
him." This brought a laugh from the executive. He dialed the number
and told Lary to pick up another phone and listen in.

"I have a former employee of yours applying for a job here. Just
how good is this Lary Cross?"

"We don't know how good he is."

"He is that good?"

"Right, and you tell that such and such that if he wants a job to come back here. I want to get back the $7 that I lost playing golf with him."

His first assignment was to produce a workable piece of equipment that would perform certain functions. He was given a room and a desk. When he looked in the adjoining storeroom or closet, there were several gadgets that newly-employed engineers had worked out to no avail. He had been working and researching on the project only a few days when they moved another desk into the large room. Lary said the new man was very sure of himself. When he looked at you with his big grey eyes, you felt he had unlimited power and confidence. The rumors about him were rather vague. They ranged from an observer, to efficiency specialist, and possibly a head hunter. He just wandered about the plant asking a question now and then. Sometimes he would write in a black notebook. He asked Lary, "What are you working on?" When Lary told him about the assignment, he said, "Cross, you'll never make it.."

"Do you want to bet?"

"Sure. I'll buy a dinner for you and your wife." Three weeks later he and his wife took Lary and Caroline out to dinner. When the notice was posted that the man was the new manager, it surprised everyone. He was a head hunter and made many personnel changes. To Lary's surprise, he was promoted to head of design over employees with much more seniority and experience.

Sanders patented Lary's creation.

POLES

Al Duke had been my supervisor as district agent. We liked each other and had worked smoothly together. His tact and ability to supervise closely and still maintain rapport and get complete cooperation from the members of his department was one of his very strong points. He moved into the State Department in Washington, D.C. Whenever delegations and officials from foreign countries wanted to visit and examine potato production in the United States, he would ask the university if they could visit me and send them the itinerary and length of the visit, and what they would like to see. Of course, the university liked the publicity and I was flattered.

The Scotchman who had won a six-month tour from the Royal Agricultural Society was a terrific entrepreneur. He was the largest spud grower in "the hull of Scotland" with 75 acres. For three days we visited farms, processing plants and equipment manufacturing plants. He never stopped taking notes and pictures. We enjoyed his company at dinner when he told us about Scotland. He said, "The salmon come upstream on the adjoining farm but are stopped from going on to my farm by the weir."

"Why don't you ask them to remove it or modify it?"

"Mon, that weir has been there for over 100 years and you just don't do that. We haven't communicated with each other in this century."

"Why haven't you?"

"Why should we?"

I drove him to a four-way road corner, stopped the car and told him to stand on the fender and take a look. Each of the corners was a corner of a mile-square potato field.

"Mon, I'm seeing more spuds than there is in the hull of Scotland!"

He copied pet food formulas that were on record and became one of the leading pet food manufacturers in the United Kingdom.

Al Duke's appointment as an attache to Poland must have accounted for the Polish delegation's three-day visit to Idaho to observe the potato industry. I received a notice from the Dean that they wanted to see culture, harvest, storage and manufacturing processes. They also wanted to see the newly-settled irrigation projects. A week before their arrival, an F.B.I. agent from Pocatello came to the office and briefed me. They could take copies of any publications on potatoes in my office. They could take pictures in the fields. No pictures could be taken in a processing plant. Under no circumstances were they to visit any potato equipment manufacturing plant. I could not invite them to my home. The agent informed me that the State Department allowed them only three stops in their two weeks' stay in the United States.

A phone call Tuesday evening informed me that the entourage had registered at the Ponderosa Motel: the Polish Secretaries of Agriculture and Economics, another official who was the interpreter, and an F.B.I. agent. All five of us could ride in one car. I decided to visit growers that were harvesting. One of these calls was to Blaine Curtis, a very successful and progressive grower. I told them through the interpreter that we were going to visit one of the big potato growers and that he was a millionaire. They talked in Russian or Polish. The interpreter said they wanted to see Mexican workers. At Blaine's they would see everything.

Blaine was running the digger and Mexicans were following and picking the potatoes into 60-pound burlap sacks. There would be considerable time, as Blaine had just started up the row for his mile-round trip. The Poles were examining the bumper crop and talking among themselves. The F.B.I. agent beckoned me and I followed him until we were out of earshot.

"Mr. Cross, you have F.B.I. clearance. The interpreter is for me. Actually, I am very fluent in Polish and Russian. They wanted to see the Mexican workers to see how downtrodden, mistreated and exploited they are, so they could make a report on it."

One of the Poles said, "You said you would show us a millionaire." I pointed to Blaine.

"Are you a millionaire?"

"I guess I am."

"Then why are you running this machine?"

"I run it because I enjoy working."

The interpreter came over and asked, "How much are the Mexicans making a day?"

I said, "You probably wouldn't believe me. That is their foreman. Go ask him." After a short conversation with the foreman, he walked back and talked to his two companions. I asked, "What did he say?"

"They are averaging about $40 a day." Later, when it was safe, the F.B.I. agent told me that the Minister of Agriculture told the Minister of Economics, "That is more than we make." They also asked about the housing and were told that the workers and their families were comfortable.

By 5 o'clock they had visited several operations. I didn't want them to think that I had picked a special one to impress them.

We had done a lot of walking and they were tired from the previous day's travel. They said, "That is enough for today." They took a lot of pictures and picked up several Idaho bulletins on potato production from my office, including some 10 publications that I had authored.

The next day I had scheduled them to tour Simplot's huge potato processing plant. They were really impressed. They had lunch at the company restaurant with Paul Hansen, manager. The F.B.I. agent said they couldn't get over the restaurant where the workers had lunch with the management and were served the same food. They sampled their first French fries and each got a small sack to nibble on.

We had been driving by two big supermarkets. The interpreter asked if they could visit one of them. I said, "You pick the one." They chose Smith's Food King. I took a cart and motioned for them to do the same and follow me. Then I waved them loose and told the interpreter they were on their own. The F.B.I. agent and I kept within hearing distance of them part of the time. One remarked, "We couldn't have a store like this in Poland or Russia. People would steal everything. This must be a special store to impress visiting foreigners."

Their interpreter said, "The signs say that this company has several hundred stores, so it must not be unusual." They laughed as they checked their carts through the check stand. Fresh fruit was very popular. Canned ham, soap and toothbrushes were in each cart. They acted like a bunch of kids at their first circus.

By the third day the Polish delegation had shed their stiffness and reserve and were pleasant and informal. They asked if I would consider working two years in Poland.

"I would consider it if you would pay all travel and living expenses as well as $100,000 for the two years."

"That is too expensive."

The third day they were scheduled to visit irrigated farms with general crop practices such as grain, beets, hay and livestock feeding. Much of Minidoka County had been recently settled by war veterans who had drawn the farms in a lottery. I told the visitors we would inspect some of these farms and they could talk with the operators. The farms had to have dwellings according to certain specifications and were generally attractive. They appeared to be skeptical when I told them the government had awarded these farms to veterans of World War II. I stopped at one of the more prosperous farms. They said, "You picked this one out," inferring that it was not typical.

"All right, you pick the stops." I drove down the road, and they pointed out a place that looked slightly less pretentious than some. I drove into the yard. Ed Zeniani was adjusting his cultivator. I introduced him to the group, explained what their mission was, and asked him to show them and explain his farming operation. I winked at the F.B.I. agent and he winked back. Ed was probably one of the most successful of all the settlers. I had been using his operation for demonstrations to show other settlers improved practices.

They asked many questions. "What does the government let you

325

plant? What does the government pay you?"

Ed laughed and said, "We are not in a dictatorship. I plant whatever I want to plant and sell to an independent buyer after bargaining."

"How did you get the farm?"

He echoed the information I had given them and added, "I got it fighting dictators."

Quietly, I told the F.B.I. man how they had really picked a ringer.

"Can we see the inside of the house?"

"I will ask the lady of the house," I told them.

She said, "Give me 15 minutes."

In the house they acted as if they were in awe about a farmer having a deep freeze, washer, drier, refrigerator, T.V., radio and tiled bathroom. Ruth told me to tell them they could open all doors and drawers and look at everything. Their inspection of the house was very thorough and they commented quietly with each other. Ruth had baked a two-layer, frosted cake from which she served generous pieces with coffee. The Poles invited her and Ed to join us in a farewell appreciation dinner at the Ponderosa Inn.

Everyone made toasts. Ethel and I didn't try to keep up with their vodka consumption, making a drink last all evening. They treated Ethel like royalty. She, being gracious and tactful, got them to talking about their families and family life. Later she said to me, "I am glad I am not a Polish wife. They are like slaves."

"You mean the Polish men are chauvinist pigs?"

"That is right. They also gulp down vodka as if it were milk. If they used the grain for food instead of making vodka, it would cut down on their huge grain imports."

Evidently they had been suspicious of everything they had seen and everything I said. They double-checked with Ethel.

"What was his father's position?" the interpreter asked her.

"He didn't have a position. He was a small farmer."

"Did the state send him to college?"

"He had no help from anyone. He worked his way through."

"Who hires him?"

"The university recommends him, but the County Commissioners have the right to reject his application."

"Who determines that he continues to be employed?"

"It is actually the farmers that he is serving and helping their programs. He brings them the findings of the experiment stations. If they decide that he is not doing a satisfactory job, they report it to the County Commissioners and they fire him. His advancement is based on his ability to serve them."

They asked about our family and what the children were doing. Obviously, they thought our sons would have reached a high rank in the Communist Party.

I appreciated their thanks and praise for our hospitality. The letters from the State Department and from the President of ɯe University of Idaho added to my ego.

My father, who still lived at Jerome, was 90 years old. He fell off a ladder while picking peaches and broke a rib which punctured a lung. He was in the hospital where they had to keep pumping fluid out of his lungs. When it was apparent that he wasn't going to last long, I called my brother Farrell who was living in Atascadero, California. When Dad heard that Farrell was coming, he demanded and got an eggnog with a shot of bourbon in it every day. When Farrell arrived three days later, he was walking to the bathroom. Al visited two days and I came down every evening from Burley. We were all tournament checker players and Dad beat both of us. On Sunday morning Farrell left. We were staying over at Norman's. That evening after dinner I visited Dad at the hospital. He told me how much he appreciated me as a son. We were holding hands as I was preparing to leave.

"Virg, look after Farrell, as he will always need help. I know you will take care of Mama when I am gone. Do you know we have been married 62 years?"

"Dad, I'll see you tomorrow night."

"Son, this is goodbye." We hugged and I left. I had been back at Norman's less than an hour when the hospital called and said, "He passed away in his sleep."

Mother lasted four years longer and was just waiting to rejoin him. Who knows how long his teachings of kindness, fair play, and helping your fellow man will prevail? One of his favorite sayings was, "A person that likes himself is a happy person. This is something you have to earn. You do it by not doing something that you will feel uneasy about afterward, because it is not right. This includes not paying a debt, breaking a promise, doing a sloppy job, or not doing one you should do, and last but not least, lying." This was something that he repeated many times to his children and grandchildren. His teachings have increased seven-fold in his grandchildren. He left the world a better place.

AUNT JANE

Guy Tobey, Ethel's father, had a brother, Tom, and a sister, Jane. Tom died in his fifties and was childless. As Aunt Jane was also childless, Ethel was now her only surviving relative. The last time they had seen each other was when Ethel was 10 years old. Jane's husband was a judge and a direct descendant of President Millard Fillmore. The judge died when he was 60. Jane Millard was also a court recorder. They started corresponding when Ethel was in high school and wrote each other regularly every month, keeping each other informed of their activities. Ethel sent Aunt Jane pictures of the children and newspaper clippings.

Several times Aunt Jane planned to visit us. Probably finances were critical and possibly her health. During the two years that Ethel could not write, I carried on the correspondence from Ethel's dictation.

When we finally got out of debt, the family was discussing Aunt Jane.

"Virg, it would be a good family outing to go to Florida for two weeks. I have wanted to see Aunt Jane for a long time."

"Let's plan it during Christmas vacation." Thanks to potato futures, we had enough money to spend for the trip. Aunt Jane's letters were ecstatic about seeing her niece and family. About a week before our scheduled departure, we received a phone call from one of her close friends in the trailer court. Aunt Jane was in the hospital. Ethel talked to her on the phone.

Aunt Jane said, "Don't worry, I will be well in a week. Go ahead with your plans. The roses you sent are simply gorgeous. I am mailing you an envelope with complete instructions about stocks, bank deposits, diamond rings and funeral arrangements."

The thick envelope arrived with minute details covering everything. Her funeral was paid for. We were to fly down and if we couldn't afford the fare, Ethel could write a check on Aunt Jane's bank because the account was joint. The letter said her diamonds were in her jewel box and her neighbor and friend would give them to Ethel. The hospital notified us of her death that evening. We flew down. The next afternoon we had been given her jewel box and contacted the funeral parlor for the services next day.

Her neighbor said, "She was always saying that she had to save for her niece." Actually, she must have lived quite frugally, as her income from stocks and social security was relatively small. Her trailer was only 18 feet long but was comfortable enough to eat and sleep in. The two diamonds were a surprise. The largest was a cluster of diamonds about the size of a large woman's thumb nail, with a center stone of over two carats. In an envelope there was a somewhat worn bill of sale for it at $1,850. That was a lot of money for the 1800s. This was the ring that Millard Fillmore gave to his fiancee as an engagement ring. The other ring was a beautiful 3/4-carat yellow stone.

The simple service in the funeral parlor was attended by several of her friends from the trailer court. The body was to be cremated. With the trailer in the park at Tallahassee as our headquarters, we rented a car and started to check out Ethel's inheritance. When Aunt Jane moved South, she still kept a bank account at Mount Vernon. The safety deposit box with the stocks was in another bank in a town nearby. This was in addition to a bank account in a bank close to her trailer. The $3,500 in cash and $4,000 in paper seemed a lot of money to a family that had been strapped as long as we had. This was all transferred to Ethel's bank account because due to potato futures we had become reasonably well off.

The warmth combined with Florida's many facets—swamps, streams, orange groves, and blooming plants—made it seem like a paradise after being in a foot of snow and below-zero temperature just a few days before. Being an ardent (Ethel would have said "fanatic") fisherman, I asked her, "Would you like to see some of the islands?"

"What you mean is, you want to go fishing."

"That is right, but just seeing them would be something." We looked over travel brochures and decided on a five-day trip to Bimini. The flight out of Miami took just two hours in a World War II DC-3.

On the plane a very friendly man was seated next to me. He was the owner of the two-plane airline and had the sole right to the route. He said that he was dickering with a larger airline that wanted to buy his franchise.

I asked, "What is your stock selling for?"

"Over the counter in Miami at $2 a share. Better buy some."

The marina with its restaurant, bar and cabins was immaculate. The purplish-blue water, dazzling white sandy beaches lined with coconut palms were all new to us and wonderful. It was pleasant just to sit in the shade of a palm tree and look. A French Canadian and I hired a fishing boat and guide. I was surprised at the fisherman's very Oxford English speech. It was a far cry from the slurring of the southern states. Actually, he was a poor but greedy guide and one day was all I could stand of him. I rented a golf cart and had the restaurant put up a lunch for us with bottled juice. We drove to the far end of the island a mile or so away. When I walked through the bar carrying my fishing pole and tackle box, someone asked, "What are you going to catch?"

"I am going to catch a bonefish on a fly." This brought a laugh.

329

After parking my cart in the shade of a palm tree and assembling my rod, I waded out into the clear water about knee-deep. Bonefish are very, very spooky. They live and feed mostly in shallow water. They are the prey of barracuda, sharks, birds and man. They are almost constantly moving. Their bodies are torpedo-shaped and so muscular and firm that their flesh gives very little when you touch them. The shadow of a bird passing over will send them scurrying for deeper water. It was only by moving imperceptively that I could get into fly casting range. I managed to catch and release three on a white fly that looked like a shrimp. A 5- or 6-pound fish would make the reel scream in a run of 200 yards or more. Two fish too large to handle ran out to the end of the line and broke off. Bonefish are not edible—you just turn them loose to catch another day.

We drove the cart deeper among the palms and scrub pines in order to eat our lunch in the shade. We still had a clear view of the beach. While we were eating, a handsome black couple anchored their boat offshore and began fishing in deeper water. They were laughing and having fun and their voices carried clearly to us across the water. He caught a nasty moray eel that wriggled up the line and tried to bite. He was having trouble getting it off his hook. In the pure British Oxford accent, she mimicked, "You fool nigger, did it ever occur to you just to cut the line?"

"You're such an intelligent woman. Why didn't I think of that?"

After a while they beached the boat, took off their clothes and started to play and swim. Either they were not looking or didn't care, or we were well hidden, as they seemed to be unaware that they were being watched. When they spread the blanket on the sand, Ethel whispered, "It looks like something is going to happen."

"I'm sure it will. Do you want to watch?"

"Why not. We might learn something." They were a very active and interesting couple. On our way back to the cabin, Ethel said, "I know what you are thinking and what I can expect tonight."

"It may be sooner than you think."

When we got back to the cabin, Ethel was tired and wanted to take a nap. I went to the bar for a drink. Someone asked, "How many bonefish did you catch with that fly?"

"I caught three and turned them loose."

There were several customers in the bar and they all laughed as if I were telling a joke. Later Ethel and I dropped in for a drink before dinner. Two men at a table said, "We are buying you a drink, as we owe you an apology. You see, no one has ever fished or caught a bonefish using anything but live shrimp. After you left, the bartender told us that it looked to him like you had a fish on all of the time."

It was a profitable trip, as I bought 500 shares of the airline at $2 and a month later after the takeover, I sold it at $4.50.

330

GADAHFY

Dr. Richard Ohms, head of the department, was one of my closest friends. He had been getting overseas assignments to the Arab nations, principally Jordan, to help them in setting up a potato production program. He had been getting some very lucrative assignments with the Agricultural Industry Development Organization, which was international. Surprisingly, Jordan, Iraq, Syria and Turkey have climate and altitude very similar to Idaho. At a banquet I met Gene Whitman, an old friend, and heard of the overseas operation for the United States. I told him I would like to finish out the last two years of my service overseas.

"Virg, that will be no problem. There just happens to be a vacancy coming up for a position in Turkey. I will notify the State Department and recommend you and they will contact you."

The State Department communique was very tempting. Not only would my federal retirement increase considerably, but I would be able to save at least $80,000. They accepted my resume and almost everything was set for my going. Because I had indicated that Ethel would accompany me, they sent a questionnaire to fill out concerning her and her health. When I wrote that she had to have a gadget to eat with, they cancelled the appointment. The reason was that a handicapped American would make a bad impression.

After I retired, a Spokane firm contacted me for an overseas assignment. Gadahfy had planted 600 acres of potatoes and 600 acres of beets in the Sahara Desert. They were having trouble. The University of Idaho recommended me. Their offer was $25,000 for a year. They had contacted Washington State, North Dakota and Minnesota. All had recommended me because of my experience in growing potatoes in sand. The Spokane firm contacted me again. I didn't like their offer so I made a counter offer of $25,000 for one month, as I was sure I could find the trouble in that time and after that the average workman could take care of the crop. The $25,000 would be free and above all expenses. In addition, I wanted plane fare, meals and hotel expenses for a two-week tour of Europe. They were to make arrangements and prepay the expenses. The firm's representative in Spokane said, "That offer is ridiculous." A few days later they telephoned me and accepted my offer and gave a date for me to meet with them in Spokane later in the week. The next day I got a call from the Dean.

"Virg, I hear you are going to work for Gadahfy."

"I am supposed to meet with them Friday."

"Don't even think about it. Two consultants have been killed on that project by snipers in the last two years." I immediately called Spokane and cancelled the deal. They were adamant and almost abusive. I told them about the snipers and said, "You can shove it." and hung up.

Gene Whitman became a close friend of King Hussein of Jordan. In fact, they played golf together, playing for an American silver dollar a hole. Gene said, "I let him beat me for a dollar or so most of the time. After all, one does not beat a king."

Gene said one of his first assignments was to teach 10 Jordanian agricultural graduates how to irrigate so they could teach others. They came out in a bus all dressed up. When Gene asked them to pick up shovels and hoes, they refused. Gene said, "How do you expect to teach field hands?"

"We will tell them."

Their attitude was that since they were college graduates, they were above manual labor. That weekend he told Hussein about the difficulty in training Arab personnel. The next Monday when the bus stopped, they practically burst out of the bus, grabbed shovels and hoes and followed his instructions. At the next golf date, Gene asked the King what happened. The King said, "I told the Minister of Agriculture. He told them if they didn't follow the American's orders, he would cut off their right hands."

RETIREMENT

My decision to retire early at the age of 60 was influenced by several factors. Ethel had been told she would live probably 10 years and now she had lived 18. The doctor warned that pneumonia almost surely would be fatal. The remaining 70 percent efficiency of her chest muscles would gradually weaken as she grew older. When we moved to Burley, I started to plan for retirement. I tried church activities, civic clubs and services, only to find that they enslaved me more. A try at several hobbies didn't pan out. Only golf was a new acquisition to my repertoire of activities.

We had taken a trip to Mexico to see if we could travel and stay in hotels and motels. We enjoyed our week's stay in Guaymas, but loading and unloading baggage, packing and unpacking, in addition to intimate care for Ethel, was just too much work. I talked to Ethel about traveling and she didn't think too much of the idea. She wanted to stay home and visit the kids by driving.

Shortly after our move from Jerome, I started pasting clippings from sports and trailering and travel magazines. The three categories, hunting, fishing, and historical places to see, interested me. By the time I was ready to retire, I had 10 years of compiling this information. The schedule that we decided upon covered almost all of the activities that were attractive—hunting, fishing, travel, prospecting with my sons, visiting and being visited by children. I felt I had served my time in civic organizations, having been a member and officer of one or more for over 30 years.

At least three years before retirement, I had decided to stay at the Key Trailer Court in Marathon, Florida, because of its location and fishing. This would be December to April. From April to August back in Burley I would spend playing golf, fishing, and a week prospecting. The month of August would be spent at Salmon Point Lodge, Campbell River, British Columbia. After returning to Idaho there would be golf, sage hen hunting, big game season, and six weeks of pheasant season which was almost a sacred ritual with Diane to hunt over. We could afford to have our children visit us or to visit them.

The refresher course at Moscow had been held until noon. On the way home, six extension agents stopped to stay overnight in a trailer court bordering the Salmon River at Riggins. It was snowing and blowing outside which dissuaded us from continuing at night. Five were playing penny ante and urging me to join the game. I was contemplating more important matters.

When the Idaho Legislature passed a new retirement bill for teachers and university personnel, we were given the option of keeping our federal retirement which was new to extension personnel and cashing in the several thousand dollars we had paid into the then inadequate state retirement fund. Only 10 percent of the personnel decided to keep their state retirement, and I was one of them. The State Legislature had just passed a new generous retirement for teachers. At the Moscow meeting a representative of the Idaho Pension Department had helped and advised personnel who were going to retire in the near future.

At the motel I was putting down figures on a sheet of stationery. The figures were about the possibility of retiring at the end of the year.

Dr. Dick Ohms, my close friend and department head, later said, "It happened like this. Virg had been busy figuring for nearly an hour, writing down a list of pros and cons. We saw him throw the papers up in the air, slam down his pencil and yell, 'I quit!' When we asked, 'What do you mean, you quit?' he said, 'I am going to retire in December. I refuse to work for $70 a month and that is all I make over what I would receive as retirement pay!'"

What I didn't mention was a safety deposit box with a really sizeable amount of money from potato futures.

When I returned home from Moscow, one of the first things I said to Ethel after our affectionate greeting was, "I am going to retire."

"When?"

"December 28. Our take-home pay will actually be more than we have now."

"Virg, you are going to miss the job and your associates. Can you cope with that?"

"Honey, what I am going to miss is having to go to the office, making reports, and having to go places I really don't want to go and do things I really don't want to do in order to satisfy someone's requirements. All these things are happy misses!"

"In order to enjoy your retirement fully, you are going to have to slow down and walk carefully through the daisies and not trample them (using your favorite expression), going like hell fighting a bear."

It took a while to change from rushing up to a stream to get in as much fishing as possible in my limited time to slow down and observe life and nature around me. Catching fish became less important. I could take time to enjoy seeing fleecy clouds floating across the sky with reflections in the clear stream, the rippling and murmuring of the stream with its many changes of current. The last of life is somewhat like early fall or autumn on the farm. The hard work of summer with its heat is over. The weather is warm but not hot in the daytime, or too cold at night. The harvest moon is beautiful. You want it never to end,

334

but you know winter is coming. Enjoy each day as if it were the last. Don't put off what you want to do—soon you may not be able to do it.

"Virg, you have really slowed down, and we both are enjoying retirement more. In fact, it is a delightful way of life!"

It was difficult to believe that after 37 years of public service I would not have to go to the office every morning and I could pursue some of the hobbies that I had not had time for in the past. It meant that Ethel and I could travel, which was something she could do and enjoy. I felt my contributions had earned a good retirement, as I had more than paid my dues. Not wanting to feel guilty about letting down on the job, I really serviced my growers. There was no use to carry on research projects or plan for schools and meetings that would be without my services. When pheasant season opened in October, I took the 30 days leave that I had coming.

After researching trailers and trailering magazines and checking with owners of trailers, I dug into the deposit box and bought a Holiday Rambler trailer and an International Travelall to pull it. It was a very comfortable and practical outfit. We took some short trips of a few days in the hills and mountains. Being self-contained, it eliminated the need for service station stops for Ethel. Our clothes did not have to be packed and unpacked. Ethel was not sold on it. She preferred the comforts of home.

I installed some safety back-up features—a gas light to supplement the electric and battery lights, a safe alcohol heater to back up the gas heater in case the battery gave out if we might be stalled for several days.

Late in December Susan came home from Salt Lake and packed the trailer with her mother's supervision. The small upright freezer was full of beef, pheasant and bacon. The trailer was hooked up to the Travelall and all I had to do was disconnect the electricity, fill the tanks with water and take off. The last days went slowly.

The potato industry held its annual meeting in Boise just before Christmas. The President of Idaho Potato Growers, Clarence Parr, called me and said that it would be important for me to attend the meeting and give a farewell speech. I really didn't want to, but the potato industry had been very good to me. I told him my talk would be very short.

Ethel went with me to Boise. Clarence told me that I would speak at the banquet. I had a feeling that something different and special was going to happen.

During the banquet Clarence went to the stage and asked me to come forward. He outlined my contributions to the potato industry and how the industry was in debt to me. Then he presented me with a solid gold Idaho potato pin. It was the third pin awarded. President Theophilus of the university received the first, Jack Simplot the second. I said I had enjoyed my association with them and it never seemed like work. I pointed out that much of my success was due to the expertise of Dick Ohms. A short thank you concluded my talk. The chairman said, "This is the first time he has ever been speechless." That brought a big laugh and clapping.

To my surprise, the university awarded me the degree of Professor Emeritus. Ethel and the children had a graduation party for me.

Don Samuelson, Governor of Idaho, sent a certificate thanking me for my long service to the people of Idaho. December 28th was the day the district agent checked me out. It didn't take long to turn in the equipment I had been using.

TO FLORIDA

Two days later we left for Marathon in the Florida Keys. We had made a deposit on a trailer space six months before. Ethel and I had been reading about historical places to visit. In fact, she was really the historian. She was also the navigator. A handy rack held the map on the dash for her to see. We had the trailer guide book with lists of trailer parks in all of the states, Mexico and Canada. Their rating was listed with stars, facilities and cost. The Travelall was packed. Diane, the Lewellen Setter, and Duchess, the Dachshund, had a bed on the full back seat that allowed them to look out to see what was going on.

We got a late start, in fact it was nearly 3 o'clock when we pulled up on the highway to Twin Falls. Ethel said, "Why don't we wait and start in the morning?"

"I would like to have one last go at the poker game in Jackpot."

"O.K., but you will have to pull the handle of the nickel slot machine for me until I have put $5 through it."

Gasoline was a nickel cheaper in Twin Falls and we filled the tanks. When we pulled into the free parking complete trailer space at Cactus Pete's in Jackpot it was nearly 5 o'clock. I turned the thermostat up to 75 degrees on the gas furnace. We had a drink and I helped Ethel to the bathroom, which solved the problem of my having to go into the ladies rest rooms with her at service stations and restaurants. The veal parmesan dinner at the restaurant was superb. Ethel won a $20 jackpot on the slot machine and insisted on keeping all of the nickels. I dropped $20 in the poker game.

We were in the dead of winter with a barren, snow-covered landscape most of the way to Las Vegas. The monotony was broken once in a great while by hills with juniper and a rare body of water. The planned route was to go through New Mexico to visit Smitty's brother Stan in Alberquerque. Shortly after Boulder City, it started to blizzard. We were driving in a storm with snow blowing and 25 below zero as we entered Flagstaff. It had been so cold and the snow so deep that no trailer parks were open. The map showed that Winslow was 2,000 feet lower. I told Ethel it would be warmer there. There was an inversion at Winslow and it had been 20 below day and night for over a week. They had cleared off the snow in the parking space of the trailer court but the only hookup was electricity.

I cooked dinner. We were very snug, as the gas heater soon warmed up the well-insulated trailer. The dogs did their puddling in a hurry and whined to be let back in. I figured that the water pipes in the trailer would freeze, but they could be fixed when we got out of the winter area. The next morning everything worked and all I had to do after breakfast was unplug the power line. The International coughed a couple of times and took off and ran smoothly. I was sure that by the time we came off the high plateau, water would be dripping from frozen pipes under the trailer. Not so. The water pipes were all inside the trailer and as long as the furnace kept the temperature above freezing, everything was all right. Ethel, who had serious doubts about traveling, decided that trailering was really great.

It was 5 o'clock and we were still 2 hours from Santa Fe. We stopped at what appeared to be a town in an Indian reservation for gas. The trailer park was close to the service station. It was Saturday night and the Indians seemed to be really whooping it up. The service station attendant said everybody would be drunk before the evening was over, and he advised us to stop and stay overnight. He said the road would be clear the next morning. We ate at a neat cafe with well-dressed Indian waitresses and were served a very appetizing meal.

In the morning the roads were almost free of traffic, but there were a lot of parked cars with people sleeping in them. On the next stop the trailer park was only a block from the old city of San Antonio and we watched the evening parade of boys going one way and girls another to the music of a Mexican band. Our sidewalk table and Mexican food took us back to another period. Ethel said, "I think I am going to like traveling." She proceeded to give me some of the history of San Antonio. We didn't hurry, but stopped to see all the historical sites. Most interesting was the Alamo, where we seemed to feel the presence of the brave defenders who were subjected to the beastly brutality of Santa Ana's Mexican soldiers. It felt like hallowed ground.

In New Orleans, the trailer park was on the edge of town. Both of us had strong stomachs and we liked to try the food of new areas. It was amazing what a large pile of crawfish shells we left on our plates. We took a bus tour of the city which was exceptionally good, with much information about the history of New Orleans. I mentioned to Ethel that my father said his great-uncle Bill Clayton fought in the battle of New Orleans and wore an iron pot on his head.

"That goes to show that there was a long line of cowards in your family."

We took the night club tour and danced a couple of slow dances to Pete Fountain's band.

After two weeks on the road, we pulled into the Key Trailer Court at Marathon, Florida. Gloria, the owner, said, "You are 10 days late."

"After all, it is over 3,000 miles."

The manager helped us hook up and showed us where to walk the dogs. I was tired because the narrow roads and especially the many long narrow bridges between the Keys made passing with a trailer difficult. A new neighbor helped me unroll the 18-foot awning and unload the deep freeze onto the wooden platform. The wooden step with a railing to assist Ethel in getting in and out of the trailer was in place. We had arrived.

To us it was a fairyland. The Keys had not become crowded with high-rises like Miami and other large Florida towns. The people that first settled the Keys probably had something to do with the lack of large buildings and even pretentious homes. The first people were Indians, then there were pirates, shipwrecked people, people wanted by the law, fishermen, and those who just wanted an easy, warm place to live. Everything was so new. The temperature about 68 degrees in the morning and 75 to 80 in the afternoon. I always thought a mangrove tree bore fruit. To my surprise, they grew in the shallow water, forming impenetrable groves. The water was warm at 70 to 72 degrees. People were very friendly and helpful to newcomers. They were busy fishing, shelling, catching lobsters, gathering driftwood—none of which we had ever done except fishing, of course.

Our trailer faced the street with trailers facing each other. The back of my trailer left me just enough space to open its trunk between it and a 40-foot wide and 40 deep canal that had been dredged for material to fill in the swampy tidal land. Almost everybody had a boat tied up to a dock back of their trailer and they used the boats to go to the many small islands to carry on their hobbies.

One of the first things I did was to spend several hours in the library reading about fishing and history in the area. Upon the advice of Harry Teebe, I bought a rod and reel. I tried to catch the tarpon that often jumped in the canal back of the trailor but never got a bite. No one offered to take me fishing in their boat. They all seemed to have a good catch of groupers, snappers, kingfish, and other kinds when they came in.

Finally, someone asked me to go fishing with him. Edgar Ashworth had a small car-top aluminum boat and since he was a very small man, he needed someone to help him load it on top of the car. We fished under the 7-mile bridge and had fair luck. I caught my first grouper. This was the start of a long, close friendship. He had been a claims adjuster and apparently very successful, as he was a millionaire when he retired at the age of 60. He and his wife both liked boats and were competent sailors on their 18-foot sailboat. For years they had planned to get a large boat and cruise the Bahamas and Carribean. In 1962, they found their dreamboat, a 40-foot yacht with everything in the way of comfort, in new condition, for half its worth from a bankruptcy sale. It had room for 10 people. He could run it, but would need a competent mechanic and engineer. They invited two couples to go along. This required a cook and a maid.

"I sold it six months later," Edgar said. "The guests ate our food, drank our liquor, didn't even offer to pay for the cleaning of their clothes or laundry. Dockage was over a dollar a foot per day. My wife and I went over the expense outlay, and she said, 'Edgar, we are still millionaires, but not for long at this rate.' We had spent over $200,000 in six month's time. We sold the boat and I bought a 10-foot car top boat. A boat is a hole in the water that you pour money into."

I had a sobering and scary close adventure with a shark while scuba diving. Edgar Ashworth had shot a grouper and it bled a lot. We saw a huge lobster and without stopping to wash my hands, I dived down about 12 feet with a long handled net. The lobster was by a 6-foot wall of coral. I was approaching him slowly when I saw a shadow and looked up to see a lemon shark cruising back and forth, picking up the scent of blood on my hands. He kept coming closer and closer to me. I crowded against the coral wall, keeping the net still and extended. When he came close enough, I slipped the net over his head and he swam off. I scrambled back into the boat. Edgar was sitting there holding the spear gun. I said, "What happened to you?"

"I was waiting so I could tell what happened to you."

It was our first winter without cold and snow. To be able to go around in shorts, a light shirt, and straw hat in January was a new and delightful experience.

If you tried to fix something on your car, trailer, or boat, there was no way you could do it alone. My gas water heater quit working. When I took the cover off, a neighbor come over and said, "I know what's the matter. I'll get my tools." Another man passing by offered the same help. In 5 minutes they were both busy working on the heater. Edgar Ashworth came by and I went with him to play golf. When we returned 3 hours later, the water heater was working. Many of the trailerites were just looking for something to do.

Ethel and I spent most of the season just looking at the endless new and interesting things.

The conch train ride in Key West was informative. Key West was at one time the richest city per capita in the United States due to the salvage of shipwrecks. Some of the wrecks were brought in by salvagers deliberately misplacing lights. It was the center of cigar-making until the workers went on strike. Hemingway's house was especially interesting to me because I had met him once on a fishing jaunt. He liked cats and set up a fund for their preservation. There were cats in all stages of growth and all possible colors. For one dollar you could buy a genuine Hemingway cat with a certificate.

Being an avid fisherman, I was frustrated about not having a boat to fish with. I found my notebook on fishing places and opened it at the tab that said Snappers. There was an article on Florida snappers that I had pasted in several years before. The author described minutely the location of a small bay and inlet about a mile from the trailer court where he had great success in catching the delicious but very wary mangrove snappers.

The next day Ethel and I drove up to a small cove that had an island in it. Wearing tennis shoes and trailing my bait bucket of live shrimp on a cord, I waded out to hip depth. On my first cast the live shrimp had barely hit the water when there was a strong jerk and bowing of my rod. It was fun reeling and listening to the reel click as the fish ran out line. It was a big snapper, enough for a big meal. I proceeded to catch several more, turning them loose and keeping only two. Several fishermen were at the cleaning troughs when I brought in my fish, which were more than twice as big as any of theirs. When they inquired where I had caught them, I pointed and said, "Over there somewhere." From past experience, I had learned that you just didn't tell people about your favorite place to fish and hunt because they couldn't be trusted to keep a secret and your fishing would be ruined in a short time.

Over the next 10 years I fished this spot, never revealing it to anyone except my sons and brother-in-law, to whom I would trust my life. A few people tried to follow me, but they didn't find out. Harry Bishop was one of the most persistent. It was fun to pick up my bait bucket, put my fishing pole in the car and have him discretely follow me to the grocery store. Other times when I knew I was being followed, I would park down the road a short distance and see who was coming out of the trailer court. One time Norman said, "Let them follow us. We will stop and fish at a different place. Then they will know where to go." It really worked with Harry and after that he stopped trying.

Charlie Bloche had a 14-foot aluminum boat with a 9 1/2-horse motor. Charley was disgusted because he couldn't catch any fish. When he offered to sell the practically new boat at about half price, I bought it. I did have sense enough to buy a life preserver and a compass.

Now I had a boat. I didn't have anyone to fish with, but I didn't care. I'd never had a boat before nor an outboard motor. The manual for the motor was brief and simple. Because of very slight tides due to the closeness of the equator, you could set a course and go almost directly to your point of destination. For the first week I fished relatively close to shore. Fishermen in larger boats were going out to the Gulf Stream's purplish blue water 4 or 5 miles from shore. There were two steamship lanes, one going up the Keys north and the other down south. They were several miles apart. Benjamin Franklin discovered the current in the Gulf Stream, noting the difference in time that sailing ships took and what routes. Close to shore there was less current, so you took the inner route if you were going south. Maps of the area giving the islands, markers, lights, buoys, and bottom depths helped me locate spots that the other fishermen talked about.

When the other fishermen started to bring in dolphin fish from an area 3 miles into the Gulf Stream, I just had to catch one. Taking a lunch, I started out early on a very calm morning. The ocean had a slight shimmering riffle with almost no wind. Gulls were skimming and diving occasionally. Frigate birds were circling high above, watching for another bird to catch a fish so they could steal it. Half an hour later I was in the dark blue waters of the Gulf Stream. I put my hand over the side and the warmth of the water surprised me. I was fascinated by the flying fish leaping and gliding above the water. Sometimes they seemed to take off just in time as there would be the swirl of a big fish that just missed. One didn't make it, as the bill of a sailfish caught it just as it left the top of a wave. I slowed the boat and shifted to neutral to watch the sailfish circle and come up to swallow the crippled flying fish.

I was looking for what they called a grassline. Grass would break loose from the sargassas sea and would float for over 1,000 miles, sometimes miles long and often 100 feet wide. The book had said little fish liked to hide in and under the grasslines, and dolphin fish hung around the edges to catch them. Birds were circling and diving about a mile ahead. Sure enough, there was a long grassline about 60 feet wide. I rigged up a bait fish called ballyhoo on the double hook combination with a wire leader. The bait trailed about 100 feet behind the boat and would run underwater for a short distance and then flop lifelike on the top of a wave. There was just time to put the rod in the holder before the click on the reel started to scream. With the motor shut off, I watched the irridescent blue, green, and yellow acrobat jump several feet in the air first on one side of the boat, then the other. After I gaffed it, I ate a sandwich and drank a Coke. A voice on a loud speaker hailed me from behind. A large Coast Guard cutter came up slowly beside me.

"Do you know what direction land is?"

"If I hold on the 0 of 330 degrees, I will hit the Voice of America tower." It was then I noticed that I could no longer see land.

"What in the hell do you think you're doing out alone in that small boat so far from shore? You're not wearing your life preserver. I am giving you a citation. You will not be grounded or fined if you attend the Coast Guard school for small boating. I am coming back here in half an hour and if you are still here, we'll take you aboard and tow your boat in and impound it."

So I took the two-week course in small boating. To pass I had to navigate between two points and handle the boat in rough water with one of the instructors. Now this farm boy was really scared as I became aware of the dangers of boating.

There is something mystical and magical about getting out early in the morning when it is calm and the water is rippling slightly in the Florida Keys. The hush just before it gets light at dawn brings on a surge of activity among the creatures. The frigate birds soar high in the updrafts, their forked tails and pointed wings enable them to do many incredible aerial acrobatics in play and pursuit to steal the prey of other birds. Gulls dive down to pick up fish from the surface and circle to locate schools of fish. The ungainly, awkward pelican turns into a lethal dive-bomber and enters the water with a big splash, coming up with a fish so large that it would seem impossible to swallow, but they do get it down. Then they sit on the water until the fish quits struggling.

There is the splash of a big fish as it pursues a victim and its momentum has propelled it out of the water. Occasionally you may see a large skate taking off and sailing or gliding 20 to 30 feet in the air to escape pursuing sharks. Flying fish take off from the tip of a wave either in fun or to escape a sail fish or kingfish, often barely escaping the swirl of its enemy.

It was such a morning when we left the canal to go to the Gulf Stream, 5 miles away. Monte didn't like to get up early in the morning any more than I did. We saw the sea awakening. Monte remarked, "According to the *Fisherman's Guide*, today is one of the best days of March for fishing."

"The *Guide* is surprisingly accurate. Today the bite will be from 6:30 to 9:00 a.m."

"Virg, I hope we run out of live shrimp. I brought six dozen."

We anchored up just over the edge of the Gulf Stream in 60 feet of water. Our chum bags were beginning to thaw and we were waiting for the small fish to start using the chum. We heard a squeaking sound. The hair on Diane's back rose straight up. She gave a tentative bark. The squeaking became a chatter. Diane was whining softly and wagging her tail. She was looking at a dolphin that was swimming around the boat with its head out of the water. The whining and squeaking increased. Finally, the dolphin came within a few feet of the boat and was laughing as if it enjoyed seeing and meeting a dog. After several minutes it left. A school of yellow tail snappers, one of the most prized Florida fish, came into our chum line. We were busy for a little while, but suddenly they stopped biting. Monte said, "There must be something in our chum line—probably a barracuda."

I pointed to a dorsal fin slicing through the water about 100 feet off our stern.

"That is a hammerhead shark. There's the cause of our fish being bitten off our lines."

"Maybe he will leave."

"Monte, he will never get full enough to leave."

"If that dolphin would come back, he would fix him good." The words were scarcely out of his mouth when 10 feet of the shark came out of the water from a butt in the midsection by a dolphin. Another porpoise on the opposite side raised him a couple of feet higher. The third hit in his midsection left the shark helpless and he sank slowly to the bottom. In a short time the snapper were back.

Portugese Man of War with their deadly tentacles many feet long were drifting by. Monte was reeling and I said, "Watch out. They will cling to your line."

"I've already got it on my hands. Do you have any meat tenderizer?"

"No, I don't. Ted Johnson borrowed mine and didn't bring the bottle back. Washing won't do any good. Pee on a Kleenex and hold it on and it will neutralize and stop the burning."

A little later he said, "It works."

A big sea turtle came close to the boat and actually acted like it was laughing. In fact, it was very funny. Monte said, "He is really high because he has been eating Portugese Man of War, and the poison really gives them a buzz."

We came in with a full box of snappers and the priceless experience of a morning on the water.

After visiting Sealand in Marathon, I ceased being surprised at the intelligent behavior of porpoises. Flipper had been trained there. Ethel said, "They have their own language. They can even communicate when they are long distances from their mates. They even love each other and have very strong and lasting attachments to their mates." One of the males at Sealand refused to do his usual act. His nose was pointed toward his mate who was about to give birth in a pen several hundred feet away. She was with two midwives who would bring her newborn to the surface at birth. The male was bothered because he couldn't patrol and guard for sharks. We were amazed at their intelligence and discussed how they should be protected against the depredations of man.

Shelling was a favorite pastime of many people. Since there were no restrictions or regulations, some of the trailerites did it commercially. Ethel could go shelling with me in the shallow water during low tides. We would anchor the boat and wade in the lukewarm water. Because of lack of use of her arms, her balance was poor and I would walk with her, holding her arm. She leaned against me when I reached to pick up a shell, and sometimes had to sit down while I chased a lobster. The large, beautifully shaded pink and golden queen conchs were much sought after and we always brought back several for friends and relatives. The early Key settlers, many of them wanted by the law, used these conch shells for communication. They made them into horns that would carry miles on a calm day. They had a signal language similar to the Africans with drums. When law officers started up the Keys in their boats, their progress was monitored by the conch horns.

On the way back to Idaho we had a four-day visit with Dallas in Kansas City. He had been promoted from a research medical biochemist to administrative officer of the Federal Medical Research Department with the Veterans. Dallas and I went to see Kansas City play Minnesota. It was my first big-league baseball game. Baseball had been my dream, but I couldn't hit curve balls when I was invited to the Giant's training camp when I was in high school. Harmon Killebrew hit two singles. Each time the ball never got over 20 feet high and hit the center field fence just beyond the fielder's reach. Harmon, though slow, got safely to first base each time. He was then nearing the end of his career and the sign on the billboard read, "There is still harm in Harmon."

THE CARRIBEAN CRUISE

To surprise Ethel I arranged for a Carribean cruise on the Viking line. Reservations were made for the late January cruise before we left Burley in October, but I did not tell Ethel until Christmas time when I gave her the brochures as a Christmas present. She was overwhelmed. This called for shopping for new clothes in Miami. Earl Hintze, my nephew, happened to be visiting. He had been working in a men's clothing store for two years while cooling off from an assignment in Europe, and was given a week off from his briefing for a new assignment in Washington, D.C. All he would say about his job was, "I am in intelligence." His men's clothing experience helped me choose some new outfits for the cruise.

We wanted to go fishing, but the weather was too rough for my small boat, so we took a charter. The six places at the stern are the choice spots, and regular customers always got them. We ran into kingfish that weighed 20 to 40 pounds and put up a very strong fight with long runs. There were many hooked at the same time and the six preferred customers at the stern would change rods and go over and under to keep from getting tangled. When the fishermen in the stern had cut my line three times as I tried to go past them, I looked at Earl and nodded. He nodded back.

He was sitting back against a bulkhead sunning himself with his shirt off. His well-muscled 175 pounds was impressive. I opened my tackle box, took out a pair of scissors, and waited until there were three fish on the stern lines. Then I went over and snipped all three lines, saying, "You should not cut the other people's lines when they have a fish on."

I backed up and shed my jacket. They were all about my age. When they complained to the captain, he said, "You had better not cut his line anymore, as he will fight, and I think he can whip any of you. Look at his backup!" Earl was grinning. "I wouldn't touch that man with a 10-foot pole." After that we had no trouble landing our fish.

The spotlessly clean cruise ship and its pleasant and courteous crew were very impressive. Our waiter was a young Jamaican pre-med student. He was very solicitous about Ethel's welfare and comfort. He told us to leave her eating gadget with him and he would take care of it all through the cruise. When we entered the dining room, he always had it set up ready to use. The many delicious entrees served at each meal made it hard to choose. The recreation director announced there would be a get-acquainted party for singles in the upper lounge.

Ethel said, "You go to the singles party."

"Why should I attend a singles party? I am legally married to you."

"Virg, I want you to have a good time."

"I am having a wonderful time and this cruise is for you."

She had felt that because she was unable to respond after polio that I should be taken care of. In fact, she had tried to set me up with her nurses, housekeepers, and even her friends in the past. Both of us had talked to Dr. Neher about the problem. He told her it was psychological. He instructed me on how to stimulate sensitive parts. Nothing had worked so far.

The dance orchestra was superb. Ethel could dance slow pieces with me. The recreation leader announced the next dance would be a Charleston contest with a bottle of champagne to each of the winning couple.

Ethel said, "There was a time when we could win it with ease. You can still do it. Go find a partner."

A voice behind us said, "I am his partner if you will let me borrow him."

"Take him."

The tall, slightly buxom blonde had a snub nose and puckish face. We started out doing the easy steps. In a little while we were really whooping it up, going through the whole repertoire. We were so busy watching each other that we didn't really look at any of the other couples. The spectators started applauding and when the music stopped, we were the only couple on the floor. We won the champagne.

On the third afternoon there was a bridge tournament. Fortunately, we had brought Ethel's card holder. She had to bid without having the cards sorted into suits. After bidding was ended, the person who was dummy would sort the hand for her. We were behind the times, as we still used the Culbertson system, but playing together for years helped. Anyway, we won the cup for first prize.

My entry into the trap shooting contest was a washout. I was sure I would win, but the rolling of the ship caused me to miss five out of 10. The two-day gin rummy tournament was a breeze until the finals. A New Jersey lawyer named Conan was by far the best player, but I out-tricked him.

On the third evening Ethel had danced her two slow dances and was sipping a Singapore sling. I would go over and talk to her between dances. I was tired after the samba contest and was sitting out. Ethel leaned over and kissed me.

"What was that for?"

"That is for being a terrific husband. Will you grant me a favor?"

"Your wish is my command."

"Darling, you deserve a night on the town. You put me to bed and come back to the dance."

"Ethel, you have the best ideas. The last one was when you called me at 11 o'clock in the morning and we got Susan. Since this is a cooperative deal we must agree on who I'm going to take to bed."

She laughed. "Why not the buxom blonde that you won the Charleston with?"

"No way. She just isn't my type. Now the girl sitting on the last seat in the front row could be interesting."

After looking at a very dark-skinned, short, wide person with a gold ring in her nose, she said, "Don't be ridiculous. How about the big, tall, beautiful brunette from Quebec that you won the samba with?"

"No way. She is just too big for the single bunk beds. Would you approve of the girl leaning against the post?"

"Virg, you are making fun of me and I am serious. She is taller and heavier than you and her ankles are as big as your knees."

"I won't break my promise and will go to bed with someone. First I'll give you your shower and stretch your neck and hands. I'll pick out the lucky girl and really surprise her. In the morning you will hear all the details."

"I'm sure she will feel that she is a lucky girl."

In the cabin I brushed her teeth. In order to give her a shower, I took one with her. After drying her with the towel, I turned back the sheets. When she sat down for me to put on her nightgown, I pushed her down on the pillow.

"You know I always wear a nightgown."

"Darling, you don't get one tonight." I got into bed with her. The cruise turned out to be our second honeymoon.

MARTINS

The second winter in the Keys was marred by Ethel's catching a cold, which meant she had to go to the hospital to avoid getting fatal pneumonia. Her stay was not a complete loss, as we became very close friends of Jim and Vi Martin. Ethel had always been the epitome of politeness and tact. Her consideration and tolerance of other people were amazing. Violet Martin was sharing the same room, recovering from a minor operation. She was fussing and complaining about everything from the food, to the bed, and neglect of the nurses if they didn't answer her bell immediately. The nurses were attentive, polite, and doing their best to care for her.

Vi said, "I had just finished giving the nurses what for, when Ethel said, very quietly and distinctly, 'Mrs. Martin, you have a fine family and an attentive and caring husband. You are going home tomorrow and you have been here only three days. You are blessed with good health. I am tired of your unreasonable complaining. If you were not going home tomorrow, I would ask to be moved to another room.' I was furious. Ethel turned her back to me. I thought, 'How dare she talk like that to me.' I said something to her and she ignored me. Then I began to think how cheerful she was. She has to be fed and dressed and taken to the bathroom. I apologized and asked her to come and visit us."

This was the start of a long-lasting friendship until Jim died eight years later.

Jim had an eighth-grade education. He built carriers for tanks in World War II and had over 40 patents. He wanted a hurricane. In the '30s a hurricane had destroyed his house on the Gulf. He said the only place you could have survived was in the bathroom standing on the stool, and the water would have been up to your armpits. He rebuilt a three-story castle of concrete heavily reinforced with steel on Marathon Key. It was complete with a power generator plant, a desalinization plant, and everything needed for survival.

He was glad to have Jim Mattox and me enter his life. His close friends and neighbors had either died or become too disabled to do the things he wanted to do. Now he had someone to fish, catch shrimp and lobsters, and talk to. He had his own little man-made bay with a 75-foot walk to a shaded bench and table where one could sit and fish.

On one of our visits, Jim said, "There is something big coming in and feeding on the fish guts that the Cubans are illegally dumping in the water across the canal."

Jim Maddox asked, "What do you mean by big?"

"BIG big. Maybe like 15 feet or more. I know it's a shark because of its big fin. If you catch a bonita, bring it over and we will use it for bait. Bonita is so bloody and a shark can follow a tablespoon of blood a half-mile or more."

Sometime later I caught a 30-pound bonita. Jim had a forged steel hook on a piece of chain. Attached to the chain was a nylon rope or cord that tested 500 pounds. I swam out into the middle of the channel and dropped the bait, anchored by a 10-pound test line and a brick. The three families had a fillet of snapper dinner, and watched the line that was tied to a concrete pier until nearly dark. Ethel and I left.

Jim said, "Right after you left the line started to move. Shorty [his ex-foreman] and I tried to hold the line but we couldn't. It got tighter and tighter and finally broke."

Several days later I was in the bait shop getting a bucket of live shrimp. I heard a man say to the proprietor, "We really caught a big one the other day."

"How big?"

"Let's say he was as big as an 18-foot boat, give or take a foot. At 9¢ a pound, they paid us $270. The beggar had a hook and a short piece of chain in his jaw." They had attached a piece of bloody meat with a short steel leader to a line hooked to a keg. They poured blood from the slaughterhouse into the water to attract the shark. They chased the keg and finally killed the shark by shooting it several times in the head.

It was then that I learned that Florida had secret shark patrols. The planes that spotted sharks for fishermen reported to them for a bonus. When I asked, "What kind?" the answer was, "White."

About a mile and a half out in the bay from Jim Martin's, there was an island of about 20 acres. Someone had dug a cistern in the coral and had a series of ditches cut into the coral to drain into it for water. Some thought it could have been made by a shipwrecked crew waiting for rescue. It was rumored that a postal worker had bought the island for taxes and over a period of months had dug up and stored in his garage over 90 bars of silver weighing 70 pounds each. Jim Mattox had a metal detector and we thought maybe the postal worker had missed something. The first day we found a piece of eight dated 1734 in the edge of his diggings. It was a week before Ethel and I were to leave the Keys and we really got excited.

At the base of a strange-looking palm tree, we got a strong reading on the metal detector. We could trace the shape of the object. It was nearly 3 feet long and about a foot wide.

Jim said, "Virg, that has to be a chest."

"Jim, can you think of anything better to mark a place than planting a tree? That is a different-looking palm tree compared to the rest of them." Now we were really letting our imagination take over.

We had a week of unusually nasty weather and were unable to get back to the location before we had to leave. Jim took a sample of the palm tree to the University of Miami. His letter to me said that it was indigenous of Yucutan.

It was seven months before we found out what was at the base of the tree. Jim didn't have a boat, and anxiously awaited my arrival back at the trailer court. The day after we arrived, we took the boat around and through Sisters Creek under the third span of the Seven Mile Bridge to the island. This time we had a pick and shovel. Sixty-year-old men don't dig very fast. After digging for nearly 2 hours, we were down about 4 feet. The detector almost screamed and we knew it was close. A few more shovels full began to show rust. When the shovel hit something hard, he pried up. We had found three hand-forged links of a huge anchor chain. Why just three links, we will never know. The only other thing of interest that we found was a pair of eroded cannons that were so rusted they almost fell apart at the touch.

MEXICO

Ethel liked Mexico and its people. She always commented, "They are so kind, polite, and so very nice to me. It seems that they have a lot of compassion for handicapped people."

I remarked, "The farther we get away from the border, the nicer they seem to be."

"Virg, that is because they haven't been contaminated by the corrupt Americans and have not adopted their chiseling ways."

We had attended a bullfight in Juarez and it seemed medieval and barbaric. I was booed by a whole arena of Mexicans when a bull got the cape from a picador and was about to get a horn in his backside. I was standing up and yelling, "Bueno, bueno, toro!" as he was chasing the man to the escape barrier. After one kill, we left and I was hearing, "Yankee, go home!" as I waved to the crowd.

Ethel said, "Remind me never to go to a bullfight with you."

"Honey, that is my last bullfight."

"You certainly know how to alienate people."

The Mexican government had completed the road down the Baja, California peninsula. Ethel read the brochure and remarked that the trip would be interesting. The brochures showed there were trailer parks and restaurants at planned intervals. "I am not tired of the Keys, but this might be a welcome change. What about Duchess [her dachshund]?"

"All we have to do is get a rabies shot and dish out a couple of extra dollars at the border."

"Why the extra?"

"That is part of the Mexican ripoff. You have to have at least 10 one-dollar bills when you cross the border. Just in case we don't like Mexico, I will pay an extra month ahead at the Key Trailer Court."

We started out the first of December on our way to San Diego, driving around Los Angeles to miss the terribly congested freeway. At the border, it seemed that everybody got a dollar. First, for escorting us to the main office for car registration, an extra dollar speeded that up. Another for checking the dog's entry visa, also for checking inside the trailer. Someone else put on a sticker. Then 3 miles past the checking point, $2 for the final looking through the door of the trailer and the gracias for the $2. A Mexican said, "These border employees live in fine homes and are rich. They even have to pay politicians to get their appointments."

352

There was a trailer just ahead of us in line and the driver said he'd be damned if he would give the thieving, grafting s.o.b.'s anything. When we stopped at the 3-mile checkpoint he was there and it appeared that he had to unload everything in the trailer for inspection. He pulled into the same trailer park with us, but 3 hours later.

I didn't take car or trailer insurance, as it is almost impossible to collect on a claim of Mexican insurance, but I did take liability because if you had an accident without it you went to jail and never got out.

The restaurants and trailer parks were excellent. The new highway without any barrow pits was smooth, but only 18 feet wide and often dropped off straight down several hundred feet. In many places on the largely backboned mountainous route there were remnants of cars and trucks way down below the road and it was only a year old. Two 8-foot trailers on an 18-foot road leaves only 2-feet clearance, so you slowed to a walk when passing. Some of the grades were very long and steep, mostly downhill as you traveled south. In three instances under-powered trailers had to have another to help pull them to the top. Mexican gas really pinged if you didn't adjust your timing. I saved 15 gallons of high test ethyl in the extra tank for the return trip, and it was a good thing, as I could switch tanks when climbing hills.

Wherever there was water, there were people. Generally these oasis-like settlements were few and far between. Where there was enough water, the vegetation was luxuriant with semitropical fruit and flowers blooming in profusion. The highway crossed and recrossed the Sierra San Pedro and Sierra de la Gigantica all the way to LaPaz. Vegetation consisted mostly of all varieties of cactus and scrubby bushes. History books report that at one time there were larger trees, but these have been long gone as they were used for firewood. Ethel remarked, "Do you know that we have seen almost no animal life?"

"Honey, you've seen a lot of very skinny cattle and donkeys."

"I didn't mean domesticated animals. I meant wildlife."

"I read somewhere that in many places the Mexicans have killed off all edible wildlife, including lizards and snakes, in order to survive."

There were many remnants of missions of the religious orders of 200 to 300 years ago. The monks, while saving the souls, enslaved the people. Being made Christian involved many drawbacks, as it exposed them to the cruelty of the Inquisition and white man's disease. These missions flourished even though they had to constantly replenish the Indian converts by force. When the supply of human workers ran out, the missions went into decay, leaving only ruins of what were imposing buildings, orchards, and vineyards, and the land turned back to native plants. Actually, the terrain around these settlements was often worse as it eroded, leaving rocks and gulleys.

I started to get very apprehensive about the wisdom of our taking this trip. I was 65 years old, traveling alone with a wife who had to be helped to the toilet, had to be dressed, and could feed herself only with the aid of a gadget. If something happened, she could not open the car door to get out. She could converse in Spanish. If she could phone, she would be able to get Dallas, Larry, or Jim down to help her in 24 hours. While driving I didn't dare turn my head, as I had to keep looking at the narrow road straight ahead. My neck was getting more and more sore every day. We had been warned not to stop at any place other than towns and rest stops because of occasional reports of bandits robbing motorists. We had stopped for lunch at a town about halfway down the peninsula. There was a grassy space and tables for tourists. While we were eating, two large Mexican boys came up to see if they could beg something. When two smaller boys who were walking by stopped, the larger boys kicked them and ran them off. This really aggravated Ethel. She called to the two small boys in Spanish, "Come back, we have something for you."

I warned the larger boys, "Vamos, mucho mala hombres."

The small boys really enjoyed ice cream and a piece of cake. We were just cleaning up after lunch when two small men wearing khaki and carrying rifles approached. I immediately blocked the door of the trailer. They pointed their guns at me and tried to enter. Several pedestrians gathered to watch the show. To my surprise, my usually quiet Ethel started to talk in Spanish so rapidly that I could not follow. The soldiers began to fidget and the pedestrians started to laugh. Finally, the two men sheepishly walked away as she continued to harangue them.

"Honey, you really saved the day. If they had gotten into the trailer they would have carried off everything. I didn't know you could speak Spanish so fast. What did you tell them?"

"I didn't know it either. I told them they were very bad men, that they were bandits. I said they were a disgrace to the great Mexican army. I asked for their number on the tags and the regiment they were in. Then I called on the Lord to punish them."

The trailer court in LaPaz had everything, even a shade tree for each space. A high brick wall topped with broken glass and a patrolling night watchman gave good security. My neck was so sore from the tension of driving that it was painful to turn my head. I told Ethel that I was going to a pharmacy to see if I could get some linament for it. I expected to have difficulty in making my needs known, so I held my neck and told the druggist, "My neck is sore and stiff, comprende?"

The druggist answered in perfect English, "I was a pharmacist in San Diego for 12 years." What a relief. I told him about my neck.

"You are an educated man. I will give you three pills, but I would give only one to a native. Under no circumstances take them closer than 12 hours apart." This he repeated twice. He brought me a pill and a glass of water which I swallowed. By the time I had walked back to the car I could turn my head. Ethel had been doing the looking on the side and back while I was driving. My neck was still slightly sore so I took the second pill the next morning. It really relaxed my body in every way. When I returned to the States and told Dallas about it, he said, "It was probably curare, the poison that South American Indians tip their blow gun darts with. If you had taken all three pills at once you would be unable to move a muscle for 24 hours." When I showed him the bottle with one pill left, he read the prescription and he was correct.

Even though everything was pleasant and the fishing was good, it bothered me to be out of the United States with Ethel in her condition. When I said to her, "I want to go back to Florida," she replied, "That is all right with me. I like it here, but you are as uneasy as a caged animal. Can we get our space back at the court?"

"Just in case, I paid an extra month ahead, so we will be o.k."

On the way back on the long, steep mountain grades, the powerful V-8 would slow down due to the low octane of the Mexican gas. It was then I switched to the high-octane tank and the speed would pick up from 10 miles an hour to 25 or 30. When I crossed the border and pulled into a deluxe trailer court that was nearby, it was such a relief to be safe in our own country, with its law, safety, and access to help and medical care. It made me aware of what a privilege it is to be an American citizen.

We drove long hours on freeways with the cruise control set at 60, and seven days later we were parked in our usual space at the Key Trailer Court in Marathon. Monte and Edgar were glad to see me and my boat, and they helped me unload and hook up lights, water, and sewage.

Edgar said, "We will get the boat ready for tomorrow."

"Edgar, make it the next day. I am going to do absolutely nothing tomorrow."

Ethel said, "Goody. I get to eat breakfast at Ted and Mary's!"

Ted and Mary were undoubtedly the bonefishing champions of the world and they had trophies to prove it. In order to be able to pursue their hobby, they served breakfast from 5 to 10 o'clock in the morning. What a breakfast—cooked to perfection in an immaculate restaurant. The place was almost always full and even at 6 o'clock you might have to wait to be seated. It was a shame when they sold out and retired. The new owners could not come close to the quality of Ted and Mary. It became just another restaurant.

The Florida Keys really felt the influence of the hippy period in the mid-'60s and early '70s. The college students from Maine on down to the ocean in southern Florida were completely uninhibited during spring vacations. They settled from one end of Florida to Key West. On the ocean side there was a man-made beach and shallow water called Sisters Creek. Ethel's friends had taken her with them to wade, bathe, and swim. When she returned, I helped her into the trailer and poured our one drink of the day.

"Did you have a good day?"

"Virg, it was quite interesting, what we saw. Some of the girls acted as if they they were deeply shocked, but I noticed that they never stopped looking."

"Looking at what?"

"I was sitting in the folding chair getting the sun to cure the psoriasis spots on my legs, and a dozen or so young men and women without a stitch on walked by carrying their clothes. They waded out to a small island about 500 feet away and disappeared into the trees. Actually, it was rather interesting."

Later in the evening we were playing bridge with Ted and Ruth Johnson in our trailer. We turned on the radio to listen to the evening news and weather report, as we wanted to fish in the morning. The commentator said, "There has been a heinous crime committed today. It happened in broad daylight and was witnessed by many shocked and deeply indignant witnesses. Here is our trusty Sheriff Mueller who investigated the crime to report on his efforts to apprehend the criminals."

The sheriff introduced himself as the duly elected officer of the law and protector of his constituents. "Mrs. Snead reported the outrage. It seems she resented her husband seeing it. I guess she didn't want him to be able to compare. Taking Butch, the only married deputy, we headed toward the scene of the crime. When we waded out to the island, the people were all wearing at least one piece of apparel, and that is all that is required by Florida law.There was no way I could identify the culprits. Doing my duty, I still tried to get incriminating evidence. I asked a very pretty middle-aged lady sitting in a chair facing the beach if she saw the streakers.

"I did see them very clearly."

"Could you identify any of them?"

"Not really, officers. But I did notice that all men are not created equal."

The sheriff's closing goodnight left us in stitches. A thought occurred to me about the pretty lady in the chair.

"Ethel, was it you he contacted in the chair?"

"If I say no, you'll never believe me. If I did make a remark to the sheriff, you'll never know."

Ruth Johnson said, "I was sitting in a chair beside her and as my lawyer husband would say, I concur."

We were planning our annual trek back to Idaho. Ethel said, "I would like to see Lary and Caroline." They were living in Nahant and Lary was working with General Electric in Boston.

356

"Why not," I said. "All we have is time." Then I found out she had made an itinerary to visit Williamsburg, Fort Sumpter, Mount Vernon, and the Capitol.

"Ethel, how long is this going to take?"

"About two weeks."

On the first day we camped in a trailer park just across the state line in Georgia. The proprietor also had a kennel of bird dogs which he rented out during bird season. I asked if it would be all right to let my dog run loose.

"It will be o.k., as the 'gators are still hibernating. It has been a cold spring."

I knew that Diane would never stray too far or get lost. I turned her loose and started to prepare dinner. It was hot and the breeze coming through the screen door was almost balmy. After dinner I suddenly realized Diane had not banged on the door to be let in. When I called and whistled, there was no answer.

"Ethel, something has happened to Diane!" I picked up my old hunting coat, attached a cord to it and walked out a half-mile and made a circle, dragging the coat. If she was lost the scent of the coat would lead her back. There was a store and service station a quarter of a mile away. They had not seen a black and white setter. The proprietor of the trailer park was notified. The next morning I started contacting the dwellings going in an increasingly large circle. Two days later I gave up. I had contacted everyone in a three-mile circle. Being Southerners, they were concerned and solicitous about my losing the dog. The local radio refused to take pay for broadcasting her loss and the $50 reward.

Ethel said, "Virg, I know how you feel about her. She has been a wonderful companion to you for 10 years."

"If she was a young dog I wouldn't worry, because the first time someone went hunting with her he would find he had a bragging dog and would take care of her. But very few would take good care of a 10-year-old dog." I told the park proprietor that I would call every evening to see if she had been returned to him. Her loss was almost unbearable. We had shared so much together. When I slipped and was swept down Snake River from Minidoka Dam, she was swimming with me when I came up. My waders kept me afloat, but I couldn't swim very well in them. She was a big, powerful dog. I took hold of her tail and she swam downstream toward the bank. We were about 50 feet from the bank when I let go of her tail because she was so tired that I was afraid she wouldn't be able to make it to the bank, and there was no use in both of us drowning. I paddled closer to the bank and tried to reach bottom. I felt that I could not swim another foot and I was so close to the shore. I told myself I wasn't going to drown because I couldn't swim another 10 feet. The next time I tried to reach bottom, my toes touched and everything was alright. When we both climbed out of the water, I held Diane in my arms while we rested.

Ethel said, "Someone picked her up and word will get to them about a lost dog."

The first day we stopped and visited interesting sites along the way. I called that night and the next morning. The kennel owner said, "I haven't heard a thing. It is still being broadcast."

The next day we were 400 miles away at Fort Sumpter. It was there that the hot-headed South Carolinians started the war. When they told how they partied on the shore as the fort was being bombarded, it occurred to me how cruel people were because they didn't think about the death and suffering that they were applauding. I called in again that night with no luck. I almost didn't call the next morning because it appeared to be so hopeless and we were going to travel to Washington, D.C., the next day. I could not give up, so I dialed the kennel. To my great joy, Mr. Jones said, "She is here in the kennel. I paid the reward."

Ethel saw my tears when I came back to the Travelall and said, "They have found her! The man said she is in the kennel."

We unhooked the trailer and drove the 450 miles in 9 hours. Diane was lying in the pen and didn't even raise her head when we drove up. She had given up. When I whistled and called her, she sat up, looked around and saw me. She slowly walked up amd jumped into the Travelall, put her head on my shoulder and cried.

She had knocked on the door of a house in less than an hour after I had turned her loose to run. It was in a town 12 miles away. Someone had picked her up and then dumped her. The lady of the house said that when she opened the door Diane went to the sink in the kitchen and she gave her a drink of water. When she told her neighbor about the smart dog which seemed to understand everything she said to her, the neighbor said, "That must be the dog that is being advertised on the radio. There is a $50 reward for her." I gave the proprietor a $20 bill and my heartfelt thanks.

DIANE THE SECOND

After hunting season in the fall, Quail became so enfeebled that it was difficult for her to move around. During the family conference, Dallas said, "The kindest thing we can do is have her put to sleep and end her suffering." We agreed.

In the spring I began to look at litters of Lewellen Setter puppies. Selecting a dog should not be a spur-of-the-moment decision. It ranks fourth in importance, with the selection of a wife, first; occupation, second; house, third. You live with these decisions.

Goss Gordon, a young potato grower at Hazelton, solved the problem. The banker at Hazelton called me, asking if I could meet with him tomorrow. I agreed. Bankers are important and essential in a farming area. When I entered his office, he looked at the other man beside him and said, "Do you know Goss?"

I shook hands with Goss, saying, "We even like each other."

Banker Evans said, "Goss wants to put in 160 acres of new land. He will have to borrow a large loan to bring the crop to harvest. His average yield in the past has been about 205 sacks per acre. If his yield is that this year it will be marginal and questionable that he can repay the loan."

"What do you want me to do?"

"Can you find time to supervise him once a week and go over with him your recommendations before planting time?"

"If it's agreeable to Goss, I would be happy to do it. I can use it as a demonstration farm for tours. With the very fertile land of his, we should be able to raise 300 sacks of high-quality potatoes per acre." We shook hands and I left them.

The Gordon field was 10 miles from the ranch house. Our contacts had always been in the field. The crop was very outstanding. The growers in the area were very impressed. Late in August I checked the field. It was getting too wet due to the shading of the rows. Goss was not there, so I drove to his house to tell him to skip irrigating for three days. I was greeted by the most beautiful, perfectly proportioned Lewellen Setter bitch followed by eight nicely marked pups.

"Goss, where did you get that Lewellen Setter bitch? She is really something."

"Virg, I sent to Georgia for her. She has the same bloodlines as the national champion gun dog. I paid a really high price for her."

"What about the sire of the pups?"

"He is of the same bloodlines."

I started to visit the pups when I made my weekly visits to the ranch. On the first visit I gave each of the pups a piece of weiner for a treat. On the next visit Goss turned the 8-week-old pups out of the pen. Two of them remembered me and came to me for their treats. A well-marked little bitch was ahead of the other. On the third visit she was at the gate, trying to get to me. I asked Goss when he was planning to sell them.

"I will keep them until they are three months old in October."

Early in October I stopped at the ranch house. Mrs. Gordon turned the bitch and eight pups out of the pen. They followed their mother into a field of short alfalfa. The bitch immediately went on point. My favorite pup honored her point. Her head was in a straight line and her tail slightly raised but straight. The rest of the pups followed suit. It was really remarkable because many bird dogs do not point until they are a year old. There was no question. I had to have that pup. I knew she would be expensive.

It was nearing noon when I contacted Goss the next week. He was running the potato digger. He stopped, shook hands, and patted me on the back. I could see the unusually large, smooth potatoes would bring a premium price. The yield would be close or over 400 sacks per acre, which meant he would gross $1,800 an acre.

"Virg, you really came through. I am going to clear over $150,000."

It was then I said, "Goss, I want to buy that bitch pup I've been playing with. How much?"

"You can't buy that pup." This really put a damper on me.

"Why not?"

"Because I am giving her to you. It is almost noon. Come to the house with me and I will make out the papers. You can take her home with you because she is old enough."

The family greeted the new pup with affection.

Ethel remarked, "She looks like our first Diane. Why not call her Diane?"

Susan said, "She has to have a middle name. She is now Diane Marie Cross."

I said, "I think she will be good enough to be named Diane."

Diane liked her bed in a box by my side of the bed. She seemed pleased to have a dish of her own and not have to compete with seven other hungry mouths.

"She doesn't seem to miss her family a bit," said Susan.

"She thinks we're her family now," Lary replied.

Getting her to go by a turkey bell hung on a long ribbon from the door knob and taking her outside when she rang it really worked. In three days she was ringing the bell for her toilet. Outside I would say,

"Puddle" when she was in the act and in a short time she knew what it meant. The first command a dog should be taught is "Come." At four months she knew this was a must, and came to us at high speed. After first showing her what to do, it took only a few repetitions and she would react perfectly. I was really amused when teaching her to heel. This meant she was to walk beside me and not ahead. I was walking along holding her leash in one hand with a light willow switch. I would pull back on the leash, say, "Heel," and tap her on the nose with the switch. After the third tap, she took the switch in her mouth and shook it. I threw away the switch and she heeled perfectly.

In her first hunting season she was unbelievably good. It was the beginning of 14 years of super hunting. She became famous when she won Field Champion in a big gun dog show in eastern Washington. Dr. Holcomb, our dentist in Burley, would reserve a hunting day with her a year ahead of time. I was more than glad to have him hunt with her. I will always be grateful to him.

My bridged front tooth had collapsed, and there was a bad sore in my mouth where it had been. The dentist in Jerome looked at it and said, "Virg, you have pyorrhea and your teeth will have to come out." He gave me a date three weeks away to start having my teeth pulled. I was playing golf with Bill Keller in Burley. When I mentioned that I was going to have my teeth pulled next week, he said, "My wife works for Dr. Holcomb and he is a very good dentist. Why don't you get a second opinion?"

Dr. Holcomb said, "Someone read the wrong X-ray. You have an infection, but not pyorrhea. I can cure it. I have bad news for you, though. Your new bridge is going to cost you $240." This was June, 1940, and the new bridge is still in place this day of July 2, 1993.

Bill Keller was an ex-Army colonel of World War II. He was a good hunting companion. I had to go to the university for a week and it was during hunting season. When he said, "My son who is a pilot in the Air Force is coming home for a week before going to Vietnam. He would like to go pheasant hunting with us. Since you are going to be gone, could I keep Diane for a week so we could hunt with her? I know this is a lot to ask." Bill was one of the few, if any, that I would trust my dog with. When I returned, his son had left for overseas. In a short time I received a letter from him thanking me for the use of a superdog and of the pleasure he and his father had hunting with her. Later on, Bill said his son had told him in a letter of the bull sessions the pilots had about dogs. When he told them about Diane, they laughed and kidded him, saying no dog could be that good.

"Bill, we can fix those fellows. We can get a portable tape recorder and take it on our next hunt and record it complete." Fortunately, we got into an abundance of birds in good cover and she was at her best at holding the birds and retrieving. We sent the two tapes to him. A letter

361

to his father said, "The homesick pilots wanted it played over and over and we finally wore it out."

My father taught me that all things, good or bad, come to an end and nothing remains status quo. This is something you have to expect, whether it is life, marriage, employment, pain, or pleasure. I was dreading Diane's getting old and being unable to hunt. When she was 11, she was beginning to slow down. When I told Ethel that Diane was still good, but could not work as fast as she used to and got tired more easily, and I could not bear the thought of her going, Ethel said, "Don't brood over it. Think of the nice life she has had, with loving care. No dog could have had a better life." After this I became reconciled.

In her fourteenth year, I hunted her sparingly, with short hunts in easy cover. She was losing ground rapidly. After the hunt I would give her a warm bath and a rubdown. She would be stiff and limp for a day or two. Bill Keller noticed this. Near the end of the season he said, "I want one more hunt with Diane." We took her to a stubblefield that was easy to hunt. Within 20 minutes she had made two sets and retrieved both birds with little difficulty.

Bill said, "That's it. She has been such a super dog and I really appreciate the pleasure that she and I have shared. Let's go home."

After that she was really stiff and sore, but I wanted one more hunt alone with her. I gave her half an Indocin pill for arthritis the evening before the last day. The next morning when I put on my hunting coat, she wasn't limping and was excited and eager to go. When I let her out of the car in the field, she worked the ground thoroughly and rapidly. She brought the first rooster back in a hurry. When she was retrieving the next bird, she brought it to me slowly and laid down. I picked her up and carried her to the car. At home I gave her the bath and rubdown and a dinner of hamburger with gravy. The next morning she could hardly walk. I called my friend Don Hanson, and he took her to the vet to be put to sleep. Wherever I go in the future, I hope they allow dogs.

A VISIT TO NAHANT

Williamsburg was a fascinating place. The introductory film depicting the life of a teenager in the colonial pre-revolutionary days set the tone and got one to reliving the past, sitting where the members of the Continental Congress sat and hearing of their debates and problems. I was very uncomfortable, as my back was so sore I could hardly move without pain. Usually Ethel was the one who asked to rest occasionally. Now I could barely get from one building to another. While we were eating lunch, Ethel remarked, "There is a barber shop just across the street and you need a haircut." As I sat in the barber's chair I noticed a shoeshine boy and asked him to shine my shoes. When he helped me take them off, he said, "Your heels are badly run down. Would you like me to put new ones on?"

"Go ahead."

Later Ethel said, "You are walking a lot better."

"It seems that my back is better." Then I realized that my discomfort had been caused by the run-down heels.

Williamsburg was interesting because it depicted many scenes and historical events that I had read about in American history classes. I was gratified to remember that I am a descendant of Samuel Adams on my mother's side.

"Ethel, I must see Manassas or Bull Run, as my grandfather Wesley Cross took part in the slaughter. He did not participate in the stupid mass frontal charges. He was a sharpshooter and was always in a strategic position on the edge or side." Our previous study of the White House and the Smithsonian helped us to comprehend and visualize the past history of our country. I am sure that many of the visitors did not notice how crude and inefficient the tools and utensils were, and how hard the housewives had to work to raise their usually large families. Ethel said, "No wonder the women were old at 35 and usually died before reaching 45."

In planning our route to Lary's home in Nahant, we chose to miss going through New York City. When we came to a tunnel, we were turned back because they did not allow propane tanks to enter. As a result, we were directed to travel right through the Bronx during the afternoon rush hour. It was a close-packed nightmare to drive in. Trucks would ease over slowly and force you to give way. Everybody was honking at everybody else. It was one hell of a place for a country boy to be in with a 30-foot trailer in tow. As a precaution I had locked of the doors. I had my window rolled down so I could signal. We had to stop for a traffic jam. A policeman was directing the four-way traffic. To make things worse we were stopped with only one car ahead of us, which meant we had to wait several minutes before it would be our turn to move. Three young blacks came up and tried the doors on Ethel's side. I reached down under the seat and picked up a big crescent wrench. When the black hand tried to pull up the door release knob on my side, I brought the wrench down on the fingers and blood and nails really spattered. He yelled, holding his hand. The policeman saw it all and waved our lane through out of turn. He waved to show he knew what was going on. I was aware that he couldn't leave his post.

When the New Englander from Vermont said, "Strangers are strangers and I don't want any truck with them," it echoed my impression of New Englanders. It seemed that we were in a different country. In the West people are friendly and helpful, usually volunteering assistance. In Boston we were actually pushed off the sidewalk in a rush period. I had to hold Ethel's arm for her balance and we probably would have fallen if it had not been for Lary's quick reflex action. At the service station where I had wheels repacked and other work done on the car and trailer amounting to about $75, they acted as if they were doing me a favor. The young attendant was filling the gas tanks and I asked him to clean the windshield. He said, "I don't clean windshields or windows."

That made me see red. I said, "You will not get paid until you do."

The proprietor winked at me and said, "You'll have to clean his windows."

Being a fishing addict, I bought bait at a local tackle shop and they were quite friendly. Fishermen were scattered along the beach. I walked up to two of them and asked, "How is the fishing?" One of them never moved nor looked up. The other one almost looked up and grunted. Farther on down the beach I asked a lone fisherman, "Are they biting?" and got a single, "No." Western fishermen are friendly and willing to pass the time of day and trade information. In the West you are quite often greeted with a "Good morning" and a smile from a passing stranger. Not so in New England. It could be the difficulty of making a living from the rocky, unproductive soil, or the handed-down superstition. After all, they believed in witches. Another theory is that the outgoing and adventuresome individuals left for greener pastures over the years and left the conservative and unsuccessful to breed.

Breed's Hill, or Bunker Hill, was a surprise. I had imagined a steep, long hill, but it wasn't very steep or very long. The U.S.S. Constitution (Old Ironsides) was something I had read about in history books and novels. Of course she had been restored. Her original oak hull that the cannon balls of the British could not penetrate was still in good condition. When I remarked to the midshipman guide that the height of the decks was only 5-feet, 6-inches and everybody had to stoop, it must have been very uncomfortable for the sailors, he remarked that it really was not. The average height of men then was less than 5-feet, 6. He added, "Goliath was only 6 feet tall, but he was fighting Jews that were only a little over 4 1/2 feet."

You never really know what your children feel about you. Larry and Caroline had a dinner party. The other eight guests were from his staff and their wives. During a break in the poker game, the men started to talk about their adolescent escapades and what they had stolen. Larry just sat and listened. Someone said, "Lary, you haven't said a word. Did you ever steal anything?"

Lary said, "Crosses don't steal. They don't have to. In fact, I got a car for not stealing." He gave a brief account of the incident, and ended by saying, "Virg would sell the car if I got a traffic ticket."

"You mean he actually would do that?"

"He would do it and not say anything. Mostly we called him 'Virg.' Sometimes we called him 'Hufad,' an abbreviation for hellfire and damnation."

"Was he unreasonably strict?"

"Not really. We had a wide circle that we could act in freely. Inside the circle anything was all right if it didn't harm you, your family or anyone else, or cause trouble. If you got outside the circle, he was Hufad. He warned us about the danger of having small portable radios in the bathroom. He came home one day and Dallas was taking a bath with his new radio on the side of the tub. He picked it up and threw it hard on the floor and walked out. Dallas knew he was right and never protested. We could always say, 'My dad or my parents wouldn't like this' and it gave us an out. We really had a very close and very pleasant growing-up period."

1975

August was the month I fished and played golf at Campbell River on Vancouver Island in British Columbia. If Ethel didn't go there with me, she visited the children. I was surprised when Susan came down from Salt Lake and packed the trailer. When I asked, "Where are your mother's clothes?" she said, "Daddy, they are in a suitcase. We are going to visit Dallas in Kansas City and Lary in New Hampshire. You will never miss us, as you have oodles of people that want to fish with you because of your expertise."

When I kissed Ethel goodbye the next morning, she said, "Enjoy your trip, and I'm sure you will." Her visiting the children during August became a ritual. She could travel alone without having to use the bathroom for 4 or 5 hours. The stewardesses on the airlines got to know her and she received the ultimate in attention. They even fed her when necessary.

When she was dressed up, she was striking in appearance. The years had not dimmed the beauty of her facial features. I remember a phone call from Susan.

"Hello, Daddy."

"What now?"

"There is a play that Mummy wants to see."

"What night did you buy the tickets for?"

"They are for Friday night. And I want to show off my special mother to my friends."

"I'll put her on the plane in Salt Lake at two Thursday. It will arrive at four."

Later in the week I met her plane in Salt Lake.

She said, "Honey, I had a wonderful time. Susan had three of her friends. We all went out for dinner and drinks after the play. It was so nice to be able to pick up the check and not worry about the cost. It is wonderful to have a husband like you!" Susan told me they were absolutely charmed with her mother.

When you are happy, busy, and enjoying life, the time goes by at an astonishing rate. Days to weeks to months almost in a blur. In spite of her tragedy, the family had a busy, happy, and never dull life together. Our 10 years of retirement was a period of delightful closeness, as we could spend more time together. We especially enjoyed our four or five months' stay in the Keys. It was so unhurried, peaceful, and tranquil that we hoped it would never end. It is hard for me to describe the pleasure of awakening to see her pretty, peaceful face sleeping on the pillow. She always woke up with a "Good morning, darling," and a smile. We both knew that it was coming to an end the last two of the 10 years of retirement. I sensed that she didn't want me away from her too long. I cut down on my fishing and golfing time. She was so intelligent and interesting to be with.

We had our 40th anniversary in 1975. It was quite an event. All of the children were present. It was evident at the party that her stamina had been declining rapidly. I noticed that she was breathing more rapidly in order to get enough oxygen. Dr. Holsinger had said that her 70 percent lung power was bound to get weaker. During the last winter in the Keys, we both sensed that she was rapidly losing strength. Neither of us wanted to be apart from the other for very long. In the past we had been as close as a husband and wife could be. She liked to sleep with her head on my shoulder and my arm around her. She said, "When you hold me, I feel that nothing can hurt me or go wrong." Now we were acting as if every moment were to be cherished and enjoyed as much as possible.

In early April she wasn't feeling very well and said she felt woozy. I decided to go early to Kansas City where Dallas lived and get her under medical care. He would know the best doctors. I hurriedly packed up and left. We were passing through Martin, Tennessee, and she fell over into my lap. Fortunately, I had just passed a hospital sign and an arrow. The hospital was only a few blocks away. I drove up to the emergency entrance, picked her up and went through the door and laid her on an ambulance cart. A nurse rushed up and started to ask questions.

"Forget the questions. Get an oxygen mask on her right now!"

In a short time her color came back and she regained consciousness. A young doctor took blood samples and reported that her electrolytes were low and she wasn't getting enough oxygen. I was doubtful about the ability of this young doctor in a small hospital, so I telephoned Dallas. He asked the name of the doctor and where he got his training. He said he would charter a plane to bring her to Kansas City. I was to stay near the phone until he called back. In about half an hour he called. His findings were that the doctor had the best grades in training and there was no better qualified doctor in Kansas City. I found out that the doctor had been sent to medical school by the little community and although he had offers from some of the top medical institutions, he stayed because he felt he owed it to the community.

They allowed me to park behind the hospital and hook up to the power. The trailer was parked less than a half-block from Ethel's room on the first floor. She recovered quickly and was her usual cheerful self in a few days. She remarked that they gave her an eggnog with plenty of Tennessee medicine in it.

I ran out of whiskey and went to the small town to buy a bottle and get a haircut. When the barber was through, I asked where the liquor store was. I was told by the barber that the place was dry. When I left, a heavyset, middle-aged man followed me out the door. Outside, he asked, "What kind of liquor do you want?"

"A fifth of Jim Beam."

"Give me $7.50 and leave your car unlocked. Wait 15 minutes in the barber shop." He had no trouble changing my $100 bill from his huge roll.

Fifteen minutes later I drove off with the fifth on the seat beside me. Later I heard one of the nurses say, "We are out of whiskey. I'll call Ronald and have him bring the sheriff a case to deliver."

I played golf every day but spent most of the time reading or talking to Ethel when she felt like it. After five days she was able to travel and we went on to Kansas City. During our three-day stay there, she had no further trouble. At Laramie, Wyoming, she had a set-back from the high altitude and had to stay in the hospital overnight. The shots and oxygen worked wonders and she wanted to go home the next morning. We reached Burley that evening. The plan was to see Dr. Holsinger the next morning. At five in the morning she woke me, shaking with a chill. I knew that meant pneumonia. In a few minutes she was in the hospital five blocks away. The respirator specialist put her in an iron lung that was small and vastly different from the old, huge barrel-like type.

She said, "I don't like this. I have served my time in the lung. Promise me that when I get out you will not let them put me back in." Of course I promised.

"You never break promises. This one may be hard for you to keep, but you have promised."

I was hoping that she could overcome the chest muscle weakness, but I knew deep down that our beautiful, wonderful relationship of 40 years was nearing an end. I dreaded the void she was going to leave in my life. The doctor didn't have much hope at first. Her recovery from pneumonia was rapid and her lungs were clear in 10 days. The children arrived on the same day to visit her. They gathered at the house and planned their visit. Susan from Salt Lake came in first, followed by Dallas from Kansas City a few minutes later. There was a break of several minutes. She was watching the door but didn't say anything. When Lary from Boston entered the room she said, "Lary, I was afraid you were not coming."

"Mummy, there was no way I could stay away and not come to see you." It was a joyful family reunion and everything seemed to be alright, as the doctor said, "We will keep her off oxygen for two days and then she can go home." He was amazed at her determination and recovery.

We all visited her the second day after their arrival. We left after 7 o'clock because the visiting was tiring her.

At 8 o'clock I received a call from her nurse, saying, "Mrs. Cross wants to see you."

She was sitting up braced by pillows against the bedstead. There was an oxygen tube in her nose.

"Hello, darling. Sit by me and hold me. When you hold me I feel that nothing can hurt me and you keep me safe from the world." We kissed and she had her head on my shoulder.

"Virg, I am going to sleep without this oxygen tube. I am wearing it now because we have a lot of talking to do. If I can't make it without the oxygen, do not let them put me back in the lung. I have had enough of that. I don't want to exist that way. You will keep your promise."

"Honey, I'll keep it." I told her what a wonderful wife she had been and that I never regretted helping her one bit. When I complimented her on her courage to live and carry on, she said, "I couldn't stop living because of the way you loved me and took care of me. You forgot about breeding stock and being a good filly. People are lucky to have one outstanding child out of three, and we have three for three!"

We talked and reminisced about the pleasant things of the past. About 10 o'clock she was getting tired. I said, "I'll see you in the morning."

"Darling, I am very tired and I am going to sleep without the oxygen. If I don't wake up, somebody is going to get a terrific husband, temporarily. If there is a hereafter, I'll be greeting you as you enter." We parted with tears.

I received a call from the hospital at 5 o'clock that morning saying she had died in her sleep.

The church was full at the funeral. Our minister of many years gave a wonderful eulogy of her life. He brought out her great courage and desire to live. He also said her cheerfulness and outlook on life was an example to everyone. She actually lit up a room when she entered it. She was leaving a wonderful family that would also continue to make the world better. He also praised the family for their loyalty, closeness, and love. Clem, Smitty, and Herb were among the pallbearers. Ethel had insisted on cremation.

The children had not left. We were gathered in the shade of the big maple tree in the backyard. They were talking about the pleasant experiences of the family as they grew up. Lary remarked, "We were a family reared in a house of love with love. The minister did a wonderful job of bringing out what a remarkable person she was. We were lucky to have her for a mother."

Her trials and suffering were over. She left me with priceless memories of the wonderful and interesting life we shared.